Globalization and the
Postcolonial World

Globalization and the Postcolonial World

The New Political Economy of Development

Second Edition

Ankie Hoogvelt

The Johns Hopkins University Press
Baltimore, Maryland

The Johns Hopkins University Press
2715 North Charles Street
Baltimore, Maryland 21218-4363
www.press.jhu.edu

Library of Congress Cataloging-in-Publication Data

Hoogvelt, Ankie M. M.
    Globalization and the postcolonial world: the new political economy
of development / Ankie Hoogvelt.—2nd ed.
        p. cm.
    Includes bibliographical references and index.
    ISBN 0-8018-6691-X (alk. paper)—ISBN 0-8018-6692-8 (pbk.: alk.
paper)
        1. Developing countries—Foreign economic relations. 2. Developing
countries—Dependency on foreign countries. 3. International
economic relations. 4. Capitalism—Developing countries. 5.
Competition, International. I. Title.

    HF 1413 .H66 2001
    337—dc21
                                                                    00-049781

A catalog record for this book is available from the British Library.

Contents

List of Figures and Tables

Figure

Tables

Preface to the Second Edition

The original aim of this book was to write a text that would be a sequel to my book, *The Third World in Global Development*, published in 1982. Like its predecessor, this text would describe recent trends in world political economy and introduce students to current debates regarding the development prospects of the Third World. The problem with this ambition is that the Third World as such no longer exists. That is to say, it is no longer there as a unitary classificatory descriptor of the economic, social and political conditions of the countries of Africa, Latin America and Asia, and with it, development studies has disappeared. Indeed, as early as 1979, Dudley Seers, one of the doyens of development studies, had written, 'Development Studies is over the hill or downright dead[1].'

At the start of the twenty-first century, we no longer encounter development studies as a body of knowledge with a coherent identity, or even coherent identities, as in competing schools of theory or paradigms. It no longer has pretensions of being, or becoming, a full-blown academic discipline. Development studies as a discrete subject in degree schools in higher education is gradually being replaced by, or merging with, other subjects, and one would be hard put to find designated Chairs being appointed to the discipline in universities. I can think of few comprehensive texts on development or the Third World published since the early 1990s. Of course, there have been collections of essays or readers still loosely gathered under the label 'development studies', but such readers reflect the fragmentation of the subject, mirroring the dissolution of the Third World itself, as some regions of the Third World have shamed the pundits of doom by becoming the dynamic growth centres of the world economy (for example, East Asia), and others have declined to the point of extinction, snuffing out all belief in progress. As

Wolfgang Sachs writes: 'The idea of development was once a towering monument inspiring international enthusiasm. Today, the structure is falling apart and in danger of total collapse.'[2]

In the early 1980s, development studies became stranded in what was widely referred to as 'the impasse', and work in the field of development studies disbanded into a diverse range of intellectual pursuits without any sense of common direction or purpose. First, it fragmented into area studies, in which the success of the East Asian 'developmental' states offered a promising focus for theoretical renewal, albeit rather more to the field of comparative political economy than to the subject of development studies itself. Second, there were meta-theoretical critiques of those theoretical constructs that had long constituted the tool box of development theory. Dependency, exploitation, unequal exchange, mode of production, modernization, rationalization, progress – all these came under the deconstructing axe of postmodernists, postMarxists and poststructuralists alike. Third, some development literature to all intents and purposes merged with international political economy literature, focusing in particular on issues of debt, poverty and peripheralization, perceived as the downside of a quickening process of globalization of the world economy. Fourth, other development literature found succour in the discovery of gender relations as welcome relief from the tedium of class relations that previously had dominated so much of the development agenda. Fifth, development studies engaged with environmental studies, as poverty in the poor world came to be seen as even more damaging to 'our' ozone layer than the pursuit of wealth in the rich world.

This certainly is not an exhaustive list, but it serves to show how development studies has been scattered by the winds of change over a wide terrain of intellectual enquiry, making the task of synthesis *a priori* impossible. What, then, should be the purpose of writing a general introductory text on the subject? And if one did find such purpose, how would it help to organize the sequencing of chapters in a manner that will ensure that at least some of the new agendas are incorporated in a coherent way?

It seems to me that an important purpose should be to understand the processes of crisis and transformation of the world economy which constitute the winds of change that are now blowing development studies into different directions. Without such an understanding we shall lose sight of the *continuity in change* of the historical process.

At the time of writing there are over 1.3 billion people in the world living in absolute poverty and immiseration, and their number is growing, increasingly enveloping those who previously formed part of the rich, First World, and of the semi-developed Second World.[3] The *Human Development Report, 1999*, notes that between 1980 and 1996 gross national product (GNP) per capital declined in no less than fifty-nine countries. It reports that the income gap between the fifth of the world's population living in the richest countries, and the fifth in the poorest, widened from 30 to 1 in 1960 to 74 to 1 in 1997, and that income disparities increased in many countries, including the rich, during the 1980s and the 1990s.[4] On the other hand, it is also the case that some countries, notably in East Asia, have grown, and are still growing, very fast indeed, and that they have managed to translate that growth into improved standards of living for the masses of the population. However, the rising fortunes of new regions or groups of countries in the world economy, and the decline of others, should not blind us to the way that wealth and poverty are connected. I remain convinced that poverty and wealth creation are but two sides of the same historical process, even if that historical process itself undergoes fundamental changes in the manner in which it is organized. But when the understanding and interpretation of wealth and poverty themselves become fragmented, divorced from one another, as they are today, there is a danger that we shall end up celebrating, in true postmodern style, poverty as 'difference'.

While there is continuity in the fact that wealth and poverty creation are connected, it is nevertheless one of the main organizing themes of the book that at beginning of the twenty-first century we are experiencing a complete, radical break, a *qualitative* change, in the historical development of capitalism. The world economic crisis that began in the 1970s has led, not just to a restructuring of the world economy, but to a major transformation of the way in which production and distribution are organized. There is a new political economy in the making. But, in contrast to the past, this new political economy is not a political economy that first developed and became organized within one specific territorial space and then expanded outwards; rather it is a new political economy that was global from the very beginning. This has consequences for our understanding of the locational distribution of wealth and poverty, of development and underdevelopment. The familiar pyramid of the core–periphery hierarchy is no longer a geographical but a social division of the world economy. The designation 'postcolonial' world in preference to 'Third World' serves to articulate at once the shift from national origin to subject-position in the global political economy, and a movement beyond a specific period in history, that of colonialism and Third World nationalist struggles.

Outline of the Book

Thus, as the subtitle suggests, the book is about the *new political economy of development*. These very words beg at least two questions: (i) that there is an understood and generally accepted meaning of the term 'political economy'; and (ii) that there is an old version of it, now distinct from and discarded by different interpretations. As we shall see in the introduction to Part I, there is no such thing as a unified methodology or theory of political economy. What there is, is a set of questions about the relationship between power and wealth, between politics and economics, between states and markets. Depending on how this relationship has been understood and conceptualized, different theories of world order have held sway for a considerable time: namely realism, institutionalism, and Marxism/ structuralism. Their common ground was the state–market interaction as the embodiment of politics and economics in the modern world. And a central question became how to grasp the conflicting logic of an evolving and progressively integrating world market, on the one hand, with the continuing compartmentalization of the world political order into sovereign nation states on the other.

Within the Marxist/structuralist tradition the evolving international state/market nexus was analyzed in terms of the *dialectical* development of capitalism in historical periods. Capitalism's inherent contradictions were said to be worked out in different phases of expansion, punctuated by crises, in which state and interstate relations were time and again rearranged as political structures that held in place the exploitative economic relationship between core and peripheral economies. In Chapters 1, 2 and 3, we look back on this tradition from the vantage point of Robert Cox's critical theory of historical structures. Thus each phase of capitalist expansion is described in turn and we review the theories that emerged, whether as hegemonic, legitimating, ideology or as counter-hegemonic critique, within each evolving phase. In this way the *historical specificity* of theories of imperialism, of modernization and dependency, of postimperialism, and world system, and of the New International Division of Labour, will become clarified.

Part II begins, in Chapter 4, with a statistical portrait of the dialectical development of capitalism since the beginning of the nineteenth century. We discover that world trade and capital flows, at first expanding to embrace ever more areas of the world, gradually turned into a process of *involution* when capital relations became intensified within the core, while selectively withdrawing from the periphery. Meanwhile, this process resulted in cumulatively growing differences in income between rich and poor nations.

The historically generated structure of deepening inequality provides the backdrop for our understanding of the present crisis and transformation debate to which we turn in subsequent chapters. By the 1970s, capitalism had reached the limits of its own expansion, and this became the crucible of fundamental change. This change is becoming visible in an information-technology (IT) driven new political economy that characterizes the production process and its global, though not worldwide, embrace. In Chapter 5, we discuss the changes in economic production and industrial organization widely referred to as flexible production, and the emergence of the new, 'knowledge' or 'digital', economy that by some accounts has been responsible for the renewed growth in the core of the capitalist system. Chapter 6 addresses the global aspects of the process of transformation. Pertinently, in contributing to a theory of globalization, I privilege the *social dimension* of globalization over the *economic dimension*. I argue that the reconstitution of the world into a single social space today drives the economics of globalization, even though the preceding period of economic internationalization has itself created the conditions for the emergence of this single social space. The contemporary process of globalization signals a 'higher' level of intensifying economic, financial, cultural and social cross-border networks than before. Meanwhile, ever larger segments of the world population, evident inside advanced countries, but more numerous still inside the Third World, are being expelled from the emerging 'thickening' network of human social and economic interaction. Rather than being a process of *expansion*, the process of globalization appears to be a *shrinking* one. How is such a system of widening global disparities managed and perpetuated? Who is in control; who runs this system? Chapter 7 discusses these questions, examines the emerging forms of transnational governance and regulation, and points to the increasing geostrategic dominance of the USA in maintaining the stability of neo-liberal regimes.

Part III of the book addresses the implications of globalization for the postcolonial world. The term postcolonial is a recent arrival in development literature. It is a term of complex origins and we shall explore these in the introduction to the final part of the book. For now it is sufficient to note that the concept has merits simply because it groups together all former colonial societies despite differences in their relationship to the global capitalist system, while at the same time offering a point of entry for the study of those differences. This point of entry is the 'aftermath' of the colonial relationship and the manner in which this becomes reconstituted *and* contested in the process of the present transformation of the global political economy. Thus we may study the postcolonial condition as a state of being that is the combined outcome of external pressures (globalization, the post-Cold War order and so on), and locally and historically specific characteristics and struggles arising out of the (neo)colonial relationship.

I consider four types of postcolonial 'conditions', 'situations' or 'social formations', each exemplified in one of four regions of the world, though not necessarily exclusive to that region. Neither are these four exhaustive of all social formations in the postcolonial world. There are plenty of postcolonial conditions that we do not discuss in this book – for example, India, China and South Africa. We shall examine in turn the following regions and conditions: Sub-Saharan Africa: exclusion and anarchy (Chapter 8); the Middle East: Islamic revolt and anti-developmentalism (Chapter 9); East Asia: state-led developmentalism and regionalization (Chapter 10); and Latin America: democracy, civil society and postdevelopment (Chapter 11).

The Conclusion revisits the various arguments and explores likely and unlikely scenarios for the future.

A Word about the Second Edition

In a world of *business@the speed-of-thought*, as in the snazzy title of Bill Gates' book, printed texts on globalization are doomed to date pretty quickly. In preparing this second edition, I have not merely needed to find last-minute factual data and statistics, more especially those pertinent to Chapter 4, but have also revised the analytic content of substantial sections.

There are several new trends in the global political economy that have needed to be addressed. First, the appearance of the new, knowledge or digital economy; second, the resurgence of the USA after decades of putative relative decline, and the question of renewed US dominance in the global system; and third, the volatility of the global financial markets culminating in the East Asia crisis of 1997. In consequence, Part II of the book has been thoroughly reconfigured and expanded.

One significant theoretical departure from the previous edition in this second part of the book, is the replacement of the concept of 'capitalist *implosion*' by that of capitalist '*involution*'. Work on the first edition developed in a time frame when the continuing crisis and instability of the global capitalist system still dominated theoretical debates. The vigorous growth of the information driven 'new economy' and its potential to overcome the crisis of capitalist accumulation, was yet to be revealed. E-business and e-commerce exploded only after 1998. Moreover, Manuel Castells' path breaking oevre, the first volume of which appeared in 1996, had not been available to me when I worked on the first edition. His work has been a profound influence on my thinking since. And thus I have come to the view, expressed in this edition, that the long capitalist crisis which began in the 1970s has temporarily been 'resolved', albeit in a manner that provides stability and prosperity for a global minority while keeping at bay the global majority.

Also amended and extended are the chapters on East Asia and on Africa. Very minor updates have been worked into other chapters. The final conclusions of the book have been rethought in light of the mushrooming cloud of anti-globalist protests.

Acknowledgements

To write about so many different parts of the world is an audacious undertaking. It would not have come to pass had it not been for the inspiration and help, direct and indirect, that has been given to me by my research and graduate students, who are a pretty international bunch. They have taught me many things I didn't know and brought to my attention literature I had never read. Where appropriate I have referred to their theses in the normal way through references in the text. Here I want to thank them: Masae Yuasa, Rongyan Qi, Lucy Walker, Gillian Koh, Rachel Tibbett, Dong Sook Gills, Fithri Othman, Anne Holgate Lowe, Mark Christian and many others, for pushing me all the time to keep up with them. In so doing they have turned teaching into a real learning experience and a delightful vocation! I also thank my friend Jan Burgess, managing editor of the *Review of African Political Economy* for her ready knowledge and the generous use of the ROAPE library and Alistair Allan of the University of Sheffeld Library, for his help in a constant stream of information retrieval!

It has astonished me that in these times of intensified workloads, and ever more oppressive working conditions in universities, one can still find colleagues willing to sit down and completely selflessly read through a long manuscript, make meticulous comments and constructive criticisms, and tune their minds to somebody else's intellectual problems. I am deeply grateful to my colleagues Tony Payne, Lena Dominelli and Nick Stevenson, who each went through some or all sections of the first edition and made helpful comments and encouraging suggestions as I went along. Naturally, they are relieved of any responsibility for the contents. But in the preparation of the second edition I did not have the heart to ask them again. Therefore, this time the entire burden of reading and advising on earlier drafts has fallen to my publisher, Steven Kennedy. Only now that the task is finished do I appreciate fully his encouragement, patient persistence and good ideas. I have, however, resisted his suggestion that selections of further reading be added at the end of each chapter. Instead, I prefer to encourage my readers to make full use of the detailed notes and references, because it is these that will guide them to what I believe are the most relevant works in a field that is rapidly being swamped by a cacophony of voices.

If I mention them last it is not because of their contribution being least, but because theirs happened to come at the very end of all the other work: scrubbing the text clean and making it presentable for the publisher. Marg Walker, Penny Draper and Sylvia McColm have been variously involved with the 'fiddly' work of presentation, and I thank them a lot.

ANKIE HOOGVELT

PART I
HISTORICAL STRUCTURES

Introduction

The term 'political economy' has a long history. It was first coined by a French writer, Montchrétien de Watteville, in 1615, when he used it to describe 'the science of wealth acquisition common to the State as well as the Family'.[1] Writing in the early period of the great transition from small primordial communities to national social formations, de Watteville's invention of the concept proved to be an expression of extraordinary vision, for it not only presaged the emergence of economics as a scientific discipline in the nineteenth century, but it also reflected this discipline's enduring preoccupation with *national territorial accumulation*.

By the term 'national territorial accumulation' we understand a process of continuous self-expansion of capital within the territorial boundedness of the nation-state. Another expression for it would be 'economic growth of the nation'. But economic growth of a nation may conceivably be achieved (at least temporarily) through a sudden growth of income, say, from natural resources such as oil, or rent income from financial investments in other parts of the world and so on. 'National accumulation', a term preferred by Marxists, tries to encapsulate the growth of productive capacity and technological advance within a national territorial context. 'National economic development' is the nearest non-Marxist synonym.

Strangely enough, in the mercantilist period in which de Watteville was writing and which lasted until Adam Smith's formal establishment of political economy in the nineteenth century, the term 'political economy' was not much used. Mercantilism, however, was a system of political economy *par excellence*.

Mercantilism is best described as the striving after political power through economic means. In the seventeenth and eighteenth centuries, the emergence of strong national states, each competing with the other, formed the backdrop of mercantilist policies designed to foster economic growth and so raise revenue – if necessary for the

3

waging of war. The economy was put to the service of the polity. In the circumstances of the time, it meant the encouragement of trade and manufacture, the pursuit of protectionist policies, and the stimulation of export trade rather than the improvement of land. International trade was seen as a zero-sum game. The mercantilists thought of wealth in competitive terms, as something taken by one nation from another, an inherently differential gain like winning a race. The words of Thomas Mun, writing in 1664, summed up the attitude towards foreign trade: 'The ordinary means therefore to encrease our wealth and treasure is by Forraign Trade, wherein wee must observe this rule; to sell more to strangers yearly than we consume of theirs in value.'[2] By the same token, a nation must try to produce at home, instead of buying abroad.

Many writers, particularly those standing in a Marxist tradition (the so-called 'world system' writers – for example, Immanuel Wallerstein),[3] also believe that capitalism is a negative-sum game, and that the rise of some nations is always accompanied by the fall of others. But it is also a view that is today shared by some conservative, nationalist elements in advanced countries such as the USA who see power and economic wealth slipping away from their nation and passing into the hands of Japanese or European nations.

If for the seventeenth- and eighteenth-century mercantilist writers and policy-makers the economy was intended to serve the power and glory of the (nation) state, with the writings of Adam Smith in the nineteenth century this picture was entirely reversed. He wrote, in *An Inquiry into the Nature and Causes of the Wealth of Nations* (1776):

> Political economy, considered as a branch of the science of a statesman or legislator, proposes two distinct objects: first, to provide a plentiful revenue or subsistence for the people ... and secondly, to supply the state ... with a revenue sufficient for the public services.[4]

For Adam Smith, the 'wealth' of a nation was different from what it had been for the mercantilists. For Smith, wealth consisted of real goods and services (not just the ability to maintain a large army), and a nation was rich or poor according to its annual production *in proportion to its population.* It is interesting that the world community has maintained this definition of wealth up to this day. This is evidenced in the universal use of the term gross domestic product

(GDP) *per capita*. Also, for Smith, the nation was co-extensive with all its people, not just the upper classes or the body politic, as had been the case with the mercantilists. The actors in the drama of political economy were households and firms.

But the biggest difference, the great watershed between mercantilist and Smith's and subsequent (classical) economist thought, lay in that the mercantilists concentrated on the *transfer of wealth* from the nation to the rulers, to enable them to wage war against the nation's enemies. In contrast, Smith, and classical economists after him, concentrated on the *production* of wealth. In Adam Smith's work, economics became the science of statecraft. It was the task of the policy-makers and legislators to ensure optimum conditions for production. But this was also the very point where Adam Smith became the founder of *liberal economics*, the view which preferred markets to politics, and which emphasized the invisible hand of the market as the best regulator of the economy. In a politically uncontrolled economy, Smith argued, the efforts of each person to better himself would lead to the distribution of capital, labour and land that maximized people's respective returns by maximizing the value of the output to the public. In a celebrated phrase, Smith said 'Each intends only his own gain', but in the end 'promotes that of society' although this 'was no part of his intention'.[5]

The subsequent development of liberal economics or, as it increasingly came to be termed, neo-classical economics – the study of production, distribution and consumption of wealth – was marked by an ever stronger emphasis on its *scientific* character, almost as through economic processes were taking place independently of human will. This led to some ambiguity and confusion over the continued prefix 'political' in the words 'political economy'. Neo-classical economists, not surprisingly, preferred to drop the prefix 'political' altogether. Consequently, when we look up the definition of political economy in a dictionary we often find a simple statement saying that it is economics as it *used* to be called in the days of the classical economists. When writers within this liberal tradition still sometimes use the words political economy, it is to indicate a much more narrow field of enquiry, namely the study of economic policy and the linkages between economic and political factors in public policy.

Karl Marx (and Marxist tradition ever since) used the term 'political economy' in an altogether different sense. After all,

Karl Marx wrote a *critique* of political economy. While he accepted much of Smith's and David Ricardo's basic premises, in particular that labour is the source of all value, he questioned the alleged positive aspects of the functioning of capitalism (or the free market economy). He used historical materialism to demonstrate the historicity of capitalism. Marx developed a theory of class struggle and he wanted to demonstrate that the individual pursuit of self-interest leads *not* to enhanced public/collective good, but to recurring crises and the eventual breakdown of capitalism.

What is important for our purposes is that Marx's generic concept of political economy was more general and *not* coincidental with the nation-state. Marx referred to the way social relations and power relations (another way of saying class relations) affect and organize the economy and, in turn, are organized by it. For Marx, in the historical evolution of human society, these social or class relations have not always been contained within the boundaries of the nation-state. When a chief in a primitive society can command respect and tribute from the people (including a substantial amount of their production), then, for Marx, that is political economy. Or when a feudal lord has domain over land which means his tenant farmers have to pay him ground rent to use the land, then that is political economy too. In capitalist societies, the fact that an entrepreneur can hire free labour and make a profit out of the difference between what is paid to workers in wages and what the products fetch in the market, that too is political economy. Marx tried to show that there have been different political economies, which he called *modes of production*, in different historical periods, and the political economy that Smith and Ricardo were writing about was just one of a sequence of five historical modes of production (primitive – slave – feudal – capitalist – communist).[6] The Marxist study of political economy involves a study of the *historical* laws of motion that govern the evolution of this sequence of modes of production and, at the time Marx was writing, more in particular from capitalist to communist.

International Political Economy

These three different conceptualizations or models of political economy came to underpin the different perspectives on what the study of international political economy is about, namely:

1. Realism;
2. Institutionalism/pluralism; and
3. Structuralism.

But whatever the perspective on the relationship between politics and economics, it was shaped and formalized by the historical experience of the nation-state. Statism came to prevail in international theory, even in the Marxist structuralist perspective. International society was generally conceived of as a society of states. The dominant motif of all three theories of international political economy became the need to explain the paradox between an economy that was clearly internationalizing amid a world political system that was continuing to be compartmentalized into separate nation-states.[7] And thus they elaborated their existing conceptual schemata to cover this historical contingency rather than to start afresh and invent new models.

Realism

The realist position is inspired by a mercantilist conception of political economy. It gives primacy to the body politic, conceives of the nation-state as actor, and imagines the world as a competition of units (nation-states) in an anarchic international arena dominated by the struggle for power among states.[8] In analogy with what Thomas Hobbes had to say about 'man eats man' (*homo homini lupus*), so the realist sees the world as a jungle of nation-states all out to further their own interests. The realist perspective focuses on interstate competition, and on the use of *power* by nations in interfering in international markets on behalf of their own states. Based on their analysis of continual interstate competition, the realist comes up with a normative theory of international *order and stability* rooted in conceptions of *hegemony* and *balance of power* (for example, American postwar hegemony; and the balance of power between the US-dominated and the USSR-dominated blocs).

Institutionalism/pluralism

The second position is that of the pluralist or institutionalist perspective. This perspective is more in tune with Adam Smith's classical liberal economics. It recognizes the increasing economic interdependence between states, and sees this as being grounded in what is regarded as the all-round growth-maximizing and beneficial operations of the now worldwide free market system. It argues that increasing economic interdependence forces states to develop and pursue policies of rational self-interest, which lead to greater economic co-operation between them rather than to conflict. Co-operation becomes necessary and institutionalized in intergovernmental regimes of governance and co-ordination. Thus, for example, the institutionalists argue that the postwar stable world order owed not so much to American hegemony and a balance of power between the USA and USSR, but rather to the development of viable international institutions, such as United Nations organizations, international treaties, regional blocs and so on. The perspective is sometimes referred to as 'pluralist' because it believes that co-operation can take place without the supremacy of any one nation, but rather on the basis of a plurality of co-ordinated and interlocking interests between nations: a plural world order. The international political economy is seen to consist of the emergence, at an accelerating pace, of international institutions for the management of the internationalized economy.[9]

Structuralism

A third perspective on international political economy is the structuralist perspective. This derives from a Marxist notion of political economy as described above. Structuralists basically apply the Marxist study of capitalist political economy to international relations. That is to say, the study of the relations between states is derived from, and subsidiary to, the concern with the development of capitalism on a global scale. It is argued that capitalism is a mode of production that has become trans-societal and which in modern times spans practically all the nations of the world. But while structuralists thus begin with a conception of the totality of the world system, they next look at states as constitutive units having a structural relationship predetermined by the world capitalist economy. It is called 'structuralist' because it challenges the assumption that national societies constitute 'independent' units whose development can be understood without taking into account the *systemic* ways in which these societies are linked to one another in the context of an ever-expanding network of material (economic) exchanges. In the view of the structuralists, it is the deep logic of the capitalist mode of production itself that yields the nodal positions (for example, of core, periphery and semi-periphery) within the global structure nations occupy. These intersocietal and trans-societal networks of material exchanges are either termed *world systems* as in Wallerstein's theory; or *global social formations*, as in Amin's terminology;[10] or *global formations*, as in Chase-Dunn's work.[11]

What is especially confusing about the three competing perspectives is that they may pair up, two against one, depending on the analytical question being posed. For example, both realists and Marxists tend to regard the outcome of international economic relations as a redistributive, non-sum game: the gain of some nations is always at the expense of others. This contrasts with the liberals, who have a more optimistic view of the outcome of international economic relations: they see it as a positive- sum game in which eventually all participants will be better-off, even if the distribution of gains is not equal. Liberals and Marxists in their turn line up together when it comes to giving primacy to the economy in shaping the body politic, in contrast to the realists, who see the relationship the other way around. But when it comes to offering an explanation of social change, both realists and liberals have nothing to present: theirs is a theory of *stasis* and *equilibrium*, while here it is the Marxists who are alone in developing a theory of social change.[12]

This incompatibility of conceptual frameworks has led over time to sterile interparadigmatic debates, and eventually to a polarization of the field of international relations into separate sub-fields. Neo-realists focused on strategic studies, American foreign policy and the Cold War; neo-institutionalists looked at international organizations, multinational companies and the developing international economy; neo-Marxists concentrated on the core–periphery hierarchy in the world economy. However, in the 1970s a powerful wind of intellectual change began to blow across the fields of *all* social sciences and eventually swept across the study of international political economy too.

Postmodernist knowledge theory began to break the hold of progressivist thinking over liberal and Marxist traditions; it opened up a space for human agency in structuralist analyses and thus made them less deterministic, and at the same time made scholars more aware of the relationship between truth and power – that is, the rules of 'knowledge' that are never far from the social context in which they operate. The outcome was a critical social theory that proliferated as an 'agenda of dissent' in the field of international political economy.[13] Soon that agenda would yield the beginnings of new theoretical approaches. For example, in the trailblazing work of Robert Cox we find critical social theory applied to the problem of world order and historical transformation. Cox has managed to synthesize and transcend the neo-realist and neo-Marxist approaches, reintegrate the separate sub-fields of international economic relations and strategic studies, and overcome the structure/agency dichotomy. Indeed, for a growing number of scholars in the field, Robert Cox has become the founding father of a *new* international political economy.[14]

The Critical Theory of Robert Cox: Historical Structure

Robert Cox's[15] main contribution lies in the development of a *methodology* for the study of historical change in international political economy. He begins by critiquing conventional international relations theory, neo-realism and neo-Marxism alike, (i) for being altogether too obsessed with the relations between states; (ii) for failing to develop conceptual apparatuses that may account for the many trans-societal linkages that are growing up; and (iii) for not being critically aware of their own historical roots. He next grapples with two problems. One is that of world order: what is it, and how can it be described? The second is that of historical change, by which he means transformative change in the organization of human affairs. Put the two together and the problematic is: how do world orders change?

What is interesting about Cox's theory is that he answers this question by a process of reversal: the question of change has to be understood from the vantage point of comprehending what makes for stability. At this point, Cox makes his most important contribution to the study of international political economy: he injects Antonio Gramsci's notion of hegemony into the study of world order. Gramsci[16] had originally developed the notion of hegemony as a 'fit' between power, ideas and institutions to explain the stability of capitalist class relations and *national* social order. Cox now uses Gramsci's concept of hegemony to explain a stable *world* order, rather than – as in conventional international relations theories – single state dominance or bipolar state balance of power, or some such.

Cox deploys the concept of 'historical structure' to examine how and why the fit comes about, and how and why it comes apart. He defines a historical structure as 'a particular configuration between ideas, institutions and material forces'. It is no more than a frame-work of action which constitutes the context of habits, pressures, expectations and constraints within which actions take place, but which does not determine actions in any direct, mechanical way. 'Individuals may move with the pressures or resist and oppose them, but they cannot ignore them. To the extent that they do successfully resist a prevailing historical structure, they buttress their actions with an alternative, emerging configuration of forces: a rival structure.'[17] Thus, we notice that the concept of historical structure is far less deterministic than in most Marxist accounts of history, and that it leaves open the possibility that history can develop in a variety of directions. The task of the critical social scientist is to uncover 'plausible' alternative futures, instead of remaining trapped in some trans-historical essentialism in which either the present is for ever (as, for example, in Fukuyama's End of History scenario), or the future is a foregone conclusion, as in orthodox historical materialism.

On the question of what is the *source* of historical change, Cox argues that historical materialism, unlike structural or (neo)Marxism, does in fact have a lot to offer to a theory of historical change. He submits that it is the foremost source of 'critical theory', for two reasons: first, because it focuses on the principle of the *dialectic* as a source of transformative changes between grand, epochal, systems of human socio-economic organization (modes of production) – the principle of the dialectic refers to the search for contradictions in social life as the mainspring of social change. And, second, because it identifies changes in social forces shaped by production relations as a prime mover in these transformations. However, historical materialism has failed in three respects: first, in the lack of awareness of its own historical boundedness; second, in the pre-Gramscian conception of a unidirectional connection between economic structure on the one hand, and institutions and ideas on the other; and third, in the altogether too abstract and deterministic presentation of an unfolding history in which the progressive transformation of modes of production through the dialectic is a foregone teleological conclusion. Instead, Cox recognizes that ideas which have become institutionalized may hang on long after the material forces that gave rise to them have been transformed, and well after the hegemonic power that institutionalized and universalized them has demised; and while rival social forces, growing out of changed material conditions, struggle for ideological and institutional ascendancy.

Thus, in line with most other contemporary postmodernist, poststructuralist thinking, Cox wants to break with the determinism of historical theory. He sees history as open-ended, and he wants us to realize that not only human structures and action but also *theory itself is part of a historical structure*, and therefore constitutes part of the problematic we are researching. This is the kernel of Cox's metatheoretical concept of critical theory: 'Critical theory is conscious of its own relativity but through this consciousness can achieve a broader time perspective and become less relative',[18] that is, it is less bound at its historical origin. It knows that the task of theorizing can never be finished in an enclosed system but must continually begin anew, beginning *not* with abstract conceptions but with a description of historical experience, ferreting out the emerging contradictions between changing material conditions and associated social forces on the one hand, and the vested interests or overhangs from past institutions and ideologies on the other.

Historical Structure and Stage Theory

I have introduced the reader to Cox's work not with the pretence of doing justice to the innovative richness of this leading theorist, but because I want to borrow his concept of 'historical structure' to look back over the history of the relationships between rich and poor countries, both materially and in respect of how these relationships were time and again institutionalized and theorized, and how they changed.

Writers standing in the structural Marxist tradition have tended to analyze the history of those relationships in terms of a dialectical development of the capitalist world system in distinctive historical *stages*. Capitalism's inherent contradictions (the driving force of the dynamics of change) were thought to be worked out in different phases of expansion, punctuated by crises, in which state and interstate relations were time and again rearranged as political structures that held in place a continuing exploitative economic relationship between 'core' and 'peripheral' areas. In each of the expansive phases of capitalism, the peripheral areas of the world were assigned a particular *function* at the service of the essential needs of accumulation at the centre, or core, of the system. Each phase of expansion, however, resulted in cumulative differences in productive capacity and income between core and periphery, leading to recurring crises of disequilibrium, after which the relationship needed to be restructured.

Thus (and very sketchily), in historical succession, the periphery is said to have served: first, in the mercantile period, as a source of primitive accumulation, financing the industrial revolution in the core; next, in the colonial period, it served as supplier of raw materials and foodstuffs; and, subsequently, in the neocolonial period, it graduated to become modernizing developmental states, providing the export markets for late industrialism's producer goods.

In Chapters 1, 2 and 3, I describe the dialectic unfolding of the relationships between core and periphery from within this stage-theoretical perspective. However, I propose that we borrow Cox's concept of 'historical structure' to distance ourselves from the determinism that is implied in this perspective. Thus, rather than viewing these stages as inevitable steps in some unfolding, progressive logic of capitalist history, let us theorize about them as periods in which there was, each time, a 'fit' between material conditions, institutions and ideology, including the reflections and 'theories' of the time. It was the 'fit' that created a momentary stability in the process of international capital accumulation (and which allows us to identify them as stages), until structural contradictions engendered by new developments in material production *or* by rivalling ideologies forced a process of crisis and change. When material, institutional and ideological elements once more fell into place, there came about the next phase, of relatively stable international capital accumulation.

1

The History of Capitalist Expansion

There is considerable agreement among economic historians that capitalism as a mode of organizing social and economic life began not only in one minuscule corner of the globe, namely north-west Europe, but from its very beginnings, while it was itself still in the process of being formed in the fifteenth and sixteenth centuries, involved outward expansion, gradually encompassing ever-larger-areas of the globe in a network of material exchanges. This network developed over time into a world market for goods and services, or an international division of labour. By the end of the nineteenth century the project of a single capitalist world economy had been completed in the sense that the grid of exchange relationships now covered practically all the geographical areas of the world.

The nineteenth century in particular stands out as the prime time for the development of an international division of labour. It is estimated that in each of the decades of that century world trade grew about eleven times faster than world production, and that by 1913, on the eve of the First World War, some 33 per cent of world production was trading across national frontiers.[1] What is even more significant for the theme of this book is the fact that in those days certain geographical areas of the world, since designated 'the Third World,' namely South America, Africa and Asia, excluding Japan, participated fully, if not on equal terms, in this international market. In 1913, the Third World captured about 50 per cent of world trade compared with about 29 per cent today.[2]

Following Immanuel Wallerstein,[3] we call this international division of labour a *capitalist* world economy because its defining criterion was the production of goods and services for sale in a market in which the object is to realise the maximum profit. In a capitalist market it is the seemingly neutral forces of supply and demand that determine the price of a product, and thereby signal to the producers whether they should expand production, cut back on output, or change production techniques and cut their cost structure and so on. In other words, through the medium of Adam Smith's celebrated invisible hand, which already by the end of the nineteenth century had become a *global* invisible hand, human activities were pretty well co-ordinated across national frontiers.

The Political Nature of the Capitalist World Economy

There should be no illusion that this co-ordination came about spontaneously or peacefully, or that it dealt a fair hand to all the players. Indeed, the merit and lasting achievement of the Marxist tradition has been to show that at all times, and at all levels, the 'invisible' hand was guided and steered by politics and power, and that it always, and indeed cumulatively so, ended up in the concentration of wealth and prosperity for some people in some places, while causing abject misery, poverty and appalling subjugation for a majority of people in most other places.

Marx's great theoretical contribution was to show how the formal equality of the market could produce socially structured inequality. Wallerstein adds to this the insight that commodity production regularly takes place in an arena that is, importantly, structured by *power relations between states*. Within the historically developing international division of labour, it was the first capitalist developers, the 'core' states, who gained the historical upper hand, and thus were able to protect and assist, with gunboat diplomacy and other forms of political coercion, their own capitalists in imposing world market relations and shaping these to their advantage. Wallerstein has shown how the interstate system is in fact the political system of the world capitalist economy, and how the core–periphery hierarchy and the exploitation of the periphery by the core are in fact necessary to the reproduction of capitalism as a system.[4]

The Dialectical Development of Capitalism as a World System

What concerns us next is how this relationship has unfolded in a *dialectical* manner. What do we mean by dialectics? Simply put, it is the study of systemic *contradictions*. An analysis that follows the dialectical method searches for inherent tendencies within a system which create and bring out their own conflicts until such a system can no longer maintain and reproduce itself without far-reaching structural adjustments. In the case of the capitalist mode of production, or socio-economic system, the question of adjustment or transformation has occupied an immense space in Marxist literature, to which we shall refer at a later stage in this book. For practical purposes it is sufficient to note at this point that so far the world capitalist system has shown amazing resilience in adapting to changing circumstances brought about by its very own laws of motion. We shall concentrate first on how it has managed to do this.

A Periodization of Capitalist Development and Expansion

A number of writers who focus on the world system have proposed a *periodization* of capitalist development in which both the characteristics of core capital *and* its relationship to the peripheral areas vary. These variations themselves are seen as a dialectical outcome of the contradictions engendered in each (previous) period of inter-

action. Neo-Marxist writers, such as Samir Amin,[5] Andre Gunder Frank,[6] Ernest Mandel,[7] Albert Szymanski[8] and Harry Magdoff,[9] commonly identify a mercantilist pre-competitive stage (1500–1800); a competitive capitalist stage (1800–80); a monopoly/imperialist stage (1880–1960); and some even a late monopoly capitalist/imperialist stage (beginning with the crisis of 1968).[10]

In each of the periods, the periphery performs specific functions at the service of the essential needs of accumulation at the centre. But these essential needs change precisely as a result of the successful outcome of the service. And because the dialectical interaction between core and periphery yields increasingly disparate levels of developments in core and periphery within each period, the core and periphery, as it were, drift further apart, each time leading to a point of crisis in the relationship which is then overcome by altering its formal structure, and the method of surplus extraction by the core from the periphery.

Here, and in the next two chapters, I shall distinguish four periods (very roughly and ignoring wide geographical variations) as follows:

1. *1500–1800 mercantile phase*: transfer of economic surplus through looting and plundering, disguised as trade;
2. *1800–1950 colonial period*: transfer of economic surplus through 'unequal terms of trade' by virtue of a colonially-imposed international division of labour;
3. *1950–70 neocolonial period*: transfer of economic surplus through 'developmentalism' and technological rents; and
4. *1970– postimperialism*: transfer of economic surplus through debt peonage.

The Mercantile Phase of European Expansion

During the mercantile phase of European expansion, from about 1500 to 1800, European merchants scoured the coasts of Africa and Asia, and the lands of South America in search of gold, spices, slaves and the conquest of existing trade routes. Paul Baran, in his famous work *The Political Economy of Growth*,[11] has drawn attention to the way this trading relationship was no more than a disguised form of looting and plundering, in which the Europeans were able to transfer the *economic surplus* of pre-industrial overseas communities back to Europe where it helped to pay for the industrial revolution. Economic surplus is investible surplus: it is that part of production that is not consumed by a community but is piled up in hoarded wealth. But this form of development was a two-way street: at the same time that the overseas lands were helping indirectly to pay for Europe's technological and industrial advance, the loss of their economic surplus removed the opportunity for economic advancement in the territories where the West traded, and so arrested their further internal development. But not only was their internal development halted, their confrontation with the West also had a *regressive* effect on the level of societal evolution they had already reached, as, for example, Walter Rodney has detailed in his book *How Europe Underdeveloped Africa*.[12]

The resulting disparity of societal advance – economic, political and social – at some stage turned into a bottleneck for the further advance of the West.[13] After 1800, Europe embarked decisively on a path of mass industrialization and it was looking for market outlets, as well as secure supplies of raw materials and foodstuffs, on a scale and requiring a degree of predictability and regularity that simply defied the arbitrary looting and plunder of the mercantile arrangement. As Magdoff comments, 'But there was a limit to the profitability of the first wave of expansion: the wealth obtained by plunder of hoards amassed over years can only be taken once.'[14] After 1875, moreover, outright territorial annexation was frequently forced upon reluctant European statesmen and public opinion by the ever more frantic rivalry between European nations.

The Colonial Phase of European Expansion

Direct political control and administration of the overseas territories was often a convenient method of organizing the production systems and laying the infrastructure in the ancillary economies at that time. Between 1800 and 1878, European rule, including former colonies in North and South America, increased from 35 per cent to 67 per cent of the Earth's land surface; and another 18 per cent was added in the new wave of annexations between 1875 and 1914.[15]

The period of formal colonialism, especially between 1875 and 1914, witnessed an extraordinary and globe-girding internationalization of capital. A handful of countries in Europe together with the USA were responsible for 85 per cent of all international lending, totalling, by 1913, $44 billion.[16] About half of this international lending went to the continents of Asia, Africa and South America. There it found its way into the building of railways, port installations, mines and factories. Capital accumulation and savings in the core of the world system were channelled to the periphery through the financial intermediation of international portfolio lending and, to a lesser extent, direct investments by emerging multinational companies. In the periphery they converted into fixed investments, laying the foundations for future wealth creation.

In a glowing tribute to Victorian attitudes towards capitalist expansion, Alex Cairncross has described the monumental quality of the effort involved:

The forty or fifty years before 1914 were clearly an exceptional period in economic history. It was symptomatic of the period that western Europe had invested abroad almost as much as the entire national wealth of Great Britain, the leading industrial country, and a good deal more than the value of the capital physically located in Great Britain. It was also symptomatic that Britain herself had invested abroad as much as her entire industrial and commercial capital, excluding land, and that one-tenth of her national income came to her as interest on foreign investments. These conditions can hardly recur.[17]

It was thus in this period that the periphery was brought into an expanding and intensifying network of economic exchanges with the core. It was incorporated in a vigorous geographical extension of capitalism that was quite the opposite of the 'imploding globalization' that we are witnessing at the start of the twenty first century, and from which most areas of the Third World are excluded.

In contrast to more recent historical narratives, which, as we shall see below, tend to play down the commercial interests involved, the colonial period itself did not lack advocates and crusaders who robustly identified the economic need for colonies and who legitimized this need to the public back home with the promise of jobs and trade, as well as with noble sentiments of civilization and universal progress.

Not only was the need for such colonies argued in economic terms, indeed it was often expressed as a vital national interest. This was especially so after 1875, when national rivalries between European states reached a frantic crescendo in the 'scramble for Africa'. As A. P. Thornton argued, the ideology of imperialism involved a legitimate attitude towards the world that was shaped by nationalistic and patriotic sentiments. For example, Houston Stewart Chamberlain and his school drew attention to the vulnerability of an England that did not command a world position. In their speeches and writings they argued that half the population of Britain would starve if the country was ever reduced to being 'Little England', if ever the British Empire narrowed down to a 'mere' United Kingdom dimension.[18]

Colonialism was seen by many not only as a form of survival but also as the sole policy of survival. Cecil Rhodes argued the same point in even stronger terms. Great Britain's world position depended, he said, upon its trade, and if its people did not take over and open up those areas of the world that were in the grip of barbarism, they would be shut off from the world's trade, since other nations would do the job for them: 'I would annexe the planets if I could', he exclaimed.[19]

The policy of territorial annexations was thus justified and defended to the taxpayers at home because it would create trade and jobs for them, and make the nation strong in its rivalry with other nations.

In this conception of imperialism as economic necessity, colonies were regarded as national property, as estates that must be developed using the most up-to-date methods. This brought with it a missionary zeal to civilize the colonized people and to bring their way of life into the twentieth century so that they would be able to participate in modern commerce and industry. Thus civilization and commercialization went hand in hand, and were generally seen as positive benefits for the colonized peoples. This indeed was the 'white man's burden', to borrow Rudyard Kipling's celebrated phrase. As Benjamin Kidd, an English sociologist at the turn of the century, wrote:

> The task of governing from a distance the inferior races of mankind will be one of great difficulty. One that will tax every resource of intellect and character. But it is one that must be faced and overcome if the civilised world is not to abandon all hope of its continuing economic conquest of the natural resources of the globe.[20]

The imperialists thus saw it as part of their mission to disseminate law, order, justice, education, peace and prosperity. Even Bernard Shaw could argue that, if the Chinese were incapable of establishing conditions in their own country which would promote peaceful commerce and civilized life, it was the duty of the European powers to establish such conditions for them.[21]

Such a view of the territorial conquest of the colonial period owes more to the notion that political rivalry, or economic and social inadequacy in the *periphery*, stimulated the drive to colonial annexation, rather than any 'necessary' causative link with the development of monopoly capital in the *core* countries.[22] The latter was the stubborn view of the classical Marxist theories of imperialism

as developed by V.I. Lenin, N. Bukharin and R. Hilferding.[23]
However, a proper analysis of the dialectically unfolding relationship between core and periphery of the developing world capitalist
system will give equal credit to both sets of reasons. For, just as
the periphery had been underdeveloped as a result of its mercantile
relations with the core (requiring 'civilisation through commerce'
in Bismarck's celebrated phrase), so the core of the capitalist system
had itself developed to a higher stage of capitalist development
in which the conditions for further accumulation of capital called
for a dramatic change of production relations, whether between
capital and labour at home (this was the preferred solution of the
social reformers in the core economies), or in a new wave and
pattern of imperialist expansion abroad. The inevitability of this
expansion was the key point of the Marxist critics of capitalist
imperialism.

Marxist Theories of Capitalist Imperialism

The classical Marxist theories of imperialism began with an analysis
of the workings of capitalism in the core countries. Interestingly, the
foundation of these theories was laid by a liberal, J. A. Hobson, in
1905.[24] While Hobson's analysis may be said to have been Marxist,
since he used the dialectic method of tracing the contradictions of
contemporary capitalism, his solution and policy prescription were
liberal and reformist. He wanted to end imperialism by changing
production relations at home.

Hobson argued that capitalist societies tend to save money and to
invest these savings as capital in order to produce more goods in the
future. Accumulation of capital is crucial if society is to progress, because otherwise production would be static. Also, it is the drive
behind the capitalist entrepreneur's profit motivation, because only
if profits are invested in more and better equipment can savings be
made on the costs of production and thereby the entrepreneur can
compete successfully with his rivals. But capital accumulation ultimately depends on the general level of profits remaining above the
point at which capitalists would prefer to consume their savings
rather than invest them. This then leads to the vital question of
whether profit rates in capitalist societies will tend to rise or decline
over a period of time.

It is in the answer to this question that we find the roots of the theories of capitalist imperialism, as developed by Hobson and many Marxist writers. They believed that the normal tendency of the rate of profit in industrialized countries is to decline over a long period. The *rate* of profit is thought to decline because the very process of capital accumulation itself increases the amount of fixed capital per worker and increases productivity. The result is the tendency of the system of accumulation to produce ever more goods with fewer income-earning workers, leading to periodic crises of *over-production* and *under-consumption*.

Hobson concentrated exclusively on the over-production and under-consumptionist aspect of the tendency of the rate of profit to decline. For Hobson, the link between under-consumption at home and imperialism was that capitalist entrepreneurs would, in consequence, find fewer outlets for their capital at home and instead would channel it into overseas investment. For Hobson, imperialism did *not* serve the nation of small producers, workers and taxpayers in the way that liberal apologists of imperialism often argued. It merely served the interests of a small ruling class – the financiers – who would usurp the taxpayers' money into overseas investments, as well as into the provision of ships, guns, military equipment, railways and so on.

In this way, Hobson turned the arguments of the liberal apologists of imperialism completely on their head. According to Hobson, investments in weak and backward countries required political control as an insurance, and the financiers and cliques of stockbrokers in the city knew how to lobby politicians into backing them. Hobson attributed the exodus of capital to *lack of investment at home* and his remedy therefore was to improve living standards in the home country. In other words: *social reform*. This remained the favourite prescription of liberals for decades to come. But the impossibility of social reform under capitalism became one of the leading tenets of Marxist theories of imperialism.

Marxist writers did not disagree with Hobson's position. However, they saw it as a kind of minimum statement, not the whole story, and they decried the conclusions as 'reformist': as if capitalism would allow itself to be reformed and mend its ways! Classical Marxist theorists of imperialism, such as Lenin, Hilferding and Bukharin, instead argued a 'necessity of imperialism' thesis.[25] In positing this thesis, these authors took their clues from Marx's own writings on the laws of motion of capitalism, even though Marx himself contributed very little to a proper theory of imperialism. These laws of motion predicted the centralization and concentration of capital arising out of the contradictions of competitive capitalism, and leading to a stage of *monopoly capitalism*. When they were writing in the early part of the twentieth century, it appeared to them that this condition of monopoly capitalism had fully arrived. Moreover, it had arrived under the compelling force of 'finance capital', which referred not to money or financial capital but to the 'merging of banking and industrial capital'. And thus, in their theory of imperialism, they came to describe the phenomenon as a necessary policy of this, the 'highest' stage of capitalism.

Classical Marxist writers were also influenced by the turbulent years of the second decade of the twentieth century, in which two puzzlingly contrasting phenomena dominated the scene. On the one hand there was the intensifying *nationalist rivalry between the capitalist countries* which boiled over into the First World War, and on the other there was the phenomenal growth, not just of a world market for commodities freely exchanged across borders, but of the *internationalization of production* itself when giant firms from metropolitan countries began to integrate mine-to-market production chains vertically across the globe, when international trusts and cartels appeared to set world market prices and allocate spheres of investments and distribution outlets, and when shares began to be traded across frontiers, and international loans became the order of the day. As Bukharin pointed out, all these were examples of an international organization of the world economy which attested to a 'thickening' network of global economic and social relations supplanting the anarchy of the world market.[26]

This puzzling paradox of nationalism and internationalization was explained with reference to Marx's theory of the laws of motion of capitalism. For Lenin, Hilferding and Bukharin, the monopoly stage of capitalism is definitive of imperialism. It was, in their view, imperialism that staved off the collapse of capitalism. How did that stage come about?

Marx had already referred to two laws of motion of capitalism whereby it would inevitably and unavoidably develop from the competitive stage to the monopoly stage. These two laws were those referring to the processes of concentration and centralization. *Concentration* refers to the enlargement of an individual enterprise's capital out of its own accumulated profits, while *centralization*

refers to the process whereby, under competition, individual capitalist enterprises lose their independence and are brought under the centralized control of one big firm. Centralization refers, in other words, to cartelization, mergers and take-overs. This process of concentration and centralization goes hand in hand with the rise of what Hilferding called *finance capital* (or bank capital transformed into and controlling industrial capital).

How does the interwovenness of industrial and financial capital, and their increasing concentration and centralization, affect imperialism – that is, the export of capital and the territorial annexation of colonies that accompanied it?

Hilferding argued that the problem with cartels was that, being so powerful, they lobbied their governments to go against the principles of free trade (characteristic of the previous, competitive epoch) and demanded *protective tariffs:* once they had the whole domestic market for themselves they wanted to keep it from intrusion by cartels of other nations. Thus competition between nations intensified. Hilferding was absolutely right about this at the time. The hallmark of the interwar period was protectionism and an increasingly souring trade relationship between nations.

Cartels, however, are also associated with an increase in the price of products: monopolistic prices are higher than would pertain under competitive conditions. The point is then reached, and this is crucial, where it no longer makes sense to produce more of the same product, or to produce the product at lower cost for the home market, because the market is controlled in any case, so why bother – the results would be to drive the monopoly price down. So what to do with the profits? Markets must be found abroad! But the opportunity for expansion abroad is limited. It is not possible to go into neighbouring advanced and cartelized countries because they have their own protective tariffs. So markets further afield must be sought, conquering overseas territories (colonies) and erecting tariffs around these too.

Both Hilferding and Lenin recognised the other reasons Marxist critiques of capitalist imperialism have brought to bear on the explanation for capital exports, namely the need for secure supplies of raw materials and foodstuffs to feed into the smokestack industries of the centre capitalist countries. But their main emphasis was on monopolies, protection, tariffs and on the manner in which *protection hinders the export of goods while promoting the export of capital.*

Thus the principal feature that classical Marxist writers identified in imperialism is that it hinges on this very dangerous paradox: namely the internationalization of capital on the one hand, and on the other the intensified nationalist struggles between advanced nations for the remaining bits of the globe – leading, for example, to 'the scramble for Africa', and eventually to imperialist wars.

Critiques of Marxist Theories of Imperialism

In the interwar period, theories of 'capitalist' imperialism became widely influential. The word 'imperialism' became a term of abuse, and its causal link with the recurring crises of modern capitalism was sufficiently widely understood to make for a growing chorus demanding social reforms and redistribution which had become an electoral platform of social democratic movements in the core countries.

It is therefore somewhat paradoxical to find that in the postwar period, which spelt the end of formal colonialism, the balance of scholarly opinion swung the other way. There has of late been considerable soul-searching over the question of why European influence converted into *formal* empire when it did; whether it was political and strategic factors that pushed otherwise (by many accounts) unenthusiastic European statesmen and parliaments into territorial annexations, or whether it was economic factors that provided the causal connection.

As V. G. Kiernan[27] has reported, modern historical scholarship, with few exceptions, has come down on the side of 'politics' as being the real villain. Sectional economic interests indeed might have been served on occasion by the imposition of direct political control, but rarely, so it is argued, did territorial conquest serve, or was directly inspired by, vital national economic interests. More often than not, the decision to occupy foreign lands came as an *ad hoc* response to local problems, such as when existing treaties or alliances with local fiefs were threatened, either by indigenous rebellions or by European rivals.

Sometimes territories were captured not because of their economic value, but because they had strategic importance as gateways to other areas where economic or security interests *were* dominant (for example, the Suez and Panama Canals). On other occasions there was a diplomatic use for colonies, such as when a threat to territories regarded by one power as a special interest could be made a bargaining point in negotiations over quite a different matter.[28] Finally, political rivalry at home could tempt nations into colonial adventures to regain a sense of glory and grandeur, or to give employment and experience to its soldiers.[29]

Not only had capitalism nothing to do with the historical accident that was imperialism, but it did not benefit from it either. Economic historians have seized eagerly on the 'evidence': trade with the colonial dependencies was generally only a small fraction of all British and French foreign trade; non-colonial powers had the advantage of having easy access to markets of colonies of other states; direct investment in raw materials (mines and plantations) was only about 10 per cent of all foreign investment in the periphery, and the share of colonial raw materials in the raw material market as a whole was relatively slight. Terms of trade were not particularly favourable to Europe during the high tide of imperialism; non-imperialist states found little difficulty in attaining a high level of growth, foreign trade, foreign investments, and so on.[30]

However, this is taking a pettifoggingly narrow view of the historical process, as if the profits from imperialism could be expected to be cashed in at the very same moment that the investments were made. It makes more sense to see the formal period as one of preparatory construction, of laying the foundations of future wealth creation and surplus extraction. Almost three-quarters of all British capital investments were in railways, canals, electricity and other social overheads, and together with the 'mere' 10 per cent that went into mines and plantations, they would not reap their full harvest until after the end of formal empire.[31]

It is in the continuing structural connections, both physical, as for example in the measurement of the gauge of railways which determines future procurement of rail coaches, *and* in terms of production relations, as in the continued metropolitan ownership and control of mineral production and exports of cash crops, *and* in the cultural and social nurturing of local élites, that we must see the 'economic' importance of the period of formal colonialism. Indeed, the importance of formal colonialism lay in the legacy of the international division of labour, of resource bondage and the westernization of the peripheral élites.

As for the Marxist contention of the causal link between the overripeness of capitalism, capital exports and the new imperialism after 1875, here too the weight of academic opinion is fully against the recognition of any such link. The grave of the Marxist theory of imperialism has been dug jointly by liberals and those standing in the Marxist tradition themselves.

For example, Bill Warren, in his powerful critique of Lenin,[32] points out, as others did before him (notably J. A. Schumpeter),[33] that the actual record of the export of capital in the period 1880–1914, however formidable, does not tally with Lenin's descriptions of monopoly capital exporting capital, nor with the idea of main rivalling imperialist countries doing the exporting, nor indeed with the notion that capital exports went primarily to the colonies.

First, many of the chief participants in the great imperialist wars that were to break out after 1914, namely Russia, the USA, Italy, Germany and Japan, contributed an insignificant proportion of capital exports (especially capital exports to the Third World), at least during the period that Lenin describes; second, the bulk, (that is, 60 per cent of capital exports from Britain) went to the New World, 40 per cent went to what is now called the Third World, but a much smaller proportion of this again went to the colonial territories themselves; and, third, most damaging of all to Lenin's theory is that before 1914, 90 per cent of all investments were *portfolio investments* rather than direct investments. Bill Warren comments:

the empirical evidence does not support the contention that monopolization was the causal link between the 'overripeness' of capitalism, capital exports and the new imperialism. The partition of the world among the imperialist powers had been largely completed before the end of the nineteenth century, by which time one-fifth of the land surface of the globe and one-tenth of the world's population were under the direct control of European powers. By 1900, some 90 per cent of Africa had been subjected to Europe and most of that part of Asia that was ever to be directly colonized. But as Lenin himself recognized, the domination of the major economies by industrial combinations took hold no earlier than the first decade of the twentieth century. Even this is too early for Britain which had by far the largest empire and exported the greatest volume of capital. Indeed, at the end of the nineteenth century the greatest imperial

powers, Britain and France, possessed the least and most recently
concentrated industrial structures of all the major powers: both
countries achieved their imperial status well before an oligopo-
listic and centralised industrial structure took root.[34]

If modern scholarship, including contemporary Marxist scholarship, denies any 'necessary' causative link between the logic of
capitalist development and the period of formal colonialism, this
is not to say that there was no *historical* connection between the
two. Alain Lipietz resolves the difference rather neatly when he
argues that we can remain faithful to a theory of the historical
dialectic while abandoning the notion of any necessary unfolding
of a capitalist logic in a *specific direction*:

> In capitalism, there are general contradictions, and if imperialism
> can resolve them, even temporarily, then it is legitimate to say
> that imperialism developed by resolving the general contra-
> dictions to the benefit of specific national capitalism. Imperialism
> was not specifically created to resolve these contradictions, but it
> continued to exist; it developed because, in fact, it resolved them.
> It could disappear, be modified, or hold on by habit if other
> solutions were found to these contradictions, or if other
> contradictions developed. Only in that sense can it be said that
> things being what they are and history having its habits, that
> imperialism's function is to resolve these contradictions.[35]

In the next chapter we shall see how the formal phase of imperialism
developed its own contradictions, to which other solutions were
found, not in any predetermined fashion, but rather as a contingent
outcome of the historical process.

2

Neocolonialism, Modernization and Dependency

Neither independence nor neocolonialism 'fell from the sky'. They did not just happen by chance, nor as the fruit of some new insight. Rather, they were the outcome of profound historical pressures and struggles. These pressures and struggles themselves, paradoxically, were engendered by the very success of colonialism as a hegemonic organization of international production relations which had permitted a vast accumulation of wealth and progress to occur in the nations of Western Europe. It is the very success of this pattern of global accumulation that brought forth its own contradictions, pressures for change and adaptation which needed to be made if the continuity of global accumulation was to be safeguarded.

We may classify these successes and the pressures that they created into three groups:

1. pressures arising from the developing material capabilities at the level of the global economy;
2. domestic political struggles relating to the organization of production relations within the colonial countries; and
3. geopolitical conflicts, relating to the interstate system and world order.

Global Economic Pressures

The imposition of the international division of labour under formal colonialism had the indirect effect of laying the foundations for

29

continued economic control and domination over colonial resources even in the absence of direct political overlordship and administration. Prime agricultural land had been passed into the possession of foreign plantation owners or otherwise directed towards the large-scale production of export crops. Long-term concessions for mineral exploration and exploitation had been granted, and mines had been established as wholly-owned subsidiaries of metropolitan firms. Capitalist markets and market institutions had been set up, and the import–export trade was firmly in the hands of such metropolitan multi-commodity traders as Unilever, John Holt or the Compagnie Française de L'Afrique Occidentale, to name but a few.

In other words, once the most important productive sectors of the colonial countries had been 'slotted' into the system of world capitalism and its institutions, control over these economic resources could be relied on to continue at 'arm's length', even without direct political suzerainty. The period of colonialism had prepared and firmed up those institutions necessary for the 'historical structure' of international capitalism in the neocolonial period. The most important of these institutions was undoubtedly the sanctity of private property abroad, which a good deal of international law and much consensus on the part of the international community had learnt to protect. It permitted the emergence of neocolonialism as the survival and continuation of the colonial system in spite of formal recognition of political independence in emerging countries. Instead, they became 'the victims of an indirect and subtle form of domination by political, economic, social, military or technical forces', as in the official declaration of the Third All-African People's Conference held in Cairo in 1961.[1] While neocolonialism was recognized as having many political manifestations (for example, puppet governments, foreign military bases, balkanization) it was the continuing 'resource bondage' that became the main plank of both Third-World solidarity and Third-World demands for global reform in the 1950s and 1960s.

If economic resource bondage merely allowed and enabled the dissolution of the formal colonial form, there were other pressures created under colonialism that positively encouraged it. The internationally imposed division of labour had relegated the colonial areas to the status of producers and exporters of primary, unprocessed commodities, and these were traded for the manufactured consumer goods from metropolitan countries. The terms of the exchange were unfavourable to the primary producers, from both the point of view of long-term price development, and that of wildly gyrating price fluctuations,[2] the reasons for which I shall discuss below in relation to dependency theory. The critical point to make here is that the 'unequal trade' charge became yet another constitutive element in the ideology of neocolonialism, a rallying cry that united the Third World around a set of demands for global reforms, and fed into a self-reliant developmentalist ideology in which import-substitutive industrialization featured most prominently.

What may only be appreciated in hindsight is that those very pressures and aspirations of the newly-emerging nations were structurally in keeping with the level of development of the productive forces in the advanced countries, and that, therefore, both the process of decolonization and the ideologies of 'modernization' and 'development' (which the colonially nurtured westernized élite sported with great enthusiasm) amounted to a historically necessary reconstitution of the international relations of production.

Already in the 1950s, in the turbulent years of independence, the leading branches of industry in the metropolitan countries had shifted from the production of consumer goods to the production of producer goods. No longer did it make sense to see the colonial areas primarily as market outlets for consumer items such as textiles, matches and cigarettes. Instead, they needed to be upgraded to being market outlets for spinning and weaving tools, match-making machines and cigarette production lines. The springing up of many small, independent national units adopting a 'development and modernization ideology' wishing feverishly to catch up with the West and seeking Western patent solutions to basic human needs, all dovetailed neatly with the level of industrialization that had been achieved by that point in the metropolitan countries.

While colonial profits continued to be made in the resources sector, a new form of surplus extraction appeared in the neocolonial period which eventually became the dominant form, namely *technological rents*.[3] These are the super profits that monopolist sellers of machines, equipment goods and 'patented' technology can harvest in the absence of competitive markets for their products. The technological backwardness of the modernizing countries created this monopoly. They had to invite foreign direct investors – multinational companies – to help them produce locally what had previously been imported.

Domestic Tensions

A second set of contradictions heralding the decline of colonialism as a formal arrangement of international relations expressed itself at the political and social levels *inside* the colonial countries. The system of European colonial rule had involved selective co-option and careful nurturing of a class 'who may be interpreters between us and the millions whom we govern...a class of persons Indian in blood and colour but English in tastes, in opinions, in morals and intellect', as one Governor of India had put it, none too delicately.[4] This class needed to be educated and ultimately it was being educated to rule. For it was not only taught to read and write in English, or French, or Dutch, but in the process also taught how to think in the best European critical traditions. Inevitably, this class discovered the contradictions between what the great European thinkers had had to say about the fundamentals of European society and culture: equality, liberty and brotherhood, and the hypocritical, oppressive, and racist institutions of European colonialism under which they were made to suffer. They drew inspiration from Western political writings on democracy, nationhood and socialism.

The awakening spirit of nationalism and independence created a momentary alliance between this Western-educated class, these '*evolués*' as the French patronisingly called them, and the masses of peasants and urban poor from whom colonial society had so carefully separated them. The independence struggle even brought together the disparate ethnic groups which the colonial powers, with their talent to 'divide and rule', had succeeded in keeping in a state of mutual animosity and suspicion. But this alliance proved to be temporary and fragile, for such was the pitfall of nationalist consciousness, in Frantz Fanon's famous description, that no sooner had the politics of take-over been exhausted than the national bourgeoisie lapsed into extreme political lethargy, motivated only by private greed and vanity.[5] With no historic mission to fulfil, the national bourgeoisie had no where to go and so did not try to take the people with them. As a class secure in the financial, political and military backing of its neocolonial paymasters, the national bourgoisie turned its back on the people and became a 'comprador' bourgeoisie instead.

Geopolitical Relations

In the period leading up to the Second World War, the economy of the USA, a late starter compared with the Western European economies, had caught up and reached a level of industrial development comparable with, and overtaking that of, the first developers. It too had reached a stage where the continued growth of its economy depended on foreign expansion, on overseas market outlets for manufactures, on access to raw materials resources, and on investment opportunities around the world.

While the USA had effectively secured its dominance over Latin America since the promulgation of the Monroe Doctrine of 1823, it was still frustrated by the continuing presence of British, French and Dutch colonialism in Asia and Africa. With respect to these territories, America championed the cause of a non-discriminating international economic system, the so-called 'Open Door' policy, expressing hostility to great power spheres of influence and supporting the calls for self-determination and national sovereignty of the colonially oppressed.

The Second World War was a watershed. There were winners and losers. There were some winners who lost all except the victory and there were some losers who eventually gained all except the victory. But there was really only one country that came out victorious in every respect, and that was the USA.

In exchange for the sacrifice of American lives in the cause of its European allies, the USA demanded a price. That price was a new international economic order under US hegemony. In the early stages of the war, the American Council of Foreign Relations had already drawn up a Memorandum to this effect. The Memorandum described the policy needs of the USA in 'a world in which it proposes to hold unquestioned power'. It outlined the component parts of an integrated policy to achieve military and economic supremacy for the United States within the non-German world, including the western hemisphere. This US-led, non-German world was to be called the Grand Area. Decolonization and the guaranteeing of markets and access to raw materials were key elements of the plan.[6]

Before the dust had settled after the Second World War, much of the Grand Area plan had been accomplished. The dying days of the war saw the coming together of all victorious nations in a remarkably swift agreement on the need to manage the world economy through effective international institutions and principles under the acknowledged leadership of the USA (for example, the Bretton Woods institutions of the International Monetary Fund (IMF) and the World Bank, 1944, and the General Agreement on Tariffs and Trade (GATT, 1947)). Barely two years later, tight political and military alliances were woven around the 'free world' economy (NATO), while the Cold War with the one group of nations not prepared to co-operate within the Grand Area became the legitimizing force behind the Truman Doctrine (1947) in which the USA formally announced its intentions to act as a global policeman, 'defending free people anywhere in the world who were threatened by armed minorities or by outside pressures'.[7]

The Bretton Woods institutions, together with the Truman Doctrine, constituted the system of informal imperialism under the *Pax Americana*, which was the hallmark of the neocolonial period and lasted until about 1970. But it was the very informality and indirectness of the system that gave it an aura of invisibility and made it so difficult for people to see through.

Of course, when indirect tactics of 'informal' imperialism failed, the USA resorted on many occasions to direct and military intervention to secure a stable investment climate and keep the lifelines of resources and markets open to the 'free world'. Between 1945 and 1970, the USA in fact intervened militarily in Greece, Korea, Lebanon, the Dominican Republic, Grenada and, of course, Vietnam. It was further involved in the destabilization of regimes in Turkey, Iran, Guatemala, Cambodia, South Korea, Lebanon, Laos, Cuba, the Dominican Republic, El Salvador, Chile, Ghana, Zaire and Mali.

Since the dominant features of neocolonialism – resource bondage, technological dependency and subjection to informal imperialism – were features commonly shared by the new nations of Africa and Asia, and by the 'semi-colonies' of Latin America, the neocolonial period was also the period that fostered and defined the solidarity of the Third World in its political and ideological stance against the First-World-dominated world order.

Modernization Theory

In the same way that the colonial period had thrown up its own theories of imperialism, of the apologetic *and* the critical variety, so the neocolonial period encouraged the development of a body of knowledge historically specific to its own time. On the one hand there were the 'modernization theories' which accepted uncritically the structure of the relationships between rich and poor countries that had evolved during the preceding epochs of capitalist expansion. They wrote a kind of 'how to develop' manual for less-developed countries. On the other hand, there were the dependency theories that critiqued the modernization theories and, by bringing the structure of unequal relationships between rich and poor countries back into the picture, demonstrated that modernization theories served to mask the continuing imperialist nature of those relationships.

Modernization theories were problem-solving and policy-orientated theories of social change and economic development. David Harrison[8] records how President Truman, in his inaugural address of 1949, announced the Point Four Programme of Development Aid. It then became the policy of the USA to aid the efforts of the peoples of economically underdeveloped areas to develop their resources and improve their living conditions. This policy was not put forward as altruism – it took place against the backdrop of the Cold War and the political independence and liberation of less-developed countries from colonialism that the USA favoured. There was an understanding on the part of policy-makers in the USA of the need to keep the Third World out of communist hands.

Economic and technological aid was at first a means of doing this. But it was soon realized that the transplantation of capital and technology to the Third World would not bear fruit unless it was accompanied by wider and *consistent* social, cultural and political changes. Early theories of the modernization school were often advanced by economists who had been hired by the USA as practical advisers: people on aid missions. It was they who observed how cultural diffusion and the introduction of technology from the outside were frustrated by the negative role that traditional culture played in 'blocking' development, and they were the first to call for 'comprehensive social and economic change'. These were continuing and recurring themes, as was the threat of Soviet influence, if development (that is, the American way of life) were to fail.[9]

It was not until the late 1950s that sociologists became involved in what proved to be for their discipline an extremely profitable bandwagon. One of the very early sociological contributions was a collection of essays by Bert Hoselitz in 1957.[10] Where the contributions of the economists had been piecemeal – never going beyond such observations that it was not possible to introduce an agricultural tractor into a community that had communal rights to land and knew no property rights, or that kinship obligations stood in the way of appointing people by merit and so on – the sociologists set about the task of developing a comprehensive all-encompassing theory of *all* the processes and structural changes required to transform non-industrial into industrial societies.

These modernization theories were in turn embedded in abstract, formal theories of societal evolution. The circumstance that these models of societal evolution had themselves been scripted from the historical experience of the development of the West did not prevent them from becoming normative and prescriptive. They turned the abstracted, generalized history of European development into necessary *logic*: the formal Western models had described the interactive processes through which undeveloped societies of all periods were thought to become developed. They theorized the compatibility or 'correspondence' between certain advanced economic institutions (money, markets, occupational specialization, profit maximization) on the one hand, and certain 'modern' political, cultural and social forms on the other, thereby turning the latter into necessary prerequisites or 'logical requirements' for the former. For example, modernization studies would examine the processes of secularization consequent upon the introduction of cash crops into traditional peasant communities, or the effect of industrialization on the nuclearization of family systems, or the need for multi-party democracy to support the division of labour. When traditional institutions or values did not fit, they were considered 'dysfunctional' to the process of development and regarded as 'problems', which comprehensive socio-economic planning could be designed to correct. Progress became a matter of ordered social reform.[11]

By highlighting the complementarity between compatible institutions and values, modernization theorists came, in practice if not always in intent, to advocate the convergence of less-developed societies to the Western model. But they also helped to strengthen the illusion of independence and of the sovereignty of the national developmental state, since they were ensconced in a theoretical framework which accorded integrity to 'society' as a self-regulating 'social whole' within which social and political institutions, cultural values as well as economic organizations, were comprehended as constituent parts.

This was a key assumption with which dependency theory took issue. Rather than perceive societies as so many independent units, *their* unit of analysis was capitalism as a world system spanning nations and placing them in different positions according to their structural place in a historically developed international division of labour.

Dependency Theory

Although dependency theory, like modernization theory, emerged in the postwar period, it had intellectual roots stretching into the past. Classical theories of imperialism (Hilferding, Bukharin, Lenin, Rosa Luxemburg) had also addressed relations of domination and subjection between nations. But the classical Marxist theories of imperialism had in the main focused on the question of what it was about the capitalist system that drove it to extend itself beyond its own borders and to expand geographically in an ever-widening circumference. And precisely because classical theories of imperialism were really only interested in the *causes* of imperialism, they did not bother overmuch with the study of the *effects* of imperialism overseas. They generally took it for granted that export of capital was the same as export of capitalist relations of production, and that therefore capitalism overseas would work up the same social tensions and class conflicts (between bourgeoisie and proletariat) as were already evident in the home country.

One exception among classical Marxists was Leon Trotsky, who in the 1920s formulated the 'unicity' of the world system in his Law of Combined and Uneven Development.[12] Trotsky argued that, with the development of capitalism as a world system through the internationalization of capital, world history would become a contradictory but concrete totality. In this totality, countries would develop at an uneven pace in relation to one another, and even inside the backward nations themselves, advanced and primitive features of economy and society would coexist. This would constitute a unique historical situation, ripe for socialist revolution. This more complex view of history enabled Trotsky to transcend the evolutionist conception of history as a succession of rigidly predetermined stages which was the received Soviet interpretation of Marx's theory of history, just as it was the liberal Western model of social evolution.

The original version of the dependency and underdevelopment theory as outlined first by Paul Baran,[13] and next more popularly and grandly by Andre Gunder Frank,[14] T. dos Santos[15] and others, was akin to this Trotskyist line of thought. But the impetus for the postwar dependency perspective was the perceived need to critique bourgeois modernization theory. Dependency theory concentrated on locating the cause of backwardness of Third-World countries (initially, more especially Latin America), within the dynamic and contradictory growth of the world capitalist system. Underdevelopment as distinct from undevelopment – it was claimed – does not result from some original state of affairs, as modernization theory had argued, but rather from the same world historical process by which the now-advanced capitalist countries became developed. Thus, from the very beginning, the dependency approach has been a world system approach, rejecting explicitly the concept of the unified state as actor and the notion of the global system as a collection of nation-states.

The essence of the dependency theory is the contention that, as a result of penetration by colonial capital, a distorted structure of economy and society had been created in the colonial countries which would reproduce overall economic stagnation and extreme pauperization of the masses for all time.

A distorted structure of economy implied two things:

1. The *subordination* of the economy to the structure of advanced capitalist countries. This had involved a reorganisation of the economy in such a way that it only produced primary goods for the industrial West, and the prevention (under colonialism) of local industrialization. Moreover, the production structure was limited in scope and diversity. As late as 1970, about ten years after the last move to formal independence, a UN report observed that, at that time, almost 90 per cent of the export earnings of the developing countries derived from primary products; that almost a half of these countries earned more than 50 per cent of their export receipts from a single primary commodity; and that as many as three-quarters of them earned more than 60 per cent from three primary products.[16]

2. *External orientation*, which meant an extreme dependency on overseas markets, both for capital and technology sourcing and for production outlets. External dependency was often exacerbated by an extreme concentration of the dependency upon few rather than many metropolitan countries (in the main as a result of continuing linkages with the colonial mother country). There were a number of empirical indicators which were said to reflect such external concentration: trade partner concentration; aid donor concentration; export product specialization; and military trade partner concentration.[17]

By a distorted structure of society, dependency theorists also referred to two main features:

1. A *class alliance* between foreign capital and comprador (mercantile and landed élites). Dependency theory argued that the export-orientated primary production structure found its handmaiden in a frozen *internal* class structure dominated by a small landed and mercantile (or comprador) élite, whose economic interests became increasingly intertwined with those of the advanced capitalist states, and whose cultural lifestyles and tastes were a faithful imitation of the same.

2. The evolution of *extreme patterns of social inequality* which in turn restricts and distorts the domestic market.

Dependency was thought to generate a structure of internal social relations which is created by and corresponds to the way a country is inserted into the structure of international economic relations. This imposed specialization of production and the continued coincidence of interests between the imperial states and the ex-colonial élites, even after independence, blocked any attempt at industrialization and internal social transformation (for example, a bourgeois revolution). It was this that resulted in overall economic stagnation and pauperization. At the time of Frank's writings, import-substitutive industrialization had, of course, begun on a large scale in Latin America, but it lasted for only a short time in the late 1950s and early 1960s, and it was quite possible to criticize it as a form of industrialization that again was 'externally dependent' and constricted (because of the internally restricted market) to produce luxury consumer goods. It also marginalized ever greater numbers of the proletariat, who were being thrown out of existing jobs because the path of industrialization was capital-intensive.[18]

So what we have here is a theory that places the cause of continued underdevelopment in the legacy of a distorted structure of economy and society; it is this distorted structure that is referred to as peripheral economy/society.

The peripheral nature of the economy and the society was said to create its own underdeveloping dynamics because it denied 'auto-centric' development. Autocentric development refers to a process of development where the whole cycle of production, reproduction, realization and valorization of capital, and the relationship between producer-goods and consumer-goods industries, are all nicely contained within the same territorial economy and society. As indeed had been the case in the 'core' economies.[19]

What the dependency theorists further argued was that the interaction between the centre countries of the capitalist system and the peripheral countries involved a transfer of value: an expropriation of *economic surplus* by the centre countries from the poor countries, resulting in capital accumulation in the advanced countries, and in stagnation and impoverishment in the others. Development and underdevelopment was a two-way affair – just as development in one part of the world went hand in hand with underdevelopment in another, so underdevelopment in the periphery contributed to further development in the advanced, core, countries. The key mechanism for this dual outcome was unequal exchange.

Dependency theorists argued that the then prevailing international division of labour involved a transfer of value from poor to rich countries because of the *unequal terms of exchange* of the commodities traded. This point had already been made in the late 1950s by liberal writers such as Hans Singer and Raoul Prebisch, when for the first time a successful challenge to Ricardo's theory of international trade and comparative advantage was made.[20] That challenge was a revelation and motivated Third-World grass roots movements in the West for decades to come. The revealing point was that, in the international exchange of primary commodities for manufactures there occurs – over a long time period – a deterioration in the prices for primary products in relation to those of manufactures. This long-term deterioration was said to occur strictly as a result of *market forces of supply and demand*, namely:

1. income inelasticity of demand for foodstuffs;
2. substitution of raw materials by industrial products and/or their replacement by synthetics; and
3. a declining ratio of raw material inputs to industrial outputs.

The first of these points represents a restriction on long-term demand for foodstuffs in a growing world economy because there is a *physiological* limit to the amount of food people are able to consume; hence a declining proportion of rising income is going to be spent on food. This is bad news for the food producers in the long run. The second and the third points refer to *technological* progress, which reduces the importance of raw materials in production. But beyond these purely market-force and technology-related reasons, Prebisch also added another reason for the deteriorating terms of trade, one which begins to move us more directly into the realm of the *political economy* of international trade. Labour emancipation in the advanced countries, he suggested, pushes up the price of their commodities in relation to those of the poor countries where no such emancipation had taken place. Since, in terms of historical social development, the periphery lags behind the advanced countries by at least a hundred years, there is no way one can bridge this gap.

This view was shared by Arghiri Emmanuel (in his *Unequal Exchange*)[21] who argued that the differential evolution of wages was a fundamental cause of unequal exchange. Emmanuel attached little importance to demand factors in explaining the worsening terms of trade of poor countries. Indeed, he criticized dependency theorists for focusing too much on the particular kinds of commodities traded. Unequal exchange, he said, does not occur between *commodities* traded, but between trading *countries*. Applying Marx's labour theory of value to international exchanges, he argued that:

1. the prices of goods produced in any country are determined mainly by the level of wages in that country;
2. the level of wages reflects historical and social conditions which vary in time and in place; and

3. equalization of wage costs at the international level is unlikely to occur because of the immobility of the labour factor (in contrast to the mobility of the capital factor).

Thus the argument here is that because advanced countries are more developed, their price of labour reflects the higher standard of living already obtained. Successful class struggles and labour emancipation in the advanced countries have made sure that what Marx called a 'historical' or 'ethical' wage has replaced the physiological wage still evident in less-developed countries. This then becomes the normal wage, not easily relinquished even in a recession. No matter what poor countries produce, and no matter how comparable their levels of productivity, their exports will always be non-equivalent in value compared with the exports of advanced countries.

The emphasis on the shaping and determining nature of the external relations between poor and rich countries led dependency theorists in the neocolonial period to advocate a radical break with the world capitalist system as a panacea to development for the poor countries. Their influence on the political ideologies of many less-developed countries at that time cannot be underestimated. It helped to underpin an already strong populist tradition favouring domestic policies of economic nationalism, self-reliance and delinking. At the international level it was – for a time – responsible for an effective 'Third-Worldist' perspective on international trade and international capital flows. In numerous international negotiating forums, organizations and discussions, the Third-World countries took a united stand in demanding fundamental changes in the world market system. They wanted better and more secure prices for their traditional exports; they wanted preferential access to domestic markets in the advanced countries for their 'infant' manufacturing industries; they asked for reforms in the international monetary system and for generous aid flows; and they proposed codes of conduct for multinational companies.

By 1974–5, these demands had been solemnly enshrined in a United Nations Charter of Economic Rights and Duties of States, and in a Programme of Action for the Establishment of a New International Economic Order (NIEO).[22] But before the ink was dry on the paper of these arrangements, profound changes in the world capitalist system had taken place which made these demands obsolete and eroded the political unity that had given expression to them.

3

Crisis and Restructuring: The New International Division of Labour

In this part of the book a stage-theoretical approach is adopted, to look at the dialectic unfolding of the world capitalist system in distinct periods or stages. In each period a particular structural arrangement between the core and the periphery succeeds for a time in achieving accumulation on a global scale. But these structural arrangements repeatedly meet internal contradictions, which are the result of the very success of the structural arrangement. The conundrum of historical progress is that 'nothing fails like success'. The failures create periods of crisis and adjustment, when the structural arrangement is realigned, and the relationship emerges in a new form.

The first neocolonial phase, which we described in the previous chapter, lasted from about 1950 to 1970. It too developed within itself contradictions that eventually required a reshuffling of the economic and geopolitical relationships between rich and poor countries. Some authors (for example, Samir Amin)[1] have described the post-1970 period as a 'second' neocolonial period. Others have used the term 'post'imperialism (for example, David Becker)[2] to denote the characteristics of this period.

Which were the constraints and contradictions of the first neocolonial period that created the crisis of the 1970s and a reconsideration of North–South relations? Again, as before, we can spot these contradictions breaking through on different, though connected, levels: the level of the development of material capabilities; the domestic or internal institutional level within the core countries;

and within the peripheral countries; and the level of economic and geopolitical relations between them.

Material Capabilities: Global Fordism

The term 'accumulation', in the Marxist tradition, refers to the self-expanding value of capital. Because of competition, the mere preservation of capital is impossible unless it is also expanded. Stage theory adds to this the notion that every phase of capitalist expansion is characterized by a particular accumulation model, a particular type of propelling industry, and a leading innovation or invention that is introduced initially into one industry before spreading to the rest.[3] In a somewhat over-simplified manner, one might say that the term 'accumulation model' refers to the dominant way in which capitalists in the leading branches of economic activity 'make their profits'.

The first neocolonial period saw an enormous expansion of producer goods and consumer durable industries stimulated by the Fordist model of production and social organization: flow-line technology; mass production of consumer durables; improved wages for workers; Keynesian forms of demand management; and welfarism.[4] But from the mid-1960s a dramatic fall in profitability was recorded more or less continuously in all advanced capitalist countries throughout the leading branches of industry. What had gone wrong?

The postwar boom had owed much to the ravages of war, which had presented a fantastic opportunity to rebuild industrial sectors. The leading technology was the assembly line, and, more generally, process technology. The whole point about mass production as a profitable undertaking is that it achieves *economies of scale*. This means that the more that is produced of a standardized product, the more the unit cost of production comes down. And more means cheaper. But the downside is that on the one hand, there is a minimum quantity required for economic operation, and on the other, that the success of the operation depends crucially on a continuous and uninterrupted expansion of market demand for that same product. The mass-production system cannot cope flexibly with cyclical recessions, increased competition, or changing market tastes. The result is under-utilization of fixed capacity, and over-production, resulting in lay-offs, losses, and ultimately closure.

For a long time in the postwar period, the rigidities of this system of accumulation had been masked by the reconstruction boom, and by the fact that the national economies of the advanced countries had put in place a supportive regulatory framework specially designed to balance mass production with mass consumption. State intervention in the economy had a Keynesian emphasis on full employment, public-sector expenditure, welfare provision, social democracy and workers' rights, and all these were novel elements in a complex societal arrangement in which socio-economic management stabilized the relationship between production and consumption. In this societal arrangement we should also mention key trade union concessions, in which protest over deskilling and alienation on the shop-floor had been abandoned in exchange for rising wages; a host of credit and fiscal institutions which helped smooth out ups and downs in the business cycle; and even socio-psychological practices of advertising and commodification of culture. All of these helped to promote and maintain a 'consumer society'. Fordism was more than a method of production; it became a whole way of life.[5] It is the merit of the Regulation School (see Chapter 5) to have drawn attention to the way in which the conditions of stable economic growth in society depend on the coming together of a distinctive regime of accumulation with a supportive mode of regulation.

The structural contradiction revealed by this analysis is that because the postwar boom period had allowed the massive expansion of the welfare state in the core countries, and because of the confirmation of the social democratic consensus there, it was very difficult to drive down wages or permit unemployment to rise during cyclical recessions. On the other hand, the technical system of production, with its vast outlays of fixed capital formation, was too rigid to respond flexibly.

It is therefore not surprising that a first response by capitalists in the core countries to the crisis was to try to export Fordism to those areas of the periphery where wage levels were very low, and could thus compensate for the loss of profitability. The material opportunity for this 'global' Fordism was created by the decomposition of the production process into simple tasks able to be carried out by unskilled labour (this itself was a key feature of the Fordist system of production, generally known as 'Taylorism'), and by technical innovations in three sectors basic to transport and communications.

Revolutionary strides in containerized shipping made the geographical dispersal of production facilities possible; improved engineering techniques provided the complex communications network crucial to the speed of operations; and pervasive computer applications permitted the virtually instantaneous data processing vital for maximization of global profits and market shares.

Hence industrial relocation to certain selected sites in the Third World, the so-called newly-industrializing economies of South-East Asia, and Brazil and Mexico in Latin America, have been highlighted as a critical feature of this period of reconstruction in global capital accumulation.[6] Multinational companies developed organically integrated circuits of production in different countries, with each country undertaking a part of the production process, but not making the whole product. The term 'new international division of labour', as this came to be called, captured the phenomenon of peripheral industrialization in which a small number of less-developed countries participated in the global dispersal of production facilities by multinational corporations.

The unevenness of industrial progress between Third-World countries in this period was described succinctly in the UNCTAD annual trade report of 1982: 'fewer than ten newly industrialised developing countries accounted in 1980 for nearly 30 per cent of developing countries' GDP and nearly half of their manufacturing output, even though their share of the population of the underdeveloped countries was no more than 10 per cent'.[7] During the 1970s, the developing world as a whole increased its share of world manufacturing exports from 7 per cent to 10 per cent, but two-thirds of this originated in just eight newly-industrializing economies.

Neocolonial Economic Relations

Throughout that first postwar period (until 1970) imperialist profit had been maintained through direct exploitation of raw material resources by multinational capital. Think, for example, of the very low costs of energy subsidized by the oil-producing countries. Between 1950 and 1970 the average price of crude oil slowly and continuously *declined*, from just over US$4 per barrel to $1.60 (at constant 1974 prices).[8] The loss in terms of trade to the developing world during the neocolonial period[9] constituted the 'hidden' imperialist profits to the advanced world which subsidized the Fordist way of life and the democratic social contract there. It has been estimated that during this period, between 25 per cent and 40 per cent of the cost of labour in the advanced countries constituted the so-called 'social' wage.[10] A good deal of that again came from imperialist profits. Another component of imperialist profits was contributed by the technological rents discussed in Chapter 2.[11]

This pattern of unequal exchange between the rich and poor worlds had been mediated by neocolonial class alliances between international capital and Third-World bourgeoisies. The downside of this was, however, that these had engendered such extreme inequalities as to block a widening of the market and a deepening of capitalist relations inside the Third World (as indeed the dependency theorists had argued). As a corollary, the peripheral Fordist strategy could only help to advance the industrial progress of a small number of less-developed countries whose industrial output as branch plant economies within the global Fordist production structure had secure access to the markets of the developed world.

It was this aspect of the crisis of the 1970s that distinguished it from normal cyclical crises of overproduction and underconsumption. The drive to expand markets could not be undertaken without major global restructuring.

Imperialism, in both the colonial and neocolonial periods, was characterized by a geographical expansion of the capitalist mode on a world scale. Time and again, geographical expansion had permitted capitalism to overcome its problems of narrowing production relations by encroaching and dominating fresh pre-capitalist areas. What characterized the crisis of the 1970s was that there were simply no more 'fresh' pre-capitalist areas available for further geographical expansion. And thus, as Samir Amin, for example, has argued, the time had come for capitalism to overcome the crisis without resorting to a new imperialism. The way to do this was to reshuffle the cards and revise North–South relations.[12]

Economic Nationalism in the Third World

A third contradiction that grew out of the neocolonial settlement of the postwar period was an increasingly strident economic nationalism in the Third-World countries themselves. There were several contributing causes. First, the postwar settlement had been overwhelmingly state-centric, and this applied to both advanced and less-developed countries. Self-determination and the sovereignty of the national state, however large or small, was the overriding principle of international relations, and the touchstone of the United Nations.

Second, state-centrism also engulfed notions of the economy. The concept of the nation-state in the postwar period carried more than the mere notion of sovereignty: it implied a neomercantilist conception of the state as having responsibility for the administration and development of the national economy. It was the universally recognized task of the state to make the nation 'stronger'. This neomercantilist conception applied equally to old and new states. The dominance of Keynesianism as macro-economic theory, with its acceptance of state intervention in the economies of the advanced countries, spilt over ideologically into and converged with the developmentalist state notions of the liberal modernization theories.[13] Less-developed countries were spurred on to take their economic destinies into their own hands.

Third, the impossibility of this task, given the economic dependency and unequal position of these countries in the world economic order, corrupted the very policies of development, including Western forms of aid, leading to a deepening chasm between state and civil society within the Third World.

Politically, the easiest option for the national bourgeoisie was to suppress internal revolt by blaming the continuation of imperialist forms of domination of their countries, while masking their own complicity in this domination. As we have seen, dependency theory did much to legitimize this analysis. In the late 1960s and 1970s, these pressures concretized importantly in a wave of nationalization and indigenization policies, in which foreign-owned companies and assets were taken over by the state or compulsorily sold to indigenous bourgeoisies. The Third-Worldist view of international economic relations culminated in the acquiescence by the international community to the right of less-developed countries to own their own resources, but there was a price to pay. Throughout the developing world the takeover of, or domestic participation in, foreign companies required financial compensation to be paid, even if the level of compensation was below market value. The financial resources were obtained from international banks eager to find outlets for accumulated euro- and petro-dollars. Whereas in 1970, foreign direct investments to the Third World were slightly larger than the flows of such *in*direct investments to them, by 1980 the latter showed a clear lead, with a ratio of 3:1.[14]

The consequence of this changed debt–equity ratio was the debt crisis of the 1980s. What was not appreciated at the time was that the changed debt–equity composition of foreign-controlled enterprises in the Third World would lead to gross inefficiencies (and deepening indebtedness) because of the institutional separation of financial responsibility from operational control. Interest on loan capital constitutes a contractual obligation that needs to be discharged irrespective of the profitability of the enterprise or project for which the obligation was contracted. At the same time, the reduced equity exposure of the foreign company which continued to run the enterprise under management contract and/or technical or service agreements, obviated the need for foreign management to worry about locally assessable profitability criteria, because dividends (return on equity) were no longer the *raison d'être* of the foreign involvement. From the parent company's point of view, the local affiliate or joint venture became quintessentially a trading partner, from whom it wished to buy cheap and to sell dear. The existence in many developing countries of centralized state financial institutions responsible for the raising of foreign credit, and the channelling of this credit to individual state enterprises, encouraged the malpractice of prejudicing one project's future viability with another project's bad debts: foreign credit raised to finance one project all too easily found its way into another project's arrears payments. As a corollary, general taxation was used by the state to finance unprofitable foreign operations.

In summary, the second neocolonial period generated a new pattern of extraction of economic surplus of poor countries by rich countries through the instrument of debt. Where 'resource bondage' and 'technological rents' had characterized the first neocolonial period, the hallmark of the second neocolonial or postimperial period is 'debt peonage'. By the early 1980s, total capital outflows from the Third World to the advanced countries began to exceed the total of capital inflows into them, for the first time since the Second World War. By the end of the 1980s, the total outstanding Third-World debt stood at US$1 trillion, or the equivalent of about a third of the combined GDP of the developing countries.[15]

But this debt peonage did not affect all of the Third World in equal measure. A second characteristic of the postimperial period was a restructuring of world economic relations characterized by a new international division of labour when 'the world factory' superseded the 'world market'.[16] Within this new world factory structure certain selected sites in the Third World, now referred to as newly-industrializing economies (NIEs), began to take part in the charmed circle of more intensively integrated world capitalist production, while other areas of the Third World became increasingly marginalized.

Changing Geopolitical Relations

A final contradiction of the neocolonial period we are discussing resulted in what has been widely referred to as the crisis of US hegemony. By the late 1960s, the Bretton Woods-managed world order that had been established under informal US imperial rule began to be challenged, both by some Western European states, and by the international capital markets in the form of speculation against the dollar, which under Bretton Woods had underpinned world monetary arrangements. Again, both challenges may be attributed to the very success of the system. For, under Bretton Woods, the USA had succeeded in re-establishing the unity of the world market, and this had encouraged a phenomenal transnational expansion of US capital.

By the late 1960s, Pierre Jalée has observed, American industry abroad had become the world's third-ranking industrial power, after the United States and the Soviet Union.[17] The transnational expansion of US capital led to an effective overvaluation of the dollar which precipitated its downfall and the collapse of the Bretton Woods system in 1971. Meanwhile, for their part, the European states had recovered their industrial strength and they began to export capital into the USA, taking advantage of the overvalued US dollar. The monetary crisis that followed testified to the autonomy of supranational market forces that in future would dominate the policies of all states, if not all equally.

The downfall of US political control over world finance was matched by the erosion of US military supremacy in the periphery. The two were linked, in fact, as Giovanni Arrighi has pointed out.[18] On the one hand, the weakening of US financial power placed limits on the escalation of the war in Vietnam. The subsequent American retreat from Vietnam marked a turning point for anti-imperialist Third-World movements. Between 1974 and 1980, Fred Halliday records, no less than fourteen Third-World states fell to national liberation forces.[19] The American withdrawal also contributed to the confidence with which the OPEC countries first unilaterally quadrupled the export price of oil, and next maintained their effective cartel in spite of mounting international pressure. They could do so precisely because of the power of stateless money. The more international dollars they earned, the more they could hold the dollar itself to ransom.

There is no doubt that, in the 1970s, Third-World developmentalism reached its apogee. The weakening of US hegemonic power, and the subsequent inter-imperialist rivalry among the advanced capitalist countries, was matched by a more robust encouragement by the Soviets of anti-imperialist revolt in the Third World. The anarchy of the international financial markets added to this the promise of alternative finance for development without political strings attached, and gave the states in the Third World a stronger, more centralized role in allocating resources and guiding the economic destiny of the nation. The intensification and the renegotiation of transnational economic linkages, both in respect of the new international division of labour and of the nationalization of the extractive resource sector, was associated with an expansion of the state's role in a range of developing countries while having a dampening effect on the expansion of the state's role in those core countries that were major capital exporters.

As Peter Evans[20] has argued, under certain circumstances transnational capital preferred dealing with a stronger, more bureaucratically capable, state apparatus. He suggests that a natural evolution or outcome of both the conflict between host countries and transnational corporations, and the alliances between them, was to enhance the organizational capacities of the state in certain Third-World countries, especially when transnational loan capital began to replace direct investment. Foreign loans (invariably underwritten by the state) substantially increase the power of the state vis-à-vis the local bourgeoisie. For example, one of the primary motivations of Korea's exceptional preference for debt in the 1970s was the leverage it gave the state over local industrialists.

The positive correlation, however, applied only to more advanced Third-World states in the postwar period.

For this, to be sure, was the lasting outcome of this period of transition: a deep division *between* Third-World countries depending on their respective insertion into the world economy, on the relative level of economic advance already obtained, on the nature of state–civil society relations, and on a number of cultural factors that became increasingly important in explaining the variation in economic progress and social advance. It was these differences that began to shape the theoretical agenda of development literature, to which we turn next.

Critical Theory: Diversity and Micro-studies

For most writers, the end of the Third World dominated the theoretical agenda in this period; the end, that is to say, of the Third World both as a unitary category of analysis, and of the mechanistic, deterministic interpretation of the historical outcome. Generalizing methodologies that had treated the 'Third World as a whole' were replaced by methodologies that homed in on the specific and the unique, and focused on the diversity of the development experience in different parts of the world. Geographic and cultural factors, long ignored in Marxist discourse, made a robust reappearance as much of the development literature became fragmented into area studies. The retreat from orthodoxy resulted in a renewed interest in anthropological, ethnographic and historiographic work. Many excellent collections of edited readers that were published in the 1980s testify to a preoccupation with national and area-specific features of the development process, rather than attempting to fit these into general patterns of structural (under)development derived from experiences in other regions.[21]

They were concerned, for example, with detailed empirical investigations of the role of the state in industrialization; of the way in which changing production relations in industry were informed by local habits and struggles; of culturally specific gender relations and ethnic relations; of agrarian transformation and differentiation; and of the role of popular culture, whether in acquiescence or protest. It was not so much that external factors of global capitalism were ignored, rather there was an understanding (often implicit) that the task of development theory was to uncover the precise interplay between external factors and internal social structures in order to explain the divergence in national historical trajectories.[22]

Some of this literature echoed the postMarxist, poststructuralist and even postmodernist turn that had begun to take hold of the Marxist debates in the mainstream philosophy and social sciences. It spawned a broad canvas of critical theory which was referred to briefly in the introduction to the first part of this book. Critical theory emancipated development theorists from overarching philosophies of progress and doom, 'development and underdevelopment', led them to explore systematic variations in development trajectories, and encouraged the study of the locally specific to combine with a celebration of the politically possible. Moving from structure orientation to actor orientation, the baton of development studies generally passed from the economics of development to the politics of development. The pursuit of such politics led, in one direction, to *micro* local action studies, highlighting, for example, the success of small-scale, 'bottom-up' community participation projects of the kind defined, funded and implemented enthusiastically by NGOs. These aimed to facilitate people's own development efforts. 'Empowerment through participation' became the clarion call of development *practice*.[23]

Gender and Development

Probably the most challenging of the new directions in development theory has been opened up by feminist scholarship, especially after its forward leap from women's studies to gender studies. It was not till about 1970[24] that women figured seriously in mainstream development literature, and their 'discovery' was flawed on at least two crucial counts.

First, it was generally but mistakenly assumed that because women had demonstrably *not* benefited from the development process, they had been 'excluded' from it and now needed to be brought in. This was a view that was seized upon with some eagerness by the international development community. The UN launched its Decade for Women in 1975 at its first World Conference on Women, held in Mexico, which followed barely a year after the 1974 UN Conference on Population in Bucharest. The ideological juxtaposition of the Third-World population explosion and the relative underdevelopment of its women led to the idea that there was a trade-off between women's productive and reproductive functions, and that raising women's socio-economic status would lower birth rates. The international aid machine revved up to combine family planning programmes with income-generating projects for women, whether in rural co-operatives or urban slum community centres.[25]

Socialist feminists soon condemned these programmes for obscuring and compounding the nature of global production relations whereby women's productive work in informal, non-organized, non-protected sectors, articulated with the global system of capital accumulation in a double, or even triple chain of super exploitation.[26]

The second problem with the 'women in development' (WID) discourse was epistemological, connected with the concept of women as a unitary, analytic category. This was blown apart by the postmodern turn in feminist critique. Why assume that women are the same the world over? What do middle-class white women in New York have in common with rural black women growing coffee for exports in Africa, or with the cloth cutters in the garment sweatshops of Asia? Radical feminists have sought an answer in patriarchy, the notion, namely, that even if women are not the same, their subordination by men is universal.

But this still left world sisterhood without a common political agenda. It was an absence camouflaged and compounded by First-World racism. As Maria Mies puts it bluntly: 'whereas Western consumer housewives are encouraged to consume more and to breed more whites, the colonial producer "housewives" are encouraged to produce more and cheaper and to stop breeding blacks'.[27]

A gradual change of focus on to broader issues of 'gender' moved the study of 'women in development' on to a less ambitious, but for all that more empowering, plane. Gender studies does not assume that there is a stable, homogeneous category called 'women', with identical interests and desires. It focuses instead on relations between men and women as these are socially constructed.[28] Gender relations vary greatly in different cultural and historical contexts. What is men's work in some places is women's work in others; in some countries, women head up households; in others, they do not. Land tenure, inheritance and usufruct rights also vary, as do legal entitlements, state provisions and marital obligations.

This realization produced an impressive range of detailed, descriptive, empirical work which showed how even well-intended development-assistance programmes targeted at women were often corrupted and deflected from their original aims by 'gender blindness', because of mistaken assumptions about women's roles and involvement in production and reproduction. For example, dairy co-operative projects for women in Andhra Pradesh (India) inadvertently increased women's workloads without giving them access to the fruits of their labour. Men controlled the paid jobs, and the income from the dairy. They (and their sons) consumed most of the milk produced. The entire setup gave many men the excuse to stop working altogether![29]

In the course of these detailed, concrete local studies, two major intellectual advances were made. First, through the gender orientation in development studies, Third-World feminists found their voice. Not only were they in possession of relevant cultural knowledge that Western researchers lacked, they also discovered that the emancipatory agendas of Western feminists were wholly inappropriate to the needs, day-to-day lives and struggles of Third-World women. Chandra Mohanty, for example, argues that the former have a singular focus on gender as a basis for equal rights, while the latter's concern with gender is in relation to race and/or class as part of a broader liberation struggle.[30] This difference explains, for example, why an issue such as a woman's right to choose, as in abortion rights, is not as clearcut for 'women of colour', whose right to bear children is often mediated by a coercive, racist state and a fertility-obsessed international development machine. J. H. Momsen and J. Townsend have found that, in fact, fertility is the most studied aspect of women's lives in the Third World.[31] In a remorselessly Foucauldian deconstruction of Western feminist writing on Third-World women (ignorant, poor, uneducated, tradition-bound, victimized and so on), Mohanty shows up and challenges its political effects, namely as being no more than a prop to a Western feminist colonialist move.[32] As Aihwa Ong puts it: 'When feminists look overseas, they frequently seek to establish their authority on the backs of non-Western women, determining for them the meanings and goals of their lives.'[33]

A second, and related, intellectual advance involved Third-World and First-World feminists engaging in what Janet Townsend remarks upon as her own conversion to the 'personal as political'. This is the insight that no outsiders can ever set the agenda for oppressed women's practical or strategic gender needs. A socialist-feminist preoccupation with production and distribution is useless when the practical need is for clean latrines. Liberal agendas of gender equality are pointless when the overwhelming strategic need is to avoid alcoholic and violent husbands. All conceptual baggage must be thrown out if researchers are to understand and empower women to take control over their own lives. And for this, only listening will do!

'Dependency Associated' Development Theory

The 'passion for the possible' was also articulated in meso-level studies of political choice, the object of which was to identify 'room-for-manoeuvre' policy alternatives at the level of state and civil society. These were particularly advocated by Latin-American 'second wave' *dependista writers*, who laid great store by the per-ceived breakdown of American global hegemony, the increase in inter-imperialist rivalry, and the new, historically specific, form of foreign capitalist penetration involving a new alliance between the state and a truly 'transnational' corporate bourgeoisie.[34]

These 'dependent development' writers went furthest in welding a structuralist analysis of the dynamic unfolding of global capitalism with an interactionist 'voluntarist' conception of domestic responses. They argued that each expansive phase of capitalism creates new forms of economic dependency, new ways in which the Latin-American economies are inserted in the world capitalist economy. Therefore, each phase brings out new class contradictions and requires new class alliances. At the precise historical moment when these new class alliances are being formed, there is scope for political action. These writers argued that what was specific to the Latin-American economies (at the turn of the 1980s) was a new dependency created by foreign penetration and control over the industrial producer-goods sector, which had to rely increasingly on an alliance with the state as a direct agent of production.

In this process, the state apparatus was becoming ever more divorced from civil society, while at the same time the very expan-sion of industrial-dependent capitalism (at that moment in time) needed members of civil society as both producers and consumers. This offered an opportunity for 'defensive alliances' or 'class com-promise' (*concertación*) on the part of the various groups of civil society (for example, trade unions as well as the bourgeoisie, and the state bureaucratic class) to pursue the objective of social democracy; or 'substantive' democratization to complement the formal democratization that had begun with the defeat of the military oligarchies. They pointed to the variety of contemporary regime types in Latin America as empirical evidence of the scope for manoeuvre and the importance of political struggle. In this way, the concern with social democracy replaced the concern with revolution in much Latin-American discourse. We shall be looking at this again in Chapter 11.

Postimperialism and World System Theories

The optimism of the 'dependent development' project was strengthened by *macro*-level theories of postimperialism, which were themselves an outcome of stage-theoretical thinking about the dynamic trajectory of world capitalism. The concept of postimperialism, clarified by David Becker,[35] refers to a still-nascent phase in the evolution of world capitalism in which relations of dominance and dependency between nations (the defining characteristic of imperialism) are being relegated to secondary importance. Instead, relations of capitalist domination and exploitation are conceptualized in terms of global class relations, which transcend national class structures. Transnational enterprises, in this view, are integrating the world economy, and during the process they create an international bourgeoisie alongside an exploited international proletariat. Nation-states mediate in the process of exploitation, but no single state is critical to it. The members of the corporate international bourgeoisie are united by mutual interests which transcend those of the states whose passports they happen to carry. They no longer need the imperialist power of their home states to gain access to resources and markets in the peripheral areas of the world. Instead, they negotiate this access by professing to an ideology which separates the political from the economic sphere.

This ideology, expressed in the 'doctrine of domicile', holds that there is no innate antagonism between the global economic interests of the transnational corporations (TNCs) and the national economic aspirations of host or home countries. TNCs are believed to transcend both: their subsidiaries are instructed to behave as 'good citizens' in any country where they do business. As good citizens they are considered able to observe national laws and regulations, and accommodate national economic and social interests. This corporate hegemonic world view reduces the nation-state of the home countries to a degree of irrelevancy while at the same time, paradoxically, opening up domestic, social and economic opportunities that did not previously exist in the colonial and neocolonial areas.

The global profit orientation of the contemporary transnational firm, coupled with a growing indifference to its national roots, implies a continuous recalculation of optimal production and profit locations. This means that developing host countries, by offering lower wage rates and competitive tax and other concessions, can achieve rapid industrialization and economic progress under the auspices of transnational capital. To the extent that the corporate national bourgeoisies in developing countries are able to consolidate these advances through informed state action, including improved bargaining with TNCs in the national economic interest, to that extent the old international division of labour will not remain fixed for ever. Although world capitalist development is uneven, some peripheral countries can attain metropolitan status, and some present-day metropoles may decay to peripheral status without contravening the fundamentals of the international order.

Another reinforcement of the dependent development approach was furnished by the American *world system theories* centred around Immanuel Wallerstein and the State University of New York's Braudel Center. The work of the school, which began in the mid-1970s, dominated the structuralist agenda in the 1970s and 1980s, spawning a huge literature, theoretical as well as substantively empirical. In basic outline the theory is not much different from Andre Gunder Frank and the dependency theory with which it is normally bracketed. It too was holistic and historical, arguing that a capitalist world economy had existed since the sixteenth century; that is, since the beginning of European overseas expansion.

In Wallerstein's terminology, the world system is 'a single division of labour, comprising multiple cultural systems, multiple political entities and even different modes of surplus appropriation' (that is, feudal, slave mode and wage labour).[36] When such a world system has a common political system, Wallerstein uses the expression, 'world-*empire*'; and when it does not, he uses the expression, 'world-*economy*'. The essential feature of the capitalist world economy is production for sale in a market in which the object is to realize maximum profit. Since its inception in the sixteenth century, the capitalist world economy has 'naturally' developed a hierarchy of occupational tasks yielding different rewards for labour. Over time, exchange has become, and remained, unequal as a result of different wage levels operating in different regions and nations. This unequal exchange, however, has been and continues to be reinforced by political interference on the part of strong states on weak ones. In this way capitalism involves not only appropriation of the surplus value by an owner from a labourer, but also appropriation of the whole economy by the 'core' areas. The core–periphery hierarchy and the exploitation of the periphery by the core are necessary to the reproduction of capitalism as a system.

From the beginning, however, the world economy has been stratified into three layers, not two: core; periphery; and semi-periphery. The reasons for the emergence of semi-peripheral nations are both political and economic: politically, semi-peripheral nations are 'go-between' nations, performing a similar function to the middle classes within national stratification systems. They form a necessary buffer in a system so based on unequal rewards that sooner or later it will lead to rebellion. Within the world system, the go-between nations also assume an economic role: they seek trade with both core and periphery, exchanging different kinds of product with each and achieving intermediate wage levels and profit margins. The *dynamic quality* of the world system is that it allows for the upward and downward mobility of nations. This is a function of the cyclical nature of the capitalist mode of production, but is made possible by the very fact of unequal wage levels, coupled with the relative rigidities in national wage levels.

It is during world economic recessions that most of the relative shifting of positions occurs. Theoretically it is not possible for all states to develop simultaneously. The rise of some nations always occurs at the expense of others that decline. Successful strategies of national upward mobility include 'promotion by invitation', 'self-reliance', and 'seizing the chance'. The successful strategy is, however, unsuccessful from the point of view of achieving national economic independence, and the participation of the masses: marginalization of the masses is a necessary condition for a country's upward mobility.[37]

Although, clearly, world system theory ran counter to both the postimperialist view of dynamism created by the transnationalization of capital, and to the political optimism of the dependent development school, it yet managed to cross-fertilize with these two currents in two fruitful ways. On the one hand, the dynamic quality of the world system that allowed for changes of position within the system suited those post-dependency analysts who tried to make sense of the reversal of fortunes evidently experienced by the newly industrializing countries (NICs) that were upwardly mobile, and some of the core countries (notably Britain) demonstrably in decline by any measure of international statistical comparison. On the other hand, many writers of the world system school began to place increasing stress on the role of the national semi-peripheral state in such cases of ascent (that is, Wallerstein's 'seizing the chance' strategy).

Ultimately, it was the case of East Asia, rather than Latin America, that clinched the deal and forced a major rethink of the relationship between global capitalism and Third-World economic development. It was a rethink that eventually also allowed a certain convergence between neo-Marxist and neoclassical understanding of why some developing countries succeeded in the world economy while others did not. The centrepiece in this new theoretical consensus was the 'developmental state', to which we shall return in Chapter 10.

PART II

CRISIS AND TRANSFORMATION

Introduction

In Part I of this book we looked at the history of capitalist expansion on a world scale. Using Robert Cox's concept of 'historical structures', we examined the material, institutional and ideological features of sequential stages in core–periphery relations. The ideological features included the intellectual traditions that grew up to explain the historical trajectory, whether as apologists or critics. Liberal and (neo-)Marxist theories of development[1] were seen as opposing 'paradigms', with all the weight of doctrinal command of emotion and thinking that the term has implied since it was first introduced by Kuhn. It will therefore come as a surprise that, with the benefit of hindsight, it transpires that more ground was common between them than that which divided them. For they both shared certain fundamental assumptions that we can only now appreciate as being 'historically bound at the origin', to borrow Robert Cox's phrase.[2]

The assumption of both liberal and neo-Marxist theories was that the capitalist system, or the world market system, was inherently *expansive* in character. As such, it was for ever driven by its own needs to incorporate (and exploit) ever-larger areas of the world. The paradigmatic controversy was over the nature of this expansive process: whether it was exploitative and underdeveloping, or progressive and uplifting. But that the process of expansion was inexorable was not questioned by either perspective. It was thought that the relentless search for raw materials, for cheap labour and for market outlets, time and again would drive capitalism *either* into fresh geographic regions *or*, when these were no longer available, into upgrading existing ones.

In their optimistic interpretation, orthodox Marxists in fact stood closer to the liberal views than did neo-Marxists, or dependency and world system writers. The liberal tradition was certainly not alone in asserting its belief in the effectiveness of capitalism in raising growth, alleviating poverty and promoting civil liberties everywhere, including the Third World. Echoing Marx's own predictions that capitalism, in spreading through imperialism to the underdeveloped lands, would stir them up and work them over in such a way as to cause social revolutions, or patterns of democratization similar to those that had happened in advanced countries, orthodox Marxists such as Bill Warren and, as we have seen, Latin American *'dependista'* writers such as F. H. Cardoso and E. Faletto,[3] assigned a positive role to capitalist imperialism. Incorporation by capitalism, they argued, in effect resulted, in *territorial economic development*, in which capitalist exploitation under foreign domination merely served as a prelude to internal social struggles and progressive democratization.

Neo-Marxist writers, on the other hand – for example, Paul Baran, A. G. Frank and Samir Amin, have generally maintained a pessimistic view, namely that incorporation caused internal blockage and distortions, and territorial underdevelopment. But even for these writers there was still light at the end of the tunnel because of the ultimate prospect of populist anti-capitalist revolutions being 'provoked' by capitalist penetration of the periphery.[4]

Thus the whole edifice of the Marxist tradition, as far as the analysis of development or underdevelopment in the periphery is concerned, was built on the assumption of capitalism as an ongoing expanding project, until it collapsed, whether nationally or internationally, under the weight of its own contradictions, after which it would be succeeded by socialism.[5]

The dogmatic belief in the ever-expanding needs of the capitalist system, and the associated 'necessity' of imperialism, was not long ago reaffirmed by Paul Sweezy, himself one of the leading architects of the tradition. Commenting on the process of globalization during the 1980s, he states categorically in an opening paragraph, 'In the periphery, foreign capital has penetrated more widely and deeply than ever before.'[6]

But do the empirical facts support the argument of continued expansion and incorporation? Is the periphery still 'necessary' for capitalism? Or can the drive to accumulation, which is central to capitalism as an economic system, survive without the periphery? Is it the case that, in the turmoil of the present crisis, a new stage of capitalism is fermenting in the core of the system, one in which the *geographic* core–periphery polarization is being replaced by a *social* core–periphery divide that cuts across territorial boundaries and geographic regions? This is the central theme of the second part of this book.

We shall map out a theory of transformation that defines globalization as a new social architecture of cross-border human interactions. It breaks down the old international division of labour and the associated hierarchy of rich and poor countries. In this process, the integrity of the national territorial state as a more or less coherent political economy is eroded, and the functions of the state become reorganized to adjust domestic economic and social policies to fit the exigencies of the global market and global capitalist accumulation. In this view, domestic peripheralization in rich and poor countries alike is not merely an unintended outcome, but performs a necessary regulatory function. And thus the new global configuration drives a politics of exclusion, contrasted with the politics of incorporation (and 'developmentalism' in the broadest sense) that marked previous periods of capitalist expansion.

The use of the term 'regulation' reveals the theoretical research agenda of the Regulation School, to which we shall refer in this part of the book. Like Robert Cox's 'critical theory' of historical structures, the Regulation School (see Chapters 5 and 7) too is a critical social theory that has been infected by the postmodernist, poststructuralist turn of the 1970s. But while Cox's theory is particularly relevant as a theory of international relations, the Regulation School has more to say about the transformation of production systems, industrial organisation and social institutional complexes that drive the present phase of globalization. We have to understand the new 'techno-economic' paradigm which began to emerge during the protracted world economic crisis of the 1970s before we can appreciate the transformation of the international political economy that accompanied it.

It has become commonplace to speak of 'crisis and transformation' as one phenomenon. It is a usage that is an indication of a particular view of the world, now widely shared, though first articulated by regulation theory, that capitalism, instead of destroying itself in consequence of its systemic internal contradiction, is repeatedly able to overcome self-inflicted crises by total renewal.[7] The word 'adjustment' does not cover total renewal, but 'transformation' does. Yet crisis and transformation are simultaneous historical processes and may only be separated for analytical purposes. There is no chronological sequence: it is *not* as though the crisis that began in the 1970s *first* gave rise to the new production systems and *next* to the new social and economic configurations, domestic and global, that have transformed our way of life. Rather, global transformations were part and parcel of the crisis itself.

In some senses they may even be said to have induced the crisis. As we shall see in Chapter 4, the expansive, incorporatist phase of capitalism had already shown signs of *involution*, when international economic interactivity and newly emerging forms of international connectivity (for example, transnational production systems) became concentrated increasingly within the core (albeit a reconstituted core) of the world capitalist system, and previously incorporated areas and regions were marginalized or expelled from it. All this began in, and overlapped with, a period that was still theorized and institutionalized as a period of 'development' of the 'Third World' as a unitary category, related objectively to the 'First World' in a homogeneously perceived way.

It is therefore pertinent that we should start our theorizing about social transformation with a hard look at the long-term empirical and statistical trends of capitalist expansion and global integration. The statistical portrait I sketch in Chapter 4 tells us about the failure of world capitalism to incorporate the periphery in its dynamic growth, which in turn set the scene for the period of crisis and transformation that has characterized the period since the 1970s.

4

From Expansion to Involution

Three key economic indicators are commonly cited to attest to the increasing internationalization of the world economy: world trade figures, in particular the rising ratio of world trade to output; the growth and spread of foreign direct investments through multinational corporations, again expressed in relation to world output and trade; and the expansion of all international capital flows and their pattern of integration. We shall look at each of these, both in relation to evidence of the general thesis of internationalization of the world economy, and in relation to the participation of the periphery in this internationalization.

World Trade: Long-term Trends[1]

The received wisdom of all the literature on the postwar period is that world trade has grown very much faster than world production, and that this testifies to 'the increased *internationalization* of activities and of the greater *interconnectedness* which have come to characterise the world economy' (emphasis in original), to quote just one, quite representative, textbook on the subject.[2]

True, world trade has grown faster than world output over most of the period since the Second World War, but it is worth going back to the nineteenth century and the early parts of the twentieth century in order to assess whether this is something new, different, more of the same, or indeed less of the same, to what happened during previous periods of internationalization.

The standard work to consult here is the contribution of Nobel prize winner, Simon Kuznets, to the quantitative measurements of world production and trade, published in 1967, in which he reviewed, compared and recalculated several longitudinal studies of world production, trade and population over the whole period 1800–1963.[3] What do we learn from Kuznets' figures?

Growth of world trade in relation to world output

For Kutznets, the nineteenth century (and more particularly the period 1880–1913) stood out as the peak period of growth of world trade. It was unprecedented and has arguably not been surpassed since then. In the period 1800–1913, world trade per capita grew eleven times faster than world output, establishing an increasingly more complex network of economic activity that eventually embraced 155 trading areas on all continents.[4] By 1913, on the eve of the First World War, the foreign trade proportion stood at 33 per cent. The foreign trade proportion is measured by the ratio of the volume of world trade (expressed as the sum total of world merchandise exports and imports at current prices) to the volume of world output. This ratio of 33 per cent had risen from about 3 per cent in 1800. During and between the two world wars that proportion fell to about a third of its 1913 level, and by 1963, the latest date in Kuznets' time series, it had recovered to about 22 per cent. For all the claims of trade expansion during the post-Second World War period, it took a further thirty years for the foreign trade proportion to reach its 1913 level (see Table 4.1).

In the 1990s, the growth of world trade surged ahead of world output faster than anything witnessed in the 1970s or 1980s. Indeed, reference is now even being made to a possible 'decoupling' of trade growth and output growth.[5] By 1996, the most recent date for which the World Bank reports the trade share of world GDP, the figure stood at an estimated 43 per cent.[6] While the East Asian Crisis of 1997–8 caused a decline in world trade of about 2 per cent, the long-term forecast is that this is just a temporary set back. The reasons for this faster pace of world trade growth are complex, but all are said to point to the effects of globalization that became manifest in the latter half of the 1980s.[7] First, a series of trade reform and liberalization measures on the part of less-developed countries, notably in Asia and Latin America, marked a shift from

Table 4.1 The ratio of commodity world trade to world output, 1800–1996 (per cent)

Year	Kuznets' figures	UN Yearbook's figures
1800	3.0	—
1850*	8.9	—
1880*	17.1	—
1913	33.0	—
1953	16.7	—
1958	19.6	24.7
1963	22.2	25.6
1975	—	28.9
1985	—	31.1
1989	—	30.5
1993	—	31.8**
1996	—	43.0**

Notes: * Figures for 1850 and 1880 derive from Kuznets' estimate of a growth rate of 7% per capita product per decade during the period, and a growth rate of 33% per capita world trade. Therefore the decennial rate of trade-to-product growth = (1.33/1.07–1) = 24.3%.
** Trade to GDP figures for 1993 and 1996 are based on *World Development Report*, (World Bank, 1995 and 1998/9).
Sources: S. Kuznets, 'Quantitative Aspects of the Economic Growth of Nations: X-Level and Structure of Foreign Trade: Long-Term Trends', table 1 pp. 4–5 in *Economic Development and Cultural Change*, 15 (2) (1967), and footnote to table 1, p. 7.
UN Yearbook figures:
Trade statistics: *Yearbook of International Trade Statistics* (New York: UN, 1963); *International Trade Statistics Yearbook* (New York: UN, 1990 and 1993).
Output statistics: *Yearbook of National Statistics* (New York: UN, 1965); *National Accounts Statistics* (New York: UN, 1982 and 1988–9).

---

inward-orientated to outward-orientated development strategies, which obviously had a positive effect on their participation in international trade. The effects of a number of regional trade arrangements, such as the European Union (EU), the North American Trade Agreement (NAFTA), and the Asia Pacific Economic Co-operation Treaty (APEC) also began to have an impact on aggregate world trade statistics. Overall, there are at the time of writing about a hundred regional trade agreements in force.[8] In addition, the accelerating flows of foreign direct investment since the 1990s, themselves the fruit of progressive capital liberalization agreements, coupled with the lowering of trade barriers, have helped the expansion of international trade. Global production structures, for example, where internationally linked firms jointly bring a product to the market after extensive cross-border exchanging of parts and semi-finished components, now account for about 30 per cent of international trade in manufactures.[9] Last, but not least, cross-border *services* trade, which previously hardly registered in world trade figures, since they used to be based on the imports and exports of *merchandise* goods, began to be better recorded and proved to be the fastest growing element of world trade, contributing about 25 per cent of the total in 1997.[10] Even so, many invisible services, particularly financial services, are still under-reported. If the internet and exploding e-commerce and e-business are taken into account (much of which includes cross-border transactions and none of which are recorded in international trade statistics), then we may certainly conclude that the foreign trade proportion of 43 per cent in the year 2000 is but a very crude underestimate of the current *intensity* of world trade.

Core and periphery: respective shares of world trade

But *intensity* is not the same as *extensity*. There is a stubborn belief that with intensity has come a geographically ever-expanding circumference of international trade. This is a view understandably held by the World Trade Organization (WTO) which exists to promote world trade, but it is also one that can be found in mainstream and objective academic texts.[11] It is largely based on a misreading of the data: after all, the postwar world has seen a multiplication of 'customs borders' which (in the statistical records) internationalize exchanges that had previously been domestic. The world knew fifty 'countries' in 1945, whereas in the year 2000 there are about 200, and the number is still growing. Inevitably, then, more countries are involved in international exchanges. It is the aim of this chapter to give the reader a sense of how globalization, in its manifestations of international trade, production and finance, in fact amounts to an accelerated withdrawing, a *shrinking* of the global map, rather than an *expanding* phenomenon, and one which expels ever more people from the interactive circle of global capitalism.

Given our interest in the core–periphery structure of the world economy, we should be examining the long-term data in respect of the participation of each of these two sub-groups, and the evolution of trade between the two, rather than looking at overall figures of world trade and world output.

Kuznets made an, admittedly crude, distinction between 'developed' and 'underdeveloped' groups of countries. The underdeveloped group covered Africa (excluding the Union of South Africa after 1880), Asia (excluding Japan after 1880, and the Communist countries after 1913), and Latin America; the developed group covered North America (USA and Canada), Europe (excluding communist countries after 1913), Japan after 1880, Australia and New Zealand (Oceania after 1913), and the Union of South Africa after 1880.[12] The trade career of these same areas, these same groupings of countries, is reviewed here.

According to Kuznets, the share of world trade contributed by the regions of Africa, Asia and Latin America was a fairly constant 20 per cent of the total throughout the period up to 1913, increasing by 6 percentage points during the period 1913–53; the share of the industrial/developed group declined correspondingly from about three-quarters of world trade to just under 70 per cent in 1953. In Table 4.2 we extend Kuznets' estimates with figures derived from the UN *Yearbook of International Trade Statistics* (the source used by Kutznets to extend his historical data up to 1960), to cover the period up to 1996. The *Yearbook* makes the same crude distinction between industrial and non-industrial areas (now relabelled 'developed' and 'developing' areas), while recording the 'eastern trading area' as a separate group. The only incongruity between these two series of data is that Kuznets has a residual category of 'other Europe/Eastern Trading Area' which includes only Eastern Europe and the Soviet Union (after 1913), but not China, which he has grouped within the 'underdeveloped' category throughout. The *Yearbook*, on the other hand, has moved China (from 1980) out of the centrally planned economies (CPE) grouping and into the 'developing' category. Since China contributed less than 1 percent of world trade until 1990 (although by 1996 it had climbed to 2.7 per cent), this should not seriously distort the picture reflected in Table 4.2.

By 1953 the share of the industrial areas in world trade was 65 per cent, and that of the non-industrial areas around 26 per cent. It is during the immediate postwar period that the share of the non-industrial group reached its peak participation level. Turning to subsequent years, there is a remarkable continuity in the historical long run, despite small periodic fluctuations. For example, in 1970,

Table 4.2   Share of commodity world trade by economic areas, 1800–1996 (per cent)

Year	Developed area	Developing area	OtherEurope/Eastern trading area*
Kuznets			
1800	65.0	18.0	17.0
1850	69.0	22.0	9.0
1880	63.0	20.0	8.0
1913	74.3	20.0	5.7
1928	68.9	23.3	7.8
1937	69.2	24.5	6.3
1953	68.9	26.3	4.8
UN			
1953	65.1	25.5	9.4
1958	65.2	23.6	11.1
1965	69.5	19.6	10.9
1970	72.0	17.2	10.7
1975	66.9	22.5	10.6
1980	66.8	25.4	7.7
1985	68.2	23.0	8.7
1990	72.0	22.7	5.3
1995	67.8	28.6	3.5
1996	67.2[a]	29.1[b]	3.6

Notes: * The 1953–75 figures included the centrally planned economies of Europe, USSR and Asia; 1980 onwards figures include only Eastern Europe and the former USSR.
[a] Of which Japan takes 11% of the industrial group's share of world trade.
[b] Of which the 4 Asian Tigers take over a third of the non-industrial group's share of world trade.
Sources: S. Kuznets' figures: 'Quantitative Aspects of the Economic Growth of Nations: X-Level and Structure of Foreign Trade: Long-Term Trends', table 2. p. 11, in *Economic Development and Cultural Change*, 15 (2) (1967).
UN figures: 1953 and 1958, *Yearbook of International Trade Statistics, 1970–71*, UN, table A, pp. xx–xxvii; 1960–75, *Yearbook of International Trade Statistics, 1982*, (New York: UN, 1963), Special table A, pp. 1124–25; 1980–, *International Trade Statistics Yearbook, 1996*, (New York: UN, 1996), Special table A, p. S2.

the share of the industrial areas had climbed back up to 72 per cent, and that of the non-industrial group had fallen back to 17 per cent. By 1990, the figures were 72 per cent and 22 per cent, respectively.

At first glance it would seem that a real recovery in the developing world's trade participation appeared in the 1990s. By 1996, respective shares stood at 67.2 per cent and 29.1 per cent, respectively.

Table 4.3   Shares of developing economies in world exports and imports, by region, 1950–95 (per cent)

	1950	*1960*	*1970*	*1980*	*1990*	*1995*
Exports						
All developing economies	33.0	23.9	18.9	29.0	23.7	27.7
America	12.1	7.7	5.5	5.4	4.2	4.4
Africa	5.3	4.2	4.1	4.6	2.3	1.5
Asia	15.2	11.5	8.5	18.4	16.7	21.4
First-tier NIEs	*2.8*	*1.6*	*2.0*	*3.8*	*7.7*	*10.4*
Imports						
All developing economies	28.9	25.2	18.8	24.0	22.2	29.1
America	10.0	7.5	5.7	5.9	3.6	4.8
Africa	5.7	5.1	3.4	3.7	2.1	1.7
Asia	12.6	11.8	8.5	13.4	15.8	22.0
First-tier NIEs	*3.0*	*2.2*	*2.7*	*4.3*	*7.5*	*10.8*

Source: UNCTAD, *Trade and Development Report* (1998), table 47, p. 183.

However, on closer inspection, it is clear that *all* the gains, and more, may be attributed to just four 'Tiger' economies in East Asia, namely Hong Kong, Korea, Taiwan and Singapore (also referred to as first-tier Newly Industrialized Economies (NIEs)). Their combined population is 71 million, a mere 1.5 per cent of the total population of the developing world, and yet they contribute about a third of all the trade of developing countries. Their overwhelming preponderance in the developing world's trade participation is ignored all too often in the hype about world trade integration. This is substantiated by an even more revealing table, this time drawn from UNCTAD's 1998 Trade and Development Report (see Table 4.3). This table shows just how much of the postwar trade growth of the developing countries has been captured by these four small economies in the 1990s.

Changes in position within core and periphery

So what has changed over this long historical period? Japan has appeared on the scene to take 11 per cent of the industrial group's share of world trade; and the four Asian Tigers have taken hold of well over a third of the non-industrial group's share of world trade. Moreover, the composition of these countries' exports, in which manufacturers dominate, suggests that, to all intents and purposes, they are now industrial/developed countries. If, therefore, these four Asian Tigers were reclassified into the 'industrial group', the share of that group in world trade would rise to 78 per cent in 1996, while that of the non-industrial group would decline to 19 per cent.

Shifts in inter-group and intra-group trade

There have been important shifts in intergroup trade. According to Kuznets, in the period 1876–80 intergroup trade (that is, between the industrial and non-industrial groups) accounted for 51 per cent of world trade, while intra-industrial group trade accounted for 45 per cent and intra-non-industrial group trade for only 4 per cent. He observed that this tripartite division remained relatively constant

Table 4.4 Inter- and intra-group trade, 1876–1996 (per cent)

Source	Year	Inter-groups	Intra-industrial	Intra-non-industrial	Total
Kuznets	1876–80	51.0	45.0	4.0	100.0
	1961–63	44.0	48.0	8.0	100.0
	1953	43.2	37.1	8.0	88.3
	1962	34.2	44.1	5.8	84.1
*GATT**	1973	25.6	51.7	3.5	80.8
	1985	28.9	49.4	5.9	84.2
	1990	26.6	55.4	5.7	87.7
*WTO**	1997	32.5	49.2	10.3	92.0

Note: * For the GATT/WTO figures, the total adds up to less than 100%, the balance being made up by trade with and within the 'Eastern Trading Area'.

Sources: S. Kuznets' figures: 'Quantitative Aspects of the Economic Growth of Nations: X-Level and Structure of Foreign Trade: Long-Term Trends' table 5, p. 27 in Economic Development and Cultural Change, 15 (2) (1967).

GATT figures: 1953 and 1962, GATT, *International Trade* (1962), table 2, p. 7; 1973: *International Trade* (1973), table 2, p. 3; 1985 and 1990: *International Trade* (1990–91), table A2. For the 1997 figure, WTO (the GATT successor), *International Trade Statistics* (1998), table A2.

over the whole period, with the respective shares by 1961–3 standing at 44 per cent, 48 per cent and 8 per cent, respectively. Looking at GATT trade statistics, we notice – as before – a brief surge in the Third World's relative participation in world trade during the immediate postwar period. In 1953, for example, intra-industrial group trade had dropped to 37.1 per cent, while intergroup trade had remained stable at 43.2 per cent. Since the early 1960s, however, there has been a slow but steady increase in intra-industrial group trade, so that by 1990 it had reached 55 per cent of world trade, while intergroup trade, on the other hand, had declined consistently, to stand at 26.6 per cent of world trade in 1990 (see Table 4.4). Again, it looks as if there was a turnaround in the 1990s. But here too this can be attributed entirely to the 'Asian Tiger' effects.

Proportions of world population involved

By far the most revealing statistic is the proportion of world population involved in the respective world trade shares. In the period before 1880, the population of the 'industrial' or 'core' group of countries included North America and Western Europe only. Their combined population rose from about 118 million in 1800 to almost 303 million in 1900. That of the 'Rest of the World' rose from 783

Table 4.5   The world population among groups of countries, 1800–1997 (millions and per cent)

Year	*(a)* Core countries		*(b)* Rest of world		World total
	Millions	*%*	*Millions*	*%*	*Millions*
1800	118.15	13.1	783.35	86.9	901.50
1850	183.20	15.2	1 019.05	84.8	1 202.25
1900	302.75	18.7	1 319.00	81.3	1 621.75
1950	471.50	18.8	2 037.50	81.2	2 509.00
1997	992.70	17.0	4 836.30	83.0	5 829.00

Notes: (a) includes North America and Western Europe 1800–1950; 1997 data also includes Japan, Hong Kong, Taiwan and South Korea.
(b) includes Eastern Europe and the Soviet Union; and Japan before 1990.
Sources: 1800–1950s data: C. McEvedy and R. Jones, *Atlas of World Population* (Harmondsworth: Penguin, 1978); 1997 data: World Bank, *World Development Report* (1997).

million to 1319 million, giving the 'industrial' group a rising share of the world population, from 13 per cent in 1800 to 18.7 per cent in 1900. By 1997, even with the inclusion of Japan and the Asian Tigers in the core, that proportion is just 17 per cent (see Table 4.5), even now remaining below the historical bench mark.

Terms of trade

Last but not least, there is the continuing nagging issue of the declining terms of trade for developing countries. It is an issue that the proponents of free trade choose to ignore. For example, the WTO annual report of 1998 produces 184 tables and charts on various aspects of world trade, but not a single one describes the evolution of terms of trade. Yet this evolution puts the purported boom in world trade participation on the part of the developing countries since the 1990s into perspective. Because, when terms of trade decline, a larger volume of exports is needed to finance a given volume of imports, and if the volume of imports increases (as indeed it has done since trade liberalization), then the result is larger trade deficits. As UNCTAD notes in the case of the developing countries (excluding oil exporters and China), income losses arising from declining terms of trade, already large in the 1980s, have grown larger still in the 1990s and trade deficits too have grown, partly as a result of the increased share of trade in GDP for these countries.[13]

The conclusion to be drawn from these various figures is that the record of world trade can neither be summoned to testify to 'the increasing interconnectedness which characterises our world economy', nor as evidence of 'the deepening and widening penetration by the core of the periphery'. Rather, it stands as evidence of a thickening network of economic exchanges within the core, a significant redistribution of trade participation *within* the core, the graduation of a small number of peripheral nations with a comparatively small population base to 'core' status, but above all to a declining economic interaction between core and periphery, both relative to aggregate world trade and to total populations participating in the network.[14]

Foreign Direct Investment (FDI) and the Growth of Multinational Enterprises

Even if world trade is not 'the most important manifestation of transnationalisation', surely foreign direct investment is?[15] Or is it? The impressive growth of the multinational enterprise in the postwar period has generally left commentators in search of superlatives: phenomenal, explosive, dramatic, and amounting to a 'complete transformation of the world economy',[16] are descriptions without which no textbook is complete.

Again, it is worth looking back in history to see whether we are confronted here with a truly new phenomenon, or a continuation of past trends. In the immediate postwar period, between 1950 and 1970, international direct investments grew at a rate just a little faster than that of the average GDP of the developed market economies (where nearly all the direct investment flows came from), but it does not follow that this presents a significant departure from the prewar situation.

In awe of the 'enormous' size and steadily growing importance of multinational corporations (MNCs) in world economic activities, a UN group of experts came to the trend-setting conclusion in 1973 that *international production* had surpassed *international trade* as the main vehicle of international economic exchange. It was estimated that international production had reached approximately US$330 billion in 1971, while the total exports of all market economies were just a little less, at US$310 billion.[17] The authors defined international production as 'production subject to foreign control and decision', and based the measurement of it on an estimate of annual foreign sales of MNCs, which in its turn was calculated from an assumed ratio of foreign sales to the book value of international direct investment stock. In this particular report, that ratio was arbitrarily set at 2:1.[18] It is interesting to compare this figure with the interwar situation.

In 1938, just before the outbreak of the Second World War, world exports totalled US$22.6 billion.[19] From John Dunning we learn that the gross value of long-term investments at that time were in the region of US$55 billion, of which 25 per cent, or US$13 billion, is calculated to have been made up of *direct* investments.[20] Applying the 2:1 ratio to this figure gives US$26 billion as the value of international production, comfortably exceeding the value of international trade at the time.

Geographic redirection and concentration

I am presenting these figures for a purpose: demonstrating that which is *not* new enables us to see more clearly that which *is*. The use of global (in the sense of 'aggregate') trade and investment flows, and expressing these as a percentage of 'global' (again in the sense of 'aggregate') world product, creates an image of a 'global' economy that stretches from Anchorage to Cape Town, from Helsinki to Santiago de Chile. It does not – *not any more!* An ambitious net of capitalist catchment may have been cast during the colonial era, but having caught the fish it has pulled back and settled comfortably on the shores of a relatively small part of the world. It is in that same part of the world that cross-national economic activity is being whipped up into a frenzy.

What is both a *new and consistent* feature of postwar foreign direct investment flows is the *geographic redirection* of such flows away from the periphery and into the core of the system. In the colonial period, up to 1960, the Third World received half of the total direct investment flows. This percentage had declined to a third in 1966, and to a quarter in 1974.[21] By 1988–9 it had dropped still further, to 16.5 per cent.[22] But over half of this remaining trickle went to the regions of East, South and South-East Asia.[23]

The 1990s have seen what appears superficially to be a monumental turnaround in fortunes, with the developing world receiving about 38 per cent of the total of world foreign direct investment (FDI) by 1997.[24] This time, Hong Kong and Singapore are no longer included in the developing group. However, this FDI-led integration, too, is a highly selective process. The opening up of China has made it a pole of attraction for FDI flows. China now accounts for two-thirds of the total FDI flow into East Asia and a third of the inflow of all developing countries.[25]

At the start of the twenty-first century, China dominates as the single largest developing host country of inward investment. Because China has a very large population of 1.3 billion, this often distorts the picture on FDI and growth in the developing world. But it is well known that in China both investment and growth are concentrated in the eight coastal provinces (mainly in the south) and in Beijing. In their book *Globalization in Question*,

Paul Hirst and Grahame Thompson have tried to discount this anomaly by including only the populations of the coastal provinces and Beijing in their summation of all populations in the ten most important developing countries in terms of inward investment. Together with the other nine most important developing countries hosting FDI, plus the population in the Triad countries (North American, Western Europe and Japan) they constituted about 30 per cent of the world population, who between them received 86 per cent of all global direct investment in the first half of the 1990s.[26] Hirst and Thompson conclude that, 'this means that between a half and two-thirds of the world was still virtually written off the map as far as any benefits from this form of investment was concerned'.[27]

Frenzied circulation

There are three further problems with the thesis of recent FDI-led world integration. The first relates to the coexistence of net *out*flows with net *in*flows. The China FDI figures are a case in point. Inflows from Hong Kong into China are counted as an FDI inflow, but many residents and companies from China use the Hong Kong financial markets as a means of 'round tripping' liquid capital in pursuit of short-term arbitrage opportunities and returning it as FDI, to benefit from tax breaks and other advantages accorded to FDI flows. The United Nations Conference on Trade and Development (UNCTAD) suggests that an important part of recorded FDI flows to China originates in the country itself,[28] while Henderson estimates that Hong Kong is responsible for 60 per cent of all FDI in China.[29]

A second problem relates to what exactly is being counted as FDI. For example, over half of US 'outward' foreign investment is not new, cross-border, money being invested, but reinvested earnings and profit.[30] Therefore, it is not an autonomous source of external financing. The third problem is that both reinvested earnings and, indeed, *new* cross-border flows are often used *not* to start new businesses (so-called greenfield investments), but to acquire existing productive or commercial capacity in the host country. It is estimated that cross-border mergers and acquisitions (M&A) have accounted for between a half and two-thirds of world FDI flows in the 1990s. UNCTAD has concluded that, with the excep-

tion of China, the 'recent boom in FDI flows to developing economies, has consisted predominantly of M&A, largely in the services
sector'.[31]

World Capital Flows: Other Resource Flows

Foreign *direct* investments are only a sub-part of all long-term
international capital flows. The aggregate also includes what used
to be called *indirect* flows – for example, bank lending, export or
commercial credits, official loans, and grants. When it comes to
assessing these wider international resource flows, it is almost
impossible to compare the past with the present. This is largely for
two reasons. The first relates to the incongruity of data collection
between historical periods; and the second relates to the cross-
penetration of resource flows between countries that has come
with the wave of liberalization and deregulation of national capital
markets in the 1980s.

New flows, new classifications

New financial instruments, new ways of borrowing and lending, and
new methods of international transfer of resources are constantly
being invented. Periodically, they come to inspire a new classification for statistical data collection by the various international institutions that make it their business to track the international
financial flows. For example, in the 1960s and 1970s it was common
to distinguish between 'direct' and 'indirect' flows, between 'public'
and 'private' flows and between 'long-term' and 'short-term' flows.
These three categorizations cut across one another, but their binary
nomenclature was fairly unambiguous. 'Direct' flows were made up
of foreign direct investment of the kind discussed in the previous
section: companies investing in wholly- (or majority-) owned subsidiaries abroad, making profits that were returned in the form of
dividends. The defining criterion here was 'equity' ownership, which
carried managerial control over the foreign operations. Indirect
investments were, by contrast, interest-bearing debt instruments,
as in bank lending, whether to governments or private firms. At
the time of writing, that distinction is becoming meaningless, as the
development of stock markets in many so-called 'emerging' mar-

kets,[32] as well as the general opening up of all the world's stock markets, means that non-residents can buy shares (or stocks, as in the American vernacular) in *any* domestic markets. Buying shares gives an entitlement to dividends, but has no managerial implications. Such 'portfolio equity' investments have become a leading component of international investments to less developed countries since the early 1990s, more especially to 'emerging markets'. But *in addition*, it has become common for governments (including those of many developing countries), and indeed for private companies, to issue bonds and 'treasury' bills (in the case of governments), certificates of deposit, or other forms of 'commercial paper' in the world's credit markets, instead of borrowing from banks. These 'IOUs' have various maturities (anything from three months to ten years) that carry interest (leaving aside exceptions such as 'zero-coupons'), but do not carry any managerial rights. This has removed the distinction between 'direct' and 'indirect'. So now it is more common to find the classification 'direct' versus 'portfolio' flows.

Then there is the distinction between 'official' and 'private' flows. 'Official' or 'public' flows used to be either multilateral – for example, from international organizations to governments; or bilateral, as in aid flows from one government to another. These were, and in fact still are especially targeted on the poorest countries which are almost wholly dependent on them for external financing. They normally carry very low interest rates, or none at all (a concessionary element). They used to be contrasted with all private flows. However, nowadays, when governments of (some) developing countries issue bonds and other securities on international financial markets, that distinction too becomes blurred, as *public* finances are raised from international *private* credit markets. Therefore, it is more common nowadays to speak of public or 'sovereign' debt versus 'private' debt.

There also used to be a very clear distinction between long-term and short-term flows. Most resource flows, whether of the direct or indirect variety, were long-term. Short-term flows constituted a relatively minor component and normally consisted of 'export credits', as when banks extended loans to exporters to tide them over the period between sending their goods abroad and receiving payment for them from the importer. But now 'short-term flows' constitute a huge variety of financial instruments, and their separation from

long-term flows is in doubt. Take, for example, the trade in currencies. In previous times, when fixed exchange rate regimes prevailed,
there were hardly any currency markets. This changed with the
collapse of the Bretton Woods system in 1971, since which time
the trade in currencies has become the fastest growing market ever,
now reaching sixty times the value of international trade in goods
and services. Currency trade is typically very short-term and often
speculative. Next, there is trading in derivatives. A derivative is a
financial contract, the value of which depends on the values of one
or more underlying assets or indices of asset values. The most
common such contracts are: forwards, futures, swaps and options.
The primary purpose of derivatives is not to borrow or lend funds
but rather to transfer price risks associated with fluctuations in asset
values. The main categories of risks are fluctuations associated with
risks in the commodity- , foreign exchange- and equity markets, and
in interest rates. The derivative markets are also a very fast-growing
element of all cross-border financial markets. The principal derivative is often classified as a long-term capital flow, while the trade in
derivatives in so-called secondary markets appears as a short-term
flow in the current account statistics.[33] However, since most financial instruments are traded in 'secondary markets', where people sell
them on long before they reach maturity, short-term movements in
financial flows can merge with long-term movements.

Cross-penetration

The second problem we have in comparing the past with the present
arises from the interactive web of cross-penetration of such flows
now, compared with the past. There was a time before the First
World War when the world was sharply and simply divided between
creditor and debtor nations. A handful of countries in Europe were
the creditor nations. Together they were responsible for 85 per cent
of international lending, totalling US$44 billion by 1913. Nearly 44
per cent of this went to the areas subsequently called the Third
World, with the bulk of the remainder going to the USA, Canada
and Russia.[34]

Today, however, creditor nations are also debtor nations. Cross-
penetration of financial flows has woven such an immensely
complex web of lending and borrowing that it has become almost
meaningless to try to trace ownership of assets and liabilities to their

respective national roots. National balance of payments statistics only give us figures for 'net' capital inflows and outflows. But these conceal a huge variety of international transactions – for example, lending by American banks operating in Britain to Americans in American dollars, or to British residents in American dollars, or to American residents in Britain in sterling. Hence the difficulties in comparing the present with the past.

The figures on gross capital flows give us a picture of the cross-penetration of the world's financial markets and are therefore a more accurate pointer to the present integrated global financial system. Already by the end of the 1980s the growth of the world's financial markets had outstripped the pace of growth and investment in the countries of the OECD (Organization of Economic Co-operation and Development) *seven* times in that decade alone. The total stock of internationally invested funds (bank lending, cross-border equity investments; derivatives, FDI) increased roughly from about US$2.3 billion to US$19 billion. Meanwhile, the combined GDP of the rich OECD countries increased from only about US$7.6 billion to US$17 billion.[35] These figures exclude the *short-term* transactions in the currency markets, which at that time were only about eighteen times the total value of international trade, but which by 1998 had reached some *sixty* times the total value of international trade.[36]

In the 1990s, and until the Asian crisis of 1997, this frenzied pace of cross-penetration continued prodigiously, with again, on the face of it, a widening rippling effect that embraced the developing world. For example, in just six years between 1990 and 1996, the *annual* value of all funds raised on the international credit markets (bonds and loans) by all countries rose by about 66 per cent to over US$1 trillion, of which the developing countries as a whole took 11 per cent.[37] The same goes for the total world stock market valuation, which by 1996 stood at a staggering US$20 trillion, of which the developing world took almost 14 per cent.[38] Meanwhile, the value of the derivative markets rose to about US$30 trillion.

Net flows to developing countries

The integration of the global financial markets is most often the reference point for the designation of the term 'globalization' in the publications of international organizations. But while gross flows are a good indicator of cross-penetration at a world level, *net* flows give a better understanding of how regions and countries share in the global circulation of funds. After all, there are two sides to liberalization and deregulation, which may be summed up in the old adage: 'what's good for the goose is good for the gander'. If foreigners can bring money in, so residents can take money out. As UNCTAD pointed out in its 1999 *Annual Report*: 'As a result of the liberalization of capital transactions and markets, outward movements of capital by residents have gained increasing importance in determining a country's net capital flow.'[39] For the developing countries as a whole, the share of recorded outflows in the total of inflows more than doubled during the 1990s.[40]

However, even going by the record of 'net' capital flows,[41] there is little argument about the fact that the developing world has recovered the ground it lost in the debt decade of the 1980s, when international private lending dried up almost completely. Excluding FDI, net long-term private flows (commercial bank loans, portfolio equity and bonds) to the developing countries increased sixfold, from US$20 billion in 1990 to over US$130 billion in 1997.[42] But, again, as was the case with trade and FDI flows, the question we must ask is whether this is a real and sustainable change, a new departure in long-term historical trends?

First, if we measure these flows in real, as opposed to nominal, money terms, taking account of inflation and the cost of living, then the improvement is much more limited. Furthermore, if we look at this measure of participation in the same way as we did in respect of trade flows, namely as a proportion of the national product of the recipient countries, then, as UNCTAD argues, the recent surge in capital inflows looks even more modest: 'Indeed, despite the much acclaimed absolute rise in capital inflows of developing countries in the 1990s, they have averaged around 5 percent of GNP since the beginning of the decade which was roughly the level prevailing before the outbreak of the debt crisis of the 1980s. If China is excluded, the ratio during 1990–1998 was more than one percentage point lower than during 1975–1982.'[43]

In addition, as was the case with both trade and FDI, the direction of portfolio flows has also been very selective, with 60 per cent going to six major recipients in the developing world – namely, Brazil, Mexico, Thailand, Argentina, Indonesia and China, and 94 per cent going to just twenty countries, including four so-called 'transition economies' in Central and Eastern Europe.[44] In fact, as the UNDP *Human Development Report* notes, today only twenty-five developing countries have access to private markets for bonds, commercial bank loans and portfolio equity. The rest are excluded for lack of a credit rating.[45]

As a result of financial openness coupled with computerization, international financial markets have also become much more volatile. What this means in simple terms is that is it easier than ever before for *short*-term capital flows to whizz around taking advantage of minuscule variations in interest and exchange rates, and commodity prices between countries. It is estimated that before the Mexican peso crisis of 1994, more than half of *all* capital inflows into Latin America were of this short-term, speculative, nature.[46] The same happened a few years later in the lead up to the East Asian crisis,[47] followed by the Russian crisis. Here is not the place to go into the highly technical, little-understood yet much-debated processes whereby such speculative flows turn into so-called 'systemic' risks that have a rapid effect on the expectations of both short-term and long-term lenders alike, causing them all to remove their money suddenly. We shall return to this in the chapters on global regulation and on East Asia. It is sufficient here to draw attention to the serious consequences for the economies concerned. For example, in the crisis year of 1997, five Asian economies (Indonesia, Malaysia, The Philippines, South Korea and Thailand) experienced a turnaround of cross-border capital flows of US$105 billion, more than 10 per cent of their combined GDP.[48] While stock markets recovered within a year or so, the damage to jobs and livelihoods will take much longer to repair.

Global Financial Deepening and the Structural Position of the Third World

In a critical review of the world's financial markets, the UNCTAD's *Trade and Development Report* of 1990 made an interesting distinction between the 'internationalization' of finance, and 'global financial deepening'. It stated that the latter occurs when – as now – the pace of growth of international financial transactions is much more rapid than any of the underlying economic fundamentals, such as trade, investment and output. For example, between 1982 and 1988 the annual increment in the stock of world financial assets was, on average, about US$3800 billion, whereas the annual average level of world fixed capital formation was around US$2300 billion. The ratio of the size of the international banking market to total global fixed investment doubled in less than a decade.[49] Fréderic Clairmont has estimated that private, corporate and household debt world-wide surpasses US$31 trillion, galloping, he says, at a compound growth of over 9 per cent per annum, or three times faster than world GDP and world trade.[50] At the time of writing, more than at any time in capitalism's history, the profits of finance capital are based on fictitious capital formation, namely on debt and exponential debt creation. What is meant by fictitious capital formation and how does it relate to the world of real money which people use when they buy their daily bread?

Surreptitiously, the phrases 'economic fundamentals' or 'the real economy', as distinct from the weird world of high finance, have crept into the vocabulary of politicians and journalists when they have to explain perplexing phenomena such as the rising value of a currency during a recession, or a stock market crash during an upswing in the economy. After the stock market crash of 1987, which wiped more than 20 per cent off the value of all stocks and shares, the UK Secretary of State for the Treasury at that time, Nigel Lawson, hastened to reassure the British public that this would not affect the 'real' economy, which was in good health and more or less independent of the goings-on in the stock market. Indeed, the financial sector is now often dismissed as a casino society where speculators play out their compulsive habits, either without much effect on the lives of the rest of the population, or with effects that can only be guessed at.[51] On the other hand, there are many who fear that an overblown financial sector sucks money away and out of productive investments and contributes to the 'short-termism' that has come to pervade the economy and the attitude of the business class. But short-termism, and so-called 'paper entrepreneurialism',[52] are mere surface phenomena. Underneath there is something more fundamental going on, namely *a change in the very nature of money, and through it a change in the relationship between rich and poor, and between the advanced and less-developed sectors of the world economy.*

In abolishing the institutional barriers between the various functions of money and removing the restrictions regarding who can deal in what kind of money, deregulation (pursued in nearly all developed and underdeveloped countries with varying degrees of robustness since 1980) has caused an enormous upheaval in the structure of finance, or in the 'financial architecture', as it has been referred to lately. Money has become more and more abstract. As a consequence, the connection has been broken between buyers and sellers, between creditors and debtors, and between the provenance and the destination of money flows.

Basically, what happened was that deregulation meant that banks were being cut out of the profitable business of borrowing and lending, since companies and all sorts of 'non-bank' banks or finance houses were able to issue commercial paper directly. This is referred to as the process of 'disintermediation'. Naturally, banks began to look for new forms of business (so-called 'off-balance-sheet' activities). What they came up with was a whole new breed of 'securities'. 'Securitization' is often regarded as the single most important innovation following deregulation.

Simply put, 'securitization' means loan selling.[53] In the traditional, literal meaning of the word, a financial security is defined as 'something being given or pledged as guarantee especially for the payment of a debt'.[54] The word 'for' is significant in the expression 'for the payment of debt'. The quantum leap in financial innovation is that the word 'for' has now been dropped. The payment of debt itself has become 'securitized' and is offered as tradable paper; effectively, therefore, as money. For example, banks can pool together a variety of mortgages on houses, stores and office buildings, or even car and credit card loans, and then sell bonds backed by these 'receivables' in small chunks to individual investors, who can either hold on to them and earn interest on their share, or sell them in secondary markets.[55] Once that principle had been thoroughly understood and learnt there were no holds barred, and an amazing variety of novel financial instruments appeared which would instantly convert any *expected future cash flow*, wherever and whenever it might occur, into instant spending power. *The Economist* summed it up: 'The truth is that there is no longer any such thing as money. At least not in the sense required by monetarism and its siblings.'[56]

It is worth reflecting for a moment on the significance of the new form in which money appears, within the context of a globalized financial structure that has evolved in a world economy in which, nevertheless, the fundamentals of trade, investment, income and productive wealth remain highly unequally distributed across regions and nations. The new financial instruments effectively delink borrowers from lenders, and they do so on a cross-national basis. The result is that people with relatively little money in one country can participate in the lending of funds to borrowers in another. Wealth, in short, has become highly mobile. The question is how the enhanced capacity of the global financial structure to switch money flows around the world economy interacts with the systemically uneven distribution of the material activities of production and consumption.

An optimistic reading might well be to agree with John Reed, the one-time chairman of Citicorp, the biggest of the American banks, that there is some good to be gained from all this frenzied careering of monies around the world: 'you can translate the saving of that Japanese household into economic well-being for somebody in Southern Italy or Spain'.[57] But note that in this particular quote the banker was careful not to mention a Third-World country. Indeed, it is very unlikely that money will flow more easily from where it is concentrated, and politically and strategically safe, to where it is scarce and subject to great political and strategic risks. Reed himself was certainly aware of this when he recognized that the Third World has become 'unbankable':

There are five billion people living on earth. Probably 800 million of them live in societies that are bankable and probably 4.2 billion are living within societies that in some very fundamental way are not bankable. I think it's a great danger as we look out between now and the turn of the [twenty-first] century that this distinction between bankable and the unbankable parts of the world could become more aggravated. We're forming this global economy which is very much a phenomenon of the northern hemisphere – Europe, North America, Japan – with some small additions . . . Many of the problems we have on the globe, be it the global environment or health, are problems of the 4.2 billion, not the 800 million.[58]

Given that much of the Third World is unbankable in the traditional sense of the word, namely offering a safe return on investment, it is more likely that élites in the Third World will buy securities in the global markets rather than in their national markets. Studies by research staff of the International Monetary Fund (IMF) on the scale of *capital flight* from the developing countries lend credence to this thesis. For example, between 1975 and 1985, an estimated US$165–200 billion were placed by individual investors from the Third World in the international financial markets.[59] UNCTAD reports that, by 1996, 300 banking entities from ten leading developing countries were operating in OECD countries.[60] This is surely the critical difference between the earlier, expansive, phase of capitalism and the present-day 'imploding' phase. In the earlier prewar period, when nearly 44 per cent of all international long-term lending (including foreign direct investments) went to the regions of Africa, Asia and Latin America, it found its way into the development of railways, port installations, mines and factories. Capital accumulation and saving in the core countries of the world system converted through the financial intermediation of international portfolio lending into fixed investments in the rest of the world, so laying the foundations for future wealth creation.

Today, however, the regime of privatization and deregulation imposed by the World Bank and IMF structural adjustment programmes have created a climate of what is euphemistically called 'financial openness', in which the Third-World bourgeoisie are freer than ever before to channel their nation's wealth into the financial markets and institutions of the core countries. In so doing, they can participate in the economies of the core of the world system, while their countries cannot. But when things go awry, as they did in the Mexican crisis of 1994, the Asian crisis of 1997, and the Russian crisis a few months later, then ordinary people are directly affected through currencies that lose their values, banks and businesses that become bankrupt, jobs that are destroyed, and ruined savings. Furthermore, each measure that domestic governments and the (helpfully standing by) international community takes, inevitably takes on the form of throwing more good money after bad and propping up the values of the financial assets of the global gamblers.[61]

Core–Periphery: From Structural Exploitation to Structural Irrelevance

I have tried in this analysis to substantiate my thesis of capitalist involution. By 'involution' I mean an intensification of trade and capital linkages within the core of the capitalist system, and a relative, selective, withdrawal of such linkages from the periphery. Looking over the longer historical period, we have examined the relationship between the core and the periphery of the world system, and found that their linkages in terms of the volume of both trade and capital flows between them, which increased during earlier phases of the period, have since diminished. Moreover, even allowing for the shift in positions of some countries from the periphery to the core, it was also found that the proportionate share of populations in core and periphery has remained surprisingly constant in the period 1880–1990.

Using the definitions of the core and the periphery adopted throughout this chapter, namely the core being Western Europe, North America and Japan, and the periphery covering all regions of Africa, Latin America and Asia, there is evidence that the gap between their respective shares of world income too has widened.[62]

Going back over a long historical period, as in the previous section when economic exchanges between the core and periphery were discussed, we have to accept that comparable statistics on world *income* are simply unavailable. Economic historians have attempted, however, to *estimate* the GNP level of per capita incomes for 'developed' and 'underdeveloped' countries in earlier periods. One such estimate was made by Paul Bairoch in 1975, and goes back to 1900 using an implicit price deflator resulting from the calculations of the US gross product at constant prices. Bairoch notes a divergence in per capita income ratios between non-Communist underdeveloped countries and non-Communist developed countries, rising as follows: 1:5 in 1860; 1:6 in 1900; 1:7 in 1929; 1:8.5 in 1953; and 1:13 in 1970.[63] This compares with the UNDP ratio of income for the same two groups of countries in 1989 of just under 1:18.[64] In more recent years, the UNDP has used a different classification, measuring the distance in income between the 'richest' and 'poorerst' countries. This distance has increased as follows: 3:1 in 1820; 11:1 in 1913; 35:1 in 1950; 44:1 in 1973; and, 72:1 in 1992.[65] Whichever way one looks at this, the conclusion is that the gap which almost a hundred years ago separated the rich world from the poor has widened continuously, both during periods of capitalist expansion and during the more recent period of 'globalization' and 'involution'.

Conclusion

Two likely counter-arguments against this very pessimistic assessment of the global economy need to be addressed. First, it might well be argued that these are *relative* proportions. In *absolute* terms, surely, the world capitalist system can be seen to have delivered the goods for growing numbers of human beings? I counter this question by asking two further questions. Is this a victory for capitalism? Is this a triumph for the free market organization of human and social life? In my view it is not. The moral justification in the liberal defence of the capitalist system is that it is welfare-maximizing in the long run. But so far all that capitalism has been able to do is just about keep pace in the Malthusian race, and perhaps not even that. Hardly a record to be proud of, particularly when bearing in mind that, to achieve this amazing triumph, the 'core' today uses 70 per cent of the world's energy, 75 per cent of its metals, 85 per cent of its wood, and consumes 60 per cent of its food.[66] It is like trying to win a race and not succeeding, despite being given a very generous headstart!

A related comment may be directed at my selective focus on the 'concentration and exclusion' aspects of the historical record, and my corresponding neglect of the 'trade and growth' literature. This literature is indeed huge. Elegant theoretical models abound, and plenty of empirical proof (no less) exists on the positive link between trade openness and economic growth, and between FDI flows and economic growth. The WTO *Annual Report 1998* sets out the case once again with implacable conviction, cataloguing some twenty cross-country case studies as supporting evidence[67] – just as UNCTAD, another of the United Nations' family of organizations, never tires of pointing out the methodological flaws of such studies.[68]

But what is the point of such a positive linkage when, undeniably, the vast majority of humanity (which now includes an expanding segment of the population of the rich countries) is getting poorer all the time? In a world so steeped in social inequality that just three super-billionaires have an amount of wealth exceeding the combined income of all the least developed nations and their 600 million population, and the net worth of another 200 equates to the income of 41 per cent of world population,[69] measures of global growth are simply offensive. In a world where the majority of developing countries have structures of inequality in which 20 per cent of the population walk away with 50 per cent of the national income, national growth accounting is perverse.

In 1990, the United Nations Development Programme (UNDP) announced the first of its annual Human Development rankings. The UNDP wanted to have a measure of progress that not only includes income corrected for internal disparities, but also real indicators of quality of life, such as literacy, longevity, and infant mortality. Year by year, the Human Development Index has demonstrated that 'even though there is a strong link between trade and growth, there is no automatic link with human development, nor is there between FDI, economic growth and human development'.[70]

Leaving aside for a moment the not inconsiderable issues of human solidarity and morality, the question we must finally pose is: does it matter? Does it matter that an intensified global capitalist system expels ever greater segments of the world population and throws them out as being structurally irrelevant?

In a lucid article on the new international division of labour in the new informational economy, Manuel Castells has summed up the structural reasons for the marginalization and exclusion of what he calls the 'Fourth World' – that is, those areas in the Third, Second *and* First Worlds that are no longer relevant to the workings of the global informational economy:

> The more economic growth depends on high value added inputs and expansion in the core markets, then the less relevant become those economies which offer limited, difficult markets and primary commodities that are either being replaced by new materials or devalued with respect to their overall contribution to the production process. With the absolute costs of labor becoming less and less important as a competitive factor . . . many countries and regions face a process of rapid deterioration that could lead to destructive reactions. Within the framework of the new informational economy, a significant part of the world population is shifting from a structural position of exploitation to a structural position of irrelevance.[71]

In the past, Marxist critics of capitalism have always relied on the contradictions of the logic of capitalist accumulation to render capitalism unviable at some point in the future, leading to collapse, and hence to socialist renewal. In the following chapters this claim will be re-examined in the light of new forms of capitalist production and organization that are coming about in the core of the world system. There is a transformation of the social organization of *industrial* production systems, variously referred to as 'lean', or 'flexible' or 'postFordist', in which information drives technologies at every stage of the industrial process from design to marketing. In this system, capital–labour relations are reorganized in a manner that seems to put paid to cherished notions of 'inescapable' class conflict, as networks of organizations, dispersed labour and output-driven reward structures render obsolete the realities of factory-based labour exploitation upon which class consciousness was built.

A second transformation has macro-economic implications that are only just beginning to be noticed. Various labels, such as the 'new economy', 'the thin air' or the 'weightless' economy, celebrate the staggering potential for commodity intensification enabled by information and digitalization in the service sectors which are said to lay to rest the age-old problem of overproduction and under-consumption, of boom and bust, of inflation as the scourge of growth, of stock market tendencies to crash after climbing to dizzy heights. Will this new economy give 'core' capitalism a renewed lease of life in the absence of expanding consumer markets in the periphery? Can the core now survive without the periphery? Or, at any rate, without the human potential of the periphery? Because the core's need for the physical resources of the periphery remains as rapacious as ever, setting the scene for a new form of imperialism to accompany the new economy.

5

Flexibility and Informationalism

The failure of the world capitalist system to expand and widen the market in the periphery, which we described in the previous chapter, led – in the 1970s and 1980s – to prolonged periods of stagnation and recurrent crises in the heartland of capitalism itself.[1] The Golden Age of Capitalism was over. But in that same period many shoots of renewal, notably in the application of new technologies in industrial production, in enterprise organization and in market strategies, were being detected. These seemed to be accompanied by a dazzling variety of other changes: lifestyle consumerism in lieu of mass consumerism; identity politics and new social movements replacing class-based politics; and globalization superseding internationalization. Thus a central question for social science theory became whether and which of these shoots of renewal would add up to a whole new configuration of economic and social life, a new 'paradigm', a new model of capitalism.

In a whirlpool of change, in which old forms and practices were still jockeying for position with the new, one had to assess whether these nascent tendencies would prove to be viable and become dominant features of a new epoch. The loose gathering of the various debates under a proliferation of labels beginning with 'post': – postFordist, postmodernist, postmaterialist, postindustrial, for example – demonstrates that there was some consensus that a social order that was pretty well understood was being left behind, and another being entered, the contours of which could only be dimly recognized. It also gives expression to the notion that history may be 'periodized' into distinct phases, each guided by a coherent frame of dominant principles, and followed by periods of uncertainty and transition during which elements of a new paradigm may or may not develop and mature. But how long is the transition? How long is a piece of string? Is the crisis over? Do we now have a new model of capitalism? As the narrative of these chapters unfolds, I hope to address these questions, but here we must begin with the key changes in the production process that have occurred during the crisis – namely, certain technological innovations and the manner in which these have become embedded in new forms of economic organization. It is changes in the 'production paradigm' that form the starting point of all contemporary analyses of social transformation, whether of the neo-Marxist or neo-liberal variety.

Pathways out of Fordism

Henry Ford's celebrated invention, in 1908, of the motor car assembly line is credited with having ushered in the great era of mass production in manufacturing. But it is worth remembering that the assembly line was a mere enabling technical device. There was a real *social* innovation that preceded it, and that was Ford's concept of standardization. As for back as 1903, Ford had recognized that, in the fabrication of complex products such as motor vehicles, the key to enhanced efficiency of production lay in the method of co-ordinating discrete sub-production processes and in the manner in which the various sub-parts were assembled into a whole vehicle. Ford reckoned that instead of making the parts first and then fitting them together to make the whole, as in craft production, to *make the parts fit prior to assembly* would make huge savings in the assembly stage. Thus he aimed for complete and consistent interchangeability of parts, and for simplicity in attaching them to each other. To achieve this, he insisted that, for example, the same gauging system be used for every part throughout the entire manufacturing process.[2]

The cost savings of standardization were subsequently enhanced further by minute divisions of labour, enabled by the time-and-motion studies of Frederick Charles Taylor, which gave title to the production paradigm as 'Fordist–Taylorist'. Eventually, each worker was responsible for carrying out one simple manipulative task. This social innovation was completed with the technical innovation of the automated, moving assembly line which delivered the vehicles in various stages of assembly around the plant from task to task. The results were awesome. In 1923, the peak year of his Model T production, Ford produced 2.1 million cars, compared with the one-car-a-day production of a craft producer such as Aston Martin.[3]

Ford's invention was so crucial in shaping the post-First World War political economy that in much modern social science literature this political economy is named after him; it was the period of 'Fordism'. But note that it took a good thirty years and the two biggest wars humankind has experienced before Ford's *techno-economic* paradigm was complemented by a whole ensemble of supporting macro-economic institutions, social organizational forms, political and class settlements, and even cultural values, which together and *only when they were in place*, permitted the economic benefits of that system to materialize to the full. In the Keynesian welfare settlement, the production consequences of technological progress were balanced by consumption in a virtuous cycle of growth. This virtuous cycle has already been described; see page 45.

However, in the organization of social life nothing fails like success. The social order of Fordism carried a number of internal contradictions which – as David Harvey comments – may be captured by one word: rigidity.[4]

The whole point about mass production as a profitable undertaking is that it achieves *economies of scale*. This means that the more that is produced of a standardized product, the further the unit cost of production comes down. More means cheaper. But the downside is, on the one hand, that there is a minimum scale required for economic operation, and, on the other, that the success of the operation depends crucially on *continuous* and uninterrupted expansion of market demand for that same product. The mass-production system cannot cope flexibly with cyclical recessions, increased competition, or changing market tastes. The result is underutilization of capacity, and overproduction, resulting in lay-offs, losses, and ultimately closure.

By the late 1960s this distinctive period of mass production and Fordist accumulation had come to an end. The rigidities of the Fordist regime showed up with irrepressible frequency, culminating eventually in economic stagnation, contraction and continuing crises. There were many instances of rigidity at all levels,[5] but the most important was undoubtedly deepening global inequalities, discussed in Chapter 4. These put a limit on the further expansion of that particular system of mass production. There was a global demand crisis, and thus capitalism had to reconstitute itself on an entirely new basis. In a world economy where the richest 20 per cent of the population had 150 times the spending capacity of the poorest 20 per cent, clearly a new production system was needed that could fully exploit consumer demand from the 'have-lots' in an ever fiercer climate of global competition.

During the crisis a series of novel social experiments and technical innovations (particularly the introduction of information-driven technologies) in the realms of industrial as well as in political and social life have begun to take shape. *The key concept that captures the nascent tendencies is flexibility*: flexible production, flexible work processes, flexible labour markets, flexible products, flexible education, flexible patterns of consumption, flexible savings and pension funds, and even flexible or multiple identities.

Flexible specialization: the industrial district model

Two early production pathways out of Fordism were identified and theorized in two models of transition that have since converged. First, pioneering work by M. J. Piore and C. F. Sabel[6] drawing on the experience of the Northern Italian industrial districts and the New York City garment district, discovered a return to industrial craft and customized production among networks of small and medium-sized business firms. These firms had previously either been integrated into one manufacturing company, or had been dependent sub-contractors of mass manufacturers.

Following decentralization, or even a full-blown company break up, the firms concentrated on niche markets by making an ever-changing array of customized products. They used numerically controlled general purpose tools that were easily redeployable, and employed skilled and adaptable workers. They linked up with one another through loose networks of co-ordination and restricted competition, which were managed and mediated by district-based agencies and brokers specializing in marketing, training, design and innovation. In this industrial district model no single institution linked the productive units formally as a group. Rather, as Piore and Sabel put it, 'cohesion of the industry rests on a more fundamental sense of community, of which the various institutional forms of co-operation are more the result than the cause'.[7] They suggested, for example, that in the 'Third' Italy of the small firms, shared politics and religion played a necessary cohesive role which in New York City was played by ethnicity.[8]

Others[9] too have made much of the role of 'trust' that nourishes from primordial affiliations. It was argued that it was this trust that permitted the smooth assignment of capacity by brokers and the tacit adherence to industry specifications by producers. Unencumbered by the constraints of legal specification, such forms of network co-ordination therefore added to flexibility and adaptability. As we enter the twenty-first century, however, there is less talk of the need for family and other forms of communal bonding, as the fusion of advanced telecommunications with information technology permits the replacement of the negotiation function of brokers by electronic markets, and computer-aided design and control systems codify specifications for producers.[10]

Flexible production: the Toyota model

A second route out of the market saturation of Fordism involved high volume flexible production along lines developed quite early by the giant Japanese car maker, Toyota.[11] In the 1950s Toyota invented a new organization of the production process that combined the benefits of mass production with those of craft production. Because Japan in those days did not have a mass domestic market, Toyota had to make the most of market segmentation, producing a wide variety of the same generic product (vehicles of all kinds) rather than, as Ford had done, using the same fixed capital investment for mass production of the same standard commodity. Toyota achieved this *not through making more of the same, but by making a whole variety of products with the same general tool.*

For example, in Fordist automobile plants 'dedicated' machines were used to produce each one of the 300 sheet steel parts that go into a motor car. Mass-producers used automated blanking presses, and stamping presses containing matched upper and lower dies. The same parts were stamped for months or even years without changing the dies. Toyota developed a simple technique for changing dies quickly so that a variety of parts could be stamped with the same machine without any significant 'downtime'. Moreover, the changing of the dies could be done by the production workers themselves. This is the essence of what some have called 'Toyot-ism'[12] and what Womack *et al.*, in their tremendously influential book *The Machine that Changed the World*, refer to as 'lean' pro-duction.[13] This is also the reason why 'economies of scope', in contrast to 'economies of scale' is probably the most accurate descriptor of the new system's method of profit maximization.

Once we understand the principle of volume through variety as the ethos that combines the best of mass production with the best of craft production, we can anticipate the next step in the logic of lean production: namely, customized production. Toyota gradually stopped building cars in advance for unknown buyers and con-verted to a build-to-order system in which the dealers became the first step in what came to be known as the '*kanban*' (or just-in-time) approach, sending orders for pre-sold cars to the factory for deliv-ery to specific customers in two to three weeks. Both dealers and customers became part of the 'extended family' of Toyota. Toyota has small or large equities in the dealer firms, while the dealers develop aggressive selling techniques which involve regular visits to customers, the build-up of massive data banks on customer households, keeping track of the changes in these households and so on. Customers, for their part, have a real role in identifying weaknesses in the cars they buy, and in specifying the changes they want. Toyota goes directly to existing customers when plan-ning new products. Brand loyalty becomes a salient feature of the lean production system. With his customary flamboyance in coining new terms, Alvin Toffler has identified the new consumer as a 'prosumer' – that is, a consumer who is indirectly, sometimes unwit-tingly, but for all that *importantly* involved in production and there-fore partly contributes to his/her own exploitation.[14]

The cost savings through the principle of volume-through-variety contrasted with volume-through-bulk are enormous. It means that less manufacturing space is needed, and little or no inventory or 'work-in-progress'. These cost savings are further increased when combined with the famous *just-in-time* (JIT) practice, where compon-ents and parts are supplied literally only hours or days before they need to be assembled. This is a big change from mass production.

In mass production, the inflexibility of tools in supplier plants (analogous to the inflexibility of the stamping presses in the assembly plants) and the erratic nature of orders from assemblers responding to shifting market demand, caused suppliers to build large volumes of one type of part before changing over machinery to the next, and to maintain large stocks of finished parts in a warehouse. Toyota developed a new way to co-ordinate the flow of parts within the supply system on a day-to-day basis. As Womack *et al.* have summed it up:

> They simply converted a vast group of suppliers and parts plants into one large machine, like Henry Ford's Highland Park plant, by dictating that parts would only be produced at each previous step to supply the immediate demand of the next step. The mechanism was the containers carrying parts to the next step. As each container was used up, it was sent back to the previous step and this became the automatic signal to make more parts.[15]

Since those early days, of course, the whole complex web of just-in-time co-ordination, inside and outside the plant, has begun to be managed by computer, a process economists have called 'systemation' (in contrast to the Fordist process of 'automation'). As Robin Murray points out, the advantage of systemated as opposed to automated production is that it speeds up the circulation of capital: 'Toyota turned over its materials and products ten times more quickly than western car producers, saving material and energy in the process.'[16]

Apart from their invention of the just-in-time system, Japanese lean production methods are probably best known for the reorganization of shop-floor management and their labour control practices. These management practices have become widely known as *total quality management*, and *quality circles, waste elimination, zero-defect* and *continuous improvement*.

Flexible, just-in-time production cannot work at all without materials and components being of a perfect quality, since there is almost no stock to replace defective parts. Faults occurring in one batch need to be discovered instantly and eliminated before the next order zooms along. This is very different from mass-production systems, where, because of the enormous investment in fixed plant and equipment, the top priority was always to keep the assembly line moving and therefore workers were discouraged from acting on their own initiative. If there were defects, and there were plenty, these were – in an accounting sense – discounted from the start, and dealt with physically at the end of the line, where there were work stations to check and repair any mistakes. This strategy, of course, had costly penalties attached to it. Errors in one part might recur over quite an extended period or series before being checked and stopped. These would become embedded in a complex vehicle before being discovered, thus adding even greater costs of rectification. Also, in order to cope with the checking afterwards and the repair, the system of mass production relied on a whole army of so-called 'indirect' workers – that is, workers who did not add value directly to the car on the line, but whose participation in the work process was simply intended to mop up the mistakes.

In flexible production, because of the small batches that are processed at any given time, this problem does not occur. Instead, the practice of checking for faults *during* the process of batch assembly instead of *afterwards* has become ingeniously tied up with an entirely new concept of 'self'-management of workers. Toyota had the idea of making the workers 'responsible' for the mistakes that were made, and 'empowered' them to do what in mass production no shop-floor worker had ever dared to do: stop the production line. The workers were also grouped into teams, not with a foreman but with a team leader/co-ordinator – all very democratic – and each team was given complete responsibility for their piece of the production line, including quality checking, tool repairs and 'housekeeping'. Each team was told that they 'owned' their product, and workers were expected to be multi-skilled and 'upskilled' (in contrast to Ford's deskilled manual workers). The next logical step was to go beyond the zero-defect principle and give the teams responsibility for quality and work flow *improvements*. The periodic brainstorm to achieve such improvements within the team is referred to in industrial history by the name 'quality circle'.

Quality circles and total quality management have been hailed as gigantic steps forward in the humanization of the shop floor. The Japanese management model has been credited with having reunified and reintegrated mental and physical labour, and with having given back to the workers technical and conceptual control over their work.[17] But the model has also attracted some of the most damaging criticism, especially during the 1990s, when Japanese lean methods were being transplanted to Western societies, where labour emancipation and trade union consciousness as well as Marxist academic interest had a more robust tradition than in Japan. An influential collection of case studies presented at various International

Labour Process conferences between 1990 and 1993, for example, detailed the intensification of the work process following Japanese-style industrial restructuring and shop-floor reorganization, and exposed the punishing regimes of 'self-subordination' and 'self-exploitation' that pass for self-management.[18]

Although the Japanese pioneered the development of flexible methods of organizing production almost forty years ago, it was not until the widespread industrial application of *information technology* from about the mid-1970s that flexible production spread to the West. Five key 'generic' technologies in particular have enabled firms to achieve the objective of flexible production. Computer-aided design (CAD) has become the principal automation technology for use in design activities, and computer numerical control (CNC) for control of machine tools. Industrial robots and automated transfer systems have almost completely replaced labour in fabrication and assembly, while process control systems have emerged as the replacement for supervisory staff, offering instantaneous monitoring and control of production.[19] The UN Centre on Transnational Corporations, in its 1988 report, recognized flexible production, together with the new information technology, as one of 'the outstanding features of world development in the 1980s'.[20]

The competitive success of Japanese manufacturing firms in global markets from the late-1970s forced companies in the West to follow suit and go 'lean'. In the initial phase, they adopted selectively some of the best-known features of Japanese 'best practice' (such as customized production and JIT), together with these smart technologies. The outcome, however, was at first far from successful. In his book *Flexible Manufacturing Technologies and International Competitiveness*, Joseph Tidd described in 1990 the growing disenchantment with the new manufacturing systems among American and European manufacturers, who had equipped their plants with ever more expensive, sophisticated technologies than the Japanese, but who nevertheless failed to match their Japanese competitors in terms of productivity or quality.[21] He argued that they failed to identify any dominant pattern of adaptation of international 'best practice'[22] and concluded that the competitiveness of advanced manufacturing technology (AMT) would ultimately depend on *organizational* issues and market strategy, rather than smart technology.[23] In other words, it was not enough to apply the new technology and to follow some new working methods. The lean production system was originally developed in Japan within a home-grown mode of regulation, and its diffusion abroad required a process of social adaptation, restructuring and reorganization, both at the level of the firm and in the wider society. In a similar vein, in 1992, the Commission of the European Communities published a report entitled *What are Anthropocentric Production Systems?*[24] The report advocated the merits of the new production system and encouraged its application through radical restructuring of industrial organizations, inventing a new term, *anthropocentric production system* (APS), to drive the point home, although the key features of this production system are no different from lean production. The report argued that the 'comprehensiveness' of twenty-first-century production methods requires not just the acquisition of leading-edge technology, but also 'the integration of cultural, work and technological factors and their organisation'.[25] This recognition, it seems, had been brought about by the 'investment disasters' of the late 1980s.[26]

There are signs that this lesson has now been learnt. At *firm level*, evidence by the mid-1990s pointed to either wholesale or selective adoption of the principal organizational features of lean production described above. Often these adoptions are couched in terms of local management discourse that disguise the degree of convergence of the process of industrial restructuring and work organization now under way. For example, in the Anglo-Saxon world, human resource management (HRM) has been hailed as a 'new' management approach involving 'employee commitment, responsibility and customer satisfaction'. A survey in 1995 by the British Labour Research Department found that no less than 87 per cent of workplaces used at least one or more of the following techniques: HRM, TQM and 'customer care'.[27] Continuous improvement practices and multi-skilling are also spreading, as are team-working and job rotation, 'single' enterprise unions, and 'no strike' clauses.[28] Japanese methods of work organization are diffusing, in both industrial sectors and service sectors, and they straddle the public/private sector divide.

Informational Production and the Network Enterprise

Even if flexible specialization and flexible production emerged initially as two distinctly different pathways out of Fordism, Manuel

Castells is probably correct in suggesting that, in the 1990s, the two models began to converge around a single organizational trajectory – that of the network enterprise.[29] Key to this convergence were two things: the fusion of telecommunications with computerized information processing, and the globalization of markets.

Castells' definition of the network enterprise is that it is 'that specific form of enterprise whose system of means is constituted by the intersection of segments of autonomous systems of goals'.[30] And he explains this rather inelegant definition as meaning that the components of the network are both autonomous and dependent *vis-à-vis* the network, and may be a part of other networks, and therefore of other systems aimed at other goals. Basically the big event of the 1990s was that qualitative advances in information technology, and more particularly its linkage with telecommunications systems, have prompted the emergence of fully interactive, computer-based, flexible processes of management, production and distribution, involving simultaneous co-operation between different firms and units of such firms.[31] Collaboration and competition, and the co-ordination of all manner of divisions of labour can now occur in *real time* through the operation of interactive computer systems.

R. Jaikumar and D. Upton have expressed what is new still more succinctly: 'production capacity itself is now suffiently flexible in some industries to be viewed as a commodity'.[32] They argue that because of the recent advances in interactive computing, two characteristics of modern product and process descriptions, namely transportability and precise reproducibility, have reduced the need to co-locate engineering and design with manufacturing, except for pilot production. The implication is that almost all activities of an industrial (indeed, *any*) firm, can be outsourced, and outsourced *competitively*. As a result, corporate organization changes to a loosely confederated network structure in which many discrete fabrication activities and services are bought in the short term, relieving the buyer of the costs of accessing capacity by committing to its continued use.

Consequently, in one path of firm evolution we encounter a dramatic reconfiguration of the corporate organizational model, from vertical bureaucracy to what some have termed 'adhocracy',[33] others, 'the horizontal organisation'[34] and still others, the 'post-entrepreneurial' firm.[35] Corporations decentralize increasingly into flexible networks of capacity in which the core firm keeps the design, marketing, R&D and finance functions, while production and distribution, and many of the old 'back office' functions, are scattered over literally thousands of companies, both globally and domestically. Much quoted early examples of such corporations are NIKE and IKEA.

NIKE, a footwear company with annual sales of nearly US$4 billion in 1993, subcontracts 100 per cent of its goods production to nearly 75 000 people employed by its independent subcontractors located in different countries. Its own 9000 workers focus on design, product development, marketing, distribution, data processing, sales and administrative tasks. NIKE has a performance-orientated inventory control system, making it possible to organize timely production from its different producers located abroad. Similarly, the Swedish furniture giant IKEA subcontracts all the actual manufacture of the goods it sells, using about 2300 firms of various size located in seventy countries. It too relies on its computer network to receive orders and monitor sales.[36]

In another path of evolution, global corporations have merged with, taken controlling interests in, or entered into long-term subcontracting relations with, existing networks of small independent businesses in nearby industrial districts who are providers of flexible capacity and who compete with one another within the (electronic) supplier and franchising network. Benetton is the favourite example here. It is a huge company that calls itself a 'clothing service company', rather than a manufacturer or retailer. Benetton has entered into collaborative arrangements with hundreds of small clothing producers in the 'Third Italy', who have become its dedicated suppliers. The firm has also built a system of flexible franchising and its worldwide shops are mostly owned by unrelated enterprises. Thus the company has become in effect the gateway to global markets for the flexible specialization districts of Northern Italy.[37]

Global sourcing and global markets are as important to the new network enterprise as the new information technology. Because of the emphasis in lean production systems on 'volume through variety', it is sometimes overlooked that these production systems are in fact *more* rather than less dependent on maximum economies of scale such as can only be offered by the *combined* market size of the core regions in the world economy. The start-up costs of the generic technologies (automation technologies, CAD, CAM and CNC) are enormous, and in fact represent a shift from labour to capital intensity of awesome dimensions. Furthermore, these generic technologies are subject to very rapid technological obsolescence; this has led to very short product life-cycles, placing an ever greater premium on access to financial resources, multiplant production and extensive marketing networks.

Thus the size of the market remains crucial. Kenichi Ohmae has coined the term 'Triad' countries to refer to the three core regions of the present world system: North America; the European Union; and the Pacific Asia Region. Ohmae argues that the global market of 'Triadian' consumers amounts to a total of some 600 million middle-class people 'whose academic backgrounds, income levels both dis-cretionary and nondiscretionary, life-style, use of leisure time, and aspirations are quite similar'.[38] In these countries, moreover, the national infrastructure in terms of highways, telephone systems, sewage disposal, power transmission and governmental systems is also very similar. This permits corporations to treat the residents as 'belong-ing to virtually the same species'. They constitute the global market.

Because of the sheer size of initial investments and the rate of technological obsolescence, today's new, high-tech, high-value-added products need to be brought out simultaneously in all three core markets of the world. This means that few companies are large enough to be independent. In addition, there is often a need to have a direct presence in each of the core regional markets because of other aspects of flexible production, such as the just-in-time supply and distribution networks, the simultaneous process of design and product development and, more important still, there is in the present ever-threatening protectionist world a political necessity for multiple home bases. Therefore, according to the leading ana-lysts, the key to competitive success in the future is for the truly global company to have top-to-bottom, paper-concept-to-finished-product manufacturing systems in each of the three great markets of the world. Womack *et al.*, for example, forecast a future dominated by multiregional companies.[39] Thus strategic alliances and other co-operative agreements between rival giants of industry, and between large corporations and complementary partners, such as cross-bor-der, cross-regional and cross-industrial independent suppliers, may be considered to be a third pathway (in addition to flexible special-ization and flexible production) towards the network enterprise.

All three evolutionary paths point to the emergence of a new polit-ical economy of 'relationship enterprising' or 'economic networking' as the fundamental form of competition in the new global economy.

Virtual teams

Until a very few years ago, these developments towards network enterprising occurred mainly within company-operated electronic communication systems in which the strategic cohesiveness of goals and functions were secured within carefully managed and in-house-accessed flows of information. However, the ubiquity of the internet, following the invention of simple-to-use browsers for surfing the World Wide Web, and the improvement of encryption technology enabling the securing of payments for services, have opened the doors (or floodgates) to what some have hailed as nothing short of a total transformation of the way business is done.

This story began, by some accounts,[40] in 1991, with the inspiring initative of one young computer whiz kid, Linus Torvalds, who out of pique because of Microsoft's monopolization of the market through the Windows operating system, made freely available on the internet a kernel of a computer operating system he had written. This was a very rudimentary version of the UNIX operating system, for long the mainstay of corporate and academic computing. He encouraged other programmers worldwide to download his software – to use it and add more features, and like him, to post their work on the internet. Three years later, this very loose, informal group of thousands of enthusiasts who shared their work freely with each other had together created one of the best versions of UNIX, the LINUX operating system.

This example of software development by freely co-operating individuals has been followed by thousands of others, even though in subsequent cases the point of the exercise has more often been to secure ownership of the joint product, to encapsulate it in a 'dot. com' company, and sell its shares on the stock market and earn millions, as anxious investors, not least a worried big business, pile in to get a slice of the action long before the product has earned so much as a penny. The phenomenal explosion of such internet-based companies since 1995 has led some analysts to argue that the fundamental unit of tomorrow's economy is not the corporation but the individual. As Th. Malone and R. Laubacher, who coined the term 'e-lance economy' for the purpose put it:

> Tasks aren't assigned and controlled through a stable chain of management but rather are carried out autonomously by

independent contractors. These electronically connected free-lancers – e-lancers – join together into fluid and temporary networks to produce and sell goods and services. When the job is done – after a day, a month, a year – the network dissolves, and its members become independent agents again, circulating through the economy, seeking the next assignment.[41]

Are traditional corporations going to dissolve into such 'virtual teams'? Or is it more likely that virtual teams are going to be controlled by big corporate interests?

Our traditional understanding of political economy as the dynamic between power and markets (see the Introduction to Part I) has ill equipped us to understand the precise nature of such networking. In the 'networked' or 'virtual' firm,[42] resources (skill, time, creative ideas, as well as finance) are allocated on the basis of a 'temporary' trust and commitment to collaboration that transcends our conventional understanding of resource allocation, either through the competitive market mechanism or by administrative fiat arising from proprietary ownership. Some observers – for example, Charles Sabel – have argued that in a setting in which the normal instruments of governance – hierarchy, legal contract and relational contracting – lose their purchase, the systemic properties of the communications technologies themselves encourage co-ordination through constant arbitration developing into a culture of 'learning by monitoring'. Sabel says that through continuous on-line discussion, individuals and groups develop a shared under-standing of the distribution of responsibilities and the mutual obligations among them.[43]

Others, more convincingly, suggest that even temporay alliances need to draw on a pool of shared common cultural values, and 'social capital'.[44] The cherished model here is Silicon Valley, the heartland of the IT revolution. In this 'intelligent region' of Cali-fornia the dynamics of spectacular profitability turns on the 'velo-city at which people and ideas move from universities to commerce, small to large businesses'.[45] While money and greed are vital lubric-ants, there is a *culture of creative destruction* in which new ideas are absorbed rapidly, venture capitalists do not hesitate to back new ideas and business failure is not frowned upon. Furthermore, loy-alty to the firm is no longer a prized asset, and large companies have learnt to accommodate constant fracturing, as when their best brains leave to start up on their own; they simply re-engage them on a short-term consultancy basis, or finance them in separate spin-off companies. All this adds up to the 'spirit of informationalism' that Manuel Castells speaks of as the cultural ethos of the new production system.[46] It is a 'state of mind, a commitment to entrepreneurial, knowledge networks', says another observer.[47] Successful companies are those that make the most of their strong core capabilities (brand loyalty, global marketing and distribution, design) and learn how to integrate the diverse sources of knowledge and input provided by the networks. They are 'a junction box', where internal and external relationships are brought together. One way in which the lubricant of money and greed ensures collaborative commitment in a system of high turnover and competitive pressures is employee ownership or stock options. Highly skilled talent is paid, not for the time put in, nor for a fixed payment on contract delivery, but with a financial share in a joint-venture company in which the corporation is the main stakeholder.

If the 'spirit of informationalism' is the cultural glue of the network economy, the social density of such networks in one location is what gives certain regions the competitive edge. Together they add up to what Robert Putnam has fashionably termed 'social capital'.[48] It is a slightly woolly concept and seems to contradict what we would counterintuitively expect in the age of the internet, but the empirical evidence points to the fact that knowledge-creating networks and the launch of innovative products still depend on intensive face-to-face interaction, on people mingling and meeting, sharing ideas and insights, and trusting one another as a result. In short, physical locations emerge as nodal points in the global economy, where those with new ideas rub shoulders with those who have financial clout, and with those who have the ability to embed creative ideas in the constant re-engineering of large-scale flows of procurement and distribution, as well as with those who work in research establishments such as universities.[49]

The New Economy

At the time of writing there is a gathering consensus that twenty-five years of investment in the new technologies and new business organizations, both in the traditional industries that manufacture producer goods and durable consumer goods, but more particularly in the new high-tech sectors, including IT, biotechnology and the media, are finally paying off. Apostles of what has been dubbed the 'new economy' point to the sustained productivity growth of the US economy since 1994, which is now said to be spreading to other advanced countries. At the macro-economic level, the 'new economy' enthusiasts celebrate the coming together, in a virtuous cycle, of this sustained productivity growth, with low inflation and low unemployment. Some even hail the end of the classic business cycle, that scourge of capitalist economy, in which short periods of boom are inevitably followed by periods of 'bust'. For these enthusiasts at least, the crisis of Fordism that began in the early 1970s is definitely over.[50]

The new economy thesis has its detractors, who argue that the US figures on overall productivity growth hide a very uneven distribution across economic sectors. One such sceptic, Robert Gorden, who is often cited in the business press, found in a recent study that 100 per cent of the productivity gains since 1995 were in fact concentrated in the computer manufacturing sector, which barely constitutes 1 per cent of the US economy.[51] However, he is in a minority, and other early sceptics, such as Alan Greenspan, the venerated Chairman of the Federal Reserve Board, are now also admitting that something very fundamental has changed.

Central to the argument of the rise of a new economy is the notion that knowledge has become the most creative, value-adding factor in production. Whereas, in the old economy, land, labour and capital were the only three 'generic' factors of production, in the 'new economy', the critical assets are expertise, creativity, and 'intelligence' or 'information'. Intelligence embedded in software and technology across a wide range of products has become more important than capital, materials or labour. As one writer put it, 'The key to economic advance are the "recipes" we use to combine physical ingredients in more intelligent and creative ways'.[52]

While knowledge or information were always present in production, what characterizes the new economy is that the production of knowledge/information has itself become the leading branch of economic activity. In the USA, software companies now employ more than 800 000 people, and employment in the industry is growing by 13 per cent a year, compared with a growth of 2.5 per cent in the rest of the private economy. At the same time, the IT sector, despite accounting for only about 8 per cent of America's

GDP, now contributes 35 per cent of the country's economic growth.[53] This is why Manuel Castells, for example, characterizes capitalism in its present stage as the 'informatio*nal* mode of production'.[54] The informational mode of production is more than just a method of production in which information is applied to production: it is one in which the production of knowledge/information itself has become the dominant sector of the economy.

The knowledge economy behaves in different ways from the traditional, three-factor-based economy. Brian Arthur, for example, argues that while the traditional economy obeys the general rules of 'diminishing' returns, the new economy obeys the rules of 'increasing' returns.[55] Knowledge is a factor of production that does not diminish, but rather increases its value by being used. The first modern fax machine was worth nothing, but each fax machine that followed increased the value of all the fax machines already in use. In the same way, one might argue that the very *suddenness* of the e-commerce and e-business explosion owes much to the fact that there is now a critical mass of users, so what was not useful before suddenly becomes valuable. Since 'prevalence' is all important to the law of increasing returns, the 'locking in' of the market (creating a network effect) is the driving business strategy associated with the knowledge economy. Microsoft's 'locking in' of internet access through its Windows software is a classic example here. As a consequence, 'increasing returns are the tendency for that which is ahead to get further ahead, for that which loses advantage to lose further advantage'.[56]

Furthermore, the information revolution has hugely extended the range of human transactions (mainly services) that can be made 'tradable' and thus be subject to market transactions and pricing. This works in two ways: on the one hand there are many new services that replace previously costly physical transactions or activities. An enormous range of recent start-ups in e-commerce and e-business are of this cost-reducing variety. By 1998 American firms were making a staggering US$43 billion worth of e-transactions, a figure that is predicted to rise to US$1.3 trillion by 2003.[57] Think of all those virtual shopping websites where the transport costs of the shopper and the warehouse costs of the seller have been eliminated. They are widely seen as having been responsible for the slashing of prices and the near zero-inflation that advanced economies – especially the US economy – now enjoy.[58] On the other hand, there is also a market *creating* variety. Because of 'digital comput-ability', many human activities that were previously free social or free public goods (basically because it was not 'worth' it to put a price on them), can now be made tradable and subject to pricing, allowing sellers to force users to pay. For example, telephone com-panies can now make customers pay by electronic pulse instead of per second or per minute, and can charge for unanswered calls. Or think of the enormous variety of customized risk assessments that make it possible to sell insurance and assurance for an expanding range of situations not previously experienced as 'risky'. Or think of financial services such as derivatives that owe their existence and profitability to the ability to calculate minuscule variations in move-ments in interest rates or exchange rates. The net result of this digitization is a *deepening of commodification* that can now override the limits to *the market widening* that brought about the Fordist crisis in the first place.

Last, but not least, the 'new economy' is a global economy, *not* in the sense of a world*wide* economy, but in the sense that has been properly defined by Manuel Castells, as an *'economy with the capa-city to operate as a unit in real time on a planetary basis'*.[59] The new knowledge-based economy is first and foremost a real-time eco-nomy that, in principle, allows all these new services to be trans-acted across borders, to be outsourced instantly, and hence subjected to one global market price.

A full taxonomy of the 'new economy' would include a much longer list of characteristics, some of which we have already touched on; for example, those relating to business organization: the virtual firm replacing the traditional company enterprise; micro-entrepre-neurialism; constant re-engineering and innovation; and many more. To my knowledge, a proper theoretical 'model' of the 'new economy' that sets out the logical relationships between its various technological, institutional, cultural, organizational and macro-economic aspects has yet to be written. However, even if there is such a thing as a 'new economy in the making, I shall argue in Chapter 7 that it responds to quite different laws of motion than those laws of capitalism which had encouraged previous generations to look forward to class contradictions as mainsprings of revolution, and to internal capital contradictions (limits to the realization of capital) as the ultimate propellant of human emancipation. The dynamics of this new economy point to a reconstitution of macro-economic equilibrium at a global level, where the global market provides for a balancing of consumption with production while majority segments of humanity are simply excluded, and political and ideological efforts are directed towards insulating this minority globalism from the majority populations.

Theorizing the Transition

Within postFordist literature there have been three broad approaches to the question of the wider social and economic embeddedness of the new production paradigm. In a concise summary, Mark Elam has distinguished between the neo-Schumpeterians, the neo-Smithsonians and the neo-Marxist perspectives.[60] What sets these three approaches apart is their answer to the question of ultimate causality: is it the technology, is it markets or is it institutions?

The neo-Schumpeterians, argue like Joseph Schumpeter sixty years ago,[61] that technical innovation is all: periodically capitalism is renewed by gales of creative destruction and the emergence of completely new production methods, new products, new industrial organization and new markets. For C. Freeman and C. Perez,[62] whose work is the most articulate and detailed expression of this school, a technological revolution carries within itself the systemic logic of a related cluster of innovations, in enterprise management, in labour organization, in market strategies and in locational patterns. All this adds up to a 'techno-economic paradigm', or a 'technological trajectory', much in the way it was described above in the section on flexible production. Correlate changes in wider socio-institutional complexes (for example, in labour markets, in credit organizations and financial structure, in government regulations and public policy, in training and education and in social policy) are largely reactive responses to the logic of the new technological regime, forced upon different environments by the demonstrable success of 'best practice'. Although Freeman and Perez have tried to defend themselves against a charge of technological reductionism by arguing that the range of suitable environments may be quite large, this scope for diversity, in my view, is very limited in a world that is dominated by a global market discipline and global standards (see Chapter 6), enforced, moreover, by inter- and supra-national agreements (see Chapter 7).

But note that, by the same reasoning, it is a mistake to blame technology for the power of politics.

The neo-Smithsonians, by contrast, are market determinists. In this broad group of approaches we may include the flexible specialization theories of Michael Piore and Charles Sabel, as well as the 'new times' perspectives of Stuart Hall, Martin Jacques and other contributors[63] to the now defunct British political magazine *Marxism Today*, whose work has been dismissed as 'pop' sociology by at least one pair of critics.[64] For these writers, the crisis of Fordism lay in the saturation of the market and the consequent need on the part of producers to pursue the consumption dollars of the affluent, which led to an emphasis on product differentation, niche marketing and the exploration of the realms of differentiated tastes and aesthetic preferences in ways that were not so necessary under the Fordist regime of standardized mass production.[65] But while the flexible specialization theorists dwelt on the industrial model best able to produce quality goods for specialist and volatile markets, the 'new times' theorists branched out into a preoccupation with the cultural diversity of consumer patterns and the multiplication of social worlds and social 'logics' that mirrored the increased production differentiation of postFordism. In short, they linked postFordist production with postmodern cultural forms – in particular lifestyle – and the politics of identity in which collectivist solidarities based on production relations are replaced by new social movements propelled by issues of gender, race and environment.

Although the 'new times' writers had some lingering notions of the Marxism they came to reject, namely in the assumption that there is some loose coherence between production and social formation, in true postmodern style they were quite unwilling to subject their theorizing to the discipline of the totalizing logic of 'modernity', which demands certainty of outcomes, and 'closure', as when one says 'this is the beginning of the crisis' and 'this is the end'. As Stuart Hall put it: 'In a permanently Transitional Age we must *expect* unevenness, contradictory outcomes, disjunctures, delays, contingencies, uncompleted projects overlapping emergent ones' (capitals and emphasis in original).[66]

The neo-Marxist approach differs from the other two, not only in its identification of the cause of the crisis, but also in its insistence on defining the conditions that need to be fulfilled before it can be said to have ended. The crisis is not over until the fat lady sings!

The Regulation School

Central to all neo-Marxist approaches is the concern with the *repro-duction of capitalism*, which is seen to be fundamentally affected by institutions. Marx's own concept of mode of production was rooted in a concept of *social* relations of production in which the *forces* of production (technology, production methods and the technical division of labour) were integrally embedded. A common concern for the regulationists, 'social structure of accumulation' theorists and 'governance' theorists has been the process by which capitalism often destroys institutions and thereby periodically obstructs its own growth and accumulation, until it finds new social supports and institutions that can temporarily overcome its own contradictions.

Of the various neo-Marxist approaches, the most influential is the Regulation School, which emerged in France in the 1970s as a loosely networked group of intellectuals who studied the Fordist crisis and the emergence of a new social, economic and political order. Prominent among them are Michel Aglietta, Alain Lipietz and Charles Boyer, of the so-called Parisian School. There is also a German School and an Amsterdam School, and in Britain, Bob Jessop's strategic-relational approach has made an important contribution to the School's research agenda.[67] Many regulation theorists stand firmly in the Marxist tradition, and acknowledge their Marxist roots. For example, Alain Lipietz, one of the pioneers of the group, describes his book, *Mirage and Miracle*, as a study about the current situation 'using Marxist analytical tools appropriately'. But in using the tools 'appropriately' they abandon the historical project for which Marx had designed the tools. There is no conception of social progress; no eschatological belief in the forward march of history; no political commitment to surrender the freedom of the intellect to a course that history has charted.

Instead, a central question for regulation theorists is how capitalism can survive, even though the capital relation itself inevitably produces antagonism, contradiction and crises. They accept here the Marxist dialectic, namely that the kernel social relation of capitalism carries within itself a contradiction that is worked out in two ways: the class struggle – that is, the *political* conflict between capital and labour over discipline, domination, control, subjugation and the profit split (the capital relation problem); and the *economic* contradiction stemming from the operation of free, price-fixing

markets (the capital logic problem). The crisis itself is conceptualized as a *simultaneous* rupture and transformation of the system that
may usher in a new mode of capitalist development in which, for a
time, the contradictions are resolved, and technological progress
and economic growth is once more possible.

There are no *certain* outcomes predetermined by inherent tendencies. What the new mode looks like is entirely *contingent*, both
historically and nationally. It depends on the outcomes of specific,
local, social and political struggles, strategies and compromises, and
the pre-existing local institutional context. This emphasis on human
agency and class struggle, and on local or national specificity, is the
voluntarist aspect of the regulation approach with which it wants to
transcend its structuralist bearings. Hence its research agenda has
been focused on precise, detailed and empirical analyses of the
content and the actual contingent movement of capital, which is
so diverse in its manifestations that it leaves considerable scope for
historical and national variation.

What is distinctive about the Regulation School, as the name
suggests, is a concern with the *regulation* of the economy, the
point being that (in their view) there is no economy (or at any rate
no stable, growing economy) without it. Periods of growth and
decline in the core of the capitalist system (the advanced countries)
are understood through two key concepts: *a regime of accumulation*
and *a mode of regulation*. A regime of accumulation is a relatively
stable and reproducible relationship between production and consumption defined *at the level of the international economy as a whole*.
Such was, for example, the case with the postwar regime of Fordism
in which Fordist mass production methods were balanced by Keynesian welfare institutions and a social democratic settlement.
According to Lipietz:

> *A regime of accumulation* describes the stabilization over a long
> period of the allocation of the net product between consumption
> and accumulation; it implies some correspondence between the
> transformation of both the conditions of production and the
> conditions of the reproduction of wage earners. It also implies
> some forms of linkage between capitalism and other modes of
> production. Mathematically, a regime of accumulation is
> describable by a schema of reproduction. A system of accumula-
> tion exists because its schema of reproduction is coherent: not all

systems of accumulation are possible. At the same time, the mere *possibility* of a regime is inadequate to account for its existence since there is no necessity for the whole set of individual capitals and agents to behave according to its structure. There must exist a materialization of the regime of accumulation taking the form of norms, habits, laws, regulating networks and so on that ensure the unity of the process, that is the approximate consistency of individual behaviors with the schema of reproduction. This body of interiorized rules and social process is called the *mode of regulation*.[68]

The merit of the Regulation School is that they have theorized this balancing of production and consumption (the regime of accumulation) as something that requires, simultaneously, a mode of regulation before it can in fact materialize and its benefits be realized. But this is where things become complicated. For 'regulation' in French means more than its English translation, which is altogether too narrowly associated with government regulation or at best 'governance', the politico-juridical norms and rules officially endorsed and prescribed by formal institutions. The French concept of regulation is broader and encompasses the wider notion of 'socialisation' or 'societalisation', as when individual agents, whether entrepreneurs, workers or consumers, learn to behave in ways that are consistent with the conditions necessary for balanced economic reproduction and accumulation.

For example, today the dominant rule of economic behaviour is to conform to international standards of price and quality. Individual agents, be they entrepreneurs or employees, are reminded continuously in the experience of their own daily lives and in the way this is being transmitted by the media, that unless they conform to these standards, they will lose the competition; they will lose their jobs. How do they internalize these standards of behaviour, and come to accept that this is only 'normal and right'? As long as they do *not* accept this as right, they will struggle against it and against new social practices, and new institutional compromises may come about depending on the struggle and local 'habits' of history, as Lipietz puts it.[69] To give another example, how do people come to appreciate, rather than oppose, the fact that they cannot look forward to a life of secure employment, but that moving from job to job in flexible labour markets and constructing a 'portfolio career' is a 'yuppie' thing to do, and is associated with 'freedom' and 'choice', creativity, excitement and adventure. Public regulation, for example, to facilitate the transferability of pension contributions, or the provision of supportive lifelong learning and training programmes, is a necessary part of the 'mode of regulation' but hardly adds up to a new institutionalized compromise around 'offensive flexibility' of the calibre of the Keynesian welfare state provisions in relation to Fordist mass production. In Chapter 6, where we describe the nature of globalization, we shall look more closely into the actual process whereby individuals internalize emerging new standards of behaviour and codes of practice, while in Chapter 7 we shall address the problematic of governance and regulation more fully.

Conclusion

In this chapter we have concentrated on supply-side changes that have emerged during the period of crisis and transformation that began in the 1970s. Summarizing, we can say that these changes were of two kinds. Both were technologically driven and were a response to market limitations that had developed as a result of inherent tendencies towards the unequal distribution of wealth and poverty that has marked the capitalist organization of economic life on a global scale. The first change occurred in the organization of production of what are now identified as 'old economy' goods and services. Here, we observed a move towards flexible methods of production, and niche marketing to cater for an expansion of élite consumption. The second involved the development of new informational products that have already entered the lexicon as 'new economy' products.

Following the Regulation School's agenda, we ended the chapter with the prospects of long-term macro-economic stability, which requires the resolution of the demand side of the equation. The two big problems for regulation theory today are theoretical and political. The theoretical conundrum is that the end of Fordism brought the end of a regime of accumulation that was, for all its international scope, *national* in the character of its social regulatory mechanisms. But the crisis of Fordism was that the internationalization of production and markets came to disrupt the possibility of national regulation of the Fordist model of development, so the problem is how to theorize an *international mode of regulation*. This then leads to the political problematic that there seems to be emerging an international *regime of accumulation*, the neo-liberal or 'liberal-productivist' regime, but for many regulationist writers this is a politically unacceptable regime. This is the nub. As Bob Jessop describes it, there is a nascent postFordist regime of accumulation that may well be based on the dominance of a flexible and permanently innovative pattern of accumulation, on rising incomes for multi-skilled workers and the service class, increased demand for new differentiated goods and services favoured by the growing discretionary element in these incomes, and, as it would be more orientated towards worldwide demand, global competition could further limit the scope for general prosperity and encourage market-led polarization of incomes.[70] Crucially, it is also a regime that is being supported by an emerging process of social regulation, notably in the development of a Schumpeterian 'workfare' state form that uses social policy instruments to encourage flexibility and that 'hollows out' the nation-state as powers are displaced upwards (to global and pan-regional bodies) and downwards (to local and regional states). Such a regime may well balance production and consumption 'at the level of the international economy as a whole', at least in the medium term. But only by excluding an ever-growing segment of the world population, including large social sectors in the core capitalist economies.

Since social exclusion is a necessary counterpart of this 'minority' regime of accumulation, instability and crises are likely to remain endemic to it. In this way, one might argue that postFordist crises have superseded the Fordist crisis. Furthermore, although the class conflicts associated with the historical capital labour relation have abated, the postFordist production paradigm has its own sources of conflict and social contradictions. For example, the petrol tax revolts that broke out all over Europe in September 2000, have exposed the vulnerability of a production system that is marked by geographic dispersal of production facilities, extensive subcontracting and outsourcing arrangements, and just-in-time supply chains. The site of social conflict has moved from the shop floor to the road, and the effective power of protest from the once mighty car workers' unions to self-employed truck drivers.

6

Globalization

In the introduction to their comprehensive volume, *Global Transformations*, David Held *et al.* present a spectrum of definitions and approaches to the study of globalization. They identify a Sceptical thesis, a Transformationalist thesis, and a Hyperglobalist thesis.[1] Somewhat loosely, I suggest that these approaches correspond to whether one views globalization as primarily an economic, a social or a political phenomenon.

The Sceptics[2] are normally to be found among those who focus on the international integration of national markets. Drawing on historical data of foreign trade and capital movements, they argue, much as we did in Chapter 4, that 'globalization', when understood as a world*wide* process of integration of *national economies*, simply does not stand up to the historical record of the late colonial period, the period of the 'gold standard', when on every proxy measure of integration, the world was just as (or perhaps even more) integrated and open than it is today, and when certainly the 'developing world as a whole' was more deeply embedded in the world system.

At the other end of the spectrum we encounter the Hyperglobalist thesis. This thesis is often advanced by writers who are primarily concerned with politics and power.[3] They compare the power of business with the power of nation states, and they argue that the growth of international business, and particularly of transnational networks of production, trade and finance have rendered nation-states practically irrelevant (the so-called *declinist view* of the state). In this view, national authorities have lost power over their own economies and act as mere transmitters of global market discipline to the domestic market.

The Transformationalist thesis, by contrast, is one that looks at globalization as primarily a social phenomenon that has brought qualitative changes in *all* cross-border transactions. This social phenomenon is time–space compression, culminating in the total 'annihilation of space through time'. It has been brought about by the fusion of telecommunications and information technology and can be dated precisely to the early 1980s. It has brought not just 'the internet', and with it e-commerce and e-business, but it has also, fundamentally, brought about the ascendancy of 'real time' over 'physical time', and with that such a transformation of the dominant sectors of economic activity that it deserves a new label: the 'new economy'. It has also brought about a transformation of *cross-border* economic activity that deserves to be identified with a new concept, namely globalization. In this sociological meaning of the term, globalization brings, in Manuel Castells' celebrated phrase: 'the capacity of the world economy to operate as a unit in real time on a planetary basis'.[4] But this capacity does not mean that the whole planet is involved: on the contrary, in this global, real time, economy, ever more people, segments, areas and regions of the world economy are systematically becoming excluded from it. In other words, a transformationalist position is not, in fact, inconsistent with the facts of economic globalization as presented by the Sceptics.

In Chapter 4 I argued that the expansive phase of world capitalism is over. The expansive phase of capitalism was characterized by the *extension* of the fundamentals of economic activity, namely trade and productive investment, into more and more areas of the globe. That phase has now been superseded by a phase of *deepening, but not widening, capitalist integration*. I prefer to reserve the term 'globalization' for this deepening phenomenon; to understand this phenomenon we have to start with the sociology of globalization.

The Sociology of Globalization[5]

Even if by now 'globe-babble' has penetrated the discourse of *all* social science disciplines, it is probably fair to say that sociologists and social geographers have been at the forefront in efforts to give it a rigorous and consistent theoretical status. In the work of prominent authors such as Roland Robertson, David Harvey, Anthony

Giddens and Manuel Castells, we find distinctive formulations that may help us to overcome the limits of the globalization discourse that has so vexed economists and international relations theorists: this is the aim of this chapter.

Roland Robertson: world compression and intensification of global consciousness

Robertson's writings[6] are firmly wedded to a conventional mainstream sociological theory of society as a social system. Social system theory is elaborated in Talcott Parsons' well-known formulation, in which any social system is thought to have four subsystems that are functionally related to serve the maintenance of the whole, namely the economic, the political, the cultural and the social.

Robertson argues that clearly for some time there has been a process of social system building at the global level. In the economic sphere it pre-dates even the rise of capitalism and the modern world because of the growing networks of international trade and production. It has also been fostered actively at the level of the political sub-system with international co-operation between states and the emergence of international organizations. But until recently, the process of globalization was still being hindered by unresolved cleavages in the cultural arena which had prevented full system development. There were three such cleavages: religious, between fundamental Islam and Christianity; legal–diplomatic, between democracies and absolutist states (the West versus East divide); and industrial, between cultures that emphasize norms consistent with industry (rationality, individualization, impersonal authority) and those that do not (the North–South divide). As we enter the twenty-first century, however, the potential for a closing of these cleavages is greatly enhanced. Globalization at the cultural level has begun because of two things, namely 'compression of the world' and 'global consciousness'. Compression of the world is the real experience of the way that interdependencies are being created in the economies of the world, to such an extent that the way people live their lives now on one side of the globe has immediate consequences for people on the other side. Shifts in preferences of consumption in Europe and America, for example, affect jobs deeply in the Far East. Industrial processes of development and growth in one country can have an environmental and ecological impact in neighbouring countries. Big dam projects in India cause flooding in Bangladesh; and the forest-burning practice of Indonesian farmers results in air pollution in Singapore and Malaysia. This is what is meant by 'compression' of the world.

World compression is not a very new idea, but what makes for novelty in Robertson's work is that he argues that world compression intensifies 'global consciousness'. Global consciousness is manifested in the way peoples all over the world, in a discourse unified through mass communication, speak of military–political issues in terms of 'world order', or economic issues, as in 'international recession'. We speak of 'world peace' and 'human rights', while issues of pollution and purification are talked about in terms of 'saving the planet'. Thus, while in Robertson's view globalization has been going on for a very long time, pre-dating even the rise of capitalism and modernity, it has accelerated only since the 1980s because it has moved to the level of consciousness.

David Harvey and Anthony Giddens: time and space

Following the works of the sociologist Pierre Bourdieu, David Harvey,[7] who is himself a social geographer, argues that symbolic orderings of space and time provide a framework for experience through which people learn who or what they are in society. Remember the commonsense notion that 'there is a time and a place for everything'. Certain behaviour that is encouraged in the classroom, for example, is not appropriate around the dinner table, and vice versa. In the past, when fewer people were students, academic tutors would sometimes try to create the informal atmosphere of home for their tutorials by inviting students to classes held in their homes, to change the 'habitus' (note that the Latin word 'habitus' means both location and habit). Ordered space is a signpost for expected social practices, and serves as a reminder of these social practices. Let us think about this a little more.

The organization of space defines relationships, not only between activities, things and concepts, but by extension, between people. The organization of space defines social relations. Harvey argues, for example, that the development of cartography during the Renaissance permitted the objectification of space and the accurate measurement of land, thus supporting the emergence of private ownership in land and the precise definition of transferable property rights, thereby replacing the confused and conflicting feudal obligations that had preceded it. Thus the organization of space holds the key to power. Five hundred years later, the freedom to move capital wherever it is needed worldwide gives the capital-owning international bourgeoisie a decisive advantage over the mass of workers who are restricted in their movements and migrations by the passports they carry.

Like space, time too represents a source of value and power. In capitalist enterprises the costs of production are calculated in terms of the time it takes to produce things, and labour is subjected to constant efforts by employers to reduce the time spent on a particular task. 'Economy of time', said Marx, 'to this all economy ultimately reduces itself.' The time-and-motion studies of Frederick Taylor's scientific management gave Henry Ford a decisive advantage over his competitors, and eventually led to Fordism. Bitter class struggles have been fought over the length of the working day. In contemporary competitive battles it is not even minutes, but rather seconds that count. In a harrowing narrative of life on the shop-floor in a flexible production plant in the UK, Rick Delbridge *et al.* report how work intensification resulted in a saving of '0.85 seconds on standard time'![8]

Time, argues Harvey, also defines the value of money itself. In capitalist economies, accountants calculate interest rates as 'the time value of money'. The time of production together with the time of circulation of exchange are referred to as the *turnover time of capital*. The greater the speed with which the capital that is launched into circulation can be recuperated, the greater the profit will be. If an investment in Britain gives me the value of my money back in five years, while in Singapore I can get it back in three years, then I am hardly likely to invest in the UK, and will prefer my money to go to Singapore.

However, the really important thing in all this discussion is the relationship between time and space itself. In capitalist economies, *space is expressed in time*. In her bestselling book *Longitude*, Dava Sobel[9] tells the story of the epic scientific quest, supported by public finance from competing seafaring nations in the eighteenth century, to map and conquer the seas by fixing the problem of longitude. This problem was ultimately solved by the chronometer, a precise marine time-keeper that effectively fixed spatial co-ordinates in terms of the time travelled from the home port. The prize of imperial rule over the oceans fell to the nation – Great Britain, that first cracked this problem.

The distance needed to travel in order to do business or to transport commodities to their final destination, or to cross-haul intermediate products for fabrication, are all calculated in terms of the time it takes to cover the distance. Anthony Giddens calls this 'time/space distantiation', which is a measure of the degree to which the friction of space has been overcome to accommodate social interaction.

Technological progress has compressed the time–space equation enormously. Harvey has illuminated this equation in a graph I shall describe here. Between 1500 and 1840 the best average speed of horse-drawn coaches and sailing ships was 10 mph. Between 1850 and 1930 it was 65 mph for steam locomotives and 36 mph for steam ships. By the 1950s, propeller aircraft covered distances at 300–400 mph, while the latest jet passenger aircraft reach a cool 500–700 mph.[10]

All this refers to the transport and the covering of distances by material commodities and human bodies. But now think of today's electronic age. Telecommunications using satellite TV and the linking of computers through cyberspace allow most 'disembodied' services – for example, technological designs, managerial instructions and operational controls, as well as media images of wars and earthquakes and representations of consumer fashions, to enter the minds of people instantly anywhere in the global system. This shrinking of the world to a 'global village' amounts to a virtual *annihilation of space through time*. Giddens sums this up:

> Globalization can thus be defined as the intensification of world wide social relations which link distant localities in such a way that local happenings are shaped by events occurring many miles away and vice versa.[11]

At the time of writing people are able to have social relations and even organized community relations regardless of space – that is, regardless of the territory they share. This has enormous consequences, not only for the role of the nation-state as a territorially-bounded community, but also for the organization of economic production on a cross-border basis. While we still have local physical lives, we also now experience phenomenal worlds that are truly global. It is this globalization of shared phenomenal worlds that drives the processes of economic globalization.

Manuel Castells: the global, informational network society

To date, the most encompassing sociological treatise on the brave new world of global capitalism has come from Manuel Castells, in a 1500-page trilogy published in the latter half of the 1990s.[12] Castells has been justly hailed as a new Max Weber. For, like Weber before him in an altogether different historical epoch, Castells tries (and broadly succeeds) to comprehend, in one unified conceptual frame, the meaningful connections between a huge number of contemporary changes: economic, social, cultural and political. Is our world new? Yes, Castells argues firmly, it is, but that is not the point he wants to make. He just wants to 'make sense' of the contemporary world,[13] namely as one comprehensive interconnected totality, ruled by a dominant logic that penetrates all spheres of life. This dominant logic is the logic of informationalism, a new technological paradigm based on information technologies. Informationalism not only intensifies the competition between capitalists in economic life, but also shapes the overall social structure of society, for it creates perpetually changing *networks* of social interaction (including cross-border networks), producing new social relationships and social norms in contrast to previous times, when the structure of society was more or less fixed in space and time as social '*order*'.

Castells' project is a triumph of bold ambition and if I have the audacity to summarize his argument in just a few pages I do this in part as a tribute to his passing at least one test of a good theory – namely, parsimony, or economy of conception. The main conceptual frame is sufficiently 'economical' in its intersecting co-ordinates of motifs and themes to have immediate heuristic value. And in part it is because of the narrowness of my own interest, which is solely with the dynamics of globalization and social exclusion, and not, in this book at any rate, with – say – the reformulation of patriarchal gender relations, or with the collapse of the Soviet state, or with US Christian Fundamentalism, or with the denial of death in modern society, or the social arrythmia of our life cycles, to mention but a handful of the mosaic of social changes that Castells draws on to his encyclopaedic canvas.

Thus selectively summarizing, we can say that, for Castells too, the point of departure is time/space compression. He describes a formal structure of an emerging network society based on the *space of flows* and on *timeless time*. Like others in the new sociology, he defines space as the material support of time-sharing social practices. But while in earlier epochs space was prescribed by physical contiguity, space is now articulated through the circuitry of electronic impulses (microelectronics, telecommunications, computer processing, broadcasting systems and so on). This space is fundamentally as borderless as it is timeless. At the co-ordinates of this circuitry there emerge 'nodes' and 'hubs' which are, indeed, specific places, with well-defined social, cultural and functional characteristics as well as physical locality. Between the nodes and hubs traverse the flows of capital, of knowledge and information, of technological designs and controls, of other organizational interactions, and of images, sounds and symbols. These flows dominate the places, and not the other way around. The nodes and hubs are organized hierarchically, depending on the weight of their relative functions in the network. Thus, for example, in the networks of the global economy, only segments of economic structures, countries, regions and populations are linked, and they are linked in proportion to their particular position in the international division of labour; other sectors, agents and local groups are disconnected and marginalized. But, crucially, the network hierarchy continually adapts and adjusts to its competitive, information-driven environment, with the result that sometimes places are switched off, or downgraded while others are being incorporated, upgraded or even created. Thus the global economy is highly dynamic, highly exclusionary and highly unstable in its boundaries. It is characterized by a variable geometry that dissolves historical, economic geography.[14]

Timeless time, or 'real time', is the emerging dominant form of social time in the network society and replaces the domination of clock time associated with modernity and industrial capitalism. Castells describes the operation of this timeless time in an understandable manner, particularly in relation to global financial markets, because this is where the global economy is now working most perfectly as a unit in real time. There are other examples, which I shall discuss later in this chapter. However, the circumstance that the financial sector has moved along furthest in respect of 'real-time' working also means that this sector now dominates and directs all other sectors. The global financial network is the mother of all networks; it strides atop the entire edifice of global economic activities. In a lucid passage, Castells argues:

> Capital works globally as a unit in real time; and it is realized, invested, and accumulated mainly in the sphere of circulation, that is as finance capital. While finance capital has generally been among the dominant fractions of capital, we are witnessing the emergence of something different: capital accumulation proceeds, and its value-making is generated, increasingly, in the global financial markets enacted by information networks in the time less space of financial flows. From these networks, capital is invested, globally, in all sectors of activity: information industries, media business, advanced services, agricultural production, health, education, technology, old and new manufacturing, real estate, war-making and peace-selling, religion, entertainment, and sports. Some activities are more profitable than others, as they go through cycles, market upswings and downturns, and segmented global competition. Yet whatever is extracted as profit (from producers, consumers, technology, nature, and institutions) is reverted to the meta-network of financial flows, where all capital is equalized in the commodified democracy of profit-making. In this electronically operated global casino specific capitals boom or bust, settling the fate of corporations, household savings, national currencies, and regional economies. The net result sums to zero: the losers pay for the winners. But who are the winners and the losers changes by the year, the month, the day, the second, and permeates down to the world of firms, jobs, salaries, taxes and public services. To the world of what is sometimes called 'the real economy'. And of what I would be tempted to call the 'unreal economy', since in the age of networked capitalism the fundamental reality, where money is made and lost, invested or saved, is in the financial sphere. All other activities (except those of the dwindling public sector) are primarily the basis to generate the necessary surplus to invest in global flows, or the result of investment originated in these financial networks.[15]

The cutting and perverse edge of timeless time is in evidence in the futures, options and other derivatives markets because here the processing of transactions is not merely instantaneous (real time), but involves the capture of *future* time in *present* transactions. But the very process of marketing and monetizing future developments affects these developments and becomes the source of increasing volatility, turbulence and economic crises which threaten the sustainability of what Castells considers to be an otherwise hugely positive and immensely productive phase in the development of global capitalism.[16]

The other source of instability is social exclusion, which results from the dynamics of global informationalism. To trace these dynamics it is important to understand that informationalism in Castells' theory is not a new *mode of production*, it is merely a new *mode of development* of the capitalist mode of production[17] which operates, even in this age, as the dominant economic form and is driven, as ever, by the capitalist's urge to accumulate profits by expoiting labour and other resources, and by relentlessly intensifying commodification to deepen, (though, in the present age, *not* widen) markets. The domination of the market as the only form of social organization, coupled with global competition and the dynamics of information-driven flexible networks, means that everything that is valuable is rewarded, while everything that is not valuable is downgraded or excluded. But what is valuable and what is not is constantly being re-evaluated and thus reorganized in the hierarchy. Under conditions of global competition and relentless information-driven innovation, only the most profitable will do. He writes:

> the ascent of informational capitalism is indeed characterized by simultaneous economic development and underdevelopment, social inclusion and exclusion, in a process very roughly reflected in comparative statistics. There is polarization in the distribution of wealth at the global level, differential evolution of intra-country income inequality, and substantial growth of poverty and misery in the world at large, and in most countries, both developed and developing.[18]

In a recent interview with the journal *New Political Economy*, Castells reiterates the view that informationalism permits – at least for the foreseeable future – 'market deepening', which will ensure that about a fifth of the world's population will be doing better and better all the time, while 40 per cent of the planet's inhabitants will be excluded. In between, there is a subordinate layer of industrial capitalism in which capital and technology continue to provide goods for mass consumption.[19]

For all the brilliance of Castells' conception, and despite the fact that he devotes one volume of the trilogy and a good part of another to a qualitative analysis of the complex interplay between economy, technology, society and politics that clarifies the multi-faceted *variety* of patterns of exclusion whereby either whole societies (for example, Sub-Saharan Africa) and/or parts of societies elsewhere, become disconnected from the global economic system, there is still a need to clarify the *generic* process that makes exclusion the inevitable counterpart of globalization. Put another way, the question is whether there are prospects for the relative proportions between top, middle and bottom layers to change towards, say, relative greater segments of the world's population being included in the top and middle parts, and fewer people being marginalized in the lowest layer. Or indeed, is there a *generic* process at work that directs an opposite trend? This question is not just academic, but has immediate policy relevance. In Castells' view, with the exception of Sub-Saharan Africa, whose very low technological base (Sub-Saharan Africa is the 'switched off' region in the world)[20] prevents it from functional participation in the new global economy, at least for the foreseeable future, other groups and places still have a hope of social inclusion, depending on a range of social, political, technological and economic strategies, the most important of which is (digital) education, as in the British government's latest project of introducing computers into all schools. However, if it is the case, as I believe, that at the present historical juncture a *fundamental* cleavage has opened up between, on the one hand, networks of capital, labour, information and markets – which link up through technology, and on the other, populations and territories deprived of value and interest to the dynamics of global capitalism. If, furthermore, this process is one that can be predicted to deepen and widen in both relative and absolute terms, then it would make sense *not* to talk about strategies of inclusion but rather to celebrate a concept of exclusion that tries to develop sustainable life on the outside. Moreover, if in capturing the fundamental logic of the system of global informational capitalism, we come to the conclusion that the systemic properties of the system not only switch off, and render as economically irrelevant, particular locales and groups, but also undermine their capacity to regroup and reorganize in alternative modes of production and survival, would it then not not be better to develop strategies of intervention that protect them from the gales of globalization threatening to overwhelm them? I return to this at the conclusion of this book. But to do so with any theoretical wit we need to exemplify first the precise process whereby the sociology of globalization drives the economics of globalization.

The Economics of Globalization

The annihilation of space through time drives the economics of globalization in three principal ways. First, the 'shared phenomenal world' supports the emergence of a global market *discipline*, contrasted with the existence of a mere global marketplace. Second, it reorders the way economic activities are being conceptualized and, as a consequence, organized. Whereas, previously it was common to classify economic activities *either* into three categories: primary, secondary and tertiary (agriculture, industry and services); *or* – as in more recent works on international economics – into a chain of high value-added and low value-added activities, it now makes more sense to reorder economic activities into two: 'real-time' activities where distance and location are no longer relevant as a determinant of economic operations; and 'material' activities where there is still some 'friction of space' that limits choice of location. As we shall see below, this twofold conceptualization is beginning to inform the organization of transnational business, and, as a result, a new global division of labour. Third, money itself has become a 'real time' resource permitting a degree of international mobility that is qualitatively different from anything witnessed in previous eras.

A global market discipline

There is an important distinction to be made between a global market*place* and a global market *principle*. A global marketplace exists when there is an international division of labour and, consequently, an international market exchange between different goods and services produced in different nations. Such international trade dominated the prewar and immediate postwar periods. It was essentially *complementary* – that is, countries specializing in the export of one type of product would exchange that product for other types that they themselves did not produce.

As a result of the growth and organizational evolution of multinational companies, this pattern of *interproduct trade* gradually has given way to *intraproduct trade*. There is no longer a neat division of labour between countries: there is now export competition between producers in different countries offering the same product lines. Countries that are high-volume exporters of cars are also high-volume importers of cars. How did this situation come about?

Liberalization and technological progress have steadily altered the way in which international production is being undertaken. At first, multinational companies adopted simple integration strategies where they set up foreign affiliates producing, typically with technology obtained from the parent company, standardized commodities that previously had been subject to cross-border trade. Second, parent companies would set up foreign affiliates engaging in a limited range of activities in order to supply their parent firms with specific inputs that they were in a more competitive position to produce.

Next, multinational companies began to adopt complex integration strategies where they turned their geographically dispersed affiliates and fragmented production systems into regionally, or even globally, integrated production and distribution networks. Thus multinational companies (by this time – that is, the 1970s – often referred to as 'transnational' companies or even 'global' companies) farmed out different parts of the production process to affiliates in different national locations. Each subsidiary took part in the production process, but no single affiliate produced the whole product from beginning to end. The hallmark of this global fragmentation and organic integration of the production process was an enormous increase in international trade in components and semi-processed manufactures. This began in the 1960s and soon overtook the growth in world trade itself.[21] Telling evidence of this global integration at the level of production is found in data on intrafirm trade. Whereas in the early 1970s, intrafirm trade was estimated to account for around 20 per cent of world trade, by the early 1990s that share was around a third, excluding intra-TNC transactions in services.[22]

For many observers and analysts of the world economy, this development of an integrated international production system was sufficient evidence of the emergence of a truly 'global economy'. And in some ways it was. That is to say, it prepared the *structural* conditions for the emergence of a global economy. Because it meant that a global market *principle* (a dominant standard of price, quality and efficiency) began to impose itself on the *domestic supply* of consumer goods, intermediate and half-processed goods, technology, and indeed the factors of production, capital, labour and raw materials. As a consequence of the shift from interproduct trade to intraproduct trade, global competition intensified. Instead of being complementary, international trade became *predatory* or 'adversarial', as Peter Drucker put it.[23]

The corollary of global competition is that even goods and services that are produced and exchanged *within* the national domestic sphere have to meet standards of quality and costs of production that are set globally. A good example is the USA, the country with the largest domestic market. As Stephen Cohen reminds us in a revealing statistic: whereas in the early 1960s only 4 per cent of US domestic production was subject to international competition, by the early 1990s over 70 per cent was.[24] The contrast between the global marketplace and the global market principle could not have been put more sharply, as in the 1960s the US-dominated international manufacturing trade contributed 25 per cent of all international trade flows, whereas by the 1990s its share of world manufacturing trade had dropped to just 12 per cent.[25]

However, of still greater significance is the manner in which such structural integration is becoming *internalized* in the behaviour of economic agents, be they entrepreneurs or workers, consumers or producers. If the expression 'market principle' refers to a structural constraint, I use the expression 'market discipline' to address the internalization of this structural constraint by individual agents in their own conduct. Writers of the Regulation School, discussed in Chapter 5, have tried to stretch their concept of 'mode of regulation' to include the internalization of relevant social values and norms. For example, Aglietta[26] speaks of the 'socialisation of the mode of life'; Boccara refers to 'anthroponomic factors',[27] while Lipietz uses the term 'habitus' borrowed from Bourdieu to indicate that values and norms that might sustain a mode of regulation are internalized in individual conduct.[28] Yet, as Bob Jessop has pointed out, none of these writers has succeeded in pinpointing the precise process of transformation because they have failed to theorise how modes of regulation in fact become internalized in individual conduct.[29]

Our discussion of time/space compression and the 'shared phenomenal world' clarifies this internalization process. It is the *awareness* of global competition (an aspect of Robertson's 'global consciousness') that constrains individuals and groups, and even national governments, to conform to international standards of price and quality. People are reminded constantly, in the experience of their own daily lives, but even more so in the way that this experience is reinforced by media coverage, of the experience of others elsewhere, that unless they conform to these standards they will lose the competition, lose their own jobs. Workers come to accept that it is 'proper' that jobs should be lost because their company 'has to' move elsewhere where wages and social conditions are less demanding.

In 1992, the American company, Hoover, was faced with pressure for higher wages from its Dijon workforce and decided to move the plant to Glasgow. The point about the 'discipline' of the global market is that such companies do not in fact have to move. It is sufficient for them to 'threaten' to move. Time/space compression has permitted us all to share in the phenomenal world of the Dijon workers (and in that of numerous other victims of company relocations elsewhere). This has imposed a social discipline on workers all over Europe, indeed all over the world, that unless they conform, companies have the power to move plant to another country. Because of the existence of a global market discipline, it is sufficient for a company merely to *threaten* to set up a plant abroad, for it to successfully drive down wages to a globally competitive level. Charles Sabel reports on German plants where charts of defect rates for particular processes are displayed on video screens next to equivalent data for their Brazilian subsidiaries.[30] This establishes a global social discipline that constrains the behaviour of Brazilian and German workers alike.

Thus, while global competition has created the structural conditions for the emergence of a global market discipline, it is time/space compression that creates the shared phenomenal world that supports and reproduces this discipline on a daily basis. And not just on workers. Companies too know they have to adopt the best quality methods and the most efficient costs, and engage in constant innovation, because they know that otherwise they will lose their markets and someone else will move in. The same holds true at the consumer end of the organization of economic life. Consumers in China can see on their satellite TV screens Western lifestyle products they want to own, regardless of their government's desire to limit foreign imports and boost local producers. The Chinese government tried to ban satellite television for this very reason, but to no avail.

A new global division of labour; a new social core–periphery hierarchy

As the costs of transporting standard products and of communicating information about them continue to drop (another example of time/space compression), modern factories and state-of-the-art machinery can be installed almost anywhere in the world. Routine producers in the UK and the USA are therefore in direct competition with millions of producers in other nations. In his book, *The Work of Nations*, Robert Reich, one time Secretary of State for Labor in US President Bill Clinton's Administration, gives spectacular examples of the speed with which factories and productive capital investments have become footloose. For example, until the late 1970s, the American telephone and telecommunications company AT&T had depended on routine producers in Louisiana to assemble standard telephones. It then discovered that producers in Singapore would perform the same tasks at a far lower cost. Faced with intense global competition they then had to switch to cheaper routine producers in Singapore. But by the late 1980s they switched production again, this time to Thailand.[31]

Such transferable routine production is no longer the preserve of deskilled jobs in 'old economy' industrial plants. The fusion of computer technology with telecommunications makes it possible for firms to relocate an ever-widening range of operations and functions to wherever cost-competitive labour, assets and infrastructure are available. The new technologies make it feasible to standardize, make routine and co-ordinate activities that previously were subject to the friction of space and therefore regarded as nontradable. They enable such activities to be turned into 'real-time' activities. Take, for example, data processing services of all kinds. Airlines employ data processors from Barbados to Bombay to key in names and flight numbers into giant computer banks located in

Dallas or London. Book and magazine publishers use routine operators around the world to convert manuscripts into computer-readable form and send them back to the parent firm at the speed of electronic impulses. The New York Life Insurance Company was dispatching insurance claims to Castleisland in the Republic of Ireland, where routine producers, guided by simple directions, entered the claims and determined the amounts due, then instantly transmitted the computations back to the USA.[32] Software firms export much of their development work to Bangalore in India, which sees itself as the Silicon Valley of Asia.

The 1970s, and still more so the 1980s, witnessed the global restructuring of industry and a redistribution of jobs through integrated international production enabled by the new technologies. The haemorrhaging of jobs in the core countries benefited the periphery, particularly Pacific Asia. A French government report in 1993 estimated that in the previous twenty years no fewer than 6.6 million jobs were lost to the EC and the USA and gained by the Far East.[33] US manufacturing employment in the developing countries as a whole grew at almost five times the rate of such employment in the developed economies.[34]

Optimists argue that the loss of jobs in manufacturing activities in the core economies will be compensated by a growth of service industries, including services related to manufacturing itself. 'New U.S. Factory Jobs Aren't in the Factory' ran a headline in *Business Week* in 1994, arguing that support industries with their high component of knowledge skills constitute a second tier of manufacturing industries. While a smaller percentage of the US workforce will be in production, a much larger percentage will be supporting this production with computer software, robot-making, and countless services that will add jobs to supply the 'leaner' manufacturers.[35] On the other hand, pessimists such as Jeremy Rifkin in his book, *The End of Work*, point to the wholesale destruction of agricultural and industrial labour as smart machines replace workers in both of these 'old economy' sectors, while the emerging knowledge sector – in Rifkin's view – will only be able to absorb a small percentage of the displaced labour.[36]

But even if the overall equation of job losses and gains is open to dispute, there is no denying that the complex integration strategies of international producers, coupled with new forms of co-ordination that are enabled by the new technologies, together with the operation of the global market principle, are altering the landscape of the global division of labour. It is no longer one that strictly follows economic geography.

There was a time when the geography of the global division of labour ran parallel with the sequential transformation of goods-in-production from low value-added activities to high value-added activities. To explain this we need to first say something about the concept of value-added.

'Value-added' is the market value of a firm's output minus the market value of the inputs it purchases from other firms. Essentially, therefore, it is the sum of the factor incomes, the wages and profits of the firm. The concept of a value-added *chain* arises because in the transformation of a raw material – say, cotton – into an end consumer product – say, a garment in a shop window – there is a *sequence* of intermediate stages of fabrication and processing: spinning, running, dyeing, weaving, designing, cutting, sewing, wholesaling, advertising, marketing and retailing. At each stage, the labour involved adds value to the process of transformation, making the product progressively more expensive to the final consumer. Moreover, at each stage, capitalist entrepreneurs intervene to organize the discrete activity in the chain, each in turn adding a mark-up to make some profits for themselves. This implies that the market price for the final product incorporates all the wages and mark-ups of all the previous stages. The history of multinational enterprise may be summed up by saying that it has moved from trying to internalize all these stage-like transactions within its own organizational embrace, to once more, as under global networking, 'externalizing' all, or many, of these stages and transactions.

So it may be seen that the concept of a value-added chain expresses a sequential progression from lower value-added to higher value-added activities. But there is more to the hierarchical progression than mere sequencing of transformation. The historical development of capitalism on a world scale, for all the reasons spelt out in the first part of this book, also concentrated 'higher-value activities' at the final, consumer, end of the chain (consumer markets in the rich countries), while largely (though not exclusively) leaving low-value activities in underdeveloped lands. There was a double effect, therefore, in so far as the wages of labour at higher stages of the transformation process are likely to be higher, and therefore also the pass-on prices, than at the lower end of the production chain. Furthermore, the more specialized the final product, again more typically at the rich-consumer end of the chain, the higher the profit mark-up for such products because of the effect of limited demand. For all these reasons, bulk or volume production, which is concentrated at the lower end of the chain, yields lower value-added than specialized, high-tech products, which are concentrated at the higher end of the value chain.

Today something curious is happening. As Paul Krugman put it, it is now possible to 'slice up' the value chain in a different way, and locate the labour-intensive slices in the production of those goods traditionally viewed as skill-, capital- or technology-intensive, in low-wage locations. A classic example is the notebook computer. It looks like a high-technology product, but while the American microprocessor and the Japanese flat-panel display are indeed high-tech, the plastic shell that surrounds them and the wiring that connects them are not, so the assembly of notebook computers becomes an industry of the 'newly industrializing economies'.[37] Furthermore, many information-intensive activities previously classed as high value-added activities have now become 'real- time' activities that may be carried out anywhere in the global system.

Thus, the global division of labour is rendering a core–periphery relationship that cuts across national and geographic boundaries, bringing on board, within the core, segments of the Third World, and relegating segments and groups in both the traditional core of the system and in the Third World to peripheral status. Core–periphery is becoming a social relationship, no longer just a geographical one.

This new social core–periphery hierarchy is set to become still more uneven than was previously the case. Many high-value-added activities that are contributed by so-called 'knowledge workers', are extremely *mobile*. Marketing experts, computer consultants, legal affairs specialists, financial accountants and top managers can go to wherever they can obtain the highest price for their services. And, because of the operation of the global market principle, payments for their services are being equalized across national boundaries, increasingly at the highest price. But at the lower end of the value chain exactly the opposite is happening. Low-value-added activities are still typically tied to tools and equipment – that is, to knowledge embodied in capital – and/or to the location where raw materials are extracted. At this end of the international production chain it is capital and not labour that is mobile, a situation perpetuated by political intervention designed to stem the free migration of labour. The mobility of capital here implies that wage rates equalize at the lowest possible denominator, and this includes wage rates for such activities in the advanced countries.

In this way, globalization alters the balance of social classes on a worldwide scale. David Coates is right to point out that, looking at it this way, 'globalization in its modern form is a process based less on the proliferation of computers than on the proliferation of proletariats ... The world proletariat has doubled in size in a generation.'[38]

Financiarization

We have referred before to the contemporary phenomenon of 'financial deepening' or 'financiarization', which occurs when the growth of financial transactions far exceeds the growth of the underlying economic fundamentals of production and trade (see Chapter 4, page 85). It too is brought about by the effects of the 'shared social space' which, in fact, is most in evidence in the timeless flows of financial capital. By financial capital we mean capital that circulates in pure money form, as distinct from capital tied up in productive assets. The annihilation of space through time by electronic means enables this money capital to scan the entire planet for investment opportunities and to move from one location to another in a matter of seconds. However, the sheer velocity of circulation of money capital does not explain by itself why this money form of capital should have become the dominant form in the age of informational global capitalism. It does not explain why, in Castells' words, 'firms of all kinds, financial producers, manufacturing producers, agricultural producers, service producers, as well as governments and public institutions, use global financial networks as the depositories of their earnings and as their potential source of higher profits'.[39] Why indeed have they become the nerve centre of informational capitalism?

It is worth trying to unravel the process whereby this has come about, if only to debunk a common myth that this is something of a historical accident, not of anybody's doing, and therefore indeed not of anybody's *un*doing. And the implication is that we are

helpless onlookers in an unfolding drama in which the world financial system lurches from crisis to crisis, repeatedly delivering shock-
ing body blows to the livelihoods of millions of ordinary people.

The reasons are in fact partly political, partly technological.
Deregulation of the financial markets put in place by the OECD
and developing countries alike during the 1980s effectively loosened
the restrictions on the form that money can take. It brought down
the 'Chinese walls' that previously had separated the various uses to
which borrowed money could be put, in particular the distinction
between long-term capital and short-term capital investments. This
topic was discussed at some length in Chapter 4. Here we might sum
up this process, which was the result of active and collective government intervention, as one that increased the *functional* mobility of
capital, contrasted with the *spatial* mobility of capital. Imagine the
functional mobility of capital as a vertical process: monies tied up in
productive assets can convert in an instant into pure money form,
escaping into the cyberspace of electronic circulation.

So what happens to money circulating in this cyberspace? Why is
it so profitable, more profitable indeed than when it is busy making
commodities and paying labour? Enter digitization, a straightfor-
ward technological process. It is best explained in a story about a
hedge fund dealer, a 'Master of the Universe', in Tom Wolfe's
novel, *The Bonfire of the Vanities*. One day this Master of the
Universe is at a family party and his seven-year-old daughter asks,
'Daddy, what is it that you do?' And the Master of the Universe is
lost for words – how indeed would one describe bond dealing to a
seven-year-old? And his wife jumps in and says, 'Well, darling, just
imagine that a bond is a slice of cake, and you didn't bake the cake,
but every time you hand somebody a slice of the cake a tiny little bit
comes off, like a little crumb, and you can keep that.'[40] Now
the point about digitization is that, in the physical world, none
of the tiny crumbs would be worth picking up and collecting, but
in the virtual world, where telecommunications combine with com-
puter-assisted data processing, money can be made by gathering up
infinitesimally fractional differences in the movement in prices, be
they interest rates, commodity prices or currency values.

The upshot is that money is increasingly being made out of the
circulation of money, regardless of traditional restrictions of space
and time, as when money transforms into bricks and mortar. Capital is being disconnected from the social relationships in which

money and wealth were previously embedded. It is because of this 'disembedding' that globalization entails a process of intensification of linkages within the core of the global system, while its counter-part, 'peripheralization', becomes a process of marginalization and expulsion that cuts across territories and national boundaries, rendering areas within the traditional core subject to the same processes of expulsion as large swathes of territory in Africa, Latin America and Asia. So here too, as was the case with the global organization of work, we see that the structure of core–periphery becomes a social division rather than a geographical one.

Let us explore the meaning of this heightened international mobility of money capital a little further. In particular, let us examine why this should represent a form of *imploding* capitalism rather than a further expansion of world capitalism.

When pension funds invest in, say, Hong Kong stocks, they can benefit from the rising values of the stocks and, if they are clever fund managers, switch out of a stock when it goes down and invest in another rising one somewhere else. There is no need for them to wait and see what happens to the companies that build skyscrapers in Hong Kong, or sell textiles back to Europe. But, of course, the connections between the world of high finance and the economic fundamentals of world trade and production are not completely severed. There is still no such thing as a free lunch. What has happened, rather, is that the integration of the world's financial markets and the development of a whole range of novel financial instruments, permitted since the deregulation of these markets, have made it possible to connect up the arteries of real production and trade, and thus squeeze the last drop of surplus out of workers and peasants all over the world, in a manner that makes these innumerable threads that lead to our pension fund invisible and therefore unchallengeable.

To stick to the same example: the rise and rise of the Hong Kong stock market prior to its dramatic fall in 1996 was due in large measure to Chinese provincial authorities investing borrowed money in Hong Kong's stock market and real estate, with dire conse-quences for the Beijing government's ability to hold the value of its currency and pay the peasants in northern China for its grain procurements. The world is now like this: if our pension fund works well for us, the peasants in northern China will just have to go a bit more hungry. If people in the West, as they did during the consumer boom of the 1980s, push up interest rates through their incautious use of credit cards, it has a knock-on effect on the interest rates that Brazil pays on its loans, and this in turn prejudices the livelihood of peasants in Brazil. The speed with which money can move across borders removes the need to anchor it firmly in (national) social relationships. Globalization makes national social solidarity (as expressed in transfer payments to the old, the sick, the unemployed, and the lower income groups) *dysfunctional* from the point of view of the rational economic interests of those who participate in the global economy. This process is being sharpened still further by recent policies of deregulation in the core countries, which encourage the globalization of small private investors and undercut the last remaining vestiges of national social solidarity. The privatization, for example, of pension schemes (a transition from 'defined benefit' or occupational and state pension schemes, to 'defined contribution' schemes or 'personal' pension schemes) is a case in point.

Thus, in the advanced countries, the pressures for globalization (maintaining liberal and deregulated markets for finance and trade, and resistance to policies of protection for national territorial economic activities) come not just from a tiny group of international capitalists – that is, from those dominant fractions of corporate capital that have global interests – but also from a broadly-based stratum of society, the 13 per cent of senior citizens and those with an eye to their pensionable future, whose continued survival, to put it bluntly, is better secured in the rising economies of the Far East than by reproduction of the labour power (and pension premiums paid) by the shrinking younger generation that steps into their shoes. As *The Economist* has put it: 'Ageing populations in rich countries and freer flowing capital the world over are changing the way people save and invest. American and British institutional money is flooding foreign markets.'[41] This deterritorialization of economic rationality as it affects not just organized capital but also the mass of middle-class individuals in bourgeois societies, is a key consequence of globalization.

Conclusion

My privileging of the sociological aspect of globalization is not to deny the importance of other factors, more especially the dynamics of historical capitalism which – as Wallerstein and many others in the Marxist tradition have argued – had a 'globalizing' imperative from the beginning. The development of transnational corporations and the growth of international finance in particular, testify to a complex multicausal logic of globalization. Rather, what has been argued here is that, through the reconstitution of the world into a single *social* space, that self-same historical process has now lifted off and moved into new territory. If, previously, global integration in the sense of a growing unification and interpenetration of the human condition was driven by the economic logic of capital accumulation, at present it is the unification of the human condition that drives the logic of further capital accumulation. It is a logic that draws a new line in the sand, a new primary cleavage in the world economy which is neither one between nations, nor between classes, but instead between those individuals and groups who can participate in the timeless, 'spaceless' flows of money, production and consumption, and those who cannot, and who are thus, in the words of Zygmunt Baumann, 'glebae adscripti' – forcibly localized. Baumann writes: 'The top of the new hierarchy is exterritorial; its lower ranges are marked by varying degrees of space constaints, while the bottom ones are, for all practical purposes, *glebae adscripti*.'[42]

Neither does this sociological take on globalization deny the role of political intervention whether in the manner of its birth, or in the manner of its future demise. What it does, however, is to take issue with those who believe that the political actors (the global business élite and their supporting political classes in the nation-states) who have contributed to its emergence can now be called upon to roll back the consequences of their ill-fated actions. For this is the nub: once the structural power of global financiarized capital was put in place successfully, it in turn began to limit the scope for action of national governments whose previous policies made it happen. The political dimension of globalization is the subject of the next chapter.

7

Global Governance:
Regulation and Imperialism

In Chapter 5 we began the story of the recent crisis and transformation process by describing the principal features of a new techno-economic paradigm of industrial production, and a new informational economy. These, however, constitute supply-side innovations. What about the demand side? Following the perspective of the Regulation School, we recall that long-term macro economic stability also requires a resolution of the demand side of the equation, with supply and demand *together* informing a 'regime of accumulation'. Moreover, a regime of accumulation in turn will only come about through an appropriate mode of regulation, in the shape of relevant norms, habits and laws, as well as governing institutions. Crucially, this mode of regulation describes not only the *micro*-institutional context of the organization of production and work, but also the *macro*-institutional context in which expanded economic reproduction takes place, namely a coherent production–distribution and consumption relationship.

There are three problems a theory of regulation has to address. The first relates to its notion of reproducibility, or of stability and sustainability. The Regulation School rejects a mechanistic and deterministic form of theorizing, where, for example, one would deduce (and thus predict) the emerging contours of a mode of regulation from an understanding of the 'logic' of the techno-economic paradigm and the way this drives the process of accumulation. Instead, the Regulation School has reserved its opinion about the shape of things to come by stressing the voluntaristic genesis of any mode of regulation as the outcome of locally and historically specific struggles. In so doing it wants to overcome its Marxist, 'structuralist' bearings, and reintroduce the role of human agency into the formulation of what constitutes a period of stable economic growth in which crisis tendencies are contained and neutralized. In other words, they couple stability with political legitimacy, and, indeed, in more recent writings, even with ecological balance. All this on an international scale. As D. Leborgne and A. Lipietz put it:

> On the ruins of Fordism and Stalinism, humankind is at the crossroads. No technological determinism will light the way. The present industrial divide is first and foremost a political divide. The search for social compromise, around ecological constraints, macroeconomic consistency, gender and ethnic equality, all mediated by the nature and degree of political mobilization will decide the outcome... The macroeconomics of the future may be based on a downward spiral of social and ecological competition, leading to recurrent financial, business and environmental crises, or an ecologically sustainable and macroeconomically stable model... Radical economists and geographers may be part of finding the better pathway, both by identifying the possibilities for prosperity and by criticizing unrealistic optimism for flexibility as a panacea.[1]

Their socio-political engagement has led many to judge, and reject, contemporary neo-liberal regimes as being internally contradictory and crisis-prone, even if according to some they do appear to be able to create a distinctive ensemble of regulatory practices which is reproducible in the *medium term*. Bob Jessop, for example, has most succinctly summarized the emerging neo-liberal, postFordist mode of regulation, describing its various features in respect of the wage relation, the enterprise system, the money form, the consumption sphere, and the state form. The latter he identifies as the emerging Schumpeterian workfare state which is supply-side orientated, promotes inter-nation competition, displaces welfarism and uses social policy instruments *not* to generalize norms of mass consumption, but rather to encourage flexibility and niche marketing for élite consumption. Meanwhile economic powers of the nation-state are 'hollowed out', as powers are displaced upwards (to global and pan-regional bodies) and downwards (to local and sub-regional bodies) which begin to integrate with one another in ways that by-pass the

nation-state.[2] Such a regime may well balance production and consumption at the level of the international economy as a whole, at
least in the medium term. But only by excluding ever-growing
segments of the world population from it, including large social
sectors in the core capitalist economies.

In the opinion of some regulationists, such a social-minority-
focused regime of accumulation is not a regime of accumulation
proper, but a 'monstrosity' that needs weeding out as part of a
political project to develop an alternative social compromise, an
alternative mode of social regulation. Many favour a new 'institutional fix' which separates the global from the local.[3] In this new
social compromise, social democracy would become embedded in
the sub-national 'local sphere', replacing the national 'organicist'
model of Fordist social solidarity and democracy. In a recent contribution, Lipietz, for example, has described the characteristics of such
a new social compromise, but in the nature of such debates it does
not add up to more than a wish list of the good life. In the conclusion
of this book we shall take up this theme of an alternative political
project implied in the separation of the global from the local.

The second problem relates to the question of where exactly is the
space in which the macro-institutional context is articulated? Is it
local, regional, national, supranational, or is it international? Early
regulation theory had taken its clues from the breakdown of the
structural coupling between Fordist production systems and Keynesian welfare modes of regulation at the *national* level, and their
search for a new 'institutional fix' was at first directed at the national
economic space. But with globalization the space problem has begun
to inspire much of the so-called 'second generation' research agendas
of the Regulation School, with work focusing on the links between
sub-national (for example, industrial districts), national, and supranational (for example, the European space) and international levels.[4]

The third, and related, problem is the one that will occupy us in
this chapter. It is a problem that arises from Regulation Theory's
original script reading of the golden age of Fordism and is related to
the question of global hegemony. Co-ordination of the international
system of global Fordism was achieved under the hegemony of the
USA. US hegemony first presented the Fordist model for development to other countries and then financed these countries with
Marshall Aid and MacArthur plans for setting up new regimes of
acccumulation. It institutionalized this international configuration

by intertwining it with US national, industrial and financial interests through the medium of the Bretton Woods agreement and the establishment of GATT, the IMF, the World Bank and the OECD. These contained disturbances and maintained a set of rules that stabilized the system through US overall hegemonic power (economic and ideological, as well as political and military). The spread of the Fordist regime of accumulation to other countries coincided with the strategic interests of the US financial and industrial community, and thus global Fordism formed an integral part of the US social transformation of Fordism itself.[5]

Between 1970 and 1990 the scholarly consensus was that the crisis of Fordism was accompanied by, and even contributed to, a decline in US hegemony – that is, the ability of the USA to 'make and enforce the rules for world political economy'.[6] Hegemony is more than rule by a dominant state. It involves the acceptance by the dominant strata in the states comprising the world system of a structure of values which they share with the dominant power, and which they regard as being legitimate and just. This US hegemony, or *Pax Americana*, was perceived to be declining, in a manner analogous to the decline of *Pax Britannica*, which had accompanied the crises of the interwar period in the 1920s and 1930s. US hegemonic decline was said to have been caused by a number of factors which indicated a relative decline in America's material strength that had underpinned its hegemonic position. For example, its loss of strategic nuclear dominance; its decline in conventional military capabilities; its diminished economic size in GNP per head relative to other countries such as Japan, Germany and Sweden; its loss of productivity and the erosion of its lead in some areas of high technology, with the gains going to Japan; its loss of influence in the UN and other international organizations; and its shift from being the world's largest creditor nation to being its largest debtor nation.[7]

In this period of the '*interregnum*', much analysis in the disciplines of international relations and of international political economy was devoted to speculation about plausible successors. For example, some considered a possible role for Japan as a world leader (*Pax Nipponica*),[8] others imagined the emergence of a multi-polar world order with balance of power being divided equally between the three regional blocs.[9] Again, others looked to an oligarchy of powerful states that might concert their powers to underpin 'international regimes' formulated under the auspices of international bodies.[10] Some even hoped for a form of post-hegemonic multi-lateralism in which there would be a broader diffusion of power between a large number of collective forces, including states, that might achieve some agreement on universal principles of an alternative order without dominance, based on mutual recognition of distinct traditions of civilization.[11]

But behind these diverging speculations, or aspirations, there was also common ground in so far as it was widely recognized that what was going on *in the meantime* was a restructuring of state and capital relations toward a more globally integrated and competitive market-driven system involving a transnational process of structural power and even of transnational class formation.

Global Governance and the Internationalization of the State

Globalization restructures relations between state and capital. It has led to what Robert Cox refers to as the *internationalization of the state*, in which the state becomes a vehicle for transmitting the global market discipline to the domestic economy.[12] Cox argues that the globalization of the world economy gives rise to a global class and social structure that deeply affects the forms of state. He suggests that globalization is led by a transnational managerial class[13] consisting of distinct fractions, but which together constitute what Susan Strange has called the international 'business civilization'.[14]

The term 'business civilization', however, has a positive ethical connotation that is arguably not warranted. It is perhaps better to refer to a transnational business 'culture' of shared norms and values that underpin and interweave with the structural power of transnational capital. Together these have become *institutionalized* in a plethora of organizational forms and practices: within international organizations such as the World Bank and the IMF; in interstate summit agendas and agreements (for example GATT, subsequently WTO) and other forms of co-operation between nations; within emerging institutional forms of 'élite interaction' between members of the international business class, state bureaucrats and members of international organizations;[15] and within the administrative bureaucracy of national governments. There is a growing body of resrach on the nature of these élite interactions and the manner in which a global business class performs an agenda-setting role within the WTO, the EU, the OECD and many other international forums that are busy deregulating and privatizing the world economy in the interest of transnational capital. To give just two examples, the European Round Table of Industrialists (ERT), comprising the leaders of forty-five key European TNCs has largely been responsible for the EU's post-1992 move towards flexibility, privatization and deregulation, as well as Monetary Union with its strict controls over national fiscal policies.[16] Meanwhile, the US Council for International Business, which includes just 150 senior-level private executives with IBM and AT&T in the lead, has played a key role in the formulation of the Multilateral Agreement on Investments (MAI) proposals.[17]

As Stephen Gill and David Law[18] have noted, there are elements of a common perspective, or a hegemonic ideology, emerging on the role of international business and private enterprise which cuts across and unites all these institutional forums. At the heart of this 'neo-liberal' political project is the idea that private property and accumulation are sacrosanct, and that the prime responsibility of governments is to ensure 'sound finance': they must 'fight inflation' and maintain an attractive 'business climate' in which, among other things, the power of unions is circumscribed. These ideas both underpin, and are the result of, the 'structural power' of capital that is so internationally mobile that the investment climate of each country is judged continually by business with reference to the climate that prevails elsewhere.

Under the previous epoch of world order, under *Pax Americana*, there was also a world economy and internationalization of production, but the role of the state was still largely autonomous. States had the *recognized* responsibility for *domestic* economic progress and capital accumulation, employment and welfare, under the aegis of the hegemonic structure of the American-led Bretton Woods-managed world economy, which laid down the rules of interstate competition and co-ordination. All states, advanced and underdeveloped alike, had a recognized 'developmental' role. Although the prevailing ideology was supportive of free markets and of the internationalization of capital, it was nevertheless, as John Ruggie has argued, a period of 'embedded' liberalism[19] – that is to say, liberalism 'embedded' in the nation-state. This contrasts with present-day globalization, which we might describe as a period of 'unembedded' liberalism.

Good examples of the institutionalization of 'unembedded' liberalism may be gleaned from the Uruguay GATT agreements, concluded in 1994, in particular the protocols relating to so-called 'trade-related investment measures' (TRIMS) and 'trade-related intellectual property rights' (TRIPS). These circumscribe severely the sovereign rights of all states (including those of the developing countries) to regulate foreign investment and external trade in the pursuit of perceived developmental needs.[20] Under the TRIMS protocol, a number of domestic measures which used to be 'normal' and 'accepted' elements in any development strategy must be phased out – for example, local content requirements, domestic sales requirements, trade balancing requirements, remittance and exchange restrictions.[21]

Equally corrosive of independent developmental state action is the agreement on TRIPS. This agreement strengthens the international property rights of foreign investment and it extends international patent protection to a whole range of products and processes previously not subject to patent. Take, for example, genetic material collected by agribusinesses or pharmaceutical companies, which are harnessed to fabricate a particular industrial process or product. These processes and products may now be patented by the corporations and sold back to the country in which the genetic material originated, under international property rights protection. Under GATT provisions, the recipient country has to allow free competitive entry for such processes and products, and, furthermore, it must prohibit the development and use by local companies of 'identical' products and processes. As Kevin Watkins has argued, this provision amounts to an act of unbridled piracy by transnational capital:

the main beneficiaries will be the core group of less than a dozen seeds and pharmaceutical companies which control over 70 per cent of the world's seeds trade . . . this attempt to incorporate into the GATT a biotechnology patenting code dictated by corporate interest appears an act of unbridled piracy. The overwhelming bulk of genetic materials used in the laboratories of western companies are derived from Third World crops and wild plants . . . Once incorporated into a patentable invention, they can become the property of the company which can claim royalty payments and restrict access to them, even claiming royalties when they are imported into the country of origin.[22]

Although developing countries, spearheaded by India, fought hard during successive phases of the Uruguay round against both TRIMS and TRIPS, they eventually bowed to the hegemony of the neo-liberal trade agenda. Nothing illustrates this better than the agreed statement of the United Nations Conference on Trade and Development in February 1992:

> The Conference recognizes that the establishment and implementation of internationally agreed standards of protection for intellectual property rights...should facilitate international flows of technology and technology cooperation amongst all participating nations, particularly to developing countries on terms and conditions agreed to by the parties concerned, and notes the important role of the World Intellectual Property Organization and the important efforts in the ongoing GATT Uruguay Round negotiations in this regard. The Conference further recognizes that a national regime for the adequate and effective protection of intellectual property rights is important because it can create market incentives for indigenous innovation and the transfer, adaptation and diffusion of technologies.[23]

Whereas, up to that time UNCTAD had been the platform where developing countries had always demanded adjustment of the international patent system to their development needs, it now expressed the belief that adoption of adequate and effective International Patent Protection (IPP) laws and related efforts in WIPO and GATT would facilitate technology transfers to developing countries.[24]

If the Uruguay GATT agreement had already achieved a far-reaching dispensation for international capital to exercise its rights over national economic interests, the subsequent proposals for the MAI, work on which was begun by the OECD and the WTO in 1995, attempted to complete the institutional framework in which the rights of international investors and corporations would prevail at all times, in all economic sectors and under all circumstances. For the MAI not only sought to make it mandatory for all member states to treat foreign investors at least as well as any local investor; it even wanted to prohibit all national or local policies that might have *unintended* discriminatory effects – for example, employment, labour and human rights, and environmental protection policies. The US Trade Secretary, Charlene Barshefsky, even went so far as to argue that all forms of labelling of consumer products could be considered a 'political' act and hence be treated as contravening pro-competition rules. And while the MAI has temporarily been shelved, thanks to a tremendously successful grassroots counter-offensive culminating in a veto by France, more or less identical proposals have been resurrected through a different route, namely an OECD-sponsored amendment to the IMF Articles of Agreement, which will force all member countries to accept the removal of all barriers to international capital flows.[25]

Hand in hand with the open trade and capital mobility agreements fostered by the WTO and IMF, are the various structural adjustment policies imposed by the World Bank and the IMF upon indebted Third-World countries since the 1980s. We shall examine these more closely in Chapter 8, but here it is worth pointing to the novelty of the *policy-based* loans that have been devised since the 1980s. New loans to help countries to pay off old debts are only disbursed if countries followed strict policy guidelines on how to introduce *overall* structural reforms of their economies. They are no longer related to investment programmes, as in conventional project lending. Furthermore, the underlying, or overarching, neo-liberal ideology ensures cross-referencing of separate negotiations between individual countries with different international institutions. The government of India went in the mid-1990s, begging bowl in hand, to the World Bank and the IMF, and returned with a deregulation and liberalization deal (the New Economic Policy) that included the signing of the GATT 1994 agreement as part of the package.[26]

The structural, and indeed institutionalized power of transnational capital has not just informed the policy agenda of *deregulation*, it is also responsible for the drive towards *privatization* of the state sector in all countries of the world. Throughout the 1980s, the advanced countries witnessed a vigorous policy of privatization of the public sector involving, first, public utilities, and then welfare services. In Britain, for example, in the 1980s, a total of £60 billion of state assets were sold at knock-down prices to the private sector.[27] In addition, Britain has pioneered 'government by contract', or 'arm's-length' government, which involves the government contracting out to the private sector everything from the issuing of passports to the prison services, setting up quasi-independent agencies (quangos), unaccountable and undemocratic, for this purpose. When the Conservative government first took office in 1979, there were about 770 000 civil servants in government service, but by 1995 there were estimated to be only around 50 000.[28]

In the indebted developing world, privatization has been imposed by multilateral agencies within policy frameworks provided by structural adjustment programmes. The World Bank and the IMF use the arguments of neo-liberalism to impose privatization. By 1992, more than eighty countries around the world had privatized some 6800 previously state-owned enterprises, mainly monopoly suppliers of essential public services such as water, electricity and telecommunications.[29] Because of the fragility of domestic stock markets in these countries, the shares of these utilities were bought by international financial conglomerates. The same processes of global governance are in evidence in the former centrally-planned economies of Eastern Europe. In total, the value of global privatizations in the developing and former socialist world amounted to over US$58 billion between 1988 and 1995.[30]

Globalization and Globalism

From the point of view of theory, we may conceptualize the emerging governance by the global capitalist class as a complex process which institutionalizes structural power through the widespread adoption of cultural values and legitimating ideology. But this legitimating ideology, while often parading under the banner of 'deregulation', draws governments into an ever-widening circumference of 'regulation' in the form of policy initiatives and legislation. These include monetary and fiscal policies, industrial legislation, social policies, the restructuring of the welfare state, and even the reconstitution of social obligations; for example, an ideological attack on alternative lifestyles, and prioritization of traditional family values through social policy initiatives.[31]

The difficulty for any theorist of regulation is that the forms of regulation of the new epoch are – compared with the past – quintessentially a form of *de*regulation. That is the paradox. Deregulation in one sense implies a dismantling of state-sponsored forms of regulation of the domestic market, a shrinking of the public sector, even a diminution of the public domain. Yet, at the same time, national governments adjust their economies to globalization by regulating *for* deregulation. It is this confusion over regulation and deregulation that explains why there is so much controversy within international relations theory and international political economy literature between those who hold so called 'declinist' views of the nation-state, and those who observe a strengthening of national authority.

In an impressive book, *The Trouble with Capitalism*, Harry Shutt catalogued the many ways in which state policy in the OECD countries since the late 1970s has been geared towards keeping the return on financial assets high, whatever the cost to the underlying economy and the livelihoods of ordinary people. His argument is that, while capitalism has always been blessed (or has blessed itself) with a ruling class in power that would look after its interests, today the dominant form of capital is the financial form (which, as we have seen before, is most completely globalized), and hence public policy is predicated on helping to maintain the value of financial assets as contrasted and even opposed to those of productive and commercial assets. Shutt's list of policies include bail-outs, as in the US government's bail-out of the Savings and Loans disaster in the late 1980s, and the more recent bail-out of the hedge fund LTCM; government purchases of securities on the stock markets; radical reforms of the pension fund regulations, moving them from pay-as-you-earn systems to other schemes run by private financial institutions and invested on the stock markets; tax breaks to investors and savers; repeal of legislation that forbade the buy-back of shares by companies; curtailment of capital gains; cutting interest rates to help unfortunate speculators to borrow money at lower rates to 'close' their positions; and, most importantly, political legitimation of all of the above through the dispersal of share ownership.[32]

The active regulation and social manipulation by governments so as to adjust their economies and societies to the forces of globalization is an entirely *political* project that is coherently, even if falsely, framed in an ideology that is perhaps best summed up as the ideology of 'globalism'. The distinction between globalization and globalism is all-important. Whereas globalization is an objective, real historical process which marks, in a sentence, the ascendancy of real-time, trans-border economic activity over clock-time economic activity (whether domestic or trans-border), globalism is the reification of this process of globalization as some meta-historical force that develops outside of human agency, conditioning and limiting the scope for action of individuals and collectivities alike, be they nation-states or local groups. Globalism as an ideology adds a belief in the *inescapability* of the transnationalization of economic and financial flows to the existing credos of neo-liberalism, namely the belief in the efficiency of free competitive markets and the belief that this efficiency will maximize benefits for the greatest number of people in the long run. These beliefs are based on what Pierre Bourdieu has described as '*doxa*' – 'an evidence not debated and undebatable'.[33]

Globalization and US Strategic Dominance

However, I would argue that the globalism discourse does more than this: it also serves to obscure the fact that global capitalism is an American political project serving the interests primarily of US capital and the US domestic economy. Set against a backdrop of twenty years of alleged US hegemonic decline, and the consequent perceived problematic of global governance, globalization is usually presented as an anarchic, chaotic, crisis-prone process in which 'the power of flows take precedence over the flows of power' in Castells' elegant phrase.[34] Global financial markets are variously described as being irrational, unpredictable and out of control. Recurrent crises such as the Mexican peso crisis of 1994, the Asian financial crisis of 1997, and the subsequent financial collapse of Russia, are all presented as testimony to the driverless machine that globalization has become.

There are other ways of looking at this driverless machine. In an important book, provocatively titled, *The Global Gamble: Washington's Faustian Bid for Global Dominance*, Peter Gowan notes that most of the literature on globalization, on international regimes and on general developments in the international political economy have simply ignored the great levers of American power.[35] He argues that there is a dynamic, dialectical relationship between private actors in international financial markets and US government dollar policy. He calls this interface the Dollar–Wall Street Regime (DWSR). In chronological order, key features of this DWSR were *deliberately* put in place, first by US President Richard Nixon when he insisted on the recycling of petro-dollars through the Atlantic's world private banks (led by US banks at that time), and next by Nixon's strategy of 'liberating' international financial markets, replacing American hegemony based on direct power over states to a more market-based or structural form of power.[36] Then came US control over IMF/World Bank and the subsequent Washington Consensus (under President Carter), in which the US government developed ways of extending the influence of Wall Street over international finance without putting its own big commercial banks at risk: 'Washington discovered that when its international financial operators reached the point of insolvency through their international activities, they could be bailed out by the populations of the borrower countries at almost no significant cost to the US economy'.[37] Third, under the Reagan and Bush Administrations there came the yo-yoing dollar–yen policy from the mid-1980s to the mid-1990s, when first the yen was made to rise against the dollar, driving Japanese companies into East Asia, and then a forced reversal of this exchange rate was followed by an imposed liberalization of the East Asian capital markets.[38] These policies may well be argued to have caused the financial collapse that ensued. And finally, this again was followed by IMF rescue packages, widely condemned but supported and upheld by the USA with very convenient consequences for US corporations and the US domestic economy.[39] Attempts by Japan and China (with strong support from governments in the region) to establish an Asian Monetary Fund to stabilize the currencies of the affected countries were immediately scuppered by the USA.[40] We shall examine these issues more fully in Chapter 10.

Thus, instead of being an unstoppable force of nature against which every nation-state is powerless, Gowan argues compellingly that the process of globalization has been driven relentlessly by deliberate US Treasury and business interests in a conscious bid to extend strategic dominance over the world economy.

Since the early 1990s, this reassertion of US power over the international economy has begun to pay dividends for the American economy. Joe Quinlan, a senior analyst for the American investment bank Morgan Stanley, fears that globalization might be coming to an end precisely because 'no one has reaped more benefits from globalization than the United States and Corporate America'.[41] Here are just a few examples of how the US economy has benefited from its super power position:

1. Since the early 1980s, net capital inflows into the USA have continuously exceeded net outflows, and yet at the same time, the economy has frequently been a net exporter of FDI.[42] What this implies is that US corporate capital has unique advantages of leverage, being able to invest and control direct investments abroad while also being able to raise the funds for it from debt in perpetuity.

2. In the short period between 1994 and 1998, US corporations resumed their previous commanding heights in the worldwide corporate hierarchy, with five corporations in the top ten (up from three in 1994); thirty-five in the top 100 (up from twenty-three), and 187 in the top 500, up from 125[43] – there are no prizes for guessing that the outcome of the East Asian crisis, when currencies collapsed and businesses were bankrupted, was that US corporations were particularly well-placed to pursue take-over activity.[44]

3. The greater the volatility of the global financial system, and hence the greater the perceived risks, the more the 'safe haven' effect kicks in. The risk premium spread on international securities is now in the region of 1500 basis points between Wall Street and many 'emerging' stock markets.[45] This has led some stock-market analysts to claim that the American stock market is even now 'undervalued'. In any case, the consensus of academic opinion is that the relationship between stock performance on Wall Street and economic growth has become essentially 'patternless'.[46] Whatever the US economy does, money from all over the world will go into American stocks.

4. The US dollar enjoys unrivalled dominance in the global financial markets, on *any* count: in 1995 it comprised 61.5 per cent of all central bank foreign exchange reserves; it was the currency in which 76.8 per cent of all international bank loans and 39.5 per cent of all international bond issues were denominated; it constituted 44.3 per cent of all Eurocurrency deposits; it served as the invoicing currency for 47.6 per cent of world trade; and it was one of the two currencies in 83 per cent of all foreign exchange transactions.[47] As Antonio Negri aptly stated: 'Money has only one face, that of the boss.'[48] No less a person than the US President, Bill Clinton himself, has admitted that there is a so-called 'seigneurial' advantage to the dollar's key currency – and international creditor status. This means that the US effect-

ively gets a zero-interest loan when dollar bills are held abroad. In the President's Economic Report of 1999 this seigneurial advantage was estimated to amount to $13 billion dollars per year.[49] In other words, this is a 'gift' from the world to the US every year to an amount that is about twice the level of total 'official' lending and grants to the whole of Sub-Saharan Africa in any one year.

5.   Linked to this there is the huge and continuing benefit of net capital inflows that permit the perpetual running of a current-account deficit. Commenting on the large capital inflows, the American President put the situation very clearly 'The investment boom that the US enjoyed since 1993 ... the growth of output and employment ... would all have been smaller had the US not been able to run a current account deficit in the 1990s.'[50] Many commentators of the 'new economy' paradigm (see Chapter 5) have noted the importance of 'venture capital' in the USA that has been there at the right time to enable the super-smart Silicon boys to get going.[51] And venture capital is what the USA has in abundance, but it would not have it had the USA not been the pole of attraction for monies from all over the world. There is a parallel here with what economic historians such as Paul Baran used to say about the decisive role played by economic surplus expropriated through mercantile adventures from foreign lands during the industrialization of Britain.[52] If indeed there proves to be such a thing as a 'new economy', beginning in America in the 1990s, future economic historians may well attribute a similar decisive role to the abundance of foreign surplus capital that flowed into the USA at this precise time.

The fiction that all of this is the product of a historical accident is constantly being peddled. The US economy just 'happens' to be the largest economy in the world; people all over the world have 'confidence' in the dollar (as the American President puts it); globalization is creating a level playing field in which the most productive economy with the most competitive conditions wins, and so on. Here is where the globalist discourse performs its most important function: it is designed to make people believe in fair play, and what could be fairer than the neutral forces of the market? The more we can be persuaded that 'the markets' control events beyond any politician's dream of intervention, the more effectively the ideology works. Indeed, the very accusation that markets behave 'irrationally', as when, for example, stock markets in East Asia collapse despite the economic fundamentals of the affected economies reportedly being sound, and nobody could have expected, or did expect, it, the more people believe in God or 'neutral' market forces commanding their destinies, rather than political thuggery. The very notion that global financial markets are subject to speculative behaviour of which nobody approves (least of all the leading speculators themselves: for example, George Soros),[53] the very admission that nobody, not even the cleverest men and women at the Bank for International Settlements, quite understands how the financial markets 'work' – all this adds up to a great narrative and theatre behind which real power, push and bullying hides. The American political scientist, Samuel Huntington, in an article in 1999, catalogues a full page of US bullying tactics that were applied at the latter end of the 1990s, including the targeting of thirty-five countries with economic sanctions.[54] Last, but not least, the resurgence of US strategic dominance is also in evidence within those international forums of élite interaction we have described above, and which some analysts have identified as a platform for a new form of global regulation. The World Bank and the IMF are dominated by the USA as a consequence of a system of voting rights that is weighted according to economic size and contribution, while the WTO, which prides itself in being an entirely democratic institution of over 130 nations with a one-member-one-vote system, arrives at decisions through a 'consensus' approach in which the capacity of large nations who can afford many legal experts and permanent representations has power over outcomes of deliberations. Such capacity is all that matters. For example, in 1997–8 the USA brought more disputes than the rest put together, and achieved more settlements in its favour (eleven out of fifteen).[55] During the ill-fated MAI drafting, the USA added over 600 pages of exceptions for itself, including a general exception for all its federal, state and local laws.[56]

Imperialism and Hegemony

What has been described as the 'deafening silence over imperialism'[57] is probably the most cunning achievement of neo-liberal brainwashing that has accompanied US corporate control over the world economy. Imperialism exists whenever there is *deliberate* transnational political interference, including (though not exclusively) military intervention, for the purposes of the mobilization, extraction and external transfer of economic surplus from one political territory to another. Those who argue that imperialism is strictly a feature of interstate relations and therefore no longer on the agenda of capitalism under the conditions of globalization[58] simply miss the point that capitalism at all times produces a network of hierarchical relations in which the wealth of some areas, groups or peoples are dependent on the transfer of economic surplus, and hence the underdevelopment of other areas, groups and people.

In the age of globalization, imperialism manifests itself in ways that are in some respects distinct from, and additional to, other forms of imperialism that have accompanied, respectively, precolonial, colonial and neocolonial times. For globalization, as we have seen, is linked systemically with social exclusion, meaning that as globalization proceeds, more and more social groups, segments of population, as well as whole areas and regions, are being excluded from its benefits.

This has two implications for the type of imperialist intervention that we see happening around us. First, it makes more (and not less) pressing the need for state-sponsored and militarily-backed strategic control over vital resources in foreign lands, as host nations in the periphery collapse into zones of instability, and fracture into rival factions and groups, warlordism and banditry. This would explain the USA's increasingly belligerent geopolitical preparedness around the world. Notably, *in 1999 alone*, there has been: the enlargement of NATO to reach a new line of defence from Estonia to Bulgaria; a new dispensation of NATO's strategic defence commitment, which now includes 'out of area' operations; a revised US–Japan security alliance, which commits Japan's military to an actively supportive role in the event of US involvement in any conflict breaking out in the 'areas surrounding Japan'. This revised security pact has rightly been dubbed: 'the Asian corollary of Nato'.[59] Next, there is the new Theatre Defence Missile Defence system in East Asia,[60] and the new 'son of Star Wars' project, the US$100 billion National Missile Defence system, the super-sensitive electronic surveillance centre of which is located high on the Yorkshire moors in the UK (at RAF

Menwith Hill), but completely under the control of the American Security Agency.[61]

It further explains why, since the collapse of the Soviet Union and the end of the Cold War, the USA has negotiated 'access' arrangements for troop and equipment deployment in thirty-eight countries (thirty in the Third World), in addition to the hundred bases in sixteen foreign lands that it already possessed. As Daniel Shirmer writes, the reasons for this type of US 'forward deployment' in the Third World have to do with what the Pentagon calls 'challenges to regional stability', but they also have direct commercial advantages, and he quotes a senior Pentagon official:

> We are protecting those countries and they owe us. Don't think it does not come up in our trade negotiations. It gives us leverage. The Japanese know we are protecting their investments in Korea, Taiwan, and all over Asia, and that gets their attention when we ask them for money. For years we had an understanding with Taiwan that if an American company's bid came within 10 percent of a Japanese bid, we could get the contracts. They would tell us: 'The Japanese make it better, but you're protecting us'.[62]

Second, social exclusion *within* nations builds up pressures for the territorial expulsion of excluded groups. The resulting spectre of economic and political refugees in turn threatens the social stability of the rich nations to which they flee. In this way, globalization, paradoxically, reinforces the need to maintain, at all costs, the *de jure* interstate system and to uphold the legal sovereignty of states (while crushing them politically, and wiping them out economically), so as to enforce the obligations of states to keep within their borders the people who carry their passports. Here is where the 'new doctrine of international community', coined by the British Prime Minister, Tony Blair, in his speech on the eve of NATO's fiftieth anniversary, comes into its own. The 'new doctrine' overrides the UN Security Council's general principle of non-interference in those cases where domestic human rights abuses present 'threats to international peace and security'.[63] The application of this doctrine, more aptly dubbed the 'new military humanism' by Noam Chomsky[64] in the recent war over Kosovo is an example that is set to be followed by others.

Conclusion

By the end of the 1990s it appeared that the long period of crisis and transformation of the world capitalist system had at last come to some sort of conclusion. New production technologies and new product innovations have combined with a reconfiguration of the map of the world economy through processes of globalization to create a new market equilibrium. A new, social rather than geographic, core–periphery hierarchy has developed which enables minority segments of the Third World to participate in the benefits of this new capitalist world economy, together with majority populations in its traditional heartlands. But this reconfiguration draws an ever-sharper divide between those who are in and those who are outside it. The longer-term *un*sustainability of this world order is witnessed in increasingly chaotic disturbances, violence and conflict in the periphery. International regulation of the globalized core of the world economy has drawn in the political class of rich countries and many poor countries alike in abandoning national programmes of economic development and social solidarity in favour of international competitiveness and transnational engagement. While the structural power of international capital has become interwoven with a culture of 'international business civilization' to become institutionalized in international regimes of governance of the IMF, World Bank and the WTO, none of this adds up to a stable, sustainable regime of geogovernance. Instead, new forms of US imperialism have taken hold, both to direct global markets and the globalist imperative, and to confront and subjugate the crises in the peripheries. Whether all this adds up to a new US 'hegemony' is a moot point, and remains for the time being open-ended. The USA prefers to have its geostrategic, and particularly its military, operations conducted with the full consent of its NATO allies, and the role of Britain, for the moment at least, seems to be as a bridging partner to an often reluctant European Union. We shall return to this question of the hegemonic nature of US resurgence in the conclusion to this book, when we discuss possible scenarios for the future.

PART III
THE POSTCOLONIAL WORLD

Introduction

In Part II we described the transformative directions of the world capitalist system. While it is over-ambitious to pin one label on the totality of all the complex, interactive changes, some writers nevertheless suggest that these changes add up to a transformation of capitalism from its modern stage to a postmodern stage.[1] This stage is characterized by new, flexible systems of production; a predominance of high-tech industries; economic enterprise orientation towards niche markets and consumerism; globalization of markets and of forms of regulation; fictitious capital formation; and the ascendancy of a hegemonic neo-liberal ideology.

Crucially, as Fedric Jameson has argued, this transformation does not permit developing countries to complete the project of modernity. For international capital, moving rapidly from one low-wage situation to the next, only cybernetic technology and postmodern investment opportunities are ultimately attractive. Yet, in the new international system, few countries can seal themselves off in order to modernize in their own time and at their own pace. Thus the disappearance of the 'Third World' is a constitutional feature of postmodern, or what I prefer to call – globalized capitalism.

Acknowledging that the Third World is no longer a unitary category or has a homogeneous identity, the aim in this part of the book is to capture the differential impact on, and responses to, globalization in those regions of the world that used to be gathered under the label 'Third World'. Nevertheless, in describing those regions and those responses as 'postcolonial' I borrow a theoretical concept for which I first must give some justification and offer clarification. For what indeed is the point of erasing one unitary label, only to scribble in another?

Part of the answer, pragmatically, lies in the popularity that the concept enjoys today. And since a central purpose of this book is to introduce key contemporary trends and issues, I cannot ignore the rising tide, even institutional endorsement,[2] of postcolonial studies, which claims as its special provenance the field that used to go by the name of 'Third World studies' or 'development studies'.

But over and above this, I do believe that the concept has heuristic value because of its timeliness: it has entered the lexicon of development studies simultaneously as the product of, engagement with, *and* as contestation of globalization. In the reshuffled order of the global economy, where First Worlds have appeared in the Third World, and Third Worlds in the First World, postcolonial studies opens up three windows, or angles of vision. First, such studies dispute that one can infer 'identity' by looking at material relations alone. The politics of cultural identity and recognition have become as important as the politics of redistribution; and, as Nancy Fraser argues, they can support the politics of redistribution.[3] Second, postcolonial studies puts a referent emphasis on the cultural *complexity* of identity formation. Cross-border migrations have resulted in fragmentation and heterogenous mixes of belonging, and loyalties and political allegiances, in which class and nation have become 'decentred' as a source of identity. Third, postcolonialism is suggestive and reflexive of a world no longer structured along binary axes, be they First World/Third World; North/South, East/West or socialist/capitalist.

The concept is, however, far from being unproblematic. While it seems to be succeeding in 'destabilizing' the development debate, it has also been accused of intellectual escapism and critical paralysis.[4] Let us first examine the concept and these debates more fully before deciding on how we can best make use of it in organizing the chapters in this part of the book.

The Postcolonial: Condition and Discourse

The term 'postcolonial' is a member of a family of 'post' literature, of which 'postmodernism' is the all-embracing generic term. And, as is the case with all this 'post' literature, the word 'post' pulls us into a semantic trap. It expresses an epistemological break with the all-encompassing totality of Western thought and scientific tradition while also signalling an epochal sequentiality. The problem, however, is that those who make the epistemological break reject the 'foundationalism' and the 'essentialism' that underpins the historical analysis by which the epochal succession is diagnosed. Needless to say, this has led to largely fruitless debates between the two camps.

In her critique of postmodernism, Ellen Meiksins Wood reminds us of how the sociologist C. Wright Mills had formulated this intellectual conundrum: the crisis of reason and freedom which marked the onset of the postmodern age, he said, presented 'structural problems, and to state them requires that we work in the classic terms of human biography and epochal history. Only in such terms can the connections of structures and milieux that affect these values today be traced and causal analyses be conducted'.[5] But, comments Meiksins Wood, 'this statement is in nearly every particular anti-thetical to the current theories of postmodernity which effectively deny the very existence of structure and structural connections and the very possibility of "causal analysis"'.[6] Exactly so, and thus it is with postcolonial theory! In fact, much of the debate surrounding the use of the term 'postcolonial' repeats *mutatis mutandis* the debates around the term 'postmodern'.

With regard to postmodernism, those writers who have engaged with it from a historical structural, or Marxist, perspective, – for example, David Harvey and Fedric Jameson – have done so by resorting to the only theoretical option available under the circumstances, namely to distinguish between postmodernism as 'condition' and postmodernism as 'critique'. And, again, so it is with the concept 'postcolonial'. Following Arif Dirlik, who has tried to bring the postcolonial discourse into the arena of global political economy,[7] I intend to treat postcolonial discourse as a 'cultural condition' or 'logic' that corresponds to the specific geopolitical and economic configuration of what we have earlier referred to as postmodern or globalized capitalism. In short, we shall understand what 'postcolonial' is from an understanding of *how*, and *why* it all began.

Based on a strict semantic interpretation one would think that the word 'postcolonial' refers to the period after independence – that is, after formal colonialism has ended. Yet this is *not* what the term is intended to mean now. Ella Shohat, in her crisp interrogation of the concept, describes it as 'a designation for critical discourses which thematize issues emerging from colonial relations and their aftermath, covering a long historical span (including the present).'[8] This also covers, pointedly, the postindependence, neocolonial, period which was stabilized under the American-led Bretton Woods postwar order.

Thus, 'postcolonial' implies a movement going beyond anti-colonial nationalist theory as well as a movement beyond a specific point in history, that of colonialism *and* Third-World nationalist struggles. Noting how historical specificity collapses under chronological diversity, Shohat asks, somewhat impatiently, 'When, exactly, then, does the "post-colonial" begin?'[9] To which Arif Dirlik quips, 'When Third World intellectuals have arrived in First World academe'.[10] The term originated, in the mid-1980s, among Third-World scholars in First-World universities, who were caught up in diasporic circumstances caused by the crisis of the Third World and the failure of the developmental and democratic project in many Third-World countries. Whether forced into exile, or as voluntary émigrés, they have regrouped around a discourse of identity that owes less to geographic location and national origin than to *subject position*. This confluence of historical and biographical details explains much of the epistemology and substantive theory that was to emerge.

As Arif Dirlik notes, the release of postcoloniality from the fixity of Third-World location, means that the identity of the postcolonial is no longer structural but *discursive*. That is to say, it is the participation in the discourse that defines the postcolonial. The postcolonial discourse or critique resonates with concerns and orientations that have their origins in a new world situation created by transformations within the capitalist world economy, by the emergence of what has variously been described as 'global capitalism', 'flexible production', 'late capitalism' and so on, terms that have disorganized earlier conceptualizations of global relations, especially relations comprehended earlier by such binaries as colonized/colonizer, First World/Third World, and 'the West and the Rest', in all of which the nation-state was taken for granted as the global unit of political organization.

But here comes the epistemological twist: even as postcolonial discourse thus engages with global times, postcolonial critics, with few exceptions, do not interrogate that relationship because they repudiate a foundational role to capitalism in history.[11] By ignoring the political economy approach they have invited criticism of being apolitical and ahistorical, and even complicit in the 'consecration of hegemony'.[12]

So much for the 'condition' of postcoloniality. Let us now turn to postcolonial discourse, or postcolonial critique, itself.

In First-World academe, Third-World scholars found a welcome home and symbiotic environment in the burgeoning discipline, and polemics, of 'cultural studies'. Cultural studies began as literature critique in English literature and linguistics departments, as did postcolonial studies subsequently. The central terrain and mode of questioning in studies such as *The Empire Writes Back*,[13] *Colonial Discourse and Postcolonial Theory*[14] and *Decolonising the Mind*[15] are literature and literature criticism. This too matches the careers of Third-World intelligentsia, many of whom first found a voice through literary writing.[16]

Cultural studies, in Raymond Williams' classic definition, investigates the creation of meaning in, and as a formative part of, a whole way of life, the whole world of sense-making (descriptions, explanations, interpretations, valuations of all kinds) in societies understood as historical material organizations.[17] Its terrain of inquiry is 'mass' or 'popular' culture in all its manifestations: language, film, magazines, TV soap operas, shopping, advertising and so on. It is political and polemical (and massively irritating to structural Marxists) in so far as it argues that the masses are not merely passive recipients of a culture wickedly designed by capitalists to suck them into consumerism, exploitation and subjugation, but instead are actively participating and contributing. Their participation can be deliberate, creative, selective and even subversive.

Culture is also the vehicle or medium whereby the relationship between groups is transacted. The emancipatory promise and purpose of cultural studies is to discover resistance and subversive creativity in the cultural relationship between dominant and subordinated groups, and help to reverse it, as when Frantz Fanon once argued that Europe is literally the creation of the Third World. Cultural studies does this *first* by deconstructing the texts, words, names, labels and definitions of the situation that have been authored by the dominant groups, and *next* by giving people of all subordinated groups – women, blacks, gays, peasants and indigenous peoples – their voices back through a 'new historicism', or through a new style of anthropology, as in ethnographic accounts of local cultural practices of resistance and protest. Third, cultural studies is emancipatory in so far as it links, through its interventions, the experience of these diverse social groups, and potentially brokers new political alliances between them.

Within this broad field and style of enquiry, postcolonial discourse nestled organically to engage in a radical rethink and reformulation of forms of knowledge and social identities authored and authorized by colonialism and Western domination. For example, it critiques both the idea and the practice of 'development' as well as the concept of the Third World as part of a Eurocentric discourse of control and subordination. Much of this literature rewrites and 'counter-appropriates' the history of the 'subalterns' (the subordinated 'others'), making their voices of resistance heard (past and present), reversing orientalist thought, and decolonizing the mind. The goal is to undo all partitioning strategies between centre and periphery as well as all other 'binarisms' that are the legacy of colonial ways of thinking, and to reveal societies globally in their complex heterogeneity and contingency. In this way, postcolonial discourse aims to reconstruct the identities of subordinated peoples, give them back their pride of place in history, and with it the confidence to build on the record of their own 'hybrid position of practice and negotiation'.[18]

The concept of 'hybridity' occupies a central place in postcolonial discourse and it is a good example of the 'reverse value-coding' that Gyan Prakash speaks of as one of the strategies of the discourse.[19] In colonial days, 'hybridity' was a term of abuse, signifying the lowest possible form of human life: mixed 'breeds' who were 'white but not quite'.[20] In postcolonial discourse, by contrast, hybridity is celebrated and privileged as a kind of superior cultural intelligence through the advantage of 'in-betweenness', the straddling of two cultures and the consequent ability to 'negotiate the difference'. Reinterpeting Fanon, for example, Homi Bhabha argues that the liberatory 'people' who initiate the productive instability of revolutionary cultural change are themselves the bearers of hybrid identity.[21] In development studies, an analysis in terms of hybrid cultures leads to a reconceptualization of established views. Namely that, rather than being eliminated by modernity, many 'traditional cultures' survive through their transformative engagement with modernity.[22] In the ensuing chapters of this book we shall encounter illustrations of this 'hybridization' in each of the 'zones' of development that we shall be discussing, whether it be the Confucianization of modernity, as in East Asia, or the postdevelopment trajectories of Latin-American peasant communities and slum dwellers.

Postcolonial Formations

One does not have to buy into the whole of the postcolonial discourse to appreciate that the concept has merits in helping us to understand the diversity of development and underdevelopment trajectories in these global times. It is the colonial and neocolonial experience, and the manner in which the aftermath interacts with globalization, that illuminates the different outcomes, namely a different postcolonial formation in various parts of the world system at the same time. As the titles of these chapters suggest, we shall study these different forms of the postcolonial condition in four major zones of the world. While the word 'zone' still carries with it a notion of area-specific location, there is nevertheless a certain fluidity and ambiguity between the area-referential emphasis and the subject-positional one.

Thus, in Chapter 8, we look at the peripheralizing consequences of globalization prevalent in many parts of the Third World, but we focus on how these have become exemplified and, in a manner of speaking, have gone furthest in Sub-Saharan Africa. Debt, and deregulation following punitive structural adjustment programmes, have more tightly integrated the wealth of many Third-World élites in the global economy, while emasculating politically the states in these regions, thus undermining their capacity to relaunch any national territorial developmental project. Moreover, the imposition of the neo-liberal orthodoxy, coupled with the insistence on electoral reform and democracy, has not only undermined the state but has also contributed directly to the descent into anarchy and civil war of many countries in Africa. The ensuing political emergencies have drawn in the international donor community in a form of containment activity that may be summed up as the *management of exclusion* rather than a programme of development and incorporation. It is a management of exclusion that is becoming characteristic of the manner in which other areas at the edge of the global system are also being treated.

In Chapter 9 we examine the postcolonial condition of militant Islam. We argue that the failure of the neocolonial, developmentalist period has interacted with the historical cultural tradition of Islamic spiritual renewal and its subjection to cultural imperialism, feeding a process of cultural denial of globalization and modernity. While we shall not develop the theme of its resonance in other parts of the world, including the diasporic Muslim communities of the

West, it is clear that this anti-developmental postcolonial position, again, is one in which the area referent and subject position become fused. The *anti-developmentalism* of militant Islam is different in its origins and expression from both the *management of exclusion* in Sub-Saharan Africa and the *postdevelopment* response in Latin America.

The global process of transformation is neither even nor unopposed. In Chapter 10 we look at the experience of the 'developmental' states in East Asia which testify to the possibilities of national territorial accumulation and defensive regional alliances. It is an experience that owes as much to the end of the Cold War and *Pax Americana* as it does to the very same historical process of capitalist expansion and integration that peripheralized and marginalized other areas and communities in the world system. Here too there are lessons to be learnt from the locally-specific contestation of this postcolonial condition that may hold out the promise of successful replication in other areas of the periphery of the global system too.

Chapter 11 looks at Latin America, where the postmodern turn in development studies has gone furthest in promoting a postdevelopmentalist philosophy of liberation. Postdevelopment theory and practice is different from anti-development sentiments in so far as it does not deny globalization or modernity, but wants to find some ways of living with it and imaginatively transcending it. Much of the creative thinking about new social movements and the development of civil society originates on this continent. Yet, as before, the hybrid forms of struggle and local experimentations with alternative social and economic organization are not exclusive to Latin America but are also found elsewhere, including the heartland of the traditional core of the capitalist system. Thus, these 'postdevelopments' also reflect conditions, and inspire responses, that may be of relevance to other social groups and localities within the global system.

8

Africa: Exclusion and the Containment of Anarchy

Debates on Sub-Saharan Africa (SSA) usually begin with a genuflexion to the size and variety of the continent, and the consequent impossibility of making generalizations. Yet once such qualifications are out of the way, the commonality of Africa's colonial and postcolonial history asserts itself soon enough, to reveal comparable economic structures and political dynamics.

Sub-Saharan Africa contains thirty-two out of the UN's forty 'least developed' member countries. Early post-independence growth, while still externally dependent, was nevertheless a source of hope and optimism. But this was followed by stagnation and negative growth in all but a very few countries (for example, Mauritius, Botswana) as earlier forms of incorporation into the international division of labour were rendered obsolete when the world economic system globalized and entered what Manuel Castells has referred to as the 'newest' international division of labour.[1] Since the mid-1970s, Africa's primary commodities trade has collapsed, from just over 7 per cent of world trade to less than 0.5 per cent in the 1990s.[2] Its share of manufacturing trade never really got a chance to lift off and went down from an already puny 1.2 per cent in 1970 to 0.4 per cent in the late 1990s. The exclusionary logic of the present globalized world order is most dramatically attested in foreign direct investment (FDI) flows. Africa's share of all FDI flows to developing countries has dropped from 13 per cent in 1980 to less than 5 per cent in the late 1990s. Private (non-public guaranteed) finance now contributes less than a tenth of the resource flows into the continent, the rest being made up of various forms of

Table 8.1. Sub-Saharan Africa: selected indicators of stagnation and decline

Production
average annual growth rate[a] per cent

	1965–73	1973–84	1980–90	1990–98
GDP	5.4	1.8	1.8	2.2
agriculture	2.7	0.9	2.5	2.6
industry	9.7	1.3	0.9	1.2
services	5.0	2.1	2.4	2.1

food production[b]
index: *1974–76 = 100*

	1982/84	1989/91	1995/97
	92	113	138

Income and consumption

GNP per capita average annual growth rates[c]

1965–84	1985–94	1996/7	1997/8
2.4	−1.2	4.2	−0.4

Average growth of private consumption per capita[d]

1965–73	1973–84	1980–97
3.8	3.1	−2.1

Per capita food supplies for direct human consumption[e]

Calories/day		protein per day, change %,
1970	1997	1970–96
2226	2205	−5.7

commercial energy use (kg of oil equivalent)[f]

1980	1996
720	670

Health and education

Life expectancy at birth[g]

1965	1986	1997
42	52	49

Infant mortality rate per 1000 live births[h]

	1980	1997
	115	91

Education: enrolment ratio of secondary pupils[i]
(percentage of relevant age group)

1965	1980	1993	1997
4	16	23	41

Sources: (a) (c) (d) (f) (g) and (i) World Bank, *World Development Report*, 1998/9 and 2000 for recent years and 1986 for preceding years (weighted averages); (b) recalibrated from World Bank, *World Development Report* 1986 and 2000 using the same index year; (e) and (h) UNDP, *Human Development Report*, 1999.

aid[3]. The vital economic statistics, portrayed in Table 8.1, sum up the calamitous reversal of economic conditions that the continent suffered in the last two decades of the twentieth century. To all intents and purposes it seems that Africa has become structurally irrelevant to the present global economic order.

Even so, Sub-Saharan Africa's foreign debt, which has trebled from US$84.1 billion to US$235.4 billion since the debt crisis first broke in 1982[4] remains its foremost intractable problem, and the noose that keeps it articulated to the global capitalist system. Africa's debt gives the international community enormous leverage over the political and economic trajectories of the inflicted countries. This is the prime reason why, for all the apparent progress toward debt forgiveness, as in the now formally endorsed highly indebted poor countries (HIPC) initiative which involves debt reduction for forty-one highly-indebted countries (thirty-three of them African), little real progress has been made, because the eligibility criteria are linked to the acceptance by the candidate countries of 'sound policies' dictated by the international community. These are focused narrowly on re-engagement with the global economy through trade-related measures, and the development of democracy and civil society, rather than poverty reduction and human development. One key question we want to ask in this chapter is what the real objective of the international community is in imposing these 'sound' policies in the context of Africa's manifest exclusion from the globalized world order.

Economic crises have bred political crises as country after country has tumbled into endemic instability, conflict or outright civil war. In his 1998 political report on Africa, Kofi Annan, Secretary General of the United Nations, noted that fourteen of the continent's fifty-three countries had been afflicted by armed conflict in 1996 alone, and that over thirty wars had occurred in Africa since 1970, mainly within states, 'counting for more than half of all war-related deaths world wide' in that period[5]. As a consequence, there are now 12 million refugees and displaced people in Africa. Julius Ihonvbere writes: 'The African condition today is to say the very least, pathetic'. And he quotes Lance Morrow: 'Africa is in a scramble for existence.'[6]

However hard one tries to discern variations in comparative politics, the dominant features of Africa's postcolonial political trajectory cannot be gainsaid. For these too stem from the structural constraints of external dependency and the imposition of foreign political models. Nation-statism was a colonial legacy with shallow foundations in Africa's own history. In the absence of a home-grown capitalist bourgeoisie and strong civil society traditions, a bureaucratic state was fashioned and financed to perform a welfare and accumulation role by an international policy consensus that cared more about land access than the promotion of democracy. As intermediaries between their people and financial resource flows from abroad, these states became the main source of income, and the control of the state became a matter of survival. Whether one characterizes the African postcolonial state as weak, patrimonial, clientelist, or merely inefficient and corrupt, the fact remains that all these states imploded when the international community, led by the IMF and the World Bank called in their loans and rolled out a new agenda for Africa. This agenda imposed the discipline of the market and sought to combine privatization and liberalization with new forms of political governance in which the state was marginalized in favour of a strengthening of civil society. As we shall argue in this chapter, in so doing, these policies had a fractitious impact on the social order and hastened the descent into tribalism and civil strife.

The purpose of this chapter is twofold. First, we need to clarify how the transition from internationalization to globalization has transformed the international community's relationship and man-agement of Africa's economy through debt-peonage. Because there are parallels in this process with the way the globalized capitalist system deals with other peripheral regions in the Third World, we shall cast this discussion in more general terms to enable us to refer back to them when we discuss similar issues and problems in the chapters on the Middle East and Latin America. Next we shall look at the structural consequences of the neo-liberal stranglehold in Africa, where it has reduced or eliminated the integrity of what were fragile national states and pushed them into anarchy and civil wars.

Debt and Developmentalism

In the 1970s, the massive expansion of Third-World debt began at the precise moment when Third-World economic nationalism reached its peak and, it seemed, its near actualization in OPEC generated petrodollar recycling. In 1974, the General Assembly of the United Nations adopted the (now defunct) Declaration on the Establishment of a New International Economic Order, followed in 1976 by the (now equally defunct) Charter of Economic Rights and Duties of States. This charter enshrined for the first time the right of nationalization and the right to regulate compensation for national-ization as a principle of international law. Petrodollars helped to fund the state nationalization of foreign-owned enterprises and ambitious development programmes.

In this same period, the international community authored a 'developmentalist' model in the Third World that effectively backed up autocratic regimes and helped to finance bureaucratic state apparatuses with a view to overcoming what in those days were perceived as 'internal blockages' – for example, the absence of a local entrepreneurial business class. State-led development spawned a plethora of government interventions in both external and internal markets, including the setting of dual exchange rates; the erection of tariffs and other import controls, as well as domestic subsidies on staple foods and petrol; and the provision of social and welfare services, such as health and education, all of this well beyond the internal financial capacity of the state. In so doing, it not only built up a mountain of external debt, but it also buttressed a bulging bureaucracy, fed a kleptocratic élite and made corruption at all levels an endemic feature. All this was condoned by an international chorus of donors and scholars, for two reasons, one scientific and one strategic. While the scientific reason hinged on a theory of 'late development', on the nature of modernization and the need to 'catch up' with the West, the strategic reason simply had to do with the realities of the Cold War and the perceived need to keep Africa and other underdeveloped lands in the capitalist camp.

Paradoxically, easy access to Arab petrodollars, which were all too eagerly recycled by international banks caught in a monetarist freeze in their core country markets, also encouraged the privatiza-tion of Third-World debt. By the end of the 1970s, commercial lending and public lending had reversed their traditional postwar positions, with commercial lending to the Third World outstripping public lending by a ratio of 3:1.[7]

As R.T. Naylor[8] has shown, against the backdrop of ambitious development programmes, the privatization of Third-World debt in its turn created the very conditions for the massive diversion of foreign borrowing by private individuals to personal deposits in foreign banks. The strategies deployed encompassed every deceitful trick: from stolen airline tickets to phoney invoicing; overvaluing the costs of imports and under-reporting the receipts from exports, with the difference stashed abroad; smuggling drugs and commodities, currencies and precious metals; and last, but not least, commissions and kickbacks price-tagged to officially-recorded borrowing but banked in safe havens abroad.

By the early 1980s, when the debt crisis broke, official estimates put the amount of capital fleeing Third-World countries at between US$80–100 billion, or about 25 per cent of Third-World outstanding debt. But, interestingly, it was not until the very end of the debt decade that the international banking community openly pointed an accusing finger at flight capital. It was only then that it became recognized as an essential cause as well as a consequence of the debt crisis.[9]

Debt, Globalization and the Neo-liberal Agenda

The moment of truth came in the early 1980s, when the failure of developmentalism to raise productivity and hard currency export earnings led to the inability to pay off the international debts incurred during the 'developmentalist' extravaganza. This failure must be understood within the context of changing world economic conditions, and of the integration and deregulation of financial markets, both of which we have identified earlier (Chapter 6) as the characteristic features of globalization. Globalization involves a seismic shift in market orientation towards intangible information-based products, while the application of information technology to the production process itself results in a long-term downward shift in prices for resource inputs. This is bad news for those peripheral regions in the world economy that have to pay their way by exporting primary commodities. Since the 1980s the terms of trade for primary commodities have begun a consistent, long-term downward trend. At the same time the information technology revolution has transformed the infrastructure of production, management and communication elsewhere in the global economy. Without the requisite infrastructure, whole regions are being excluded from participation in the new global division of labour. And in respect of network capability and network connectivity, Sub-Saharan Africa is, as we noted earlier, the 'switched off' region of the world.[10]

The earnings shortfall was compounded by the combined process of integration and deregulation of the world's financial markets which facilitated the merging of two streams of capital flow: private capital fleeing the Third World (some of it quite illegal from the national treasurer's point of view – in fact, diverted booty), and mainstream corporate and institutional funds that are raised on the money markets. As Naylor has put it:

> Recycling had taken a bizarre new twist. An ever growing number of off-shore banking centres and tax havens competed for the increasingly large supply of hot and footloose money fleeing the developing countries. The hot money was then lent through the eurobanking system funding loans to developing countries in need of hard currency to bolster their foreign exchange positions drained by capital flight.[11]

Money laundering became easy as it was progressively more difficult for public or national regulatory bodies to track illegal funds; indeed, with deregulation, the concept of illegality was whittled down to its minimum moral denominator, namely to include only those monies that were clearly derived from drug smuggling. After all, the emerging worldwide ideological regime of monetarism dictates that money must be free to flow across frontiers. Since the core of the capitalist world system has now moved to this higher level of financial integration, its institutions no longer recognize or respect the right of national governments in the periphery to control their currency areas.

The core creditor countries, among which the USA is still dominant, issue and control the value of the currencies in which most debts are denominated. In a world economy dominated by global financial markets, by money careening around the globe at a frenetic pace, the principal national economic objective of the core countries has become to maintain the competitive strength of their currency *vis-à-vis* each other, fighting domestic inflation that threatens this competitive strength, and trying to catch as much as possible of the careening capital flows in the net of their domestic currency areas. The trade wars of the past have been replaced by investment wars. However, the prevailing monetarist ideology with its emphasis on deregulation and privatization, and on the reduction of the size and influence of the public sector, permits only one instrument to achieve this objective: manipulation of interest rates.

It is therefore no coincidence that the 1980s, at least until the Louvre Accord in 1986, stand out as a period of historically unprecedented high and rising interest rates of the core currencies. Most of the outstanding stock of Third-World debt was originally contracted at low, fixed interest rates in the mid-1970s. They were, however, rescheduled in the early 1980s when floating (and rising) interest rates prevailed. The sharply increased commercial world-market interest rates of that period (of between 13 per cent and 16 per cent) coupled with the resulting improvement in the value of the core denomination currency (the US dollar) throughout the 1980s *added* to the debt service burden of the Third World.

The outcome was that, since 1983, and for the first time in the postwar period, *officially recorded* capital outflows from the Third World countries to the core countries annually exceeded the monies flowing into them.[12] F. C. Clairmont and J. Cavanagh,[13] in an article published in 1987 and covering the period 1981–6, have added to these figures an estimate of flight capital and profit remittances. Together these lifted the total net financial transfers over the period 1981–6 to a figure well over US$250 billion, representing the total financial contribution of the Third World to the advanced, core countries over that period. Allowing for price inflation, this figure was four times that of the US$13 billion in Marshall Aid with which the United States financed postwar recovery in Europe.

The Role of the IMF and the World Bank

Since the debt crisis broke in 1982, the year Mexico first declared a moratorium on its international debt payments, the IMF and World Bank have been commissioned and dispatched to the frontiers of the global economy to exact payments from and supervise the credits to the Third World. In this capacity they have been able to affect profoundly the organization of production and trade in the periphery to the benefit of the core of the world capitalist system. In all debt rescheduling exercises in the 1980s it has been the seal of approval of the IMF/World Bank as expressed in official memoranda of agreement and letters of intent exchanged between them and the debtor countries that has released, in complex and inter-active packages, official and commercial credit flows.[14]

Structural adjustment is the generic term used to describe a package of measures which the IMF, the World Bank and indi-vidual Western aid donors persuaded many developing countries to adopt during the 1980s, in return for a new wave of loans. As Adrian Leftwich notes, the aim of adjustment was to shatter the dominant postwar, state-led development paradigm and overcome the problems of developmental stagnation by promoting open and free competitive market economies, supervised by minimal states.[15] Between 1980 and 1990, World Bank structural adjustment loans increased from seven to 187 in sixty countries.[16]

The inventory of IMF/World Bank prescriptions is by now well known. It includes currency devaluation, deregulation of prices and wages, reduction of public spending on social programmes and state bureaucracies, removal of food subsidies and others on basic neces-sities, trade liberalization, privatization of parastatal enterprises, and the expansion of the export sector; the latter – in the case of agriculture – often at the expense of food production. The officially-stated aims of these policies was to stabilize domestic economies, to stimulate economic growth, and to ensure the country's ability to earn the foreign exchange needed to service its foreign debts.

However, there is another way of looking at this. According to critics,[17] debt peonage has given the international financial institu-tions (IFIs) a stranglehold over states and economies, especially in Africa. In a joint declaration to UNCTAD IX, held in Midrand, South Africa in 1996, African NGOs condemned the imposition of the neo-liberal paradigm through structural adjustment programmes (SAPs) as no less than a form of *re*colonization of the continent.[18] SAPs, it is argued, amount to the pillage of what remains of Africa's economic wealth.

Structural Adjustment in Africa: the Social and Economic Record

The 1980s saw twenty-nine Sub-Saharan African countries accept the IMF/World Bank medicine. Even in the stated objectives of the multilateral agencies themselves, the results were very disappoint-ing. Hewitt de Alcantara and Dharam Ghai estimated that, in the region as a whole, per capita incomes declined by 30 per cent over the period 1980–8,[19] and while it is true that political crises and civil wars in many countries have contributed to this staggering loss of income, the adverse international economic environment (as partly mediated through structural adjustment and debt management policies) can be held responsible for most of it. They argue that this is so, first, because of the *simultaneous* deterioration in nearly all of the countries of the region, including those relatively free from internal turmoil; and second because of the *magnitude* of the deteriorating external financial position of Sub-Saharan Africa over the period. Based on UN figures, they note an annual loss of US$6.5 billion over the period, even without taking into account capital flight. This total amounted to roughly a third of total annual imports, 45 per cent of export earnings, 10–11 per cent of the region's combined GDP, and 60 per cent of gross capital formation.[20]

The result was, in fact, so disappointing that a World Bank-sponsored report in 1992, given the frank title 'Why Structural Adjustment Has Not Succeeded in Sub-Saharan Africa', was retrieved from the publishers, reissued with a less controversial title and embellished with an introduction which pointed out that the analysis was in any case flawed, because it failed to distinguish countries that merely signed up to a reform programme from those that carried it out.[21] It next issued a more optimistic report on the lessons of structural adjustment in Sub-Saharan Africa.[22] Unsubtly shifting the blame for failure on to the governments of the countries themselves (for not having implemented the World Bank/IMF adjustment policies properly), it argued that only six countries got their macro-economic fundamentals 'about' right (Ghana, Tanzania, Gambia, Burkina Faso, Nigeria and Zimbabwe). This, the report claimed, has resulted in restored export competitiveness with low inflation and improved fiscal balance. But even these star performers, although eventually returning to positive GDP per capita growth rates, had deteriorating rates of investment. The other countries which implemented the policies only partially or not at all, or which backslid, the report argued, paid the price with negligible or deteriorating growth. But, as UNCTAD noted five years later, the 'recent faster growth' that has taken place in Sub-Saharan Africa 'has occurred in countries that were not among the World Bank's "core group of adjusters" and most of the countries that were thought to be pursuing relatively sound policies at the time, are not among the strong performers today'.[23] In any case, the UNCTAD report argues that the observed surges of growth can be explained by one-off factors and are unlikely to be sustained. The critical point is that, despite the implementation of structural reforms in about two-thirds of the Sub-Saharan Africa countries, the private investment response to SAPs continues to be weak.[24]

By the end of the millennium, the average growth rate for the continent had yet to catch up with population growth.[25] Its debt burden in relation to both GDP and in relation to export earnings had risen steeply. Indeed, as a proportion of GDP and of exports, the debt burden is the highest for any developing country.[26]

Outside IMF/World Bank circles, few observers have a positive word to say about structural adjustment. Non-government organizations (NGOs) working in the field in Africa are particularly scathing in their criticism, none more so than Kevin Watkins of British Oxfam. He sums up his devastating critique as follows:

> the application of stringent monetary policies, designed to reduce inflation through high interest rates, has undermined investment and employment. At the same time, poorly planned trade-liberalisation measures have exposed local industries to extreme competition. Contrary to World Bank and IMF claims, the position of the poor and most vulnerable sections of society have all too often been undermined by the deregulation of labour markets and erosion of social welfare provisions, and by declining expenditures on health and education. Women have suffered in extreme form. The erosion of health expenditure has increased the burdens they carry as carers, while falling real wages and rising unemployment have forced women into multiple low-wage employment in the informal sector.[27]

Structural Adjustment: Intensifying Global Relations

Even if the structural adjustment programmes (SAPs) achieved little or nothing from the point of view of national territorial development and the improvement of standards of living of the masses in

African countries, the programmes were a resounding success when measured in terms of the acceleration of the process of globalization. Structural adjustment has tied the physical resources of Africa more firmly into servicing the 'old' segment of the global economy. At the same time, it has oiled the financial machinery by which wealth is being transported out of the region, thereby removing the very resources which are needed by *dynamic* adjustment to the 'new' global economy.

Commodity specialization and debt go hand in hand. Both the World Bank and the IMF have used their leverage on indebtedness to require that production be concentrated on commodity exports. The consequence of this has been a flooding of the commodity markets which forced prices downwards. During the 1980s, the terms of trade for Sub-Saharan African commodities fell more rapidly than for any other region of the globe.[28] In fact, the terms of trade of Sub-Saharan Africa in the late 1990s were lower than in 1954.[29] This is by far the most pertinent criticism to make against the SAPs, namely that the excessive focus on export-orientated production has contributed to a decline in food production, thus making many countries vulnerable to famine and epidemics during periods of drought, war or other catastrophes. Food production per head was lower at the end of the 1990s than it was in the early 1970s.[30]

Second, forced privatization was a standard feature of all SAPs. In the words of one senior World Bank manager who resigned after twelve years' service: 'Everything we did from 1983 onwards was based on our new sense of mission to have the south "privatised" or die; towards this end we ignominiously created economic bedlam in Latin America and Africa.'[31] According to the World Bank, 400 industries were privatized in Africa in the 1980s. These included public utilities such as telecommunications, electricity companies, railways and credit organizations.[32] Inevitably, while national stock markets are still small and in the process of being formed, these privatization policies ensured that foreign investors got a large slice of the action. The under-capitalization of the emerging stock markets proved an attractive hunting ground for the active money managers of core countries' investment funds and more speculative instruments such as hedge funds.[33] The World Bank reports that between 1989 and 1995 US$1630 million-worth of foreign exchange was raised through privatization in Sub-Saharan Africa, well over half of the total of privatization revenues in the continent.[34]

Third, imposed devaluations and interest rate liberalizations have been justly criticized as encouraging high profits for the largely foreign-owned financial sector, while production is undermined.[35] Devaluation increases foreign debts in local currency terms while interest rate liberalization means that governments have to pay higher interest rates on domestic debt. The net result is that budget deficits actually worsen, and because governments are not allowed under SAP rules to print money they find themselves eventually borrowing more from the IFIs and the private financial markets.[36]

Democracy and Economic Reform

As the debt decade of the 1980s wore on, the political nature of the structural adjustment programmes, and of bilateral and other multilateral (for example, EU) programmes, became ever more strident and outspoken. Previously, Western governments and multilateral agencies, while professing a genuine interest in liberal democracy and human rights, had nevertheless been quite happy openly to sponsor repressive authoritarian regimes for the sake of a stable political climate. US President Bill Clinton, on tour in Africa in 1997, in candid contrition, even apologized for past US 'support' for brutal African despots because of his country's obsession with the Cold War. The World Bank, forbidden by its own articles of agreement to use overtly 'political' criteria, had similarly been uninterested in the nature of regimes.

However, in the drive for structural adjustment, Western governments from the late 1980s became increasingly outspoken in their preference for electoral, multiparty democracy as a precondition for further loans and grants. The World Bank, while still unable to insist on 'political' adjustment, began to favour a none-too-subtle form of 'good governance', which it defined as including the following features: an efficient public service; an independent judicial system and legal framework to enforce contracts; the accountable administration of public funds; an independent public auditor, responsible to a representative legislature; respect for the law and human rights at all levels of government; a pluralistic institutional structure; and a free press. All this adds up, as Adrian Leftwich writes, 'to a comprehensive statement of the minimum institutional, legal and political conditions of liberal democracy, though the Bank never stated this explicitly'. [37]

For its part, the European Union (EU) formally adopted political conditionality as an 'aid regime principle' in 1989, while the United States added a 'democracy initiative' under the auspices of USAID in 1991. [38] At the time of writing, almost without exception, African states have moved in the direction of competitive multiparty systems, with contested elections either having been held or due to be held in the near future. Between 1988 and 1993, the United Nations monitored ballot-box elections in some thirty Sub-Saharan countries.

What could explain this curious change of heart? Adrian Leftwich identifies four main influences: the experience of structural adjustment lending; the resurgence of neo-liberalism in the West; the collapse of official Communist regimes; and the rise of pro-democracy movements in the developing world and elsewhere. In short, we might say: the new world order. [39]

How does this 'democracy is good, state is bad' agenda assist economic reform? The link between democracy and debt restructuring in the case of Africa is very puzzling, since it assumes a positive correlation between democracy and economic development. But such assertions were not made by the leading international organizations when commenting on and 'explaining' the success of economic development in the newly-industrializing countries of East Asia. As we shall see in Chapter 10 on East Asia, in relation to that part of the world, the new orthodoxy singled out the virtues of strong, authoritarian and dirigiste states as the most important factor contributing to the development of the region.

Many analysts have focused on this apparent contradiction, arguing that while prescriptions of a minimal liberal state treat the state as a pariah, economic reforms nevertheless depend on a proactive interventionist government. Reform cannot be delivered without local capable hands bolstered by an efficient bureaucracy. [40]

For such authors, the suspicion then arises that there is a hidden purpose behind the ostentatious ignoring of this obvious contradiction. Falling back on classical structuralist explanations, some have explained away the contradiction in terms of concepts such as 'low intensity democracy', arguing that electoral reforms merely permit changes acceptable to international capitalism to be put in place with greater case and less resistance than in more overtly authoritarian regimes.[41] They have also pointed out that economic reform policies benefit certain factions of African élites with close links to international capital.[42] Others have argued that the emphasis on quality of governance merely serves 'as an efficient means of focusing responsibility on governments of developing countries, both for past ills *and* for implementation of reform packages'.[43]

While thus, one view in the academic literature regards the new political conditionalities in the manner of serving up old wines in new bottles – that is, as new ways of serving the interests of international capital – there is also a new turn in the analytical literature on Africa which explores the 'new donor agenda' more widely and rather differently, namely as being reflective of a generalized reconsideration and reformulation of bilateral and multilateral relations with Africa and, indeed, with other marginalized, politically unstable, areas of the global economy. As we shall see further below, there is a new kind of postmodernist type of analysis that examines the political conditionality of the economic reform agenda as a *discourse* which, whether intended or not, both creates and manages a new relationship between the 'new world order' and Africa. This is a relationship of *exclusion*, rather than of continuing incorporation. But before we turn to this literature, we examine how far economic reform itself has contributed to fragmentation and political instability.

Economic Reform and Anarchy

In many African countries, the imposition of a neo-liberal orthodoxy, including privatization of the public sector, the emasculation of the state apparatus, and the insistence on electoral reform, has contributed directly to the descent into anarchy and civil war. Recent wars have scarred Angola, Sudan, Sierra Leone, Liberia, Somalia, Rwanda, the Democratic Republic of Congo, and Ethiopia and Eritrea. Banditry, warlordism and low-intensity conflict have come to prevail in some other parts of the continent too.

What is the link between neo-liberal reform and the descent into chaos? Surprisingly, there is relatively little theoretical literature available that addresses this question. Although there are studies that report on the empirical connection between structural adjustment and food riots,[44] there are few attempts to theorize the link between reforms, weakened state apparatuses and disintegrating state–civil relations. One plausible explanation, however, is offered by William Reno.[45]

In a compelling study of the reform process in Sierra Leone, Reno argues that neo-liberal reforms dissolve the 'patrimonial' state form that emerged after decolonization and encourage disaffected élites to strike out on their own. After independence, the newly-independent states in Africa were typically weak, they lacked legitimacy and were confronted by formidable coalitions of rent-seeking strongmen using alternative, often tribal, power bases. The patrimonial state form emerged naturally to deal with this situation. In the patrimonial form, rulers use the state's resources available to them to buy off the opposition. The larger the state sector, the greater the amount of money and lucrative positions of privilege in the gift of the rulers. Undoubtedly, this state form created unwieldy, inefficient and corrupt administrations, and led to economic decline and debt. But what is often overlooked is that *it also kept the peace.*

Imposed neo-liberal reform, by contrast, attacks the patrimonial state, removes the corrupt bureaucracy and pulls state officials out of the framework of patron–client politics. In its efforts to get the state budget under control, the IMF has even negotiated with governments to subcontract tax collection to foreign firms. But this manner of reining in the rent-seeking state and its officials dissolves the patrimonial glue that holds the society together. It brings about fragmentation as erstwhile clients are forced to seek their own benefits independent of the central authority. This hastens the collapse into 'warlordism'. As Reno sums up the situation for Sierra Leone:

> much recent fighting, especially its territorial spread, is directly related to the elimination of opportunities for powerful strongmen under 'reform' and the efforts of these strongmen to strike out on their own for personal gain. Meanwhile, ordinary citizens conclude that Freetown has less and less to offer in the way of services or protection from predations of wayward élites. The reformist state is attacked from two sides – from below, by those who believe it will have little to offer them, and from above, by clients who make irresistible claims on reform policies.[46]

World Bank and IMF officials protest their innocence as country after country tumbles into civil strife and despair. After all, all *they* want to do is to 'free' poor peasants from corrupt state marketing boards, and liberate urban enterprise from the punitive shackles of bureaucratic licences and petty government regulations. Their grand design is to use the economic discipline of global markets to promote social restructuring. But this strategy backfires, because Africa is simply too far behind to make a living in the global market. Because of its structural irrelevance to the global economy, any enforced return to global markets as agents of economic discipline cannot even be excused on the grounds that the adverse effects of adjustment will be 'temporary'.

Nor, it seems to me, can the officialdom of the international institutions be excused on the grounds that they could not have foreseen the political consequences of their neo-liberal programmes. Theories of the patrimonial state and the positive function of corruption were part of mainstream political development literature in the 1960s and 1970s. Political scientists such as Samuel Huntington had commonly viewed political corruption as the only means of integrating marginal groups into a disjointed social system.[47] Some were objective enough to recognize that the growth of corruption, for example in England in the seventeenth and eighteenth centuries, was a necessary alternative to violence, an historically inevitable step in the long haul towards the institutionalization of a political structure and administration relatively independent of the competing demands of economic agents.[48] It is the tragedy of Africa that history has not given it time to catch up.

Imperialism and Resource Wars

Even when critical academic analyses do have a background understanding of the wider adverse international context, the portrayal of contemporary African communal violence itself is nevertheless one that is often focused, even if not entirely blamed, on the victims. It is an analysis that stubbornly ignores the *direct* imperialist connections that stoke the fires, supply the weapons, purchase the commodities (oil, diamonds, gold) and in so doing erect a self-reproducing architecture of a war economy. The expanding killing fields of Africa are ultimately attributed to resource scarcity pushing primordial ethnic cleavages towards escalating violence, while the battlefield itself is often characterized as being of a premodern 'formlessness', or as 'criminal anarchy', in which hordes of men move around like 'loose molecules in a very unstable social fluid',[49] and for whom fighting and killing becomes, not a means to an end, but a purpose in itself and even a 'liberating' experience.[50] To the casual observer, this descent into barbarism is complete when one encounters evidence of a revival of the irrational spirit power of animist beliefs.[51]

Belatedly, however, analysts are beginning to describe, as Reno indeed himself does,[52] the numerous ties that cement the private interests between state officials, rulers and warlords on the one hand, and foreign commerce and investors on the other. In Sierra Leone, for example, where rebels have controlled the diamond areas, the profits of war have been fostered by clandestine supplies of diamonds smuggled across the border into Liberia and sold to a number of Canadian companies, with links to the central selling organization of the De Beers Company.[53] There are other studies that lay bare the murderous intertwining of international rivalries for Africa's mineral wealth, and the fractitious explosion of resource wars on the ground.[54]

Angola is probably the country that has most clearly advanced to a self-perpetuating war economy. On one side there is the MPLA government in Luanda, and a war oligarchy comfortably endowed with oil wealth obtained through the operations of Shell, while on the other side, Jonas Savimbi's UNITA rebels control the diamond areas in the interior which wind their way through circuitous routes to the central selling organization of De Beers. Arms are smuggled through equally circumspect and illicit trails from Eastern Europe.[55]

The essential characteristic of a functioning war economy is that neither side has any real incentive to end the fighting, not even with the prospect of winning a decisive victory. Since an arms-for-resource economy is relatively simple in its transactional infrastructure, it offers massive opportunities for primitive accumulation by a very small social minority. War also offers an eminent excuse for the neglect of expenditure on public works or social welfare, or on forms of national productive accumulation. At the same time, the technological affluence of the globalized world economy enables the élites of each warlord domain to maintain a comfortable and secure lifestyle amid the debris of the public landscape. Cocooned within their gated enclaves they simply import all the technological fixes necessary for their own private state-of-the-art participation in the global system: foreign bank accounts, computers, mobile phones, advanced technological security systems, electric generators, water supplies, helicopters and even private jets to take their families out of the country for hospital treatment in the West, and their children to schools abroad.

As two recent reports on the wars in West Africa conclude, until the international connections of the war economies are dealt with decisively by the international community, the prospects for peace are bleak.[56] A third study confirms this finding with an instructive counter-example. Braathen, Boas and Saether compared the civil wars in Mozambique and Angola. They point out that, in the case of Mozambique, a UN-mounted peace operation was genuinely supported and completed successfully, whereas in the case of Angola, UN intervention proved to be a complete failure. The big difference is that, in the case of Mozambique, the FRELIMO state was almost entirely dependent on foreign aid, and the opposition party RENAMO, with little outside funding, had to make do with a 'beggar's barefoot army'. This meant that both parties were amenable to a foreign-assisted peace deal. By contrast, in Angola, the MPLA finances 95 per cent of its state and war machinery through oil revenues, and UNITA has become one of Africa's largest traders in diamonds and ivory. This encourages both sides to pursue the war indefinitely.[57]

The Reverse Agenda of Aid and Global Management

As was intimated earlier, some of the present-day analytical literature on Africa explores the political conditionality of the 'new donor agenda' in a wide sense as articulating a generalized reconsideration and reformulation of bilateral and multilateral relations with Africa and, indeed, with other marginalized areas of the global economy. Ground-breaking theoretical work by Mark Duffield, for example, theorizes that the new aid agenda reverses earlier developmentalist goals of 'incorporation' of peripheral areas into the world system, and instead now serves as a policy of management and containment of politically insecure territories on the edge of the global economy.[58]

What is particularly striking about some of this literature is its epistemological orientation, which is reminiscent of, though not openly indebted to, postmodern 'discourse' critique. That is to say, there is a preoccupation with *when* and *why* particular statements, such as 'pluralist democracy', or 'institutional capacity', 'strengthening civil society', and 'human rights' came about, how these statements have merged into a consensus agenda mediated through collective structures of consultation and co-ordination between previously disparate donor countries, and – last but not least – how these statements translate into practices of policy which, using Michel Foucault's phrase, 'systematically form the objects of which they speak'.[59] For this is the epistemological difference between the modern (Marxist) and postmodern critiques of knowledge, namely that, where the former merely expose the use of theories, policy statements or doctrinal assertions as ideologies that legitimate anterior, existing social practices, the latter study such statements as constituting the very conditions of their historical appearance. And thus, some analytic studies of the 'new aid agenda' now seem to appreciate that social relations within African countries, and between Africa and the global economy, are being shaped through the discourse of the new aid agenda itself.[60]

Political conditionality is the deliberate use of 'aid' to improve 'governance'. We have already discussed the definition of 'governance' in World-Bank-speak. Ostensibly, it is aimed at creating an enabling environment for economic reforms. Leverage through 'aid' may be achieved through threats of withdrawal of promised monies in the event that certain conditions of project or programme implementation are not met. Some people may be quick to retort that, in this sense, aid was always politically conditional. This is true, but the difference is that, in the past the recipients of aid were mainly national governments or programmes designated with their approval, and this offered the donors the excuse to say that aid was 'nonpolitical' – that is, not interfering in the internal affairs of state.

However, what characterizes the new political conditionality, is that through its own conceptualization of good governance and an enabling environment, it wilfully and openly *does* meddle in the internal affairs of state, targeting a plurality of actors, be they nongovernmental organizations, micro-businesses, local communities or grassroots organizations. In addition, they pay for programmes and projects that stimulate and strengthen pluralist local structures. This redirection of 'aid' away from national governments and towards civil society has become known as the 'reverse aid agenda'. As the British Overseas Development Institute (ODI) put it in 1995:

One manifestation of a growing common ground has been the way that most donors have broadened their aid objectives...[they] now view action to enhance human rights and democratic processes as a constituent part of their development agenda. Additionally, many donors have taken up 'strengthening civil society' as a specific aid objective.[61]

NGOs and the Politics of Exclusion

In *Symphony of the Damned,* Mark Duffield[62] uses discourse analysis to deconstruct the new, or reverse, aid agenda. He argues that with economic globalization has come a new discourse of development. Previously, development was theorized as a process of societal convergence between hierarchically conceptualized state-societies (rich–poor; developed–underdeveloped). In this theorization the state was seen as the accepted engine of growth. The failure of modernization in many parts of the Third World, however, brought criticism of 'top-down' approaches, and the disparagement of big government and the state, thus making way for 'bottom-up' interventions concerned with the vulnerability of the poor, which aim to strengthen local structures and empower local communities.

Duffield next contextualizes these donor adaptations within a wider, reshaped world view, in which cultural pluralism has replaced universalist preoccupations and goals. In the West, cultural pluralism, or multiculturalism, has been the liberal establishment's answer to racism. That is to say, it has replaced biologically-derived notions of racial superiority with an appreciation of cultural difference. On the positive side, the discourse of multiculturalism aims to promote societal harmony and integration by encouraging mutual respect and recognition. The idea that violence can be avoided fosters the organizational adaptations among international aid agencies and donor governments towards civil society and democratization in the periphery, in the same way as it supplies the motivation and operational logic for multicultural activities at home.

Unfortunately, the fundamental premise of multiculturalism has also bred a darker, oppositional structure of beliefs that has been labelled 'the new racism'.[63] The basic, generic assumption, namely that cultural difference is both natural and unavoidable, has also fed into notions that these differences are immutable and that they have an innate and non-rational quality that leads 'inevitably' to inter-ethnic conflict. This new racism has come to underpin popular explanations of growing political instability and intercommunal conflict in the marginal areas of the global economy. A special variant of the new racism as applied to contemporary Africa has come to be called 'the new barbarism'.

One influential version of this theory appears in the work of Robert Kaplan,[64] who interprets the collapse into anarchy as an unfocused and instinctive response, to mounting pressures resulting from environmental and economic collapse. However, other writers give the 'new barbarism' a positive connotation. Paul Richards, who is credited with having coined the term in 1995,[65] in fact welcomes the new barbarism as a form of liberation. He describes the often grotesque acts of warlord violence and terror as rational responses to the failure of modernity, and as exhibiting potentially new and innovative ways of knowing and interacting with the environment. Thus, argues Duffield, both assertive cultural plural-ism *and* the new racism are mirror images of a common structure of beliefs. They share a common glass of cultural pluralism, yet each foretells a different future.

Humanitarian Relief and Complex Political Emergencies

Drawing conclusions from the previous sections, we may argue that both the economic reforms imposed under structural adjustment and the new or reverse agenda of aid have, at the minimum, put an extra spin on the centrifugal forces already present in the weak, underdeveloped states of Africa. The advent of humanitarian relief to cope with the ensuing political emergencies, furthermore, has the effect of protracting such crises by making them more 'complex'. According to Duffield, the possibility that humanitarian interven-tion encourages fragmentation is a factor that makes a political emergency 'complex'.[66]

Since the mid-1980s, as several countries in Africa have fallen into chaos and political conflict, humanitarian relief operations have increased sixfold. As emergency food and medical aid has been rushed in to support war victims, the legal mandates of relief agen-cies (UN-connected *and* independent NGOs) have been reframed: whereas previously it was nearly impossible to operate in non-government controlled areas, today the organizational options have been widened to include effectively all situations of contested governance. This further undermines the responsibilities previously held by governments.

The agenda of cultural pluralism again informs the nature and direction of relief operations. That is to say, it is avowedly apolitical – less concerned with power and power relations, or with rights and wrongs, or with human rights abuses, than with managing and containing the situation. Relief agencies intervene in the hope that, by feeding the victims, they will in some way free the warring parties and allow them to resolve the conflict eventually. In this way, cultural pluralism translates into cultural functionalism: the idea that natural order and stability will resume in due course.

However, because of their robustly apolitical stance these agencies are unaware that their humanitarian aid is gradually being incorporated into the socio-political fabric of the internal conflict. For cultural functionalism prescribes a stance of balance and even-handedness that legitimizes both, or all, of the warring factions. Such legitimation operates not only at the ideological level, but also materially. For example, humanitarian relief agencies negotiate access for emergency deliveries of food and medicine equally with all warring parties, routinely having to offer a proportion of the aid to warlords. Such aid is diverted immediately and commutes into a fresh supply of arms. A further step in this process of 'incorporation' occurs when warring parties use the promise of relief aid as a means of mobilizing local populations for practical and political purposes.

Conclusion

Thus, with Duffield, we conclude from this sorry tale of the West's recent relations with Africa that there is an emerging system of global governance with methods and instruments geared to containing and managing symptoms rather than removing causes.[67] The lack of political will to remove such causes attests to a process of disengagement from the periphery of the world economy. The agonizingly thin line of UN peace-keeping in countries such as Sierra Leone ('keeping the peace' that is not there, while lacking the mandate or military wherewithal to enforce peace) has been contrasted rightly with the swift and decisive NATO intervention in Kosovo which *is* within the heartland of the global system.

A further cynical example of this disengagement is reflected in the politics surrounding the AIDS epidemic. The World Health Organization estimates that 23 million people are infected by AIDS in Sub-Saharan Africa, with new cases running at 5000 per day. One in four Africans is expected to die of the disease. Even so, 90 per cent of AIDS research and investment is spent on the development of expensive drugs for the treatment of the 8 per cent of people who have contracted the disease in the rich countries, thus squeezing out the funds and the research agendas for cheap vaccines to prevent its further spread in the Third World. When the government of South Africa, where the rate of AIDS is rising fastest, passed legislation to enable the domestic production of generic drugs, the USA and the EU immediately applied pressure to have the legislation rescinded, on the grounds that the South African legislation violated the international patent rights of the big international pharmaceutical firms.[68] It was only when a US government study identified the AIDS pandemic in Africa as a potential national security problem for the USA[69] that a dramatic change of heart followed and pharmaceutical companies were armtwisted into making their drugs available at very low concessionary prices, on condition that the recipient countries would desist from contravening established international trade laws. Profits definitely remain more important than the lives of millions in Africa where, as one World Bank official observed: 'if Aids disproportionately fall on the poor in these countries then the fact they they will die of it will have a positive impact on the economic growth of these nations'.[70]

9

Islamic Revolt

Today there are twenty-eight countries in the world, with a total population of 836 million, in which Muslims have an overall majority, and many more countries have sizeable Muslim minorities. The total world Muslim population is around 1.2 billion, or a quarter of the total world population. Even in Europe, the heartland of Christianity, Muslim immigration and conversion has led to Islam being the second largest religion.

Since around the mid-1970s a number of apparently related political and social events all over the world have led Western commentators to speak of a militant Islamic revival. The defining moment was no doubt the overthrow, in 1979, of the Shah of Iran's pro-Western monarchy, and the establishment there of the modern world's first theocratic Islamic Republic. In Lebanon, the Hamas movement sponsored by the Muslim Brotherhood has since forced an increasingly bitter split within the Palestinian struggle against Israel. In Sudan, Islamists are preventing the military junta from making concessions to the non-Muslims of the south, thus dragging out the civil war there. In Algiers, the fundamentalist party, the FIS, won the elections in 1990 only to find its victory at the ballot box snatched from it by the imposition of martial law (backed by Western governments), resulting in near civil war. In Egypt, the tourist industry has been badly affected by attacks from fundamentalists, and the Mubarak regime only holds on to power by a massive, and precarious, security clampdown involving the imprisonment, without trial, of thousands of fundamentalist Muslims. In India, tensions between Muslims and Hindus, always simmering just below the surface, have been threatening to boil over since the Muslim revolt in Kashmir, and the destruction by Hindus of the mosque in Ayodhya. The disintegration of the Soviet empire has created new Muslim states searching for an identity in Islam. In Afghanistan, an especially virulent and extreme fundamentalist Islamic movement, the Taliban, have taken power, and allegedly given sanctuary to Osama bin Laden, widely suspected of having masterminded the bombing of the American embassies in Kenya and Tanzania in 1998. Terrorist attacks in the West, alleged or real, have raised the spectre of the *jihad*, or holy war, being fought out abroad as well as at home. As *The Economist* in 1995 summed up in colourful language: 'Islam at its most ferocious is cutting a blood-stained path to the front of the world's attention.'[1]

In a provocative article in *Foreign Affairs* in 1993, Samuel Huntington predicted a new clash of civilizations.[2] The nation-state, he said, is disappearing as the primary unit of international relations and therefore conflict and competition between the world's peoples will in future be worked out at a different level, chiefly among the larger units known as cultures or civilizations. He identified as the most important among a total of eight, three such civilizations: the West (the Euro-American culture); the East (the Confucian culture); and Islam. His article is well worth reading, particularly as a counter-argument to the facile statements of the 'end of ideology' or 'end of history' theologians (for example, F. Fukuyama).[3] The latter are based on an economic/technological deterministic interpretation of an inevitable course of human evolution. Huntington, on the other hand, says, 'The great divisions among humankind and the dominating source of conflict will be cultural.'[4]

Huntington argues that, precisely because of economic modernization and social change throughout the world, people are being separated from long-standing local identities, while at the same time the nation-state is weakened as a source of identity. Religions move in to fill the gap left by the nation as a source of identity. A complementary factor about which he theorizes relates to what Anthony Giddens, David Harvey and other writers on globalization have variously referred to as the 'time/space compression' or 'distantiation' phenomenon.[5] Increased cross-border social interaction of people around the world has the paradoxical effect of signifying the larger social, cultural or ethnic group to which people belong as a source of identification for 'the other'. By way of example, Huntington quotes Donald Horowitz: 'an Ibo may be ... an Owerri Ibo or an Onitsha Ibo in what was the Eastern region of Nigeria. In Lagos he is simply an Ibo. In London he is a Nigerian. In New York, he is an African'.

Civilization, according to Huntington, is the 'highest' cultural grouping of people and the broadest level of cultural identity people have short of that which distinguishes humans from other species. It is defined both by common objective elements, such as language, history, religion, customs and institutions, and by the subjective self-identification of people.[6]

As far as the immediate future is concerned, Huntington expects the clash between civilizations to rage between the West and Islam. However, it is a mistake to argue, as he does, that this is so because of the potent contradiction between oil and poverty, since, apart from the combined population of 10 million who live in six very rich Gulf states, the vast majority of Muslims live in countries with minimal or no oil resources. These countries belong to the world's poorest and middle-income groups.

More decisive for a correct analysis of the roots of the contemporary Islamic revolt, in my view, is the circumstance that the Islamic world contains within it millions upon millions of people who do not have any prospect of being incorporated into the new global system, while – similarly – Muslim minorities in the advanced countries often find themselves also excluded from the global system. The analysis presented in this chapter is that, rather than the West's domination of oil, it is the failure of the national developmental strategies in the neocolonial period, coupled with the recent episode of globalization, that drives the contemporary Islamic crescent. Islamic resurgence is best understood as a politics of identity in response to exclusion, rather than (as was the case during the heyday of Arab nationalism) as a response to subordinated incorporation. But this politics of identity has not brought a new model of society, nor has the organizational programmatic unity become a geostrategic factor.

In developing this analysis I put forward two themes that appear to prevail in much recent discourse about the Islamic revolt:

1. The continuity of spiritual renewal throughout Islam's history; and
2. The cultural impact of the West's historical confrontation with Islam.

Spiritual Renewal

Islam is more than a religion; it is a complete way of life. It concerns not only God's relationship with His people, but it also orders social relations among people, including legal, contractual institutions, social and political institutions, and issues of economic propriety and practice. G. H. Jansen, in his book, *Militant Islam*, quotes two fundamentalist Islamic scholars as saying that 'Islam provides guidance for all walks of life, individual and social, material and moral, economic and political, legal and cultural, national and international'.[7] Islam is particularly detailed about matters relating to family, marriage, divorce and inheritance; it also addresses questions of dress and etiquette, food and personal hygiene – in short, the obvious and public signifiers of identity and belonging, potentially therefore the insignia of lifestyle politics.

The two principal sources for Islam are:

1. The *Qu'ran*, the book of direct revelations by God to the Prophet Muhammed through the Archangel Gabriel; and
2. The *Sunna*, literally, the 'trodden path', a compilation and codification of the sayings of the Prophet plus the official biography of the Prophet's life, this including all the things He *did* as well as said.

After the Prophet's death in 632BC (AH10) naturally it took some time to compile and codify the entire body of holy scriptures. There was confusion, interpretation and counter-interpretation, by competing schools of law, until, some time around AD900, consensus among the scholars triumphed. From that moment 'the Gates of the *ijtihad* were closed' (*ijtihad* meaning independent judgement). This implied that, from then on, no further augmentation to the scriptural body could be countenanced, and that henceforth only past precedent counted.

As an aside we should note at this point that while the above description of religious authority holds for the vast majority of Muslims, who are called Sunni, there is a sizeable minority, called Shi'ites, for whom, by contrast, religious authority centres on an inspired person, the Imam. Shi'ites have constituted themselves as a separate sect since the early days of Islam, and at first traced the authority of religious inspiration through a direct line of succession from Ali, cousin and son-in-law of the Prophet Muhammed. The fact that the twelfth and last Imam, Muhammad al-Mahdi, disappeared in AD 878, did not become an effective bar to this divine basis of authority. On the contrary, He became the 'Hidden One', still in this world and in contact with his chosen agents, who have the right to pronounce *ex cathedra* an opinion on any matter affecting the *Sharia*, or canon law. In Persia, at an early date, the Shi'ites lent themselves to the nationalist movement, which in time displaced Arab domination by purely Persian rule. In this way, Shi'ism ultimately became the national religion of Persia, later Iran.[8] The Ayatollah Khomeini successfully led the revolution that overthrew the Shah, with the Ayatollah claiming to be the incarnation of the twelfth Imam.

Although the system of authority thus differed between Sunnis and Shi'ites, and led to mutual enmity between them, both systems have features that make for powerful religious revivals. In the case of the Shi'ite religion, the withdrawal of the Imam and his continued existence as the 'Hidden One' would periodically fire up hopes of a messianic return and salvation that enabled strong personal leaders to emerge as new Imams leading a social revolt against the orthodox establishment. In the case of the Sunni religion, as we see below, it was the doctrine of the *ijtihad* that allowed social protest to be battled out at the level of theological disputes, and in this way challenge existing powers.

According to Ernest Gellner,[9] the sociological significance of the *ijtihad* was twofold, and it implanted a deep dialectic into the very heart of Islam: on the one hand it provided a power-base for the scholar/jurists, the learned men, *ulema*, who could pontificate on the basis of analogous reasoning, and declare any conduct or event in changed historical circumstances to be, or not to be, in accordance with Islamic law. This gave them a power-base independent of temporal authorities, and there was therefore always an institutional separation between political and religious authority. On the other hand, the subordination of the former to the latter meant that, in principle, as Gellner has put it, 'a socially and politically transcendent standard of rectitude was ever accessible, beyond the reach of manipulation by political authority, and available for condemning the *de facto* authority if sinned against it'.[10]

Thus, despite the *institutional* separation between politics and religion, there was never a *cultural* separation between the two. In this sense, Islam was not a secular civilization. Where Christ had accepted the separation between God and Caesar and had advised people to 'render unto Caesar the things that are Caesar's', Muhammed and Islam never recognized such separation in their universe of discourse and belief.[11] Further, the non-manipulability of divine law proved time and again to be a source of legitimacy for acts of self-correction, as when the disgruntled, oppressed masses could translate their grievances into the discourse of theological disputation, challenging political authority on those grounds. As we shall see below, much of the present-day Islamic revolt may be interpreted in precisely those terms.

Thus the spirit of renewal has been immanent in Islam as a cultural belief system. But it was also sourced by the peculiar material circumstances and social relations of production of the historical environment in which it developed and was consolidated. As Simon Bromley writes, in the course of its history, Islamic civilization came to straddle two social formations, each grounded in a different ecology and economy. On the one hand, there was the urban society of the Sultanates (consolidated during a five-century-long period of rule in the Ottoman Empire). It was a society of state officials, military personnel and Islamic scholars *(ulema)*. Together, in tacit co-operation with the merchants, they maintained order, networks of trade and finance, and exacted tribute from the surrounding peasantry. On the other hand, beyond the compass of the urban social formation lay the tribal forces that remained outside central control. In these regions, 'the tributary state was unable to control the rural areas, essentially because of the greater weight of pastoral nomadism with its mobile means of production, armed populations and absence of urban growth'.[12]

These two different social formations, Gellner states with absolute confidence, gave rise to, 'the really central, and perhaps most important feature of Islam namely that it was internally divided into a High Islam of the scholars and the Low Islam of the people'.[13] While high Islam was puritanical, scripturalistic and mindful of the prohibition of claims to mediation between God and man, low Islam (or folk Islam) was simple, adaptive and flexible, inspired by saintlike mystic heroes *(sufis)* and centred on grassroot *tarikas* (Muslim brotherhoods). Periodically the two religious styles would clash, as when the scholars of high Islam would launch 'a kind of internal purification movement' in an attempt to reimpose itself on the whole of society.[14]

The West Confronts Islam

Compared with all other areas of the world, the world of Islam has had the unique, if dubious, distinction of having always been regarded by the West as a cultural adversary – a cultural 'other'. No doubt rivalry over exclusive claims to a single, indivisible transcendent God had a lot to do with this, as had their claims on the Holy Land, and their geographic proximity. And no doubt the original contest of wills on the battlefield during the Crusades helped to strike enduring terror in the hearts and minds of Europeans and Muslims alike.

But probably of greater significance is the fact that, in confronting Islam, from the time of the Crusades and in distinct episodes since, the West has come to define itself. The need to know the enemy also became an inspiration for self-identification. While it can be argued, as in Edward Said's celebrated account,[15] that 'orientalism' was a product of Western culture, equally it may be said that the West's concept of its own culture and society derived from the same discourse. It is this dependency engendered through binomial opposition, in different phases of their intertwining histories, that explains the West's special fear of Islam, and Islam's enduring search for self-identity.

In his overview of the history of the West's image of Islam, Maxime Rodinson opines that: 'The image of Islam arose, not so much as some have said from the Crusades, as from the slowly welded ideological unity of the late Christian world which led both to a clear view of the enemy's features and also to a channelling of effort towards the Crusades.'[16] The fight having become more concentrated and better-focused, the enemy must of necessity be given sharper, more specific, features and thus its image simplified and stereotyped. In these stereotypes, Islam was given a systemic civilizational unity it did not possess.

Later, in the medieval period, when Latin Europe was beset by internal factions and struggles, the ideological conflict with Islam lost its pre-eminence. But in Europe, internal ideological strife also sowed the seeds of a relativity of belief that in fact opened up a certain ideological space for Christian scholars to pursue the study of Islam with some 'objectivity'. From there, Islam graduated to become a subject of curiosity and exoticism, as witnessed in the flourishing of Arabian scholarship, notably in the fields of philology, arts and religion. With the birth of the sciences, followed by the Age of Reason, Islam even became an unwitting partner in the project of Enlightenment: 'People could now view the religious faith which competed with Christianity in an impartial light and even with some sympathy, unconsciously seeking (and obviously finding) in it the very values of the now rationalised trend of thought that was opposed to Christianity.'[17]

However, in the nineteenth century, specialist knowledge about Arabia and Islam turned into 'orientalism', a special discipline devoted to the study of the East. But it was a special discipline which would serve European imperialist conquest from that time onwards. While buttressing the confidence of Europe in its own cultural superiority, it cast the Muslim in the role of contemptible victim, in need of correction. This was so because the specialist knowledge of Arab language, customs, religion and art transmitted itself to other fields of scientific enquiry (notably social philosophy, later sociology and economics) in its most vulgarized, mechanistic form, driven as it was by the general ideas of the time, which attributed a boundless influence to religion, language and race as explanatory factors in the diverse trajectories of human social evolution.[18]

This particular form of social theorizing climaxed in Max Weber's enduringly authoritative typification of West and East, whereby the Oriental became no more than a mirror image of the Occidental. As Edward Said writes:

> Weber's studies... threw him into the very territory originally charted and claimed by Orientalists. There he found encouragement amongst all those nineteenth century thinkers who believed that there was a sort of ontological difference between Eastern and Western economic (as well as religious) 'mentalities'.[19]

This ontological difference became theorized in a self-serving contrast of identity and progress: while the West was economically dynamic *because* it was universal, rational, pluralist and secular, the Orient was economically stagnant *because* it was particularistic, traditional, despotic, wallowing in religious obscurantism, and therefore stagnant.

As Rodinson writes:

> In the Middle Ages, the Oriental had been regarded as a fierce enemy, but nevertheless on the same level as Western man; in the

eighteenth century enlightenment and the resulting ideology of the French Revolution the Oriental was, underneath his disguise, essentially a human being; but in the 19th century he became a creature apart, imprisoned in his specificity, an object of condescending praise. Thus the concept of *homo islamicus* was born, and is still far from being overthrown.[20]

The end of the First World War resulted in the demise of the Ottoman Empire. Against the backdrop of fierce competition between European nations, the scramble for the Middle East and its vast oil resources began. Everywhere the Europeans established two new principles: the freezing of boundaries, and the freezing of dynasties. Arbitrarily drawing lines in the sand, they made permanent territorial boundaries that had either been non-existent or were constantly shifting.[21] In a cynical move that would pre-empt any future pan-Arabism or pan-Islamism, the colonial powers drew the borders of states in such a manner as to ensure that there were oil-rich territorial states with small populations and oil-scarce states with large populations.

This new age of imperialism again changed the cultural and political relationship between the West and Islam. This time it was marked by an 'active tide of imposing responsibility on the local peoples', turning the unchanging Oriental passivity into militant modern life.[22] In the creation of Arab protectorates, mandates and outright colonial territories there began the process of imposed political state formation, which grew dialectically into independence movements,[23] and was sealed by constitutional sovereignty granted at various moments in the interwar and postwar epoch.

We shall return to the refractory effect of the imposition of artificial nation-states shortly. First a word about how the impact of the West was received and resisted in the Islamic world. G. H. Jansen reminds us that since 1500 scarcely a decade, or even half a decade, has passed without a Muslim area somewhere fighting against encroachment by some Western power.[24] Rioting and internal armed uprisings were endemic, especially after the First World War. For the Muslims these were all wars, both in defence of Islam and in defence of hearth and home. They mainly took place at the local level, at the grassroots of popular 'low Islam', rather than at the level of the urban scholars of 'high Islam'. This was hardly surprising, since European conquests were frequently accompanied by a vigorous policy of support for the Christian missionary effort. Many a time this forced the Muslim brotherhoods to go underground, and to become 'secret' societies. The creation, through conversion, of Christian communities, deliberately fostered and favoured by the colonial powers and living as separate enclaves amid the mass of Muslims, had the paradoxical effect of keeping Islam militant.[25]

Education and Orientalization

It is probably a function of the rising pre-eminence of cultural studies in the Humanities that recent literature on the Arab world singles out European education and European cultural domination generally as the most important, lasting and damaging legacy of the colonial period. In the introduction to the third part of this book we have referred to cultural studies and its connection with postcolonial studies, so we shall not dwell on that here. Edward Said, in his ground-breaking book, *Orientalism*, and again in its sequel, *Culture and Imperialism*,[26] has probably done more than anyone to redefine imperialism in terms of cultural power. Taking as his frame of reference Michel Foucault's notion of 'discourse', he has examined Orientalism as a discourse in which power and knowledge are linked dialectically. European imperialist power in the nineteenth and twentieth centuries drew on knowledge of the Orient to rule and manage, and in so doing *produced* the Orient: politically, sociologically, militarily, ideologically, scientifically and imaginatively. While European culture gained in strength and identity by setting itself off against the Orient as a sort of surrogate and even underground self, the Orient itself became 'Orientalized'.[27]

The most tangible concretization of this Orientalization was effected through colonial educational policies. Jansen writes: 'foreign rulers with rare unanimity and unusual purposefulness and pertinacity, sought to give as little education as possible, the wrong sort of education when it had to be given, and also to bring about a schism in the soul of the Muslim community'.[28] The local education system was either destroyed or allowed to collapse through benign neglect, while new schools using European languages and curricula were introduced. A new breed of intellectual élite was selected, nurtured and sent abroad for higher education, including, perversely, for the study of subjects such as 'Islamic' and 'Oriental' studies. There they learnt to see the Orient through Occidental eyes. Jansen turns up the arresting statistic that until 1955, 95 per cent of all books written about Islam were written by Western scholars.[29]

The colonially-imposed, yet arbitrary, process of state-formation combined with this conscious policy of educating native élites who would see their own world through European eyes; it succeeded in forging a deep rift between modernizers and reformers on the one hand and traditionalists and neofundamentalists on the other. Nevertheless, all these movements also had a common origin. Indeed, in one sense, all these groups may be classed as 'Islamists', or representatives of 'political Islam'. As Oliver Roy points out, from a sociological and intellectual point of view they were products of the modern world, and more particularly of their subordinated position in the West-dominated world system. Thus, in this sense, the Islamist movement was and still is a Third-Worldist movement. It conceives of itself explicitly as a sociopolitical project, founded on an Islam defined as much in terms of political ideology as in terms of religion.[30]

But where the modernizers (in different ways and with different emphases on secularization) sought to reform or rationalize Islamic thought and institutions in order to bring them into line with the new order introduced by the Europeans (particularly the 'order' of the interstate system and of developmentalism), and the reformers sought to Islamize the Western model, attempting to create a synthesis between modernity and Islam, the neofundamentalists and traditionalists are obsessed with the corrupting influence of Western culture. They reject the Western model and eschew any compromise with it. Instead, they seek a return to the scriptures and a lifestyle signifying, in dress, in body language, in social practices of conviviality and prayer, and most prominently in respect of the status of women, the exclusivity of the true believer as a member of a select and holy community. As Roy says, 'Neofundamentalism entails a shrinking of the public space to the family and the mosque.'[31]

After independence, in the neocolonial period, the modernizers were in the ascendancy, but in more recent times radical reformers and neofundamentalists have begun to hold sway. The reasons for this are both external and internal: the dependent development project of the modernizers was corrupted by continuing and divisive interventions of the West in the pursuit of its strategic interests in oil, and 'legitimated' with reference to the Cold War. For its part, the political establishment failed to deliver material benefits or a coherent system of meanings.

The Failure of Dependent Development

The defeat in the Yom Kippur War and the economic crisis that followed put paid to fragile attempts at pan-Arab unity which had been the hallmark of the radical reformers in the immediate post-independence era. It meant that everywhere Arab nationalism had to give way to ever more 'pragmatic' and corrupted leaderships dancing to the tune of the USA and IMF/World Bank donors and aid givers. As their hold over their populations weakened, they became still more dependent on military and other handouts from their Western masters.

Meanwhile, the conservative regimes of the oil-rich Gulf states became increasingly implicated in the geostrategic interests of the USA and the West. The Shi'ite Islamic revolution in Iran was followed by a cynically-exploited divide-and-rule-backed war with Iraq which did much to identify the Iranian revolution with Shi'ism and Iranian nationalism. Conservative Arab states financed a Sunni fundamentalist pole of attraction outside their own borders in order to break the momentum of the Islamic revolution. The second Gulf War spread even more confusion in the Arab world by organizing a conservative Arab and Western coalition against Iraq.

A structuralist understanding of the geopolitical dynamics that led to the Gulf War of 1991 may help us to understand the forces that gave rise to the present-day neofundamentalist crescent as well. In the structuralist perspective we have adopted in much of this book, the advanced capitalist countries, with the USA at the head, form the core of the system, the rest is either semi-periphery or periphery. But we have also seen that the capitalist world system is continually developing towards higher, more complex forms of integration. Periodically this forces a reshuffling of the relationships between the parts, and a destruction and reconstruction of the formal political organization of these relationships.

Following the Second World War, and within the context of the emerging bipolar world order, the process of decolonization and the creation of a multitude of sovereign states within the periphery of the capitalist system was an appropriate reconstruction of formal political relations which served to maintain the interests of the core within the periphery. But inevitably it also opened up opportunities for national development and liberation for those peripheral states which played the sovereignty card to the full, and which knew how to play off the superpowers to their nation's advantage. There is no doubt that Saddam Hussain and his Ba'athist Party had succeeded in doing just that. We may not like the way he set about this task, and morally condemn the fascist brutality that accompanied the building of a militarily-powerful, industrially-advancing and even socially-commendable welfare state, but we cannot deny that national economic and social progress had been made.

The pertinent historical, as opposed to moral, question one should ask is: what was it that blocked internal advance towards progressive democratization and instead propelled this brutal leadership into external aggression? It is here that a structuralist analysis, without condemning or condoning, directs attention to the entire web of core–peripheral and semi-peripheral relations in the region which had reached a crisis point because of the combined effect of global capitalist integration and the collapse of the bipolar world order. What was the structure of these relations and why was it in crisis?

The core has, of course, economic interests in the oil of the Middle East. But this is only a starting point. In order to access the oil, in the past it was in the interest of the oil companies backed by the political power of the imperialist core countries to make deals with local feudal rulers, kinglets or sheiks in exchange for concessions for exploration and so on. Now, when one is only interested in a raw material such as oil, and not in labour or consumer markets, one's profit strategy at that stage dictates a preference for dictatorships rather than democratic regimes. A sovereign ruler is all that is wanted: *Oil and dictatorship go together.*

Similar reasons prompt a divide-and-rule strategy – that is, an uneven distribution of populations over the oil-rich regions. Small countries with large quantities of oil and small populations are less demanding than large ones. After the demise of the Ottoman Empire at the conclusion of the First World War, such deliberately uneven divisions of states were drawn up under British and French colonial rule. There are six very rich Gulf states (joined together in the Gulf Co-operation Council) with a combined population of ten million; and six very populous states outside with a combined population of about 200 million. It is these latter states that particularly have to cope with the displaced and restless Palestinians within their borders who lost their land to the Israelis.

When, however, oil prices did eventually increase as a result of organized cartel-type rebellion in the oil-producing countries (1973), the links between the peripheral and semi-peripheral states in the region, and between them and the core became more complex. Arms trade and financial links, *in addition to* oil now formed a triangle of interests, consolidating the interests of the rulers of the small states with the core. This is the significance of the developing integration of the world capitalist system.

For every hundred US dollars the West spends on oil in the Middle East, US$40 comes back through the arms trade, and roughly another US$40 comes back into Western banks, underpinning the financial system in the core nations. Noam Chomsky nicely illustrated this point with a joke going around on Wall Street at the time of the second Gulf War: 'Why do the United States and Kuwait need each other? Answer: Kuwait is a banking system without a country and the United States is a country without a banking system.'[32]

While a blanket of secrecy is wrapped around the exact amount of oil dollars invested in the West, the highest estimate of Gulf countries' investments in the USA alone amounts to US$1 trillion. In 1989, Kuwait earned more income from its vast overseas investments located in the capitalist metropoles than from its domestic oil production (US$8.8 billion, compared with US$7.7 billion).[33]

The interwovenness of the 'reformist', 'modernising' Muslim élites in the Third World with the core of the Western capitalist system widened the gap increasingly between them and the masses of the population whom they rule and who are dispossessed. Much of the rise of neofundamentalist Islam can be understood as a popular and anti-imperialist protest movement. But two features that are unique to the Islamic tradition give it its vitality: the tradition of spiritual renewal and the concept of '*umma*' (the community of the faithful). While the former permits, at least in principle if not in practice, as we shall see below, the conversion and reabsorption of governmental élites and 'exploiters' in the revivalist movement, the latter gives priority to the world-wide community of Islam and denies its nationalist or even supranationalist (as in pan-Arabic) pretensions. This, I believe, makes a historical fit with the denationalizing forces of globalization.

What has been worrying the West since the late 1980s is that increasingly within Sunni territory a fundamentalist interpretation of Islam as a potent, popular, anti-Western force is rising. For the real strength of neofundamental Islamists lies in their peaceful, community-based activities. The Muslim Brotherhoods, so-called, offer welfare, health care and educational services to thousands of people neglected by the secular state.

The Rise of Islamist New Intellectuals and the Politics of Anti-developmentalism

After independence, having been given the mantle of sovereignty, the modernizing, Westernized élites set about the task of social and economic development. As Simon Bromley has noted, whether they adopted a capitalist or a socialist model, the outcomes in terms of social structure were not all that different. First of all, the state everywhere became the main site of surplus appropriation. This was the case regardless of whether the source of revenue was oil exported under the aegis of international oil cartels, with the state thus becoming a 'rentier-state', or whether, in the absence of oil, nationalist élites – as in Egypt, Iraq and Sudan – occupied the state centre to secure more or less complete control over internal resource mobilization, if not state control over all property. The point is that, in both cases, what was lacking was a degree of separation between the institutions of rule and surplus appropriation. This, as Bromley points out, led everywhere to an absence of the conditions for democratic participation, and ushered in the politics of clientelism.[34] Second, in the oil-poor, populous countries, strategies of import-substitutive industrialization became stranded on the same rocks of deepened foreign indebtedness as they had in Latin America. By contrast, the oil-rich countries with small populations had an income far in excess of their needs. Possession of vast oil reserves in fact reduced the incentive to rely upon the skills and quality of the people. The oil-rich Gulf states invested their money in the metropolitan countries, and imported labour from elsewhere in Arabia and the Indian subcontinent, thus creating enclaves of second-class, disenfranchised non-citizens. The obvious solution should have been some form of regional economic integration, and for a time pan-Arab nationalism was a potent rallying force in the postwar settlement. But, time and again, the West, and more especially the USA and its bridgehead client state, Israel, managed to divide and break the incipient regional solidarities.

A third characteristic consequence of the dependent development strategies of the neocolonial period was the process of urbanization coupled with a rapid population explosion. Dependent incorporation into the world capitalist economy implied a neglect for subsistence agriculture, rural–urban migration, and swelling numbers of unemployed and underemployed city-dwellers. This movement of the social location of Islamism engendered an important shift in the ideological realm as well. Today's masses who follow the Islamists are not 'traditionalists', writes Oliver Roy, instead:

> they live with the values of the modern city – consumerism and upward social mobility; they left behind the old forms of conviviality, respect for elders and for consensus, when they left their villages ... they are fascinated by the values of consumerism imparted by the shop windows of the large metropolises; they live in a world of movie theatres, cafes, jeans, video and sports, but they live precariously from menial jobs or remain unemployed in immigrant ghettos, with the frustration inherent in an unattainable consumerist world ... Their militant actions exist in symbiosis with their urban environment: except in Afghanistan and Kurdistan, the guerilas of the contemporary Muslim world are city-dwellers.[35]

A fourth social structural characteristic of dependent development in the neocolonial period is the emergence of a new category of educated individuals produced by the expansion in state-funded education established along Western lines. Roy variously refers to this class of intellectuals as 'lumpen intelligentsia', or the 'Islamist new intellectuals' or 'neofundamentalists'. They are young people with school, and even university, education who cannot find positions or professions that correspond to their expectations or visions of themselves, either in the saturated state administrative sector or in industry because national capitalism is weak, in the traditional network because of the devaluation of religious schools, or in modern universities which are also saturated and experiencing a loss of social status. Thus, the newly-educated of the Muslim world find no social ratification, either real or symbolic, for what they perceive as their new status.[36]

In an unusual and provocative analysis of the Islamic world today, Roy dissects the ideological pretensions, the social basis and the political project, of this lumpen intelligentsia that forms the core of the contemporary neofundamentalist crescent. In doing so, he debunks as a myth the theory that it could consolidate into a new force in international relations or indeed pose a threat to the West.

According to Roy, the lumpen intelligentsia are differentiated from, and resent, the clerical scholars (the *ulema*, or scholars of high Islam) because, unlike these scholars, they have no state-legitimated and supported relationship to that corpus of knowledge.[37] At the same time they have smatterings of Western education without, again, having an institutional connection to that body of knowledge.

Roy makes the important point that there is a direct relationship between the configuration of the new intellectual's 'conceptual' space and the social space that he occupies. As a self-proclaimed mullah or as a militant he preaches among the urban poor. He operates in meeting houses, sites of worship, educational centres, and new suburban settings not yet socialized by the state. He rejects, and is marginalized by, both the Westernised professionals and the governing class on the one hand, and the state-legitimated clerics (the *ulema*) on the other. His conceptual apparatus reflects how he operates on the fringes of both.

The Western-style intellectuals and the clerical scholars have in common the fact that both their social status and their methodology is guaranteed by processes of investiture and authorization that distinguish them from the masses. Their claims to truth, each in their own way, albeit in methodological opposition to each other, have an assured connection to their own procedures of acceptance and institutional validation, whether these are the rules of logic and objectivity and peer scrutiny, as with Western science and intellectual positions, or the norms of analogous reasoning and peer consensus within the clerical community of the *ulema*. They are both validated by examination and titles that accord social positions to them. But the neofundamentalist, small-time mullahs operate outside these approved networks of knowledge transmission. And thus, argues Roy, the neofundamentalist intellectual is quintessentially an *auto-didact*. He is a tinkerer, creating a montage of fragments of knowledge combined from these different conceptual universes, using a method of invocation and incantation as emblematic *display* of knowledge, rather than as an object of systematic study. Fragmentary modern knowledge drawn from an immense variety of immediately accessible (through TV, newspapers and so on) fields of Western knowledge, including economics, sociology, nuclear physics and biology, is immediately integrated within a Qu'ranic framework in which claims to truth drawn from the Qu'ran or the Tradition and cited as verses, are positioned as the equivalents of concepts drawn from modern science and ideologies.

There is nevertheless a unity in this montage of borrowed fragments. It is the mystical site of the divine *Tawhid*, the Oneness of God which extends to all his Creation, including, most importantly, the Perfect Man (*Insan Kamil*). According to the myth of the Perfect Man, it is the ethical disposition of one's soul that gives unity to one's knowledge and practice. Hence there is an emphasis on mental conversion, on devotion, on lifestyle and on purity. But there is no political programme of action, no model of a new civic society, no worked-out alternative system of economic and social organization.

As the radical or 'political' Islam of the postindependence years slides into neofundamentalism, it assembles the outcasts of a failed modernism, mobilizing them around the myth of a return to an Islamic authenticity that has never existed. Such Islamism, Roy concludes, is not a geostrategic factor: it will neither unify the Muslim world nor change the balance of power in the Middle East. For it cannot withstand power. What today's Islamists advocate: 'is not the return to an incomparably rich classical age, but the establishment of an empty stage on which the believer strives to realize with each gesture the ethical model of the Prophet'.[38] The empty stage is that of civic society which is non-existent. The Islamization of officially secular and moderate regimes targets personal law and penal law, leaving intact the existing economic formation and the political model inherited from previous regimes. Through processes of globalization, the business élites and governing classes may continue to be picked off, divided against one another, corrupted and incorporated into the global system.

Conclusion

Islamic fundamentalist projects have emerged in all Muslim societies, and among Muslim minorities in non-Muslim societies. These projects have originated as a socio-cultural movement of protest and frustration of a generation of youth that has been excluded socially, economically and politically from the accelerated modernization of Muslim societies and their partial and disjointed articulation to the global economy. However, for reasons to do with the cultural history Islam, the exclusion from modernity takes a religious meaning, and self-immolation becomes the way to fight against exclusion.[39] In this way, as Castells writes, 'Through the negation of exclusion, even in the extreme form of self-sacrifice, a new Islamic identity emerges in the historical process of building the *umma*, the communal heaven for the true believers.'[40] But the preoccupation with the politics of identity by making politics sacred and by transforming Islamic pseudo-legal institutes into 'social devotions', also means that Islamic fundamentalism cannot be taken seriously as a geostrategic counter-hegemonic project.

10

The Developmental States of East Asia

In the 1980s and 1990s, and until the crisis of 1997, the fast and sustained pace of growth of seven countries in East Asia, collectively sometimes referred to as the seven 'Dragons', had forced a major rethink in development studies. The seven countries were: Singapore, Hong Kong, South Korea, Taiwan, Malaysia, Thailand and Indonesia. Curiously, it took rather a long time for the rethink to occur. Because, as a World Bank study in 1993 discovered, since 1960 these high-performing East Asian countries (HPEAs) had grown faster than any other group of countries in the world, including the rich countries (see Figure 10.1).

One reason for this lag between reality and our perception of it owes something to the statistical presentations of world order produced annually by international organizations in their 'state of the world' reports. For over thirty years it had been commonplace to rank the nations of the world *not* by growth rates or economic performance, but by economic groupings based on income. The ranking of the world's economies in ascending order of gross national product (GNP) per capita yielded classifications of economic groupings by arbitrary cut-off points in the ascending order of GNP per capita.

Conventional World Bank rankings used to be low-income, middle-income and high-income countries but, as the World Bank itself acknowledged in its 1993 report, *The East Asian Miracle*, classification by income does not necessarily reflect development status. Moreover, 'once the classification is fixed for any publication, all the historical data presented are based on the same economic

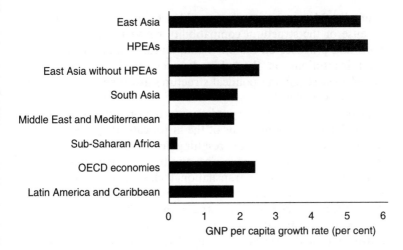

East Asia

HPEAs

East Asia without HPEAs

South Asia

Middle East and Mediterranean

Sub-Saharan Africa

OECD economies

Latin America and Caribbean

0   1   2   3   4   5   6

GNP per capita growth rate (per cent)

Source: World Bank, *The East Asian Miracle* (New York: Oxford University Press, 1993) p. 2. Reproduced with permission.

Figure 10.1   The economic growth of the world's regions (average growth of GNP per capita, 1965–90)

grouping'.[1] Thus, presentation by economic income grouping can hide and prevent other possible classifications, such as those based on growth, changing composition of structure of production, distribution of income, and so on.

Classifications are the cornerstone in any theorizing. For a long time, development theory took as its starting point the income gap between rich and poor countries, between North and South, First World and Third World. It was this gap that prompted the search for the 'sameness' within each group as well as the differences between them. The task which development theory set itself was to theorize, and explain, what made the former rich, and what the latter had to do to become rich (modernization theory), or what made the former rich and kept the latter poor (dependency theory). Modernization theory was closely allied to neoclassical liberal economics, which stressed the benefits to developing countries of participating in the international economy, on the basis of their comparative advantage arising from natural factor endowments. This theory advocated the pursuit of open-door policies towards trade and investment, emphasizing the growth-related benefits of receiving technology and capital inputs from the advanced countries. Modernization theory added to this the argument that, because of the structural compatibility between economic institutions and practices on the one hand, and political, social and cultural institutions on the other, less-developed countries should model their social and political structures after the example of the West (see Chapter 2).

Dependency theorists argued exactly the opposite: they pointed to the debilitating limitations of the historically-developed international division of labour, the resulting deterioration of the terms of trade for less-developed countries, and the distorted internal social structure dominated by transnational class alliances which prevented internal autonomous development and industrialization. Their policy prescription was either a radical break with the world system or, in watered-down, more pragmatic versions, policies of self-reliance and selective delinking. Thus they placed emphasis on import-substitutive industrialization with all the price-distorting state intervention in the economy that this entails.

The Role of the State in Economic Development

By the mid-1970s, some East Asian states – South Korea, Hong Kong, Singapore and Taiwan, collectively known as the 'four Tigers' – had notched up a decade of near double-digit growth. In contrast to the Latin American newly-industrializing countries (NICs) of that period, this growth was export-led, and at first glance seemed to confirm the thesis of orthodox neoclassical writers, that the fast pace of economic development in these countries resulted from liberal, 'market conforming' regimes and 'open-door' policies towards inward investment and foreign trade. But the neoclassical tradition gradually had to come to terms with the incontrovertible evidence of extensive direct government intervention in the East Asian economies. In an effort to salvage the neoclassical tradition, the nature of state intervention was at first argued to be in line with the prevailing orthodoxy, rather than going against it. Thus Bela Balassa,[2] Chalmer Johnson,[3] E. K. Y. Chen,[4] and various World Bank documents of the period argued that government interventions were merely of the kind that aimed at creating macro-economic stability, and a suitable environment for entrepreneurs to perform their functions by providing certain public goods, such as basic education. Where interventions in credit and fiscal policies did occur, these were said to be mainly in order to 'get the prices right' (in line with international prices and not as a distortion of them).

Eventually, some writers within the neoclassical tradition, dubbed revisionists or institutionalists, came to admit that state interventions in East Asian economies were not merely 'market conforming' but rather 'market guiding', even deliberately 'market distorting'.[5] It was beginning to be appreciated that East Asian countries used very selective financial instruments (credit and tax policies), trade policies, inward investment screening policies, and industrial relations policies to channel investment decisions into directions that conformed with national priorities. These interventions did not just remain at the level of macro-economic policies but were sector- and firm-specific.

This marked the beginning of an understanding of the nature of 'state capitalism', in which the primary purpose of government intervention was to promote the interests of the business sector as a whole, and to do so by creating conditions for capital accumulation and productivity improvement, even if this meant extensive bureaucratic regulation and neglect (or repression) of the interests of specific sectors and groups.

For their part, neo-Marxist dependency writers had for a time dismissed the success of the East Asian Tigers as an underdeveloping by-product of the productive decentralization of multinational corporations from the core of the world system. These writers had argued that the 'success' of these countries resulted from a temporary comparative advantage based entirely on the super-exploitation of cheap labour in specially-designated 'free export processing zones' with few linkages to the surrounding economy, and that it eventually deepened inequalities and marginalization. This position came to be known as the new international division of labour (NIDL) thesis (Fröbel *et al.*).[6]

In applying the dependency paradigm to diminish the achievements of the observed process of industrialization, NIDL theorists contended that the stimulus for the industrialization of certain peripheral countries came from the deepening crisis in the core economies of the world system, and the associated problems of valorization of capital. This pushed core capital into the periphery in search of large amounts of unskilled labour power. Technological advances in global communications and transport permitted the spatial dispersal of intermediate production processes, creating branch-plant industrialization massively dependent on corporate decisions and technical inputs from the core economies. The originators of the NIDL thesis (Fröbel *et al.*) asserted that the 'world factory' had overtaken the world market. As to the question of why some peripheral nations were selected in this way rather than others, or all, NIDL theorists merely pointed to the availability in these countries of vast armies of cheap, unskilled labour helpfully offered to international capital by repressive regimes that restricted trade unionization and offered tax incentives to boot.

In the course of the 1980s, as the economic success of these countries was consolidated in real, autonomous upgrading of productive capacity as well as in undeniable, if yet limited, social and civic advance of the masses, the NIDL thesis looked increasingly threadbare. In the generalist versions of the world system and dependency theses, the states of the core countries had been regarded as being 'strong', while those in the periphery were naturally assumed to be 'weak' – that is, a mere instrument of international capital. But in the more detailed, specific examinations of real cases, it was now admitted that, while some developing states were 'weak', others were 'strong'. Writers standing in the neo-Marxist tradition began to take a closer look at the social origins and functions of the state in these countries. Historical structuralist analysis showed that strong states were associated with a degree of autonomy of the state bureaucratic apparatus that owed to a specific class composition, coupled with a specific geopolitical situation.[7]

Theories of the Developmental State

The two intellectual traditions converged somewhat in theories of the developmental state. This convergence broke the debilitating mould that had dominated the agenda of development studies for so long and that had up to that point equated capitalism with democracy, and state bureaucracies with socialism. But this is not to say that the convergence settled on only one theory of the developmental state. Rather, there were variations on a theme: neoclassical and neo-Marxist traditions did not so easily relinquish their methodologies or their world views.

One way in which the neoclassical argument tried to square the circle was by reintroducing Listian political economy into the debate.[8] Friedrich List was a nineteenth-century German political economist who was concerned with how Germany could fashion national policies to develop its manufacturing industry in the face of competition from the more advanced industries in Britain, in a world where a belief in free trade was enshrined in the canons of classical economics. List had argued that when societies at different levels of development come into contact with one another, the more highly-developed society and the more productive economy unleashes a process of 'displacement competition' within the less-developed and less-efficient society and economy. This results in peripheralization and structural deformation unless it is counter-acted by effective political steering (strong state intervention) aimed at temporarily 'dissociating' the economy and society from the international competition.

Neo-Listian theory added to this the observation that, in the contemporary world, 'delayed' development had become increasingly more difficult, and in the process the salience of dissociative conditions for such development has become more pronounced. As a result, development strategy had to become even more 'political'. That is to say, the social agents of delayed development had changed, from private enterprise needing a little mercantilist state protection (as in List's days) to the strong nationalist state.

Neo-Listian theory explained the success of the East Asian countries with reference to the strategic role of the state in taming domestic and international forces and harnessing them to a national economic interest, coining the term 'the developmentalist state' for this purpose. It was pointed out that the developmentalist state had a role different from that of the Keynesian welfare state in the already advanced countries. The Keynesian welfare state, it was argued, serves to restrain market rationality by measures to protect groups vulnerable to the consequences of market rationality. By contrast, the developmentalist state restrains market rationality in order to pursue a policy for industrialization *per se*.[9] The difference between the two forms is made evident in the difference in the sizes of the public sectors: in the advanced countries the public sectors are twice as large as those in the developmentalist countries. In the developmentalist state it is not the size of the public sector that counts but its use in subsidizing certain strategic industries and sectors.

However, to credit the state with developmentally successful intervention in the economy still left a lot of questions unanswered. What are the conditions that give rise to a developmental state? Why did it emerge in East Asia and not, say, in Latin America or Africa? What is the nature of government–business relations and of state–civil society relations? Broadly speaking, the answers to these questions drew *either* on cultural- or 'area'-specific factors *or* on historical–structural and geopolitical factors. I classify them as excursions into comparative political economy, and international political economy respectively.

Comparative Political Economy

One school of thought began to argue that East Asian capitalism was a model of capitalism quite different from the model of capitalist development originating in the West. Peter Berger,[10] for example, says that East Asian capitalism presents a 'second' case. It is a case of successful industrialization that (unlike the Western case) combines growth with equity from the beginning of the modernization process. East Asia is also 'exceptional' in so far as public authority and state intervention have led the modernization process rather than individual enterprise, the free market and representational democracy.

In Berger's view, cultural norms and values derived from the Confucian ethic explained both the public spiritedness of officialdom (that of the developmentalist bureaucracy), and the obedience of the populace, who were said to prefer social harmony to conflict. Berger admitted that there was some irony in the way that Confucianism was now presented (including by himself) as a cultural factor explaining successful economic development, when previously, following Max Weber, theoretical analyses had always pointed to Confucianism as one of the *obstacles* to economic development of East Asia. Confucianism had been dismissed by Weber for its conservatism and antagonism to economic activity. But, at least until the Crash of '97 it was widely praised for its 'respect for superiors, its collective solidarity, and its emphasis on discipline'.[11]

It requires a considerable stretch of the imagination to spread a hypothesis of postConfucianism (that is, modernized Confucianism) to include an entire region noted for its multiple and competing religions, and to maintain, in Peter Berger's words, that 'Confucian-derived values hold sway in the lives of ordinary people, many of whom have never read a Confucian classic and have little education.'[12] Nevertheless, other scholars too, and not least 'postcolonial' Chinese intellectuals,[13] have asserted that, in the melting pot of East Asian culture, Confucianism has mixed syncretically with other religions and traditional value systems such as Buddhism, Taoism, Shintoism, folk religions and even Christianity, creating a unique system of ethics characterized by diligence, respect for authority, familism and a positive attitude to the affairs of the world.

This kind of simplistic social science theorizing, in the view of others, merely served as an ideological prop to repressive regimes in their suppression of unpalatable facts. Such facts, for example, included the existence of martial law in Taiwan, which was not lifted until 1987, after which Confucian values of 'obedience' spontaneously gave way to a storm of labour and environmental protests; the all-pervasive censorship in Singapore which gags the media, the churches and the public, and prompts many to vote with their feet and emigrate; or the fury of democratic movements in Korea which in the late-1980s successfully confronted the authorities with a forth-right militancy that achieved some timid democratic reforms.[14] Indeed, it is testimony to organized union militancy in at least three of the four 'Tiger' economies (Korea, Taiwan and Hong Kong) that wages have been driven up to the point where capital (including not least domestic capital) has been forced to seek cheaper locations further afield, in Malaysia, Indonesia and Thailand. There, the entire cycle of boot-camp-managed export-industrialization and the struggle for democratization started all over again.[15]

International Political Economy

Analysts standing in the Marxist tradition have predictably not paid such attention to cultural explanations of the emergence of the developmental states in East Asia. Rather, they have tended to emphasize geopolitical and historical–structural factors.

Many analysts argue that the legitimating basis for government authority in directing East Asian capitalism has rested not so much on Confucian values as on the geopolitical reality of US Pacific dominance in the postwar period.[16] This Pacific dominance was articulated in strategic military and economic aid to the postwar regimes, the object of which was to develop Japan, South Korea and Taiwan as bulwarks against Communism. For example, the USA provided economic and military aid to South Korea totalling US$13 billion or US$600 per capita in the period 1945–79, and during the 1950s US aid accounted for five-sixths of Korean imports. The comparable figure for Taiwan was US$5.6 billion.[17]

Admittedly, while American aid was a major contributor to the economies of South Korea and Taiwan during the 1950s, this was not the case with Hong Kong and Singapore, whose economies had previously served as regional entrepôts and who still retain entrepôt functions to this day.[18] But both prospered as small enclaves at the cutting edge of the US containment policy of Communism in the Far East. Hong Kong became the gateway for Communist China's clandestine commercial exchanges with the West, while Singapore's take-off in the mid-1960s owed in no small measure to its profitable oil, and ship-repairing commerce with American forces in Vietnam.[19]

American geopolitical interests in the region did more than contribute military and economic assistance and provide commercial opportunities. More important perhaps than the power of the USA to shape international security arrangements was that it understood with remarkable enlightened self-interest that security arrangements depended on shaping international economic arrangements. As Stephen Krasner has noted:

> Economic prosperity was thought to be a prophylactic against communism. American policy makers promoted European economic unification even though this was, in the long term, bound to place American products at some comparative disadvantage; and they tolerated explicit Japanese discrimination against American exports and direct investment. Their basic objective was to increase the level of absolute well-being in the western alliance.[20]

Other countries in the region benefited in the same way from American security-inspired largesse. As a benevolent hegemon, the USA was prepared to allow relative political autonomy in economic matters and tolerate the mercantilist policies of the regional states in an otherwise Bretton Woods-supervised free trade world. As Stephen Haggard writes:

> These strategic considerations dictated significant exceptions to the liberal, multilateral norm in East Asia just as they did in Europe. Trade, financial and aid links were self-consciously developed to serve three mutually supportive goals: economic reconstruction, strengthening the internal political position of pro-American political élites, and cementing strategic relations through economic interdependence.[21]

Under these circumstances, mercantilism, or state-directed economic development, became for the externally politically supported regimes the legitimating basis for their intervention in the economy and the restructuring of government business relations. Over time, their survival came to be dependent on economic success. Instead of having to 'buy out' rent-seeking strongmen as the fledgling national regimes in Africa had to do (see Chapter 8), they could, from the beginning, command authority and resources to a degree sufficient to protect policy-makers from clients demanding payouts.

Freed from these political pressures, decision-makers and technocrats were better able to direct economic policy and state intervention in ways that were not only efficient but also profitable for the business class. In directing businesses to adapt to the opportunities available in export markets, former clients were forced out of rent-seeking and into productive activities. Over time, this helped to develop a business class who identified their own interests with those of the state as an autonomous organization. Export success and economic expansion financed subsequent market interventions by the government and helped further to insulate bureaucrats from the temptations of corruption. Fast economic development, in turn, generated a broader 'growth coalition' supportive of policies geared towards promoting economic efficiency, which sustained an institutional and political framework that enabled bureaucracies to follow through with successful policies.[22]

To such geopolitical analyses must be added the *historical–structural* analysis of the development of capitalism on a world scale. While geopolitical forces helped to firm up the early regimes and motivate their interventions in directing their economies and fashioning

state–business and state–society relations, equally there were confluent forces at work in the way international capitalism had reached
a level of development of productive forces and relations of production which gave rise to 'peripheral Fordism'. In Chapter 3 we
described how peripheral Fordism came about, and how it selectively
homed in on *some* but not all developing countries, depending on the
availability of a docile labour force, authoritarian regimes sympa-
thetic to international capital and supportive of a business class
willing to seize the chance to participate on a subcontracting,
junior-partner basis to the accumulation of capital on a global scale.

Globalization and the Limits of the East Asia Developmental Model

The question as to what extent the developmental state phenomenon in East Asia was historically specific, rather than culturally
specific, is important in determining both the limits of this model for
the future of the developmental states themselves and the emulation
of their model by other, second-generation, industrializers in the
region. After all, a model, as Berger helpfully reminds us, is a term
that has two connotations: 'on the one hand it means a specific
pattern or type, on the other it means an example to be emulated'.[23]

The historical specificity of the 'model' relates both to the external environment of the geopolitics of the Cold War and its unique
conjunction with a certain phase in the development of capitalism
on a world scale. By the late 1980s, well before the crisis of 1997,
critics such as Walden Bello and Stephanie Rosenfeld, were talking
about *Dragons in Distress*, as in the pithy title of their excellent
study of three NICs – Korea, Taiwan and Singapore.[24] They argued
that a comprehensive alternative vision and model of development
was needed because the external environment of these countries had
changed radically, and in the attempt to redirect developmental
strategy their states also came up against the limits of the internal
environment.[25]

Geopolitically, the USA had ceased to be the guardian of the
liberal trading order and in fact had become aggressively protectionist, blaming the NICs, together with Japan, for its huge trade
deficit. The end of the Cold War and the extinction of the Soviet
threat undermined any last vestige of US strategic interest in maintaining the exceptionally favourable trading and currency status of

the countries in the region, or in bolstering their authoritarian regimes. A battery of punitive US trade measures and currency manipulations, coupled with the deep recession in the mid-1980s, forced Korea, Taiwan and Singapore into rethinking their strategy away from export-orientated industrialization for mass markets abroad, and towards either seizing a commanding role in the new high-tech-driven world economy (as in Singapore's strategy), and/or a deepening of the domestic market, as in the more populous Taiwan and Korea.

However, according to Bello and Rosenfeld, these strategies now threatened to unravel because of the social and ecological consequences of the previous phase: repression had disenfranchised the middle classes, had alienated the poor from an 'economic miracle' built on their backs, and had caused a collapse of the agricultural sector and environmental degradation that choked off further growth. Well before the financial crash of 1997, they predicted a growing crisis of political legitimacy intertwining with a developing economic crisis.

It is true that, judging by conventional measures of quality of life, namely life expectancy, mortality rates and literacy rates, all seven Dragons had scored undisputed successes, but the downside was evident in appalling air and water pollution, deforestation and overcrowding.[26] Moreover, the record of social progress as measured by declining income inequality and poverty levels continued to be a matter of interpretation and dispute. The statistics were not robust: the World Bank made much of the claim that all the high-performing East Asian economies (HPEAs) had combined high-speed growth with equity, but in its trailblazing report published in 1993 it relied on figures that cover only the period 1970–80, where attributed, or did not attribute them at all.[27]

For example, in relation to Korean data, Bello and Rosenfeld used statistics collected and analysed by various South Korean writers, in unpublished manuscripts,[28] which pointed to *increasing* income inequality over the period 1970–81, which the World Bank claimed to record *declining* income inequality. Others, too, doubted the reliability of the claim of reduction in income inequality in South Korea, arguing that the data had been 'derived from surveys that exclude wealthy households, single person households, nonfarm households in rural areas and small farmers'.[29] Singaporean claims of narrowing income inequalities have been questioned by E. Paul.[30]

But even if we accept the consensus which, rightly or wrongly, has developed in respect of the 'combined equity with growth' thesis of the East Asian model, it can hardly be disputed that the region as a whole, on the eve of the 1997 crash, still faced an uphill task in lifting the mass of the population above subsistence level. The question to ask in the context of a globalizing economy is, under what conditions can the developmental states complete the project of national developmentalism? In a globalized world economy, it becomes increasingly difficult for the state to subordinate business interests to its own strategic concerns. As Nigel Harris has noted, the endeavour of building competitive capacity through state-assisted economic development has a contradictory result. To the extent that the private sector has been encouraged to survive as a means of accelerating growth, to that extent governments have been successful in creating a strong private capitalist class ultimately capable of challenging the priorities of state policy. Moreover, the change in the social weight of the business class *at home* is not the only implication. As Harris put it:

> As the world economy becomes increasingly integrated, the mark of maturity of a national capitalist class is that world competition drives it to operate internationally, to merge increasingly with global capital. This is only feasible with the liberation of capital from all that mass of restrictions which national governments seek to impose in order to capture a larger share of any surplus for the nation ... National liberation freed the State; restructuring and liberalization now freed capital ... Thus paradoxically, national economic development that was impelled by the rivalries within the State system now produces a new component in the market system that in part contradicts the independence of the State.[31]

The rising figures of regional and overseas direct investment by the Tiger economies in the 1990s is testimony to their deepening participation in the process of globalization. For example, annual FDI flows from the Republic of Korea, Singapore and Taiwan were US$5.7 billion during 1988–92, compared to US$0.4 billion during 1983–7. And while most of this outward investment was located in the East Asian region, such investments also increased in Europe and North America.[32]

But as the 1990s proceeded, the interweaving of East Asia's official and private sector savings with the global circulation of capital took on gigantic proportions. During the September 1997 IMF/World Bank meeting in Hong Kong, the Chief Executive of the Hong Kong monetary authority, Joseph Yam, questioned publicly the foreign investment of the region's foreign reserves, arguing that more than 80 per cent of total Asian foreign exchange reserves (including that of Japan), amounting to US$600 billion were invested mainly in North America and Europe.[33]

Globalization not only affects the developmental process through the increasing interweaving of global and domestic capital. Equally important is the reshaping of the world economy into high-value producers and routine, high-volume producers, as discussed in Chapter 6. Modern factories and state-of-the-art machinery can be installed almost anywhere around the globe, throwing 'routine' producers into competition with one another in capital's relentless search for the cheapest locations. Thus competition from low-cost producers had already begun to frustrate the completion of the developmental project in the successful East Asian economies.

Regionalization: the Next Lap?

In the 1990s it seemed that the best hope for the multitudes in the East Asian region who were not yet benefiting from the economic growth that had taken place, was an accelerating process of regional economic integration. While the developmental possibilities of export-orientated industrialization are limited, productive upgrading and internally-based growth are constrained by the limits of national markets and consumer demand. It was therefore important that the drive to maturity of East Asian capitalism became locked into a wider coherent territorial space in which the positive social dynamics of capitalist development might be played out. What were the chances of such regional integration?

One major problem is what is sometimes referred to as the 'variable geometry' of the region. What, indeed, is the region? Where does it begin; where does it end? And which countries belong to it? For reasons of both political history *and* of economic realities, there are several competing, if loose, regional groupings (sometimes no more than *initiatives* for regional groupings) with part-different, part-overlapping membership. The fact that these initiatives coexist despite conflicting conceptions of the region, and of the nature and extent of wished-for economic co-operation, is testimony to the fluidity of the present time when globalizing and regionalizing forces take turns to wax and wane.

The hardiest of the groupings is the Association of South East Asian Nations (ASEAN), originally formed in 1967, and until the late 1990s more preoccupied with anti-Communist security issues than with economic integration. ASEAN includes the Philippines, Malaysia, Thailand, Singapore, Indonesia, Brunei and, of late, Vietnam. Tellingly, it *excludes* three of the four Tigers: Hong Kong, Taiwan and South Korea. In 1989, the Prime Minister of Malaysia, Mahathir Mohamed, set up the East Asia Economic Grouping (soon to be watered down to a mere caucus, EAEC) with the specific aim of developing a trade bloc, dominated by the yen, as a counterweight to the EU and NAFTA, and seeking to include, besides ASEAN, South Korea, Hong Kong, Taiwan and, eventually, China. Japan was invited to lead the caucus, and while at first very cautious, has since shown signs of warming to the concept. Meanwhile, China too has become a leading actor within the variable geometry of the region by actively pursuing a concept of 'Greater China' or the 'China Circle', mapping within its sub-regional orbit southern China, Taiwan and Hong Kong–Macau as one viable growth triangle.[34]

Anxious not to be left out and to pre-empt protectionist moves, in 1992, Australia, with the wholehearted support of the USA, proposed the Asia Pacific Cooperation Forum (APEC), striving to include all of the above countries apart from Vietnam, but plus the USA, Australia, New Zealand, and, more recently, even Mexico and Chile. APEC's expressed aims are to promote 'open regionalism', emphasizing the neo-liberal creed of liberalization, privatization and open markets. ASEAN countries reacted coolly to the APEC initiative, fearing marginalization by the larger players, notably the USA. In 1993, they responded by setting up the ASEAN Free Trade Area (AFTA), agreeing to reduce tariffs on intra-ASEAN trade goods over a fifteen-year period, with about 40 per cent of this trade being targeted for accelerated reductions.[35] This move was parried by APEC, in 1994, when it announced the formation of a (non-discriminatory) Asia-Pacific trade liberalization scheme aimed at producing free trade by 2020. AFTA responded by extending its effective preferential list of trade goods and shortening the implementation period to ten years.[36]

Thus competing conceptions of the 'region' dovetailed with competing economic ideologies of discriminatory versus non-discriminatory trade, or regional trade integration versus global liberalization of trade. Meanwhile, there were changes in political economy happening on the ground that make these competing configurations of regionalization less critically different. As Paul Bowles and Brian MacLean[37] argue in a persuasive review of emerging trading arrangements in the region, much of our second-guessing of the evolution of trade blocs is based on *de facto* analyses of cross-border trade culled from statistical examinations of customs books. However, such analyses often fail to capture the extent and depth of intra-firm trade (trade occurring within multinational enterprises) spread across countries in one region.

Since the revaluation of the yen following the Plaza Accord of 1985, Japanese foreign direct investment in the whole of Asia jumped from 50 per cent to 80 per cent of all Japanese FDI flows.[38] In absolute terms, it went up two and a half times, from US\$2.9 billion to US\$8.1 billion between 1991 and 1995.[39] As William Tabb notes, East Asia has emerged as an increasingly tightly co-ordinated manufacturing bloc, exhibiting a complex regional pattern of production and distribution, with Japanese multinationals cross-exporting and importing parts from and between their facilities in the region, assigning to each a specific role within a dynamically flexible but coherent strategic plan organized and administered from Japan.[40] This 'flying geese' pattern of regional trade has, according to one estimate, increased the index of intraindustry trade by 91 per cent for the Philippines; 90 per cent for Indonesia; 85 per cent for Thailand; and 64 per cent for Malaysia during 1979–88.[41] According to Lim, these intraindustry trade patterns make the logic of regional trading arrangements (for example, as in AFTA's or EAEC's proposals) more compelling in so far as the ASEAN countries 'as a group can offer investors . . . a combination [of advantages] that no member individually possesses'.[42]

Thus the fact that the division of labour within the region has become more a *process* rather than a *product* division, makes the case for regional trade integration of the AFTA and EAEC variety more compelling; yet it is *also* a case, as Bowles and MacLean point out, that is qualitatively different from past objectives of trade integration. Whereas in the past regional economic integration initiatives were meant to maximize *inward looking trade creation* as the reason for forming a trade bloc, the objective is now one of *outward looking investment creation.*[43]

The Crash of '97

The East Asian financial crisis of 1997 began on 2 July, when the Thai currency, the baht, relinquished its historic peg to the US dollar, and took a nosedive on the foreign exchanges which quickly spread to the regional currencies of Indonesia, Malaysia, South Korea, the Philippines and Hong Kong. As currencies fell, foreign capital exited, stockmarkets crashed, companies were bankrupted and millions of people lost their savings and their jobs. At the time, the first reaction of analysts and commentators was one of surprise: who could have suspected this when the 'economic fundamentals' had been so sound? This was rapidly followed by a blaming discourse, in which two opposing camps pointed the accusing finger either at 'internal', institutional and political factors, or at 'external' factors, in particular short-term and speculative international capital movements.[44]

The reaction in the Western press was, by and large, one of triumphalism: the mystique of Asian values had at last been shown to add up to no more than warm words wrapped around plain cronyism, corruption and an appalling lack of accountability. If only they had adopted Western values and the Rule of Law! For example, it was 'suddenly' discovered that state support for private enterprise (praised and admired up to that point) had never much been targeted using criteria of entrepreneurial merit, but rather had often been a matter of personal connections and political patronage determining the access to credit and other resources, and on which terms. It was also 'suddenly' discovered that the much applauded role of industrial policy had in effect been to provide implicit guarantees to investment projects in government-favoured industries, thus encouraging their managers to take excessive risks.[45] As the Economic Report of the President (USA) to Congress in February 1999 summed it up:

First, connected lending and, at times, corrupt credit practices rendered the financial sectors of the crisis economies fragile.

Loans were often politically directed to favored firms and sectors. In addition, regulation and supervision of banking systems were notably weak, and implicit or explicit guarantees that the government would bail out financial institutions in trouble created moral hazard. These weaknesses contributed to a lending boom and over investments in projects and sectors, especially real estate and certain other sectors not exposed to international competition.[46]

This view was widely shared by other protectors of the global capitalist community, notably the IMF, who seized the opportunity to make emergency assistance, in the shape of stabilization packages, conditional upon far-ranging liberalization of trade and investment flows, and on 'deregulation' coupled with 'transparency' and 'accountability' of the domestic banking systems in the affected countries. As the Under-Secretary of the US Treasury Department, Larry Summers, candidly and contentedly admitted: 'In some ways the IMF has done more in these past months to liberalise these economies and open their markets to US goods and services than has been achieved in rounds of trade negotiations in the region'.[47]

The other side was led by Mahatir Mohamed of Malaysia, who equally robustly blamed hot money and fickle international investors, and more especially the Quantum hedge-fund chief, George Soros. The argument here rested on the empirical evidence that, in just the three years leading up to the crisis, net private capital flows to the region's economies had more than doubled,[48] that much of it had proved to be of a short-term, speculative kind, gravitating not to the productive sectors but to the stockmarket and real estate,[49] and had exited with indecent haste at the first signs of currency devaluation.[50]

Each side of the paradigmatic divide had its own chorus of academics who turned 'paradigms into parrot times', in Robert Wade's witty paraphrase.[51] It is not necessary here to repeat the various arguments. The essential point is that the very fact that these two factions were still separated analytically showed that people had not quite grasped the nature of globalization.

The conceptual image that drives this analytical distinction is still one of globalization as an intensification of flows (whether of capital or trade) *between* nations, as if traversing some vacant space between principally bounded, regulated (or not so well regulated as the case may be) markets. However, the growth of risk arbitrage by hedge funds[52] (see Chapter 6), and particularly the rapid proliferation of custom-based derivative instruments in international financial markets,[53] bears witness to an increasing intertwining of these markets in such a way that borrowers and lenders are scattered even while they are connected, and counter-parties are concealed from one another even while they are being joined at the hip.

Add to this the lack of adequate separation between onshore and offshore activities of a country's (*any* country's) banks, and the picture of a truly global financial whirlpool is complete. The UNCTAD Trade and Development Report of 1998 reports at length on the participation by East Asian banks in the global banking business through such offshore activities. For example, it singles out for scrutiny the Bangkok International Banking Facility (established in Thailand in 1992), which 'increasingly served as a conduit for interest rate arbitrage between domestic and international financial markets, much of the financing made available through such arbitrage being used to finance speculation in stocks and property'.[54] In short, in the global financial markets, the distinction between 'international' lenders and 'domestic' borrowers falls away: they become one and the same.

What became better understood in a second round of analyses after the dust had settled, was that these globalizing pressures had in fact, been targeted on the region's economies *well before* the crisis, and perhaps even deliberately so by the political manipulations of the US government and the IMF. Peter Gowan, for example, asserts that the East Asian crisis resulted from 'what might be called the teamwork between the spontaneous drivers of the financial forces of Wall Street and the political will and ingenuity of Washington'.[55]

This, in one view, is how it happened. Throughout the 1980s the USA and Japan had a strong symbiotic economic–financial relationship which steered the dollar–yen exchange rate.[56] As the USA grappled with budget deficits, and with trade account deficits mainly with Japan, it was in the USA's interests to channel the increasingly large Japanese trade account surpluses into dollar holdings, for example US Treasury bonds. This was achieved by the Plaza Accord in 1985, which pushed the yen up against the dollar for the following ten years, and by a related and none-too-subtle message from the MITI (the Japanese Ministry of Trade and Industry) that coaxed companies to buy US Treasury bonds. The new dollar–yen exchange rate in turn led Japanese producers to relocate core manufacturing to East Asia, where currencies were pegged to the dollar, this itself being a legacy of the postwar geopolitical settlement under US hegemony discussed earlier (see page 224), thus making these economies competitive export platforms for Japanese products. But by 1995 the Japanese economy was close to a financial meltdown,[57] and this time a joint US–Japanese political intervention in the foreign exchange markets deliberately reversed the dollar–yen exchange rate to loosen Japanese monetary policy. An arguably *unintended* side effect was that Japan's loose monetary policy created huge amounts of liquidity in the international credit markets, with much of it being exported to Japan's East Asian neighbours as portfolio investment and short-term loans. It also fuelled the hedge fund 'financial warfare' against the East Asian currencies.[58] At the same time as exports from the East Asian economies, being pegged this time to a declining dollar value, were becoming increasingly uncompetitive in international markets, the USA and the IMF put pressure on their governments to liberalize their capital accounts, allowing the free movement into and out of domestic currency areas. Thus money was drawn in by a strong currency and it contributed to the export collapse which undermined confidence that the debts would be repaid, while the liberalization of the capital accounts permitted the exit of funds when the rot set in.[59] Telling evidence that the *antecedent* pressures for liberalization were a huge contributory factor in the crisis comes from the comparison with those countries in the region that had ignored such pressures, and which escaped largely unscathed: India, China, Taiwan and Vietnam.

In sum, it is inappropriate to blame either Asian countries or international lenders for the crisis. The conclusion rather would be either to see it as a crisis typical of capitalism in this particular globalized phase, or to regard it more suspiciously as a deliberate attempt by the US government to engineer a downfall of what was rapidly becoming an all-too-competitive region in the world economy, regain its hegemonic status in that part of the world, and force down the value of the assets in the region to where they would prove to be easy pickings for US capital rolling in on the coat tails of the IMF's rescue packages.

The economic conditionalities of the IMF assembled rescue packages (to the tune of US$120 billion for Korea, Indonesia and

Thailand – Malaysia did not join the party and introduced temporary capital controls) consisted of the usual 'austerity' prescriptions: savage cuts in government expenditure coupled with the maintenance of high interest rates and the raising of taxes. Together they pushed the affected economies into depression. For example, the IMF calculates that the 'cumulative' output losses over a four-year period after the crisis amounted to 82 per cent in the case of Indonesia; 27 per cent for Korea; 39 per cent for Malaysia; and 57 per cent for Thailand.[60] The World Bank estimates that the percentage of the population living below the nationally defined poverty line, as an immediate result of the crisis, rose by 5.4 per cent in Indonesia; just over 10 per cent in Korea (urban population only); and about 3 per cent in Thailand (where the middle classes were affected disproportionately).[61] Unemployment totals rose variously by between 6 per cent in Thailand; 9 per cent in Korea; and up to 60 per cent in Indonesia.[62] Meanwhile, the financial rescue package itself guaranteed the repayment of debt to international private investors, thus ensuring that they would be happy to come back in the future in the secure knowledge that they would always be rescued.

It remains a moot point whether the whole sorry saga was indeed a deliberate geopolitical strategy on the part of the USA: coherent, thought-out, and conspiratorially put together. Peter Gowan, who has unearthed many incriminating documents and statements uttered by key personnel, nevertheless states cautiously that there is no conclusive evidence that 'the Clinton administration acted strategically from 1995 ... to bring East and South-East Asia to its knees', although he says there is much 'circumstantial evidence' to suggest that strategic planning played a part.[63] On the other hand, there is little doubt that the fall of East Asia was both opportunistically and strategically seized upon by the USA to reoccupy the economic high ground, and that its discourse and analysis of the crisis (crony capitalism) was fulsomely applied to hammer home the virtues of globalism in a region that had come dangerously close to developing its own near-independent integrated pattern of production and trade. The most telling pointer here is is that when Japan, during a G7 meeting in Hong Kong in September 1997, floated the idea of an Asian Monetary Fund to stabilize the financial systems in the region, the proposal was immediately shot down by the IMF with strong US backing, on the stated grounds that two rival monetary funds would create 'moral hazard' by allowing countries access to emergency funds even if they failed to adopt tough economic reforms.[64] The real reason was more probably concern about US reliance on Japan's and other East Asian dollar holdings, which might have been sold to finance such a fund, and the consolidation of regional integration that such a fund would have implied.

But whether or not the USA acted with malice aforethought is not really what matters. It is not important whether Bill Clinton sat in his Oval Office thinking what he could do for American capital. Indeed, the really interesting and relevant twist in this particular story of globalization is that neither the US President, nor the National Security Council, the State Department, not even the CIA, all of whom are traditional participants in the making of US foreign policy, contributed anything much to the negotiations, and when they did they were overruled.[65] By all accounts, it was the US Treasury and the Wall Street financial firms who, together with and through the IMF, shaped the reform agenda. It was this cabal that had both the crucial relationships with finance ministers and central bank directors, and understood the technical details and policy issues.[66] In Chapter 8, on Africa, we have already had an opportunity to learn that discourse analysis is a helpful methodology to describe how social and economic relations come into being as a result of the way they are being spoken of. Herein lies the power of the international 'donor' agenda. Discourse creates facts on the ground. The unremitting word-fall about 'cronyism' by the USA, the international financial institutions and press, in the aftermath of the 'crisis' evolved into a wider agenda about structural reform and about rebuilding 'confidence' in the markets that went way beyond the cleansing of corrupt banking practices, to include punishing monetary and fiscal policies (raising taxes and interest rates, and cutting government spending) and opening previously closed sectors of the financial and economic sectors to global capital. Governments in receipt of international rescue packages had their arms twisted into accepting these political and economic conditionalities that created new realities. These proved to be most beneficial for global capital, and more especially US capital. In the first half of 1998, US companies bought up double the number of Asian businesses they had bought in any previous year, prompting Hiromu Nonaka, Secretary-General of Japan's ruling Liberal Democratic Party, to observe: 'There is an invasion of foreign capital, especially US capital, under way. A type of colonisation of Asia has started.'[67]

Conclusion

At the time of writing, it is too soon to tell whether the crash of '97 has dealt a definitive blow to the developmentalist model, the drive for regional coherence, and the extension of the project to provide real and sustainable advances for the mass of the populace in the region. On the plus side, the signs are of recovery on all the usual indicators so beloved of the liberal press: currencies have stabilized; stockmarkets are rising; exports have resumed their upward trend; GDP is back on track, with an average of 3.4 percent;[68] and even poverty indicators are improving, according to the World Bank.[69] Most important of all, the 'Asian eclipse' has strengthened pro-democracy movements, notably in Indonesia, which saw the departure of President Suharto and his cronies (for thirty years supported and protected by the USA and global capital), but also in other lands, where legal measures have been put in place to break the link between vote-buying and government corruption (as, for example, in Thailand), or opposition parties have been able to join the fray with more muscle than before. On the downside (again, according to the liberal press) there is foot-dragging on the promised structural reforms, although the IMF's recent assessment shows some satisfaction with the reform of the banking sector and the liberalization of capital accounts in Korea and Thailand, and, more tellingly, even in Malaysia, which initially pursued an unorthodox agenda.[70] Evidence that even without arm-twisting the discourse of the crisis itself has had the desired effect of moving East Asian economic practice closer to the US model.[71]

As for the prospects of regional coherence, here the longer-term picture seems more contradictory, and indeed hopeful. The IMF-imposed solutions to the crisis have met with deep political resentment, which has undermined the credence of APEC and in fact reinvogorated the search for regional co-operation through exclusive Asian regional groupings such as the EAEC and ASEAN.[72] In this way, paradoxically, the East Asian crisis, which was triumphantly seized upon to force through a globalist agenda, may well end up as the foundation for a new regionalism.

11

Democracy, Civil Society and Postdevelopment in Latin America

In this part of the book we illuminate, in separate chapters, the manner in which globalization has an impact on and is responded to in different regions of what used to be called the Third World. Each time we select a dominant theme as a conduit for our inquiry. These themes are not chosen arbitrarily. Rather, they reflect the preoccupation in the literature with what is happening in various parts of the world. They are intended to convey a kind of summary statement of the intellectual consensus, a sound-bite characterization. Africa is 'about' the disintegration of the state and the collapse of civil society; East Asia is 'about' the success of state-led development; the Middle East is 'about' the Islamic anti-developmentalist revolt. Similarly, Latin America is about the return to 'democracy' and the birth of 'civil society'. As Norbert Lechner has put it: 'If revolution was the articulating axis of the Latin American debate in the 1960s, in the 1980s the central theme is democracy.'[1]

This debate about the democratization of Latin America is, first and foremost, a debate among Latin American intellectuals themselves, and more strongly the Latin American left. As such, the debate cannot be divorced from the particular historical circumstance, post-Cold War and postmodern, in which the Latin American left tries to accommodate and transcend the forces of globalization and the legitimating mantle of neo-liberal ideology. As we shall see, this situation is not without irony, but neither is it without hope, for it signals that at the precise historical juncture when structural forces appear to be at their most imperative, human agency may yet find its political moment.

The Latin American Intellectual Left

Why should we privilege the Latin American intellectuals in our understanding of Latin America? And why the left? It is because, as Jorge Castañeda, in his comprehensive book on the subject, *Utopia Unarmed*, tells us, they have always fulfilled a central, and even disproportionate, role in Latin American societies and politics. They are an entity unto themselves; they make up a separate estate.[2]

As to the reasons why this should be so, Castañeda points to two: the postcolonial domestic social structure; and the particular relationship of Latin American intellectuals with the outside world. The postcolonial domestic social structure has always been characterized by a strong state and a weak civil society, in which political parties were often unrepresentative, civil institutions (judges, courts, a free press and trade unions) weak or absent, and nation building incomplete. In this situation the intellectual stood out, Castañeda argues. But the term 'intellectual' encompasses a broad spectrum: almost anyone who writes, paints, acts, teaches, or speaks out, even sings, becomes 'an intellectual'.[3] They write, speak, advocate, or do what is accomplished elsewhere by more specialized institutions or groups. And, he continues, from the early part of the twentieth century most of the better known Latin American intellectuals were on the left of the political spectrum, even if they did not always dominate the region's thinking or politics.[4]

On the other hand, the prominence of these intellectuals stemmed from 'their role as a conduit between a region avid for ideas, experiences, and doctrines from abroad, and an outside world where these commodities were produced and generated'.[5]

I would add that this intellectual articulation with the West, sometimes confrontational, sometimes accommodating, but often at the cutting edge of political theory, arises from a different postcolonial condition from that found in other regions of the world. In Latin America, colonialism has succeeded more or less completely in wiping out native culture and society, and the present population, certainly those strata of the urban middle class from which intellectuals are chiefly drawn in any society, are of European descent. Thus, in the main, they did not draw on native roots, culture or religion, in their search for national identity and self-expression.

This double positioning of the Latin American intellectual left on the seam between Latin America and the rest of the world, and between a strong state and a weak civil society, helps us to understand the tumultuous trajectory of the region's postwar transition from developmental aspirations through the long night of the generals and the debt débâcle of the 1980s, to the contemporary accommodation with, and struggles to transcend, neo-liberal challenges. While as a class or stratum the native intelligentsia served, as Castañeda has put it, as mediators or interlocutors between two sets of actors who often proved incapable of communicating directly with each other (that is, state and society),[6] it has also to be recognised that *individuals* from these strata were frequently co-opted by the political class and drafted into office, or were otherwise seduced into participating in the leadership of political parties, writing their platforms and giving direction to the policies that shaped the region. Thus they often had political power. Castañeda quotes the writer Garcia Márquez:

> There is a curious relationship between intellectuals and political power in Latin America. The State and the powers-that-be both need us and fear us. They need us because we give them prestige they lack, they fear us because our sentiments and views can damage them. In the history of power in Latin America, there are only military dictatorships or intellectuals. No wonder then – and it is a fascinating thing – that there was so much coddling of the intellectuals by the State. Under these circumstances, one cannot be always completely independent.[7]

There is another reason for singling out the Latin American left. It is my view that the neo-liberal adjustment of Latin America to the world economy has in fact preceded and pre-charted the neo-liberal integration of the advanced countries as well. And much of the experience with the return to democracy, particularly the rise of new social movements and the changing role of civil society, is a foretaste of things to come in the 'old' democracies of the West as well. The Latin American left's reflection on the nature of the new political economy therefore becomes an invaluable inspiration to those who search for ideas about social reconstruction in the old democracies too.

Postwar Developmentalism and Dependency Theory

Before the Second World War, Latin America occupied a position in the world economy much the same as other colonial areas (hence Lenin's designation of Latin America as a 'semi-colony').[8] It produced primary exports in exchange for manufactured goods from the West; its mines and plantations were either directly owned or controlled by foreign companies; its ruling landed oligarchies were a handmaiden to Western interests; and national policies of exchange rates, tariffs and taxation favoured the export sector over the interests of the native urban industrialists and workers. However, the depression of the 1930s and the subsequent war years forced Latin American countries on to a path of import substitution as an emergency measure to produce goods that could no longer be obtained from abroad. The experience with this effective, if historically contingent, structural break with the world capitalist system was positive, and in the aftermath of the Second World War it grew into a fully-fledged model of development.

The theoretical foundations for this model were laid by Raoúl Prebisch, an Argentinian economist and one-time director of the Economic Commission for Latin America (ECLA – or CEPAL, to give it its Spanish acronym). In a seminal paper published in 1950, Prebisch[9] argued that the classical Ricardian theory of international trade was not applicable in the context of the existing international division of labour, and instead contributed to trade-generated inequality and structural underdevelopment. Prebisch and his colleagues at ECLA favoured import substitution as a means of helping the process of infant industrialization of underdeveloped countries, and they assigned a leading role to the state in pursuing policies of inward-directed development combining state-protected industrialization with import substitution, under the aegis of foreign investment.

Elsewhere I have described how the 'structuralist' analysis of Prebisch and his colleagues in ECLA were not only influential in shaping early postwar policies in Latin America, but also became the crucible from which later neo-Marxist dependency theory was cast.[10] Indeed, dependency theory was principally a Latin American theory of development.

There were other influences, however, which *ab initio* reinforced the state-centric nature of postwar policies. Duncan Green recalls the way Soviet industrialization and the heavily state-led revival of the European economies after the Second World War further established the centrality of the state in successful economic planning. He sums up the comprehensive catalogue of state policies: investment in infrastructure required by industry; subsidizing basic foods and imposing price controls to keep labour costs down in urban areas; protection of local industries against foreign competition; nationalization of key industries, such as oil, utilities and steel, and establishing new ones; and supporting an overvalued exchange rate, making Latin America's exports expensive and imports cheap.[11]

The model of 'import substitutive industrialization' (ISI) became the trademark of Latin America in the 1950s and 1960s, and while it was subsequently discredited and compared negatively with the ostensibly more successful export-oriented strategy of industrialization (EOI) of the East Asian economies, it was, as Green reminds us, successful on its own terms, and it transformed the region's economies:

> By the early 1960s, domestic industry supplied 95 per cent of Mexico's and 98 per cent of Brazil's consumer goods. From 1950 to 1980 Latin America's industrial output went up six times keeping well ahead of population growth. Infant mortality fell from 107 per 1000 live births in 1960 to 69 per 1000 in 1980, life expectancy rose from 52 to 64 years. In the mid 1950s, Latin America's economies were growing faster than those of the industrialized West.[12]

The ECLA theorists, however, had failed to address the issue of class and income distribution. Indeed, the political companion to the economic theory of ISI in those early days was populism: a concerted effort by the ruling élite to mobilize and unite industrialists, urban masses and peasants alike around the message of nationalism and national development, while conveniently blaming imperialism (more particularly, American imperialism) and unequal exchange for any policy failures. But, over time, the issues of class and income distribution would rebound on their policies with a vengeance.

By the mid-to late 1960s, the ISI model began to falter: balance-of-payments problems worsened; real wages did not rise sufficiently quickly to stimulate domestic demand; unemployment grew more acute, and income inequalities ever more severe; and industrial production became increasingly concentrated in products typically consumed by élites.

It is at this point that dependency theory came into its own, injecting class into the analysis of underdevelopment. André Gunder Frank,[13] T. dos Santos,[14] Celseo Furtado,[15] Norman Girvan,[16] Osvaldo Sunkel[17] and many other left-of-centre intellectuals pointed out that the ISI model had in fact led to a deepening of dependence and to further underdevelopment because the existing, colonially-inherited class structure had rendered a highly unequal income distribution which limited internal domestic markets. This, in turn, they argued, had two related effects: on the one hand, it had skewed the industrialization process towards meeting the needs of the élites, while such a pattern of production involved heavy reliance on imported producer goods, spare parts, technology and so on. On the other hand, the increasingly severe balance-of-payments problems resulting from this pattern of industrialization made for ever-greater dependency on foreign firms which had been invited to set up their producer-goods plants and technology locally. The combination of a limited domestic market with foreign industrial subsidiaries encouraged a grotesquely inefficient system of production and a net outflow of resources. Latin American subsidiaries became the dumping ground for obsolete foreign plant and machinery, their capacity was grossly underutilized and their labour absorption rate became regressive. Over time, remitted returns on foreign investment came to exceed net inflows several times over.[18]

Military Regimes, Internationalization and US Imperialism

Industrialization and social modernization in the postwar era led to the emergence of new middle- and working-class sectors which demanded the right to participate in the political life of their countries. Populist political parties, peasant and labour unions, and progressive sectors of the Church all encouraged the mobilization of the lower classes. Their demands for land and income redistribution, for higher wages and social programmes, threatened the property rights and accumulation potential of the dominant coalitions. During the course of the 1960s the developing political crisis deepened, with the emergence of guerilla warfare and urban terrorism, and the threat of Cuban-inspired subversion, even though, as Richard Gott has argued, Cuba's support for the guerrilla movements, especially in the early years, was more imagined than real.[19]

Meanwhile, high inflation, serious balance-of-payments difficulties and economic stagnation further buffeted the populist regimes in countries such as Brazil, Bolivia, Argentina, Ecuador, Uruguay and Chile. In these conditions, a return to authoritarian rule by military dictatorships was seen by many élites, including the nascent middle classes, as a bulwark against the capture of the state by revolutionary forces. They thought it would help to restore the conditions of social and political stability that were prerequisites for capital accumulation and economic growth.[20]

By the middle of the 1970s, many Latin American countries and several of the Caribbean states were run by military governments (Venezuela, Colombia, Mexico and Costa Rica being exceptions). Between 1969 and 1978, it is estimated that imports of military equipment and arms of various types grew by more than 300 per cent in real terms, with Argentina, Brazil, Peru and Chile being the leading purchasers.[21]

Military coups, of course, were nothing new in Latin America. They had been a major theme of Latin American political life for more than 150 years. Even so, the return to military rule came as something of a surprise to political observers, because it had been assumed that economic modernization would be accompanied by the consolidation of civilian government and the 'professionalization' of the armed forces. Moreover, the military interventions that heralded the 'long night of the generals' of the 1970s were unusual in so far as they departed from the previous pattern, in which the military had been content merely to take 'temporary custody' of the national constitution. The new wave of military regimes instead announced their intentions to stay in power as long as was 'necessary' to carry out social and economic reforms. Hence their designation as 'garrison' states, or even 'military developmental' states.[22]

The nature of these social and economic reforms, and the repressive severity with which they were imposed, cannot be understood without considering the changing international context in which they took place. They coincided with the beginning of the world-wide economic recession, the collapse of the Bretton Woods system, the oil price hikes and the recycling of petrodollars in the 1970s, and the acceleration of the internationalization of capital. To this potent cocktail must be added the renewed and aggressive interest of American foreign policy in the region, whether exemplified by armed invasion, as in the Dominican Republic in 1965, or covert interventions by the CIA in toppling, for example, Presidents Goulart in Brazil in 1964 and Allende in Chile in 1973,[23] or whether typified in countless instances of financial backing for dictators, the training of (and assistance to) their armies and police for rural 'pacification' programmes (Honduras, El Salvador, Nicaragua) and the higher education of the generals and officer class in neo-liberal economics.[24] In the words of Robert McNamara (US Defence Secretary in the 1960s, and President of the World Bank in the 1970s): 'They are the new leaders. I don't need to expiate on the value of having in leadership positions men who have previously become closely acquainted with how we Americans think and do things. Making friends with those men is beyond price.'[25]

The Dance of the Millions

The oil price hikes and the petrodollar recycling in the 1970s changed the size and composition of foreign investments in Latin America dramatically. Along with other non-oil-producing countries, most Latin American countries needed to borrow heavily to cover balance-of-trade deficits. For their part, international banks were falling over themselves to lend. Before the 1970s, the bulk of Latin America's foreign capital had come from public sources (bilateral and multi-lateral aid) and direct foreign investment; by the end of the decade the proportions had reversed.[26] What is more, the bulk of new lending went to private companies and parastatal enterprises; relatively little ended up covering government deficits. Spectacular waste and corruption fed a spiral of inflation and a frenzy of capital flight in which 'much of the money being borrowed from abroad was funnelled straight out again', as the World Bank itself admitted.[27] Perverse Reaganomics[28] in the early 1980s, which increased dollar interest rates to dizzying heights, massively increased the debt burden and set the scene for the harrowing 'de-development' of the debt decade.

In Chapter 8, on Africa, we introduced the reader to the general forces underlying the debt crisis and the principal features of IMF/ World Bank debt management policies of the 1980s. What it is necessary to point out here is that the renegade insertion of Latin American economics in the new world system of maniacal capital integration explains the support for the administrative terror of the generals by the global capitalist élites, and made them turn a blind eye to horrendous human rights abuses, including torture, killings and disappearances, as well as the systematic exclusion of large sectors of the population. James Petras recalls an interview with an international banker who said: 'We lend to Chile because whatever problems they have down there [those little things like torture] we're the first on the list to get paid before anyone else.'[29] Thus, wrote Petras, the social sectors on which the junta depended – the financiers, the multinationals, the banks – were the very ones who were its main beneficiaries. They were also the instruments of inflation: 'By increasing profits, through price gougings, not through increases in production; through speculation, not through innovation, and through loans, not through investments, they generated the inflationary spiral.'[30]

Even a cursory examination of the region's political economy in the run up to the debt crisis and the imposed structural adjustment policies of the 1980s cannot fail to notice variations in political style, economic policies and performance. Some regimes (for example, Brazil, or Venezuela) were labelled 'bureaucratic authoritarian'[31] because they continued with state-centric development programmes, while others (General Pinochet's Chile, or Argentina after 1976) were ultra-monetarist, combining export-orientated accumulation with a strident form of privatization. Some regimes were less repressive than others, giving encouragement to the 'voluntarist' theories of development and dependency that we noted in Chapter 3.[32] While some regimes had no economic record of which to boast, not even in terms of the paper exercise of national account statistics, others recorded very high rates of economic growth (for example, Brazil, Mexico [up to 1979] and Chile), even though deep reversals during the adjustment years that followed exposed these achievements as superficial.

The New Democracy: State, Civil Society and Market Reforms

None the less, these variations were as nothing compared to the outcome when, in the 1980s, the austerity programmes imposed by the IMF and World Bank led to economic contraction, deindustrialization, savage reduction in wages, declining living standards, and popular revolt *everywhere*; and when *all* governments had to withdraw or reduce subsidies and funding for the social sectors, including health, housing and education, laying bare a wasteland from which new shoots of democracy and civil society would spring.

Duncan Green, in his lucid and commanding study of the economics and politics of neo-liberal reform in Latin America, observes the 'cruel twist of history that made the debt crisis and structural adjustment coincide with Latin America's return to (more-or-less) democratic rule'.[33] The nature of that democratic rule, and the forms of civil society that have emerged, or are emerging, is what now captures the attention of the Latin American left.

However, it is wrong to speak of 'coincidence'. The word 'coincidence' carries a notion of an accidental and chance happening. This prevents generalizations being made about other situations and parts of the globe. Yet this is precisely what we must do. Because the neo-liberal adjustment in Latin America is a precursor of the neo-liberal integration of other parts of the world, particularly the advanced countries themselves. By understanding the dynamics of the relationship between economic and political forces in Latin America, much may be learnt about the new forms of democracy that could be, and are, emerging there too. In this sense, Latin America is today 'ahead' of the game, as it were, and this is why the reflexivity of the left in the emerging Latin American political economy should engage the attention of people in the West, the traditional core of the world capitalist system.

The neo-liberal agenda imposed by the joint IMF stabilization programmes and the World Bank structural adjustment programmes, and backed by the USA (dubbed 'the Washington Consensus') forged new relations between state, society and the market. In the interstices of this trio, new forms of political mobilization occurred, new democratic rights were prioritized, and new demarcations between public and private domains were drawn. To capture the democratization process in Latin America in the later decades of the twentieth century we shall make a distinction that some writers[34] have made between political democratization and social democratization. Whereas the former refers to the establishment of a principle of autonomy in a constitution, with a bill of rights and the reform of state power to maximize accountability to elected representatives and ultimately the citizen body, the latter refers to an experimentation with different democratic mechanisms and procedures in civil society.[35]

Civilian Rule and Political Democracy

The apparent paradox of the return to civilian rule at the very time that structural adjustment programmes came into operation dissolves if we consider that structural adjustment policies by their very nature require a measure of popular legitimation that the dictatorships who had contracted the debt burden had not needed. After all, contracting debt is a highly private, invisible and unaccountable affair, but paying the money back would bear down directly on every section of society, through devaluations, hyperinflation, wage reductions, public-sector cutbacks and so on. The debts had to be socialized or 'nationalized'.[36] This was made very clear in the very first round of debt rescheduling negotiations in the early 1980s: fresh loans (if only to repay old debts) were made conditional upon an acceptance on the part of the debtor countries of national – that is, *government* – responsibility for all outstanding loans, including private-sector loans.[37] The international gulag of World Bank, IMF and US bankers were shrewdly aware of the political implications, which is why, by the 1980s 'human rights' suddenly appeared on the US Administration's agenda. Where President Jimmy Carter led, Ronald Reagan followed, with the establishment of the National Endowment for Democracy.[38] The World Bank too spent much energy during the 1980s driving home the virtues of electoral democracy.

International 'concern' was confluent with mounting internal opposition to the regimes from people in all walks of life. The once-broad support for the juntas among the middle classes disintegrated as the arbitrariness of the human rights abuses affected many of their class as well as those of the lower strata,[39] and the economic depression of the early 1980s dragged down all but the very few who had been able to avail themselves of pseudo-legal

channels to transport their wealth (and that of their country)
abroad.

Much has been made in the literature of the fact that the struggle
against the dictatorships took place outside previously existing left-
wing party and organizational structures, and that in their place
new forms of grassroots and human rights movements swept across
Latin America. There was a difference between what Salvador
Samoya has called 'the party left' and the 'movement left',[40] and
since the dying days of the military regimes and their return to the
barracks, the 'movement' left has been the fulcrum of the region's
redemocratization. In some respects this is not surprising, since the
juntas had either obliterated or crippled the traditional left's party
organizations, and the foreign, capital-intensive, export-orientated
industrialization of the junta years had stripped the trade unions of
much of their membership. But it is certainly interesting that intellectuals from the traditional Marxist-Leninist (party) left joined the
grassroots movements in a struggle for electoral democracy, in what
appears to have been a lasting reversal of traditional priorities.

In the past, left-wing parties in Latin America were often led by
Communists, or had proto-socialist leanings, in which electoral
democracy was subordinated to demands for social justice and
national independence. And, while in the revolutionary days of
the 1950s and 1960s many Communist parties had been anti-Soviet,
this had not prevented them from adopting the Marxist-Leninist
conceptions of a 'vanguard' party, with the overriding aim of capturing the state apparatus. However, the arbitrary jailings and killings, the gagging of the media and the all-pervasive censorship
exercised during the junta years awakened the intellectual left to
the virtues and significance of bourgeois-democratic values. They
quickly began to acquire notoriety for their advocacy of democracy,
and, as Castañeda suggests, they played a key role in the grassroots
explosion: 'conceptualizing it, narrating it, and socializing it
and . . . channelling it into political expression and structured political parties'.[41]

The intellectual left's support for, and even coalition with, demo-
cratically elected governments who, *nolens volens*, had to preside
over a brutal reversal of economic fortunes, a staggering widening
of inequalities, and a deepening misery of the masses,[42] has perforce
led them to rethink the relationship between state and market as
well. It is a rethink that is proving particularly challenging, because

of the collapse of the socialist world and the absence of alternative existing models to the neo-liberal agenda. They have to do their rethinking all on their own!

Thus far, the results of this rethinking have been confusion and disarray. Steve Ellner, in an introduction to an edited volume, *The Latin American Left*, observes that its response to neo-liberalism and *perestroika* has been far from uniform. While nearly all leftist spokespeople are opposed to the elimination of social welfare programmes, and many favour lengthy moratoria on payments of foreign debt, there is no consensus on privatization or the role of the state in promoting economic development.[43] Indeed, some of yesterday's radical populists have been transformed into neo-liberal protagonists, while others continue to make clarion calls for a 'popular economic alternative'[44] even though the 'big idea' remains elusive.

Duncan Green has classified the left's responses to the present-day neo-liberal realities of Latin America by using a simple and useful, but theoretically not very sophisticated, dichotomy: short-term tinkerers and long-term utopists:

> there are those concerned with short term improvements within the existing global and national economic frameworks, and those who think in the longer-term, and believe the existing order must be swept away and a new society built from scratch in order to achieve any lasting improvement in the lives of ordinary Latin Americans.[45]

The former, not surprisingly, are those who are either in power or hoping to achieve it at the next election. Their concept of democracy is one of a 'democratic pact', in which the various parties commit themselves to an overriding allegiance to the procedural norms of democracy and the rule of law, in order to rebuff threats from the old military regime. The democratic pact may lead to a further social pact (*concertación*) intended to bring the state together with capital and labour in a bid to regulate wages and profits.[46]

Paradoxically – and this is the truly arresting difference compared to the situation in the past – the utopists, those who take a longer view, are to be found among the proponents of grassroot, local alternatives. They are suspicious of state power of *any* kind and look instead to a strategy of local organization and mobilization.

The practice of these grassroots movements, and the theories of civil society and democracy they have spawned is what we turn to next.

The New Social Movements and Civil Society

The extraordinary increase in the organizational capacity of civil society in the Latin American region since the 1980s is both a source of hope and a key point of departure in much theorizing about a postmodern social reconstruction. What is civil society? The philosopher Hegel once defined it as everything 'beyond the family but short of the state'.[47] Civil society encompasses all voluntary associations, organizations and networks engaged in some form of collective action. In Latin America today the terms 'voluntary organizations', 'grassroots movements', 'new social movements', 'popular movements', and 'non-governmental organizations' (NGOs) are all used interchangeably with 'civil society'.

How do we explain this growth, and what pointers does it hold for the future? And, more crucially: what are the connections between it and the still-fragile process of political democracy? The movements vary in origin and collective purpose, and hence in the form of politicization and empowerment that may be ascribed to them. Nevertheless, they have a number of shared characteristics: they are issue- rather than class-orientated; they have formed at local, grassroots level; they operate largely outside the prevailing state structures; and originate mainly in the experience of poverty and exclusion. Castañeda identifies four broad categories: the ecclesiastical base communities; the neighbourhood and urban dwellers' movements and 'self-help' associations; the women's movement; and environmental associations, Indian groups and human-rights organizations.[48]

The CEBs (ecclesiastical base communities – from the Spanish *comunidades eclesiásticos-de base*) are probably the earliest and best-known grassroots movements. They emerged in the mid-1960s, and grew in strength and number until their heyday in the early 1980s when, it has been estimated, as many as three to four million people were active in many tens of thousands of such groups located in rural areas or on the outskirts of the region's larger urban centres.[49] They had their origins in pastoral work, when priests and nuns began to break out of the traditional mould 'to go to the people'.[50]

They divided parishes into local units and got to know the people through house visits, learning their vocabulary, views and popular culture. They organized discussion meetings in which the Bible served as a guide to reinterpret the experience of people's everyday lives and as a methodology for raising people's social and political consciousness. The emphasis was on dialogue: equally as much on the priests being 'evangelized' by the people as vice versa. Paulo Freire's early theorization of this methodology of *Conscientization and Evangelization* took a full political turn in the liberation theology of Camilo Torres, Leonardo Boff and many other Church leaders, who argued as a matter of theological principle that there could be no reform without taking power.[51]

The CEBs, however, were diverse: many remained devotional groups without any overt political, let alone revolutionary, aspirations. Others blended with, or inspired, urban dwellers' groups and neighbourhood associations with more modest social goals: housing, public transportation and other urban services, land, clean water, electricity, health and education. These urban movements sprang up precisely because the exclusionary politics of the military regimes, and of the structural adjustment democracies that followed, withdrew state support and subsidies for such services. They combined self-help programmes with active campaigning at the local, municipal level. The tremendous growth of large cities in the region has given such movements an added political importance. It is estimated that the percentage of large-city inhabitants living in shanty towns varies from 30 per cent in Bogota to 70 per cent in Caracas.[52] Moreover, well over 70 per cent of the population of Latin America now live in cities.

The movements have led to leftist coalitions taking power at municipal level in contrast to the rightist coalitions that rule the national state. In some countries, the leftist coalitions have placed the effective decentralization of the state on the agenda.[53] More importantly, some of the larger such movements have grown into financially viable and accountable non-governmental organizations (NGOs). Their financial backing from international NGOs,[54] (and – by a truly perverse twist – sometimes the World Bank itself)[55] have made it attractive for municipal governments, beset by austerity, to enter into 'negotiated interactions' and collaborative arrangements with such NGOs over the provision of services.[56] The consensual, participative or 'consociational' democracy[57] characteristic of the grassroots days has, however, many times been subverted through political clientelism, corruption and co-optation at the local level. The women's movement in Latin America deserves a place of its own in the annals of the resurrection of civil society. It is a unique collection of diverse groups with quite different goals. They came together during the years of struggle against the military and have continued to co-operate, though less successfully, since.[58] There were women's human-rights groups organized by the mothers and grandmothers of the 'disappeared';[59] and neighbourhood-based groups of poor women (housewives' committees)[60] who had to band together to ensure the daily survival of their families. In coming together with feminist groups, often drawn from teacher and student movements, their political consciousness was raised in societies characterized by centuries of male domination and church-supported gender exclusion.

A final category of grassroots movements includes environmental groups, Indian-rights groups and native peasant movements. The coalition of such movements is particularly interesting, partly because they are of more recent origin, and are therefore still on the ascendancy, and partly because it is these movements in particular that those who have tried to theorize a postmodern, postdevelopmental path seem to have in mind as examples.

Imagining Postdevelopment

Social movements have become a privileged arena for Latin American social enquiry today. The most comprehensive study of recent social movements is a ten-country study carried out by the Latin America Social Science Council under the general direction of Fernando Calderón.[61] The study examines the relationships between crisis, social movements and democracy, and explores to what extent they are 'constructing new social orders, propitiating new models of development and promising the emergence of new utopias'. It seeks in the movements 'evidence of a profound transformation of the social logic . . . a new form of doing politics and a new form of sociality . . . a new form of relating the political and the social, the public and the private'.[62]

Sadly, there is not much evidence as yet of such a profound transformation. In his own survey of Latin American social movements, Abby Peterson concludes that: 'at the end of the day, the social changes generated by the social movements are functional to the continued existence of present-day society – their explosive or transcendental power is nonexistent.'[63] But if Utopia has not yet arrived, there is no denying the intellectual enthusiasm for trying to imagine its birth in the spaces that have been vacated by the withdrawal of capitalism and modernity from much of the periphery. As Arturo Escobar put it, in a riposte to Jürgen Habermas: 'In the Third World, modernity is not "an unfinished project of Enlightenment". Development is the last and failed attempt to complete the Enlightenment in Asia, Africa and Latin America.'[64]

Many Latin American utopists stand in a postmodern tradition, using Foucauldian discourse analysis to 'deconstruct' the development discourse of the last four decades. They critique it as a system of knowledge produced by the First World about the 'underdevelopment' of the Third World, not only as an instrument of economic control and management, but also as a knowledge 'discipline' which marginalizes and precludes other ways of seeing and doing. This deconstruction, or 'context smashing', as Roberto Unger[65] prefers to call it, is a necessary first task in order to free our imagination and make it ready for a 'reverse discourse'. It is a bit like stripping walls before putting fresh paint on. It is also a task that many of these writers carry through with remarkable persuasion. I particularly recommend Escobar's wonderful critique of developmentalism in *Encountering Development: The Making and Unmaking of the Third World*. Escobar concludes that, rather than searching for development alternatives, we need to speak of 'alternatives *to* development' – that is, a rejection of the entire paradigm. This radical move away from development and towards postdevelopment is seen as an historical possibility already under way in innovative grassroots movements and experiments.[66]

But what, exactly, is there to see? What *are* these alternatives? Anyone asking this question and reading this literature will be disappointed by the paucity of the examples. What utopian alternative is there in, say, the 'hybrid experience' of the popular resistance of the Kayapo Indians, who use video cameras and planes to defend their culture and ancestral lands in the Brazilian rain forest?[67] Or in the inventive nature of 'coping strategies' in slums, or in the use of local native knowledge of healing practices, or the new political culture in which 'identity construction is more flexible, modest and mobile, relying on tactical articulations arising out of the conditions and practices of daily life'.[68]

But we are asking the wrong question. The future is not yet here and remains open-ended. The real strength in the postmodernist turn in Latin American development discourse is precisely that it wants it to remain so in order to give the social movements a chance to speak. Their advocacy of ethnographic methodology, and 'nomad' science is genuinely meant to be subservient to the marginalized and oppressed. Rather than summoning the power of a conceptual apparatus or a pre-established form of intervention, nomad science stays close to the everyday life experiences of the people, seeking not to extract constants but to follow social life according to changing variables.[69] As David Slater sagely comments: 'Perhaps, after all the words, all one can say is that the movements *are* there, and they *move*.'[70]

Conclusion

The dismantling of the developmentalist model and its replacement by the neo-liberal model has thrown the region into a spiral of peripheralization and pauperization that has led some observers to remark on its increasing structural similarity with Africa. Globalization, as William Robinson[71] observes, has led to a polarized model of accumulation in which the domestic market is no longer seen as being strategic to development. For the ruling class, all that matters is to create the most profitable conditions to attract mobile international capital: cheap labour, lax and flexible working conditions, the elimination of environmental controls, little or no taxation, and the abandonment of public obligations and provisions to the poor majorities. Some 20 per cent of the population are enriched by this deepening integration into the global charmed circle; the rest are thrown on the scrapheap.

Thus the 'lost' development decade of the 1980s has persisted in the 1990s despite the seemingly enormous political turnaround. In its authoritative review of the region in 1999, the UN Economic Commission for Latin America and the Caribbean (ECLAC) catalogues the continuing social decline, even while its sibling organizations in the UN system, the World Bank and the IMF, applaud the region's nations on the renewal of economic growth and the resumption of exports and foreign capital inflows. According to ECLAC, income inequalities have increased in seven out of the twelve countries it studied; the region's level of poverty in 1997 was, at 36 per cent, roughly the same proportion as in 1980, while in absolute terms the numbers of those living in poverty rose to 204 million in 1997, compared to 135 million in 1980.[72] Four out of every five new jobs in Latin America are in the informal sector – irregular, unregulated and with wages below poverty level, and below the minimum wage. Even *The Economist*, not noted for its social concerns, was driven to exclaim: 'Great reforms, nice growth, but where are the jobs?'[73]

But the difference compared with Africa is nevertheless historical, and for all the reasons spelt out in this chapter remains decisive and hopeful. While Africa is no longer of interest to the global system, Latin America's wealth, its (social minority) markets and its labour remain targets for exploitation. While in much of Africa, the post-colonial social formation has imploded and driven out the state as a relevant administration, in Latin America the state remains the most powerful instrument of global domination, and because of this it is the perceived locus of oppression. This, coupled with the cultural legacy of political intellectual protagonism, means that the social movements, for all their present-day fragmentation, hetero-geneity, diversity and decentralization, may yet come together in a broad social alliance that can oppose the neo-liberal order and challenge the logic of the prevailing system.

Conclusion

In this book I have tried to do two things. First, to navigate students of 'development' through recent currents of literature, and, second, to reorganize the field in a manner that I believe to be consistent with emerging agendas reflecting a variety of development situations and options. What are these new agendas, situations and options? Let us revisit the argument briefly.

In the first part of the book I used Robert Cox's concept of 'historical structures' to look back on the development of world capitalist relations between rich and poor countries, and the manner in which these relations have been understood and theorized in the past. For a long time, until about the 1970s, the material conditions and social forces of this relationship inspired a view of the world order as one of a geographical core–periphery hierarchy, pyramidal in shape.

While radically opposed theories and ideologies argued over the rights or wrongs of this pyramid, projected diverging historical trajectories, and came up with different policy prescriptions, they still shared some fundamental premises. First, theirs was a universalist and inclusive credo: all human beings on the planet had a right to partake in the fruits of technological and economic advancement. Second, the world pyramid was envisaged as an overall structure of nation-states, and the state was accorded a central role as arbiter of human affairs and agent of development. Third, worldwide social progress was assumed to be possible because the 'logic' of the capitalist system was thought to have an inherent drive to expansion and incorporation.

Globalization (discussed in Part II) has rearranged the architecture of world order. Economic, social and power relations have been recast to resemble *not* a pyramid but a three-tier structure of concentric circles. All three circles cut across national and regional boundaries. In the core circle we find the élites of all continents and nations, albeit in different proportions in relation to their respective geographic hinterlands. We may count in this core some 20 per cent of the world population who are 'bankable'. They are encircled by a larger, fluid, social layer of between 20 per cent and 30 per cent of the world population (workers and their families), who labour in insecure forms of employment, thrown into cut-throat competition in the global market.[1] State-of-the-art technology, frenzied capital mobility and neo-liberal policies together ensure both a relentless elimination of jobs by machines, and a driving down of wages and social conditions to the lowest global denominator.

A recent study warned of the global gales ahead. The move to market-orientated production in South America, Indonesia, India, parts of China and the rest of South East Asia taking place at the start of the twenty-first century, is likely to put 1.2 billion Third-World workers into worldwide product and labour markets over the next generation. The vast majority of them earn less than US$3 per day. As a consequence, wages in the traditional advanced countries are set to fall by as much as 50 per cent.[2] This is entirely consistent with our discussion in Chapter 7 of the global division of labour.

The third, and largest, concentric circle comprises those who are already effectively excluded from the global system. Performing neither a productive function, nor presenting a potential consumer market in the present stage of high-tech, information-driven capitalism, there is, for the moment, neither theory, world-view nor moral injunction, let alone a programme of action, to include them in universal progress. Developmentalism is dead, containment and exclusion rule OK! The present commitment by the various standard-bearers of the international community – for example, the World Bank – to target aid flows on poverty alleviation, and the 'social protection' measures that are currently on the agenda of global agencies, are testimony to a fundamental shift of social policy away from redistribution and towards residualization.[3]

In the third part of the book, I described a variety of situations and options that are present in different parts of the postcolonial world. I used the term 'postcolonial' to capture the notion that the distinct social formations that have emerged are a result of the way in which the aftermath of colonialism interacts with the forces of globalization and responds to it. I identified four such postcolonial conditions or situations.

A first condition, that of 'exclusion and anarchy', is exemplified in Sub-Saharan Africa, where, all too frequently, the patrimonial state form emerging after independence proved too weak to produce a viable political unity or civil society from the mosaic of ethnic fragments bequeathed by colonial administrations. The failure to progress from a juridical to an empirical state derailed the state-led developmental project. It made countries in Africa particularly vulnerable to the deepening dependency characteristic of the neo-colonial period. Globalization, including structural adjustments imposed since the 1980s, has overwhelmed the fragile social and political orders, while further peripheralizing their economies. The combined outcome of these external and internal forces manifests itself in a zone of civil collapse, anarchy and instability on the edge of the global system. And, while there *are* forms of constructive contestations in existence – for example, in innovative coping strategies at the micro level,[4] my own view is that these are not indicative of what is going to happen in the foreseeable future. Rather, *other* forms of contestations, frequently expressed in resource wars, fragmentation into warlordism, banditry and large-scale population displacements are more likely to characterize the region for some time to come. In emerging international practices of conditionality, aid and humanitarian relief, we discern policies of management and containment rather than of incorporation of the region in the global economy.

I sketched a second postcolonial condition in the anti-developmentalism of fundamental Islam. Here, the failure of the developmentalist project, coupled with the exclusionary effect of contemporary processes of globalization, has interacted with the spirit of renewal ever-present within Islam *and* with its long history of cultural confrontation with the West, to render a quite different social formation. It is one in which the politics of religious identity and lifestyle has gained pre-eminence in the private sphere without, however, yielding a political project to (re)create civil society and rearrange state–society relations. As long as the state élites continue to be co-opted into the global élite system there is neither much hope for constructive rebellion nor any threat to established geopolitical relations. In the latest round of OPEC negotiations in which Western pressure for increased production has been applied to bring down the world price, it was once again the Arab oil producers (Saudi Arabia, Kuwait and the United Arab Emirates) that have yielded to the US demand for cheaper oil.[5]

In East Asia, the state-led developmentalist project has succeeded in catapulting the economies of a small number of NICs into the heartland of the reconstructed global capitalist system. A unique postwar configuration of geostrategic forces has assisted the emergence of a state apparatus relatively independent of civil relations, and hence relatively free to steer an export-orientated path to industrialization at a precise historical juncture, when the world capitalist system of production underwent transformative change. However, the sweep of globalization is threatening the drive to maturity of the developmentalist project (and the social emancipation of the masses) unless this drive becomes anchored in a regional division of labour. At the time of writing, despite the temporary integrationist success of the neo-liberal containment of the East Asia crisis, there is a prospect that a resurgent Asianization may provide the glue for just such regionalization.

We encountered a fourth and final postcolonial condition in Latin America. For reasons peculiar to its own colonial history, the continent has a long intellectual tradition of absorption, experimentation and revolt against Western models of modernity and progress. This intellectual commitment has helped to politicize the process of impoverishment and exclusion as the counterpart of Latin America's dependent insertion in the world economy. In recent decades, as Latin America has become a testing ground for neo-liberal policies of globalization and privatization, democracy and the strengthening of civil society have become an arena for intellectual and political renewal.

Reconstructing Universalism, Regional Mercantilism or Postdevelopment?

A major proposition of this book is that the reconfiguration of capitalism through globalization, coupled with the advent of the 'knowledge' or 'new' economy has concluded the long period of crisis and transformation that has characterized the world capitalist system since the demise of its postwar Fordist-Keynesian settlement. In other words, it is plausible, in the view of this author, that the virtuous cycle of capitalist production and consumption for the time being continues its present growth path as a relatively stable regime of accumulation, to use the conceptual schema of the Regulation School, while the hegemonic neo-liberal mode of regulation provides an adequate governance framework for this regime of accumulation. However, and it is a *big* however, it is a growth regime that embraces only a globalized social minority and has no economic need for the excluded majority. In consequence, it will rely increasingly on American military dominance to hold it in place.

What then, are the options for the future? Can we construct a new political project of engagement in today's polarized world? Social-democratic arguments for emancipation and universalist participation *perforce* do so on the basis of an a priori determining position of the economy. They take the formal capitalist market economy as a given, and attempt to squeeze the excluded back into it. They start from the premise that it is possible to involve the whole population in 'economically viable' activity, mainly through investment in human capital, training increasing numbers of people to chase after dwindling numbers of global jobs. Such a political project either implies a return to a Keynesian welfare state form that ignores the historical realities of globalization or, as in the British government's 'third way' it is a political project in which equality of *outcome* is sacrificed in favour of equality of *opportunity*,[6] and is combined with a ratcheting up of the nation's competitive advantage within an Olympic model of inter-nation competition which itself is at odds with at least one essential characteristic of globalization, namely the international mobility of human capital. It is often forgotten that the model of global success, Silicon Valley in California, has imported no less than a third of its talent from overseas.[7]

Alternatively, appeals from the internationalist left to transnational labour solidarity of anti-systemic movements rely, equally naïvely, on some magic wand that waves away the fragmentation of class, gender, ethnic and nationalist loyalties, and single issue politics that constitute the very counterpart of globalization. As we have seen, capital works globally as a unit in real time, but labour has dissolved its collective identity into an infinite variety of individual existences. While capital is co-ordinated globally, labour is individualized. This process of fragmentation is the very condition, or 'situatedness', to use David Harvey's terminology,[8] that gave rise to the epistemology and the politics of postmodernism. Even our individual positionality in relation to capital accumulation is fragmented and chaotic. Each one of us is a bundle of multiple roles in relation to different circuits of capital. As a holder of shares in an active pension fund with assets in Hong Kong, one will have conflicting interests, even with oneself as an employee about to be made redundant, when one's company moves to the Far East; as a purchaser of garments that have been cross-hauled between different locations, one may curse oneself for causing pollution. We can no longer achieve political solidarity even between our various multiple selves, let alone with others. Small wonder, then, that in the post-structuralist world in which we live, the politics of identity has displaced that of collective struggle.

Regional capitalist alliances, such as those emerging in East Asia, may extend the progressive drive to maturity and social emancipation of capitalist relations of production, but only if they are not overrun by the integrationist imperative of global capital. This, as I have argued elsewhere,[9] will only happen if the regionalization impulses there are matched and strengthened by regional competitive bloc formations in other parts of the world. Such a neo-mercantilist scenario would see the world disintegrate into regional competitive blocs, each with its own periphery. Trade wars could be expected to spill over into investment wars, and the existence of divisive and mutually-exclusive currency areas would rein-in the present untrammelled growth of speculative global finance.

The neomercantilist competitive agenda of each bloc would set up political pressures for a regaining of control by the public domain (for example, of supranational bodies, such as the EU) over regional markets and money flows, and set up systemic pressures to reabsorb these flows back into production and trade within each of the respective regions, including their peripheries. The advantage of such a scenario and political strategy would be that it buys time for the progressive promise of capitalism to be fulfilled. The downside is that such a political project is likely to feed the most destructive of intercapitalist rivalries on a diet of nationalist and racist loyalties, which the history of the twentieth century can hardly be expected to recommend.

All of the above political strategies remain entrapped in structuralist thinking, in so far as they take for granted the determining logic of market competition and capitalist accumulation. By contrast, as in Latin America, those intellectual activists engaged with the excluded sphere have the advantage of poststructuralist 'imagination'. They can play with the tasks of articulating alternative productive strategies and rationalities – autonomous, culturally grounded, democratic and ecologically friendly – without having to worry overmuch about overthrowing or taming the global capitalist system, because the capitalist system is not anywhere near where they are playing.

The only thing they have to worry about, but it is a serious worry, is how far their efforts 'to stop being what we have not been, what we will never be, and what we do not have to be ... namely (strictly) modern',[10] dovetails with the containment policies of the global capitalist system and leaves the excluded zone 'free' from the undoubted advantages of technological and economic progress. The quip attributed to Fidel Castro many years ago, that there is only one thing worse than being exploited by the multinationals, namely *not* being exploited by the multinationals, is as true now as it was then.

Yet I believe there are merits in these postdevelopment experiments. First and foremost, they free our imagination. They dare to experiment with community exchange systems, establishing working links between unmet wants and needs, and unused resources. There are already many examples in the developed countries of 'time-dollar' projects, where volunteers who take part in charitable work are paid in time donated by other volunteer workers. A computer system registers every time-dollar earned and spent, and provides participants with regular accounts.[11] Provided payments are made tax free, and not deducted from money income obtained from unemployment benefits, time-dollars should be able to be accumulated to pay for an expanded range of services in the public domain.

In the excluded zones, we can think imaginatively about money and the function of money. One might imagine the development of 'twin' or 'parallel' economies in which circulation money is divorced from interest-bearing money, and where the leakages between the formal and the informal economy are strictly controlled. Geoff Mulgan reminds us of the long, if largely forgotten, history of imaginative thinking about money, from Silvio Gesell in the 1930s, to Claus Offe's work on alternative monies, and to Robin Murray's work on municipal money in the 1990s. J.M. Keynes predicted sagely that the future will learn more from Gesell than from Marx.[12]

The Global and the Local

In the past, experiments with local monies, and with local efforts to revitalize local communities, came to nothing because the national state, acting on behalf of national capitalist interests, suppressed them. At the turn of the twenty-first century, the national state, being more interested in assisting the internationalization of domestic capital, may be pressured to leave well alone. This offers a window of opportunity that dovetails with the new division, described in Chapter 6, between real time (global) economic activities and material (local) economic activities. Let us end this book by thinking imaginatively and optimistically about this division.

A social perspective on globalization, which we have privileged throughout in this book, tells us that one of the enormous advantages of the real-time economy is that it is potentially free of the friction of space, and therefore of environmental stress. When buyers and sellers meet on the internet, at least one thing that can be said for them is that they are avoiding travelling miles and avoiding all the environmental pollution this entails. Of course, when dispatch and delivery of purchased commodities take place there are yet again all the consequences of cross-hauling and transporting, and indeed, at the time of writing, global informationalism is interwoven with existing historical structures of capitalist economy, with all the centralizing tendencies that this implies. Thus, at present there are no environmental gains when an internet purchaser of, say, widgets in France, or Brazil, takes delivery of widgets produced in Sweden. But the potential of the internet economy is such that production sites *could* be organized locally, while expertise, managerial functions, and other associated services could be dispersed globally via the ether highways. So what would be needed to make this happen?

The answer to this question is blindingly simple, and yet for the moment appears to be utopian: make local production and exchange economically competitive. How? By taking away the present advantage offered to capitalist companies to make free, uncosted use of the earth's environment. In an interesting book, *Natural Capitalism – Creating the Next Industrial Revolution*, P. Hawken, A. Lovins and L. Hunter Lovins, estimate that at present capitalist business is a free rider on the earth's resources to the tune of roughly US$36 trillion, about the same as world GDP.[13] If these free resources were costed, on a polluter-and-user-pays principle, I believe there would be an enormous stimulus to big business to re-engineer economic activity, growth and jobs down to a very local scale.

Such a proposition is not as far fetched or utopian as it may seem. I believe that it marches in step with both the logic of the historical process of *globalization*, and with the political challenges that are fomenting against the *globalism* of the transnational capitalist class (for the distinction between these, see page 153). First, as a result of globalization, national authorities are increasingly unable to tax corporate profits. Wondering how it has come to pass that the EU countries are unable to finance a reconstruction of their social security system when, in fact, since the 1980s they have become 50 per cent to 70 per cent richer, Andre Gorz notes the decline in revenue from corporate taxes which, in Germany, for example, has fallen by half.[14] And it is not only corporations that can avoid domestic taxation; personal wealth and income has become equally footloose and mobile. As a consequence, I believe that national taxation is bound to drift away from income and profits, and towards transactions, as in value added tax. This is already happening, in fact. But the problem with value added tax is that it is still predicated on a notion of gain that is very difficult to assign and levy in cross-border transactions. A logical next step is therefore to tax costs and burdens rather than gains or profits. So-called 'hypothecated' taxes, where the taxation is linked to the specific public costs arising from private consumption goods, are becoming more attractive all the time. Think of how duties on tobacco are defended with reference to the public health costs of lung and heart disease, or motor taxes to pay for roads. A logical evolution of the principle of hypothecated taxation is to levy pollution and other environmental costs on the production and consumption of material commodities, at the place where they are incurred. This would have an enormous bearing on the relative competitive advantages of location of production. Local producers of, say, yoghurt in Yorkshire, would find themselves able to compete very effectively with some brand name yoghurt that has travelled from German cows to Greek factories to supermarket shelves in Leeds or Sheffield.

Second, this downward pressure towards the *economics of place*, which I believe is a logical counterpart of the very process of globalization, will merge with a *politics of place* that is becoming the crucible of resistance against globalism on the part of the 'mosquito cloud' of protesting citizens who are successfully challenging the neoliberal hegemony of the corporate gulag and their international political servants, the IMF, the World Bank, the OECD and the WTO. By a 'politics of place' I mean a programme of action that unites people around the sustainability of their physical lives in a shared location. There is much evidence that the social energy for such political action is being galvanized. The 1990s saw a stupendous increase in locally-based environmental protest groups. In the UK alone, it is estimated that the number of such groups grew from 500 in 1986 to over 10 000 by 1997.[15] And this is nothing compared to the estimated 1 million of such grassroots groups in India, and the surging increase of others throughout the developing world.[16]

It is true that in the temporary coalitions of consumer rights, environmental issues and worker rights movements that in the 1990s targeted international summits successfully, as in the battle of Seattle (WTO) in 1999, such *locally-based* groups are only minor players. The 'NGO swarm'[17] that really worries the international establishment includes the political leverage, the money and the membership of huge international organizations, such as Oxfam, Greenpeace, Friends of the Earth, Médecins Sans Frontières and many more. The number of such non-governmental international organizations (NGOs) is reckoned to have more than quadrupled, from 6000 in 1990 to 26 000 in 1999.[18] While the capitalist press has been quick to dismiss the periodic coalitions of these citizens' protest groups as amorphous and anarchistic, and lacking any central leadership or command structure, their success in halting the onward march of globalism cannot be denied. In the late 1990s alone, the defeat of the GM giant Monsanto; of Shell's planned disposal of the Brent Spar oil rig in the North Sea; of the Multilateral Agreement on Investment; and Jubilee 2000's success in forcing through debt reductions for the poorer countries are all testimony to agenda-setting by international protest groups, as well as their full and expert use of the positive aspects of information technology – that is, the internet – which overrides the need for enduring collective organization for political purpose.

The fact that these citizens' groups and NGOs have very different and certainly sometimes even conflicting long-term organizational goals, (for example, environmentalists versus labour groups), and yet can and do co-operate over immediate issues, points to a much more important, fundamental, shift in cultural values. Put simply, what they share is discontent with global capitalism: with its acceleration and environmental destruction; with the ruthless piling up of marginalized numbers, wretched lives, dire poverty and war-related deaths, and, with its being out of democratic control. And where these citizens' groups are frustrated in achieving global political change, their membership goes back to their local, grassroots concerns and translates this discontent in their own daily lives. They want none of it, they want out! This is where, I believe, the emotional fuel behind the politics of place will come from, and strengthen the effort of will needed to re-establish quality of life on an environmentally sustainable, democratic basis, and one that does not suck the life blood out of everybody else on the planet.

Notes and References

Preface

1. Dudley Seers, 'Introduction', in D. Seers (ed.), *Dependency Theory, A Critical Assessment* (London: Francis Pinter, 1979).
2. Wolfgang Sachs, 'Development: A Guide to the Ruins', *The New Internationalist*, June 1992, p. 5.
3. In 1991, the United Nations Development Programme (UNDP) estimated that about 100 million people in the rich industrialized countries and another 100 million living in the erstwhile socialist countries of Eastern Europe had joined the ranks of the poorest in the world (UNDP, *Human Development Report, 1991* (Oxford University Press, 1991), pp. 23–6). The 1999 Report notes that, measured by the Human Poverty Index, 'one in 8 people living in the rich, OECD countries is affected by some aspect of poverty: long term unemployment, a life shorter than 60 years, an income below the national poverty line, or a lack of the literacy needed to cope in society' (UNDP, *Human Development Report, 1999* (Oxford University Press, 1999), p. 28).
4. See UNDP, *Human Development Report, 1999* (Oxford University Press, 1999) overview and ch. 1.

Part I Introduction

1. B. Horvat, 'Political Economy', in *Encyclopaedia of the Social Sciences* (New York: Collier Macmillan, 1968), p. 611.
2. T. Mun, *England's Treasure by Forraign Trade* (1664) (Oxford: reprinted for The Economic History Society by Basil Blackwell, 1928), p. 5.
3. I. Wallerstein, *The Capitalist World Economy* (Cambridge University Press, 1979).
4. A. Smith, *The Wealth of Nations*, book IV, quoted in B. Horvat (1968), 'Political Economy', p. 611.
5. A. Smith, *The Wealth of Nations* (New York: Random House, 1937), p. 423, quoted in T. Sowell, 'Adam Smith in Theory and Practice', in Gerald P. O'Driscoll, Jr (ed.), *Adam Smith and Modern Political Economy: Bicentennial Essays on The Wealth of Nations* (Ames, Iowa: Iowa State University Press, 1979).

6. On Marx's concept of mode of production and its historical evolution, see Eric Hobsbawm's edition of Marx and Engels' *Pre-capitalist Economic Formations* (London: Lawrence & Wishart, 1964); see also Barry Hindess and Paul Q. Hirst, *Pre-capitalist Modes of Production* (London: Routledge & Kegan Paul, 1975), and Umberto Melotti, *Marx and the Third World* (London: Macmillan, 1977).

7. R. Gilpin, *The Political Economy of International Relations* (Princeton, NJ: Princeton University Press, 1987), p. 15.

8. K. Waltz, *Man, the State and War* (New York: Columbia University Press, 1959), and *Theory of World Politics* (Reading, Mass.: Addison Wesley, 1979). Among the principal early prophets of these realist perspectives are H. Morgenthau, *Politics Among Nations* (New York: Knopf, 1948); K. Thompson, *Political Realism and the Crisis of World Politics* (Princeton, NJ: Princeton University Press, 1960); and E. H. Carr, *The Twenty-Years' Crisis, 1919–1939: An Introduction to the Study of International Relations* (London: Macmillan, 1939).

9. R. O. Keohane, *After Hegemony: Cooperation and Discord in the World Political Economy* (Princeton, NJ: Princeton University Press, 1984).

10. S. Amin, *Class and Nation, Historically and in the Current Crisis* (New York: Monthly Review Press, 1980).

11. C. Chase-Dunn, *Global Formation, Structures of the World Economy* (Oxford: Basil Blackwell, 1989).

12. For a schematic comparison of the three conceptions of political economy, see Robert Gilpin, *US Power and the Multinational Corporation: The Political Economy of Foreign Direct Investment* (London: Macmillan, 1976), p. 27, table 6.

13. See J. George and D. Campbell, 'Patterns of Dissent and the Celebration of Difference: Critical Social Theory and International Relations', *International Studies Quarterly*, 34, 1990, pp. 269–93.

14. For example, the relatively recent journal *Review of International Political Economy* claims to represent this 'new' international political economy; see the Editors' Statement, 1, issue 1.

15. In a seminal paper in 1981, Robert Cox outlined the first brush strokes of the new theory. The discussion that is presented here is based on this article: R. Cox, 'Social Forces, States and World Orders: Beyond International Relations Theory', *Millennium: Journal of International Studies*, 10(2), 1981, pp. 126–55. See also his 'Multilateralism and World Order', *Review of International Studies*, 18, 1992, pp. 161–80, and his book *Production, Power and World Order: Social Forces in the Making of History* (New York: Columbia University Press, 1987).

16. A. Gramsci, *Selections from Prison Notebooks* (originally written 1929–35) (London: Lawrence & Wishart, 1971).

17. R. Cox, *Social Forces*, (Note 15 above), p. 135.

18. Ibid.

1   The History of Capitalist Expansion

1. S. Kuznets, 'Quantitative Aspects of the Economic Growth of Nations: X-levels and Structure of Foreign Trade: Long-term Trends', *Economic Development and Cultural Change*, 15 (2) part II, January 1967, pp. 1–45.
2. In 1996, the latest year for which the trade figures are available. See ch. 4, table 4.2 for notes and references.
3. I. Wallerstein, *The Capitalist-World Economy* (Cambridge University Press, 1979), p. 15.
4. I. Wallerstein, ibid. For an excellent discussion on Wallerstein's additions to Marx's model, see Christopher Chase-Dunn, *Global Formation, Structures of the World-Economy* (Oxford: Basil Blackwell, 1991), esp. part I, ch. 1.
5. S. Amin, *Imperialism and Unequal Exchange* (New York: Monthly Review Press, 1977).
6. A. G. Frank, *Dependent Accumulation and Underdevelopment* (New York: Monthly Review Press, 1979).
7. E. Mandel, *Late Capitalism* (London: New Left Books, 1976).
8. A. Szymanski, *The Logic of Imperialism* (New York: Praeger, 1981).
9. H. Magdoff, *Imperialism: From the Colonial Age to the Present* (New York: Monthly Review Press, 1978).
10. For a discussion of these periodizations, see C. Chase-Dunn, *Global Formation* (Note 4 above), ch. 3.
11. P. Baran, *The Political Economy of Growth* (New York: Monthly Review Press, 1967) (originally published in Spanish in 1957).
12. See W. Rodney, *How Europe Underdeveloped Africa* (Dar es Salaam: Tanzania Publishing House; and London: Bogle L'Ouverture, 1972). See also A. M. M. Hoogvelt, *The Sociology of Developing Societies* (London: Macmillan, 1976), ch. 4.
13. Ibid. for a more extensive discussion.
14. H. Magdoff, *Imperialism*, (Note 9 above), p. 102.
15. Ibid., pp. 29–35.
16. See B. Thomas, 'The Historical Record of Capital Movements to 1913', in J. H. Adler (ed.), *Capital Movements and Economic Development* (London: Macmillan, 1967), pp. 3–32, reprinted in John H. Dunning, *International Investment* (Harmondsworth: Penguin, 1972), pp. 27–58.
17. A. K. Cairncross, *Home and Foreign Investment* (New York: Harvester Press, 1975), p. 3; first published by Cambridge University Press, 1957.
18. Quoted in A. P. Thornton, *The Imperial Idea and its Enemies* (London: Macmillan, 1985), p. 76.
19. See H. Wesselinck, *Verdeel en Heers, De Deling van Afrika 1880–1914* (Amsterdam: Bert Bakker, 1991), opening citation.
20. B. Kidd, *The Control of the Tropics* (1989), quoted in A. P. Thornton, *Doctrines of Imperialism* (New York: John Wiley, 1965), p. 85.
21. A. P. Thornton, *The Imperial Idea and its Enemies*, (Note 18 above), p. 76.

22. See Fieldhouse on the difference and complementarity of peripheral or core explanations of colonial imperialism, in D. K. Fieldhouse, *Economics and Empire 1830–1914* (London: Macmillan, 1973), esp. ch. 4.

23. See V. I. Lenin, *Imperialism, the Highest Stage of Capitalism* (Moscow: Progress Publishers, 1978; first published 1916); N. Bukharin, *Imperialism and World Economy* (New York: International Publishers, 1929; first published 1917); and R. Hilferding, *Finance Capital, a Study in the Latest Phase of Capitalist Development* (London: Routledge & Kegan Paul, 1981; first published 1910).

24. J. A. Hobson, *Imperialism, a Study*, 3rd edn (London: Unwin Hyman, 1988 first published 1905).

25. 'Necessity' as being a necessary policy of finance capital, not, however, in the sense of 'not being able to be overcome'. Bukharin condemned this meaning of 'necessity' as a limit to action, as semi-imperialism. Imperialism was the policy of finance capitalism which was itself a highly-developed capitalism implying the ripeness of the objective conditions for a new socio-economic form. And while finance capital cannot pursue any other policy (this is the meaning of necessity) it is not necessary in terms of not being able to overcome it. Bukharin, *Imperialism and World Economy* (Note 23 above), pp. 141–3.

26. N. Bukharin, ibid., p. 28.

27. V. G. Kiernan, *Marxism and Imperialism* (London: Edward Arnold, 1974).

28. Fieldhouse, *Economics and Empire*, (Note 22 above), p. 66.

29. For example, France after the the Franco-Prussian war – see H. Daalder, 'Imperialism', in *Encyclopedia of the Social Sciences* (New York: Collier Macmillan, 1968).

30. Ibid., pp. 103–4.

31. For a critique of the alleged refutations of economic theories of imperialism, see P. Baran and P. M. Sweezy, 'Notes on the Theory of Imperialism', *Monthly Review*, 17 (March 1966), pp. 15–31. The authors argue that there is a fatal methodological error in comparing costs and rewards for nations as a whole, because the relevant actors on the imperialist stage are classes and their sub-divisions down to and including their individual members.

32. B. Warren, *Imperialism, Pioneer of Capitalism* (London: Verso, 1980).

33. J. A. Schumpeter, *Imperialism and Social Classes* (New York: Kelley, 1951).

34. B. Warren, *Imperialism, Pioneer of Capitalism* (Note 32 above), p. 65. Note, however, Anthony Brewer's observation that this line of criticism follows in part from a semantic confusion caused by different uses of the term 'imperialism'. For Lenin in particular, imperialism did not refer specifically to the possession of colonies. He recognised explicitly that earlier stages of capitalism also involved colonial expansion – just as he recognized that the 'semi-colonies' of South America were really victims of imperialist control and domination. See A. Brewer, *Marxist Theories of Imperialism* (London: Routledge & Kegan Paul, 1980), p. 117.

35. A. Lipietz, 'New Tendencies in the International Division of Labour: Regimes of Accumulation and Modes of Regulation', in A. Scott, M. Storpor and contributors, *Production, Work, Territory: The Geographical Anatomy of Industrial Capitalism* (Winchester, Mass.: Unwin Hyman, 1988), p. 21.

2. Neocolonialism, Modernization and Dependency

1. J. O'Connor, 'The Meaning of Economic Imperialism', in R. Rhodes, *Imperialism and Underdevelopment* (New York: Monthly Review Press, 1970). See esp. p. 117, which lists the chief manifestations of neocolonialism as identified by the African leaders at the conference.

2. For confirmation of both the long-term downward trend, and the fluctuations of all non-oil commodity prices since 1950, see World Bank, *World Development Report* (Oxford University Press, 1987), p. 17, fig. 2.3, and the Appendix on the terms of trade, p. 176.

3. Ernest Mandel first coined this term. He defined 'technological' rents as

> surplus profits derived from the monopolization of technical progress, from discoveries and inventions which lower the cost price of commodities but cannot (at least in the medium run) become generalised throughout a given branch of production and applied by all competitors, because of the structure of monopoly capital itself: difficulties of entry, size of minimum investment, control of patents, cartel arrangements and so on. See E. Mandel, *Late Capitalism* (London: New Left Books, 1978), p. 192.

4. P. Worseley, *The Third World* (London: Weidenfeld & Nicolson, 1964), p. 52.

5. F. Fanon, *The Wretched of the Earth* (Harmondsworth: Penguin, 1963), ch. 3.

6. N. Chomsky, 'Foreword' in Y. Fitt, A. Faire and J. P. Vigier, *The World Economic Crisis* (London: Zed Press, 1972), p. 4.

7. Quoted in Jenny Pearce, *Under the Eagle: US Intervention in Central America and the Caribbean* (London: Latin America Bureau, 1981), p. 27.

8. D. Harrison, *The Sociology of Modernization and Development* (London: Unwin Hyman, 1988).

9. See W. W. Rostow, *The Stages of Economic Growth* – somewhat superfluously subtitled 'A non-Communist Manifesto' (Cambridge University Press, 1960). This work has no doubt been the most influential. Other important economists who brought social and even psychological variables into their economic development theories were: A. Lewis, *The Theory of Economic Growth* (London: Allen & Unwin, 1955), and E. E. Hagen, *On the Theory of Social Change* (Homewood, Ill.: Dorsey, 1962). By far the most comprehensive of all these approaches was Gunnar Myrdal *et al.*, *Asian Drama*, vols I–III (New York: Pantheon, 1968).

10. See N. J. Smelser, 'Towards a Theory of Modernization', in A. Etzioni and E. Etzioni, *Social Change* (New York: Basic Books, 1964), pp. 258–74. This is probably the most widely quoted theoretical text on modernization. Another early work of great influence was B. F. Hoselitz and W. E. Moore (eds), *Industrialisation and Society* (The Hague: Mouton, 1963). For an extensive discussion on modernization theories, see A. M. M. Hoogvelt, *The Sociology of Developing Societies* (London: Macmillan, 1976), ch. 3.

11. For an excellent discussion on the historical specificity of the idea of development as a form of Western-imposed administrative reform of the Third World, see P. W. Preston, *Theories of Development* (London: Routledge, 1982), ch. 2 (the idea of development).

12. L. Trotsky, *The Permanent Revolution* (1928) (New York: Merit Publishers, 1969). See also M. Lowy, *The Politics of Combined and Uneven Development* (London: Verso, 1981), ch. 2.

13. P. Baran, *The Political Economy of Growth* (New York: Monthly Review Press, 1967) (first published in Spanish in 1957).

14. A. G. Frank, *Capitalism and Underdevelopment in Latin America* (New York: Monthly Review Press, 1967).

15. T. dos Santos, 'The Structure of Dependence', in C. K. Wilber (ed.), *The Political Economy of Development and Underdevelopment* (New York: Random House, 1970).

16. L. Pearson *et al.*, *Partners in Development* (London: Pall Mall, 1970), p. 81.

17. R. Jenkins, *Exploitation* (London: Paladin, 1971).

18. For a further discussion, see Chapter 11 of this book.

19. For a discussion on autocentric versus peripheral development, see S. Amin, *Unequal Development* (New York: Monthly Review Press, 1976).

20. R. Prebisch, *The Economic Development of Latin America and the Principal Problems* (New York: UN Economic Commission for Latin America, 1950); and H. Singer, 'The Distribution of Gains between Investing and Borrowing Countries', *American Economic Review*, Supplement, May 1950.

21. A. Emmanuel, *Unequal Exchange. A Study of the Imperialism of Trade* (London: New Left Books, 1971).

22. For an extensive discussion on the programmatic achievements of the Third World in putting its case on the agenda of the international community, see A. M. M. Hoogvelt, *The Third World in Global Development* (London: Macmillan, 1982), ch. 2. See also P. Willets, *The Non-aligned Movement: The Origins of a Third World Alliance* (London: Frances Pinter, 1978); and M. Ul Haq, 'Intellectual Self-Reliance', opening speech at the establishment of Third World Forum in Karachi, January 1975; printed in *International Development Review*, 1, 1975, pp. 8–13. About a hundred leading Third-World scholars and officials of international organizations attended this conference.

3 Crisis and Restructuring: The New International Division of Labour

1. See S. Amin, *The Law of Value and Historical Materialism* (New York: Monthly Review Press, 1978), ch. 6.
2. D. Becker, 'Development, Democracy and Dependency in Latin America: A Postimperialist View', *Third World Quarterly*, 6(2), April 1984, pp. 411–31.
3. S. Amin, 'Towards a New Structural Crisis of the Capitalist System'; Paper submitted to the Third World Forum, Karachi, Pakistan, 5–10 January 1975; and *The Law of Value and Historical Materialism*, (Note 1 above).
4. We shall return to the definition and description of 'Fordism' extensively in Chapter 5 of this book.
5. D. Harvey, *The Condition of Postmodernity* (Oxford: Basil Blackwell, 1989), p. 135.
6. See A. Lipietz, 'How Monetarism has Choked Third World Industrialization', *New Left Review*, 145, 1984, pp. 71–88, **73**.
7. UNCTAD, *Trade and Development Report* (1981), p. 102.
8. P. R. Odell, *Oil and World Power* 7th edn (Harmondsworth: Penguin, 1983) figure, p. 138.
9. For a discussion of the relative price movements between primary products and manufactures over the colonial and neocolonial periods, see M. Barratt Brown, *The Economics of Imperialism* (Harmondsworth: Penguin, 1974), ch. 10.
10. On the concept of the social wage, see I. Gough, *The Political Economy of the Welfare State* (London: Macmillan, 1979), pp. 108 ff. and Appendix D. On the link between the social wage and imperialist profits, see R. Sutcliffe, *Hard Times* (London: Pluto Press, 1983).
11. An oft-quoted study by Vaitsos in 1970 propelled 'technological rents' to the forefront of the dependency debate. Vaitsos discovered that, in the pharmaceutical industry in Colombia, for example, as little as 3.4 per cent of effective returns to the parent company consisted of 'declared' profits. Another 14 per cent were accounted for by royalty payments, while 82.6 per cent were contributed by the parent company's overpricing of its sales to the affiliates. See C. V. Vaitsos, 'Bargaining and the Distribution of Returns in the Purchase of Technology by Developing Countries', *Bulletin of the Institute of Development Studies*, 3(1), 1970, pp. 16–23.
12. S. Amin, *The Law of Value and Historical Materialism*, (Note 1 above), p. 77.
13. See, for example, the argument developed by J. Toye in 'Development Policy in the Shadow of Keynes', ch. 2 in his book *Dilemmas of Development* (Oxford: Basil Blackwell, 1987).
14. This calculation is based on the statistical tables in Annexes of the 1970 and 1982 issues of *Development Cooperation: Review of the OECD Development Assistance Committee* (Paris: OECD, 1970 and 1982).

15. S. George, *A Fate Worse than Debt* (Harmondsworth: Penguin, 1988), esp. ch. 1.
16. The term 'world market factory' was first coined by F. Fröbel, J. Heinrich and O. Kreye, *The New International Division of Labour* (Cambridge University Press, 1980), p. 6.
17. P. Jalée, *Imperialism in the Seventies* (New York: The Third Press, 1972), p. 83.
18. See G. Arrighi, 'A Crisis of Hegemony', in S. Amin, G. Arrighi, A. G. Frank and I. Wallerstein, *Dynamics of Global Crisis* (New York: Monthly Review Press, 1982), pp. 55–108.
19. F. Halliday, *Cold War, Third World* (London: Hutchinson Radius, 1989), p. 33.
20. P. Evans, 'Transnational Linkages and the Economic Role of the State: An Analysis of Developing and Industrialised Nations in the Post-World War II Period', in P. Evans and D. Rueschemeyer *et al.*, *Bringing the State Back In* (Cambridge University Press, 1985).
21. A good example are the regional volumes of the 'Sociology of Developing Societies' series, edited by T. Shanin, published by Macmillan and the Monthly Review Press in various years in the 1980s.
22. A pathbreaking essay on the new approaches to development theory in this period was D. Booth, 'Marxism and Development Sociology: Interpreting the Impasse', *World Development*, 13(7), 1985. See also his contribution to F. J. Schuurman (ed.), *Beyond the Impasse, New Directions in Development Theory* (London: Zed Books, 1993).
23. For examples of this bottom-up 'empowerment approach', see R. Chalmers, *Rural Development, Putting the Last First* (London: Longman, 1983); and P. Oakley and D. Marsden, *Approaches to Participation in Rural Development* (Geneva: ILO, 1984).
24. E. Boserup is widely credited with having been the first writer to explore systematically the role of women in economic development. While her work was a *tour de force* in its novelty, it was underdeveloped theoretically. Nevertheless, it alerted donor agencies to the exclusion of women from the benefits of progress and is said to have inspired the 'UN Decade for Women' that was to follow. E. Boserup, *Woman's Role in Economic Development* (London: Earthscan, 1970).
25. M. Mies, *Patriarchy and Accumulation on a World Scale, Women in the International Division of Labour* (London: Zed Books, 1986), pp. 122 ff. See also B. Mass, *The Political Economy of Population Control in Latin America* (Montreal: Women's Press, 1975); and N. Kardam, 'Bringing Women In', in *Women's Issues in International Development Programs* (Boulder, Col.: Lynne Rienner, 1991). While most literature is confident about the 'double' burden of women in the Third World, the concept of 'triple' exploitation has been developed by D. Gills in 'The Forgotten Workers: Rural Women in Korean Development', (PhD thesis, University of Sheffield, 1994).

26. M. Mies, *Patriarchy and Accumulation on a World Scale, Women in the International Division of Labour* (London: Zed Books, 1986); see also V. Bennholdt-Thompson, 'Investment in the Poor: Analysis of World Bank Policy', *Social Scientist*, 8(7), February 1980, part I; and 8(8), March 1980, part II; C. von Werlhof, 'The Proletarian is Dead. Long Live the Housewife?', in I. Wallerstein *et al.* (eds), *Households and the World Economy* (New York: Sage, 1984); and K. Young *et al.* (eds), *Of Marriage and the Market: Women's Subordination in International Perspective*, 2nd edn (London: Routledge, 1984).

27. M. Mies, *Patriarchy and Accumulation*, (Note 25 above), p. 127.

28. For a good coverage of the issue of women versus gender in development, see G. Waylen, *Gender in Third World Politics* (Buckingham: Open University Press, 1996); a good introduction is also R. Pearson, 'Gender Matters in Development', in T. Allen and A. Thomas (eds), *Poverty and Development in the 1990s* (Oxford University Press and Open University Press, 1990).

29. M. Mitra, 'Women in Dairying in Andhra Pradesh', Term paper, Mimeo, Institute of Social Studies, The Hague (1984), cited in Mies, *Patriarchy and Accumulation*, (Note 25 above), p. 131.

30. C. Mohanty, 'Introduction', in C. Mohanty, A. Russo and L. Torres (eds), *Third World Women and The Politics of Feminism* (Bloomington and Indianapolis, Ind.: Indiana University Press, 1991), p. 11.

31. J. H. Momsen and J. Townsend, *Geography of Gender in the Third World* (New York: SUNY Press, 1987).

32. C. Mohanty, 'Under Western Eyes', in C. Mohanty, A. Russo and L. Torres (eds), *Third World Women*, (Note 30 above), pp. 51–80.

33. A. Ong, 'Colonialism and Modernity: Feminist Re-presentations of Women in Non-western Societies', *Inscriptions*, 3–4, 1988, pp. 79–93; cited in J. Townsend, 'Gender Studies: Whose Agenda?', in F. Schuurman (ed.), *Beyond the Impasse, New Directions in Development Theory* (London: Zed Books, 1993), pp. 169–86, **183**.

34. The Brazilian sociologist and politician (later elected President of Brazil) Fernando Henrique Cardoso was one of the key contributors to the 'dependency associated development' vision. See F. H. Cardoso, 'Associated-dependent Development: Theoretical and Practical Implication', in A. Stepan (ed.), *Authoritarian Brazil: Origins, Policies, and Future* (New Haven, Conn.: Yale University Press, 1973). Together with Enzo Faletto he wrote the classic text *Dependency and Development in Latin America* (Berkeley, Calif.: University of California Press, 1979; translation, with new introduction and post-scriptum of their original Spanish volume published in 1969).

35. D. Becker (1984) 'Development, Democracy and Dependency in Latin America' (Note 2 above).

36. I. Wallerstein, *The Capitalist World Economy* (Cambridge University Press, 1980), p. 5.

37. This section is a summary of Wallerstein's arguments in Chapters 4 and 5 of *The Capitalist World Economy*.

Part II Introduction

1. A. M. M. Hoogvelt, *The Third World in Global Development* (London: Macmillan, 1982), p. 208.
2. R. Cox, 'Social Forces, States and World Orders: Beyond International Relations Theory', *Millennium: Journal of International Studies,* 10(2), 1981, pp. 126–55.
3. See B. Warren, *Imperialism, Pioneer of Capitalism* (London: New Left Books, 1980); and F. H. Cardoso and E. Faletto, *Dependency and Development in Latin America* (Berkeley, Calif.: University of California Press, 1979), esp. the Preface to the American edition.
4. For an example of the restatement of this view, even after the collapse of the socialist experience, see S. Amin, 'The Future of Socialism', in *Monthly Review,* July/August 1990; also S. Amin, G. Arrighi, A. G. Frank and I. Wallerstein, *Transforming the Revolution, Social Movements and the World System* (New York: Monthly Review Press, 1990).
5. For a repeat of this ingrained view, see S. Amin, G. Arrighi, A. G. Frank and I. Wallerstein, *Transforming the Revolution,* (Note 4 above).
6. P. Sweezy, 'Globalization – To What End?', *Monthly Review,* 42(9), February 1992, p. 1.
7. R. Boyer, 'Technical Change and the Theory of "Regulation"', in G. Dosi and C. Freeman *et al.*, (eds), *Technical Change and Economic Theory* (London: Pinter, 1988).

4 From Expansion to Involution

1. I am indebted to Dr Rongyan Qi for her kind help with some of the tables in this chapter.
2. P. Dicken, *Global Shift, The Internationalisation of Economic Activity* (London: Paul Chapman, 1992), p. 16.
3. S. Kuznets, 'Quantitative Aspects of the Economic Growth of Nations: X-level and Structure of Foreign Trade: Long- Term Trends', *Economic Development and Cultural Change,* 15 (2), part II, January 1967.
4. Ibid., pp. 7–8.
5. For a discussion, see Shigeru Otsubo, *Globalization, Accelerated Integration through World Trade, A New Role for Developing Countries in an Integrating World,* (Washington DC:World Bank, International Economics Department, Discussion Papers, November 1995).
6. *World Development Report* (Washington DC: World Bank, 1999), table 20.
7. Otsubo, *Globalization,* calculates that, of the 16% rise in the trade integration ratio of low and middle income countries since the mid-1960s, 15% was observed only after the mid-1980s and resulted from the developing countries' shift in development strategy.
8. World Trade Organization, *Annual Report 1998* (Geneva: WTO, 1998), p. 29.

9. A.Yeats, *Just How Big is Global Production Sharing?* World Bank Policy Research Paper No. 1871, (Washington DC: World Bank, 1988), cited in WTO, *Annual Report 1998*, (Note 8 above), p. 36.

10. WTO, *Annual Report 1998*, pp. 15 and 16.

11. For a good example, see David Held *et al.*, *Global Transformations* (Cambridge: Polity Press, 1999), p. 167, where the authors cite T. Nierop, *Systems and Regions in Global Politics: An Empirical Study of Diplomacy, International Organization and Trade 1950–1991* (Chichester: John Wiley, 1994). As Held *et al.* put it: 'over the postwar period, trade has become much more extensive than ever before as a world wide network of trading relations between regions and countries has developed.'

12. S. Kutznets, 'Quantitative Aspects of the Economic Growth of Nations' (Note 3 above), p. 10.

13. UNCTAD, *Trade and Development Report 1999* (UN: New York and Geneva, 1999), p. 85.

14. Other academic authors have come to similar conclusions. For example, Paul Hirst and Grahame Thompson, in *Globalization in Question* (London: Polity Press, 1995), p. 28, argue that using gross figures of ratios of trade relative to output 'confirms unequivocally that "openness" was greater during the Gold Standard period than even in the 1980s'. The second edition (1999) of this book confirms their position even regarding the 1990s and they critique in even greater detail than before the methodologies used by those who take trade/GDP ratios as a proxy for 'globalization'.

15. UNCTC, *Transnational Corporations in World Development, Trends and Prospects* (New York: UN, 1988), p. 16.

16. C. Tugendhat, *The Multinationals* (London: Eyre & Spottiswoode, 1971), p. 24.

17. UNECOSOC, *Multinational Corporations in World Development* (New York: UN, 1973), pp. 13–14.

18. For a discussion of the methodology used, see the footnote on p. 135 of the sequel to the report, *UNCTC, Transnational Corporations in World Development, a Re-Examination* (New York: UN, 1978).

19. UN Department of Economic and Social Affairs, *Economic Report 1947* (Lake Erie, NJ: United Nations, 1948).

20. J. H. Dunning, *Studies in International Investment* (London: Allen & Unwin, 1970), see pp. 23 and 19, respectively. See also *The Problem of International Investments, A Report by the Study Group of Members of the Royal Institute of International Affairs* (Oxford University Press, 1947).

21. For the 1960 figure, see M. Barratt Brown, *The Economics of Imperialism* (Harmondsworth: Penguin, 1974), pp. 206–7. For 1966, see L. B. Pearson, *Partners in Development* (London: Pall Mall Press, 1970), p. 100. For 1974, see *Transnational Corporations in World Development* (as in Note 18 above), p. 242, table III. For 1989, see UNCTC, *World Investment Report* (New York: UN, 1991), p. 11, table 4.

22. See UNCTC, *World Investment Report* (1991), p. 11, table 4.

23. Ibid., p. 68.

24. Based on UNCTAD, *Trade and Development Report* (1999), p. 116, chart 5.10.
25. Ibid., p. 116.
26. P. Hirst and G. Thompson, *Globalization in Question*, 2nd edn, (Note 14 above), pp. 73/4.
27. Ibid., p. 74.
28. UNCTAD, *Trade and Development Report* (1999), p. 107.
29. J. Henderson, 'Danger and Opportunity in the Asia-Pacific', in G. F. Thompson (ed.), *Economic Dynamism in the Asia-Pacific* (London: Routledge, 1998), cited in Paul Hirst and Graham Thompson, *Globalization in Question*, 2nd edn (London: Polity Press, 1999), p. 156.
30. UNCTAD, *World Investment Report* (1997), figure 1.2.
31. UNCTAD, *Trade and Development Report* (1999), p. 118.
32. The term 'emerging markets' refers to those countries in the developing world as well as among the so-called transition economies of Central and Eastern Europe which have either set up or opened their stock markets to foreign penetration since the wave of free market reforms began in the 1980s. The main emerging markets are: China, Malaysia, South Africa, Taiwan, Thailand, Indonesia, India, Mexico, Brazil, Korea, Argentina, Russia and the Czech Republic.
33. For this classification, see International Monetary Fund, *Balance of Payments Statistics Yearbook*, (Washington: IMF; 1997), annex III.
34. B. Thomas, 'The Historical Record of Capital Movements to 1913', in J. H. Adler (ed.), *Capital Movements and Economic Development* (London: Macmillan, 1967), pp. 3–32, reprinted in J. H. Dunning, *International Investment* (Harmondsworth: Penguin, 1972), pp. 27–58, **34**, table 1.
35. C. Crook, 'Fear of Finance', *The Economist*, 19 September 1992.
36. State of the Union Address, *Economic Report of the President* (Washington DC, US Government Printing Office, January 1999), p. 224.
37. UN, *World Economic and Social Survey 1997* (New York: UN; 1997), p. 267, table A31.
38. International Finance Corporation, *Emerging Stockmarkets Factbook, 1997* (Washington DC: IFC, 1997).
39. UNCTAD, *Trade and Development Report* (1999), p. 99.
40. Ibid., p. 106.
41. The term 'net capital inflow' denotes acquisitions minus sales of domestic assets by non-residents, while the term 'net capital outflow' denotes acquisitions of foreign assets minus sales of foreign assets by residents. Thus the term *net capital flow* refers to net capital inflow minus net capital outflow. See ibid., p. 100.
42. *Economic Report of the President, 1999* (Washington, DC: US Government Printing Office, 1999), pp. 221–2.
43. UNCTAD, *Trade and Development Report* (1999), p. 101.
44. United Nations Development Programme, *Human Development Report 1999* (New York: UN; 1999), ch. 1, figure 1.1.
45. Ibid., ch. 1.
46. UNCTAD, *Trade and Development Report* (1995), p. 77.
47. UNCTAD, *Trade and Development Report* (1999), p. 61.

48. Dani Rodrik, 'Who Needs Capital Account Convertability?', *Essays in International Finance*, 20–27, May 1998, p. 55. See also, *Economic Report of the President*, (see Note 42 above), p. 241.
49. UNCTAD, *Trade and Development Report* (1990), p. 110.
50. F. F. Clairmont, *The Rise and Fall of Economic Liberalism* (Penang: Southbound Press/Third World Network, 1996), p. 29.
51. On the orthodox economics distinction between 'real' and 'monetary' economy, see H. Magdoff and P. M. Sweezy, 'Production and Finance', *Monthly Review*, May 1983, reprinted in H. Magdoff and P. M. Sweezy, *Stagnation and the Financial Explosion* (New York: Monthly Review Press, 1987), pp. 93–105. See also S. Strange, *Casino Capitalism* (Oxford: Basil Blackwell, 1986), p. 118, where she says the consequences for the real economy, for production, trade and employment can 'only be guessed at'.
52. P. Volcker, Chairman of the US Federal Reserve Board during much of the 1980s, is quoted in an interview with Anthony Sampson as saying: 'it seems to be easier to make money in some sense, with paper chasing paper, than in investing in real goods and services. If you're doing some research and the pay-off is coming in fifteen years or twenty years at today's interest rates, it's hard to envisage a big enough pay-out to justify the investment that you make today'. Quoted in A. Sampson, *The Midas Touch: Money, People and Power from West to East* (London: Hodder & Stoughton, 1989), p. 13.
53. For a simple explanation of securitization, see A. Hamilton, *The Financial Revolution* (Harmondsworth: Penguin, 1986), esp. pp. 71–2. See also Barclays Bank *Briefing* No. 87, January 1992 and *The Economist*, 'Corporate Finance', June 1986, pp. 7–13.
54. Longmans, *Dictionary of English*.
55. *The Economist*, 'Corporate Finance', Survey, 7 June 1986, p. 23.
56. *The Economist*, 19 September 1992, p. 30.
57. Quoted in A. Sampson, *The Midas Touch*, (Note 52 above), p. 179.
58. A. Sampson, ibid., p. 179.
59. UNCTAD, *Trade and Development Report* (1990), p. 35, table 17.
60. UNCTAD, *Trade and Development Report* (1999), p. 107.
61. For example, after the East Asian Crisis of 1997, the governments of both Japan and Hong Kong piled taxpayers' monies into their stock markets to buy falling stocks and support the markets. The US Federal Reserve bailed out LCTM, the hedge fund that collapsed as a result of the crisis, with US$3 trillion worth of 'uncovered' 'positions'. For details about the regular support for financial markets by governments, see Harry Shutt, *The Trouble with Capitalism* (London: Zed Press, 1998), pp. 124–31.
62. UNDP, *Human Development Report 1992* (Oxford University Press, 1992), p. 36. Note that the UNDP in this report includes the countries of Eastern Europe and the Soviet Union in the industrialized group. For confirmation of the widening gap in incomes between traditional core and periphery countries, see also P. Sweezy, 'Globalization to What End?', part II, *Monthly Review*, 43(10), March 1992, p. 10,

table IX; and G. Arrighi, 'World Income Inequalities and the Future of Socialism', *New Left Review*, 189, 1991.

63. P. Bairoch, *The Economic Development of the Third World since 1900* (London: Methuen, 1975), p. 193.
64. UNDP, *Human Development Report 1991* (Oxford University Press, 1999), p. 23.
65. UNDP, *Human Development Report 1999* (Oxford Univeristy Press, 1999), p. 38.
66. UNDP, *Human Development Report 1992* (Oxford University Press, 1992), p. 35.
67. WTO, *Annual Report 1998*, pp. 62–3.
68. See P. Mosley, 'Globalization, Economic Policy and Growth Performance', in UNCTAD, *International Monetary and Financial Issues for the 1990s*, vol. x, UN publications, ref. E.99. II.D.14, (New York and Geneva: UN, 1999). For a critical assessment of the empirical evidence, see also F. Rodriguez and D. Rodrik, 'Trade Policy and Economic Growth; A Skeptic's Guide to the Cross-national Evidence', National Bureau of Economic Research Working Paper No. 7081 (Cambridge, Mass., April 1999).
69. UNDP, *Human Development Report 1999*, p. 3.
70. Ibid., p. 39.
71. M. Castells, 'The Informational Economy and the New International Division of Labor', in M. Carnoy, M. Castells, S. S. Cohen and F. H. Cardoso, *The New Global Economy in the Information Age* (New York: Pennsylvania State University Press and London: Macmillan, 1993), p. 37.

5 Flexibility and Informationalism

1. Throughout the 1970s and 1980s, 'crisis' literature dominated the general social science agenda. In journals such as the Marxist *Monthly Review* not an issue could pass without some reference to it. For comprehensive guides to the 'crisis', see Y. Fitt, A. Faire and J. Vigier, *The World Economic Crisis: U.S. Imperialism at Bay* (London: Zed Press, 1980); S. Amin, G.. Arrighi, A. G. Frank and I. Wallerstein, *Dynamics of Global Crisis* (New York: Monthly Review Press, 1982); R. J. Johnston and P. J. Taylor (eds), *A World in Crisis?* (New York: Basil Blackwell, 1986); and R. Sutcliffe, *Hard Times, The World Economy in Turmoil* (London: Pluto, 1983).
2. J. P. Womack, D. T. Jones and D. Roos, *The Machine that Changed the World* (New York: Rawson Associates, 1990), p. 27.
3. J. P. Womack *et al.,* ibid., p. 37.
4. D. Harvey, *The Condition of Postmodernity* (Oxford: Basil Blackwell, 1989) p. 142.
5. See D. Harvey, ibid. The summary of 'Fordism' in this chapter owes much to Harvey's excellent discussion in ch. 9 of his book.

6. M. J. Piore and C. F. Sabel, *The Second Industrial Divide* (New York: Basic Books, 1984).
7. Ibid., p. 265.
8. Ibid., p. 266.
9. For a full discussion, see F. Fukuyama, *Trust: The Social Virtues and the Creation of Prosperity* (London: Hamish Hamilton, 1995).
10. R. Jaikumar and D. Upton, 'The Co-ordination of Global Manufacturing', in S. P. Bradley, J. Hausman and R. Nolan, *Globalization, Technology, and Competition* (Boston, Mass.: Harvard Business School Press, 1993), pp. 178–9.
11. The description of the Toyota model in this chapter draws substantially on the excellent book by J. P. Womack *et al. The Machine that Changed the World* (Note 2 above) on the same subject.
12. K. Dohse *et al.*, 'From "Fordism" to "Toyotism"? The Social Organisation of the Labour Process in the Japanese Automobile Industry', *Politics and Society*, 14 (2), 1985, pp. 115–46.
13. J.P. Womack *et.al.*, *The Machine that Changed the World*, (Note 2 above), ch. 3.
14. A. Toffler, *Power shift, Knowledge, Wealth and Violence at the Edge of the 21st Century* (New York: Bantam Books, 1992) pp. 102 and 239.
15. J.P. Womack *et al.*, *The Machine that Changed the World* (Note 2 above), p. 62. Note the authors' use of the word 'machine' in this context. A deliberate, if mistaken analogy.
16. R. Murray, 'Fordism and Post-Fordism', in S. Hall, D. Held and T. McGrew, *Modernity and its Futures* (Cambridge: Polity Press and Oxford: Basil Blackwell in association with Open University Press, 1992), p. 218.
17. Good examples of such advocacy are J. MacDonald and J. Piggot, *Global Quality, The New Management Culture* (London: Mercury, 1990). See also C. Lorenz, 'Power to the People', *Financial Times,* 30 March 1992; T. Stewart, 'A User's Guide to Power', *Fortune,* Spring 1991; A. Toffler, *Power shift,* (Note 14 above) p. 210.
18. See the collection of contributions in T. Elger and C. Smith (eds), *Global Japanization: The transnational transformation of the labour process* (London: Routledge, 1994); see also R. Delbridge, P. Thurnbull and B. Wilkinson, 'Pushing Back the Frontiers: Management Control and Work Intensification under JIT/TQM Factory Regimes', *New Technology, Work and Employment*, Autumn 1992, pp. 97–107; and H. Williamson and G. Coyne, *New Management Techniques: New Union Strategies*, (Liverpool: CAITS/MTUCURC; 1991).
19. UNCTC, *Transnational Corporations*, Fourth Report, 'Trends and Prospects' (New York: UN, 1988), p. 42.
20. UNCTC, ibid., p. 42.
21. J. Tidd, *Flexible Manufacturing Technologies and International Competitiveness* (London: Pinter, 1991).
22. Ibid., p. 92.
23. Ibid., p. 96.
24. Commission of the European Communities, Directorate General Science, Research and Development, *What Are Anthropocentric Pro-*

duction Systems? Why Are They a Strategic Issue for Europe? Report EUR 13968 EN (Brussels; 1992).
25. Ibid., p. 3.
26. Ibid., p. 2.
27. Labour Research Department, *Human Resource Management Survey, Bargaining Report* (London; February 1995).
28. UNCTAD, *World Investment Report 1994, Transnational Corporations, Employment and the Workplace* (New York and Geneva: United Nations, 1994), p. 271.
29. M. Castells, *The Rise of the Network Society*, vol. I of a trilogy *The Information Age: Economy, Society and Culture* (Cambridge, Mass. and Oxford: Basil Blackwell, 1996).
30. Ibid., p. 171.
31. Ibid., p. 170.
32. R. Jaikumar and D. Upton, 'The Co-ordination of Global Manufacturing' (Note 10 above), p. 169.
33. A. Toffler, *Future Shock* (New York: Bantam Books, 1970); and H. Mintzberg, *The Structuring of Organizations* (Englewood Cliffs, NJ: Prentice Hall, 1979).
34. F. Ostroff, *The Horizontal Organization: What the Organization of the Future Actually Looks Like and How It Delivers Value to Customers* (Oxford University Press, 1999).
35. R. Moss Kanter, 'The Future of Bureaucracy and Hierarchy', in P. Bourdieu and J. S. Coleman, *Social Theory for a Changing Society* (Boulder, Col.: Westview Press, 1991).
36. UNCTAD, *World Investment Report 1994*, (Note 28, above), pp. 193–4.
37. 'Benetton: The Next Era', *The Economist*, 23 April 1994.
38. K. Ohmae, *Triad Power, the Coming Shape of Global Competition* (New York: The Free Press and Collier Macmillan, 1985), pp. xvi–xvii.
39. J. Womack *et al.*, *The Machine that Changed* (Note 2 above), pp. 218–22.
40. See for example, Th. Malone and R. Laubacher, 'The Dawn of the E-lance Economy', *Harvard Business Review,* September/October 1998, pp. 145–52.
41. Ibid,. p. 146.
42. C. Freidheim, 'The Global Corporations – Obsolete So Soon?', quoted in *The Global Firm R.I.P.', The Economist*, 6 February 1993.
43. C. F. Sabel, 'Experimental Regionalism and the Dilemmas of Regional Economic Policy', Paper presented to the Conference on Socio-Economic Systems of Japan, the United States, the United Kingdom, Germany and France, at the Institute of Fiscal and Monetary Policy, Tokyo, Japan, 16 February 1996.
44. C. Leadbeater, *Living on Thin Air: The New Economy* (London: Viking, 1999), pp.137–8.
45. Ibid., p. 143.
46. M.Castells, *The Rise of the Network Society*, (Note 29 above), p. 199.
47. C. Leadbeater, *Living on This Air* (Note 44 above), p. 143.
48. R. Putnam, *Making Democracy Work: Civic Traditions in Modern Italy* (Princeton, NJ.: Princeton University Press, 1993).

49. There are many 'Silicon Valley' imitations all over the world, from Cambridge in England to Bangalore in India; see C. Leadbeater, *Living on Thin Air*, (Note 44 above), p. 143.

50. From the annals of general business and management literature the new economy voices have been heard for longer than those emanating from the general economic discipline. Among the former, useful general introductory books are: D. Coyle, *The Weightless World* (Oxford: Capstone, 1997); John III Hagel, and A. Armstrong, *Net Gain* (Boston, Mass.: Harvard Business School Press, 1997); K. Kelly, *New Rules for the New Economy* (New York; Viking, 1998); and B. Davis and D. Wessel, *Prosperity: The Coming 20–Year Boom and What It Means to You* (New York: Times Business, 1998); Bill Gates, *Business @the Speed of Thought, Succeeding in the Digital Economy* (Harmondsworth: Penguin, 1999). Among economists, see R. Lester, *The Productive Edge: How U.S. Industries Are Pointing The Way to a New Era of Economic Growth* (London: W.W. Norton, 1998). For a sober assessment of pros and cons, see OECD, *The Future of the Global Economy*, 1999. Surveys of the new economy debates may also be found in recent issues of *The Economist*: for example, 'Business and the Internet Survey', 26 June 1999, and 'The New Economy', 24 July 1999.

51. Cited in 'How Real Is the New Economy?', *The Economist*, 24 July 1999; p. 17; also in 'The New US Economy, Part ɪ', *Financial Times*, 13 December 1999, p. 8.

52. C. Leadbeater, *Living on Thin Air*, (Note 44 above), p. 9.

53. *The Economist*, 24 July 1999, p. 21.

54. M. Castells, *The Rise of the Network Society*, (Note 29 above), p. 91.

55. W. Arthur, 'Increasing Returns and the New World of Business', *Harvard Business Review*, July/August 1996.

56. Ibid., p. 100. Also Dan Schiller, in *Digital Capitalism: Networking the Global Market System* (Cambridge, Mass.: MIT Press, 1999) argues much the same thing and points to the consequences of increased corporate control over expression and education.

57. *The Economist*, 24 July 1999, p. 21.

58. In a glowing article on the new economy, Willam Sahlman says 'inflation is dead – dead as a doornail'. He lists a number of online auction companies that push prices down. There is even one in which consumers themselves post what they are willing to pay for products or services (www.priceline.com). See W. Sahlman, 'The New Economy Is Stronger Than You Think', *Harvard Business Review*, November/ December 1999.

59. M. Castells, *The Rise of the Network Society*, (Note 29 above), p. 92.

60. M. Elam, 'Puzzling out the Post-Fordist Debate: Technology, Markets and Institutions', in A. Amin (ed.), *Post-Fordism* (Oxford, UK and Cambridge, Mass.: Basil Blackwell, 1994), pp. 43–70.

61. J. Schumpeter, *Business Cycles: A Theoretical, Historical and Statistical Analysis of the Business Cycles* (New York: McGraw-Hill, 1939).

62. C. Freeman and C. Perez, 'Structural Crises of Adjustment, Business Cycles and Investment Behaviour', in G. Dosi *et al.* (eds), *Technical*

Change and Economic Theory (London and New York: Pinter, 1988), pp. 38–66. See also C. Freeman, 'Preface' to part II of that volume.

63. S. Hall and M. Jacques (eds), *New Times: The Changing Face of Politics in the 1990s* (London: Lawrence and Wishart, in association with *Marxism Today*, 1989).

64. P. Hirst and J. Zeitlin, 'Flexible Specialization versus post-Fordism: Theory, Evidence and Policy Implications', *Economy and Society*, 20(1), 1991, pp. 1–55, **11**.

65. See Hall and Jacques, (Note 63 above), p. 129.

66. Ibid., p. 127.

67. For a concise summary of the Regulation School's main conceptual apparatus, see R. Boyer, 'Technical Change and the Theory of "Regulation"', in G. Dosi *et al.* (eds), *Technical Change and Economic Theory* (London and New York: Pinter, 1988). For a *comprehensive* review of the diverse approaches loosely federated under the label "Regulation School", see R. Jessop, 'Regulation Theories in Retrospect and Prospect', *Economy and Society*, 19(2), May 1990, pp. 153–216. See also his more recent update in R. Jessop, 'Twenty Years of the (Parisian) Regulation Approach: The Paradox of Success and Failure at Home and Abroad', *New Political Economy*, 2(3), November 1997. For a *critical* review of regulation theories in comparison with other contemporary crisis and transformation theories, see P. Hirst and J. Zeitlin, 'Flexible Specialization versus Post-Fordism: Theory, Evidence and Policy Implications', *Economy and Society*, 20(1) February 1991 pp. 1–55. A thorough critique of the substantive theses of the Regulation School has been written by R. Brenner and M. Glick, 'The Regulation Approach: Theory and History', *New Left Review*, 188, pp. 45–99. Finally, some more recent regulation contributions can be found in the excellent Reader edited by A. Amin, *Post-Fordism* (Oxford: Basil Blackwell, 1994).

68. A. Lipietz, 'New Tendencies in the International Division of Labor: Regimes of Accumulation and Modes of Regulation', in A. Scott and M. Storper *et al.*, *Production, Work, Territory* (London: Allen & Unwin, 1986), pp. 16–39, **19**.

69. A. Lipietz, *Mirages and Miracles* (London: Verso, 1987), pp. 12–16.

70. R. Jessop, 'Post-Fordism and the State', in A. Amin, *Post-Fordism*, (Note 60 above), pp. 251–79.

6 Globalization

1. D. Held and A. McGrew, D. Goldblatt and J. Perraton, *Global Transformations: Politics, Economics and Culture* (Cambridge: Polity Press, 1999), p. 8.

2. A clear exposition of the Sceptics' view is in P. Hirst and G. Thompson, *Globalization in Question*, (London: Routledge: 1999).

3. For a classic statement, see S. Strange, *The Retreat of the State: The Diffusion of Power in the World Economy* (Cambridge University Press: 1996).
4. M. Castells, *The Rise of the Network Society* (Cambridge, Mass. and Oxford, UK, 1996), p. 92.
5. For a compact review of sociological theories of globalization, see M. Waters, *Globalization* (London: Routledge, 1995).
6. See R. Robertson, *Globalization* (London: Sage, 1992), and J. Nettl and R. Robertson, *International Systems and the Modernization of Societies* (London: Faber, 1968).
7. D. Harvey, *The Condition of Postmodernity* (Oxford: Basil Blackwell, 1989). The summary here is based on chs. 14, 15 and 17 of his book.
8. R. Delbridge, P. Turnbull and B.Wilkinson, 'Pushing back the Frontiers: Management Control and Work Intensification under JIT/TQM Factory Regimes', *New Technology, Work and Employment*, Autumn 1992, pp. 97–107, **104**.
9. Dava Sobel, *Longitude* (London: Fourth Estate, 1998).
10. D. Harvey, *The Condition of Postmodernity*, (Note 7 above), p. 241.
11. A. Giddens, *The Consequences of Modernity* (Cambridge: Polity Press, 1990), p. 64.
12. M. Castells, *The Information Age, Economy, Society and Culture*, volume I, *The Rise of the Network Society* (Cambridge, Mass. and Oxford, UK: Basil Blackwell, 1996); vol II, *The Power of Identity* (Basil Blackwell, 1997); and vol. III, *End of Millennium* (Basil Blackwell, 1998).
13. M. Castells, *End of Millennium*, (Note 12 above), p. 336.
14. M. Castells, *The Rise of the Network Society* (Note 12 above), p. 106.
15. Ibid., pp. 471–2.
16. Ibid., pp. 436–7.
17. Ibid., p. 14.
18. M. Castells, *End of Millennium*, (Note 12 above), p. 82.
19. *New Political Economy*, 4(3), November 1999, p. 385.
20. M. Castells, *End of Millennium*, (Note 12 above), p. 93.
21. UNECOSOC, *Multinational Corporations in World Development* (New York: UN, 1973).
22. UNCTAD, *World Investment Report, 1993* (New York and Geneva: UN, 1994) p. 143.
23. P. Drucker, *The New Realities* (London: Heinemann, 1989), pp. 123–5. See also K. Ohmae, *Triad Power, the Coming Shape of Global Competition* (New York: Free Press, 1985); and *The Borderless World: Power and Strategy in the Interlinked Economy* (London: Collins, 1990).
24. S. S. Cohen, 'Geo-economics and America's Mistakes', in M. Carnoy *et al. The New Global Economy in the Information Age* (London: Macmillan, 1993), p. 98.
25. For the figure for 1990, see P. Dicken, *Global Shift, The Internationalization of Economic Activity*, 2nd edn (Manchester: Paul Chapman, 1992) p. 30, table 2.5.
26. M. Aglietta, *The Theory* of *Capitalist Regulation* (London: Verso, 1976), p. 122.

27. P. Boccara, 'Qu'est-ce-que l'anthroponomie?', in *Cahiers du l'IRM, Individues et Société*, 1; and cited in R. Jessop, 'Regulation Theories in Retrospect and Prospect', in *Economy and Society*, 19(2), May 1990, pp. 153–216, **168**.
28. A. Lipietz, *Mirages and Miracles* (London: Verso, 1987), p. 15.
29. R. Jessop, *State Theory* (Oxford: Basil Blackwell, 1990), pp. 317–18.
30. C. Sabel, 'Experimental Regionalism and the Dilemmas of Regional Economic Policy', Paper presented at the conference, 'Socio-Economic Systems of Japan, the United States, the United Kingdom, Germany, and France', at the Institute of Fiscal and Monetary Policy, Tokyo, Japan, 16 February 1996.
31. R. Reich, *The Work of Nations* (London: Simon & Schuster, 1991).
32. Ibid., p. 211.
33. UNCTAD, *World Investment Report 1994, Transnational Corporations, Employment and the Workplace* (New York and Geneva: UN, 1994), p. 188. The report refers to the much-publicized study by a special committee of the French Parliament under the direction of Senator Jean Arthuis, which gave a very pessimistic assessment of the link between relocation and unemployment.
34. P. Dicken, *Global Shift*, (Note 25 above), p. 67.
35. *Business Week*, 19 December 1994 pp. 28–30.
36. J. Rifkin, *The End of Work, The Decline of the Global Labor Force and the Dawn of the Post-Market Era* (New York: G. P. Putnam's Sons, 1995).
37. P. Krugman, 'Growing World Trade: Causes and Consequences', in *Brookings Papers on Economic Activity*, 1, 1995 pp. 327–77.
38. D. Coates, *Models of Capitalism, Growth and Stagnation in the Modern Era (Cambridge: Polity Press, 2000), p. 256.*
39. M. Castells, *End of Millennium*, (Note 12 above), p. 343.
40. Tom Wolfe, *The Bonfire of the Vanities* (London: Pan 1988), p. 260.
41. *The Economist*, 27 November 1993.
42. Zygmunt Baumann, *Globalization, the Human Consequences* (London: Polity Press, 1998), p. 105.

7 Global Governance: Regulation and Imperialism

1. D. Leborgne and A. Lipietz, 'Conceptual Fallacies and Open Questions on Post-Fordism', in M. Storper and A. Scott (eds), *Pathways in Industrialization and Regional Development* (London: Routledge, 1992), p. 347–8. Cited in J. Peck and A. Tickell, 'Searching for a New Institutional Fix: The After-Fordist Crisis and the Global–Local Disorder', in A. Amin, *Post-Fordism, A Reader* (Oxford, UK: and Cambridge, Mass.: Basil Blackwell, 1994), pp. 280–315, **283–4**
2. Bob Jessop, 'Post-Fordism and the State', in A. Amin, *Post-Fordism, A Reader*, pp. 251–97. See also Bob Jessop, 'Post-Fordism and Flexible Specialisation: Incommensurable, Contradictory, Complementary, or Just Plain Different Perspectives?', in H. Ernste and V. Meider (eds),

Regional Development and Contemporary Response: Extending Flexible Specialisation, (London: Belhaven Press), pp. 25–44.

3. J. Peck and A. Tickell, 'Searching for a New Institutional Fix' (Note 1 above), pp. 280–315.

4. For a review of the second and third generations of regulation theory, see R. Jessop, 'Twenty Years of the (Parisian) Regulation Approach', *New Political Economy*, November 1997, pp. 503–26.

5. M. Aglietta, *A Theory of Capitalist Regulation: The US Experience* (London: Verso, 1979), p. 32.

6. R. Keohane, *After Hegemony: Cooperation and Discord in the World Political Economy* (Princeton, NJ: Princeton University Press, 1984), p. 37.

7. For various conceptions of the term 'hegemony', see D. Rapkin (ed.), *World Leadership and Hegemony* (London: Lynne Rienner, 1990). For debates on US hegemonic decline, see A. O. P. Kennedy, *The Rise and Fall of the Great Powers: Economic Change and Military Conflict from 1500 to 2000* (London: Fontana, 1988); R. Keohane, *After Hegemony*, (Note 6 above); R. Gilpin, *The Political Economy of International Relations* (Princeton, NJ: Princeton University Press, 1987).

8. See, for example, E. Vogel, 'Pax Nipponica?', *Foreign Affairs*, 64, 1986.

9. See R. Gilpin, *The Political Economy of International Relations* (Princeton, NJ: Princeton University Press, 1987).

10. R. Keohane, *After Hegemony*, (Note 6 above).

11. R. Cox, 'Civilisations in World Political Economy', *New Political Economy*, 1(2), July 1996; and 'Towards a Post-hegemonic Conceptualisation of World Order: Reflections on the Relevancy of Ibn Khaldun', in J. Rosenau and E. Czempel, *Governance Without Government: Order and Change in World Politics* (Cambridge University Press, 1992).

12. R. Cox, 'Social Forces, States and World Orders: Beyond International Relations Theory', *Millennium*, 10(2), 1981 pp. 126–55, **139**.

13. R. Cox, 'Structural Issues of Global Governance: Implications for Europe', in S. Gill (ed.), *Gramsci, Historical Materialism and International Relations* (Cambridge University Press, 1993), p. 261.

14. S. Strange, 'The Name of the Game', in N. Rizopoulos (ed.), *Seachanges: American Foreign Policy in a World Transformed* (Washington, DC: Council on Foreign Relations, 1990), p. 260.

15. See S. Gill, 'Hegemony, Consensus and Trilateralism', *Review of International Studies*, 12, pp. 205–21; and K.V.D. Pijl, *The Making of an Atlantic Ruling Class* (London: New Left Books, 1984). See also H. Sklar (ed.), *Trilateralism, the Trilateral Commission and Elite Planning for World Management* (Boston, Mass.: South End Press, 1980).

16. On the élite interactions in the European Union, see L. Sklair, 'Transnational Corporations as Political Actors', *New Political Economy*, 3(2), 1998, and B. van Apeldoorn, 'Transnational Class Agency and European Governance: The Case of the European Round Table of Industrialists', *New Political Economy*, 5(2), 1999, pp. 157–81.

17. See J. Davis and Ch. Bishop, 'The MAI: multilateralism from above', in 'The Threat of Globalism', *Race & Class*, special issue, 40(2&3), 1999, pp. 159–70, **168**.

18. S. Gill and D. Law, 'Global Hegemony and the Structural Power of Capital', *International Studies Quarterly*, 33, 1989, pp. 475–99.

19. J. Ruggie, 'International Regimes, Transactions and Change – Embedded Liberalism in the Post War Order', *International Organisation*, 36, pp. 379–414.

20. K. Watkins, *Fixing the Rules, North–South Issues in International Trade and the GATT Uruguay Round* (London: Catholic Institute for International Relations, 1992).

21. GATT, Uruguay, Final Protocol, quoted in L. Walker, 'Gatt: The Uruguay Round and the Developing Countries', PhD thesis, University of Sheffield (1996) ch. 7, section 4.

22. K. Watkins, *Fixing the Rules*, (Note 20 above), p. 95.

23. UNCTAD, *Strengthening National and International Action and Multilateral Cooperation for a Healthy, Secure and Equitable World Economy*, Eighth session, Cartegena de Indias, 8 February 1992, UNCTAD/TD/L339, 24, pp. 62–3; quoted *passim* in J. van Wijk and G. Junne, *Intellectual Property Protection of Advanced Technology, Changes in the Global Technology System: Implications and Options for Developing Countries*, Report prepared for the United Nations University's Institute for New Technologies, INTECH, contract no. 91/026, Maastricht, The Netherlands, October 1992.

24. J. van Wijk and G. Junne *Intellectual Property Protection*, (Note 23), p. 61.

25. J. Davis and Ch. Bishop, 'The MAI', (Note 17), p. 168.

26. See M. Thekaekara, 'Global Free Trade, the View from the Ground', *New Political Economy*, 1(1), 1996 pp. 115–18, **116**.

27. H. Hyman, 'Privatization: The Facts', in C. Veljanovski, *Privatisation and Competition: A Market Prospectus* (London: Hobart Paperbacks, 1989). See also J. Vickers and G. Yarrow, *Privatization, an Economic Analysis* (Cambridge, Mass.: MIT Press, 1988). Note, however, that the 1990s saw further swingeing privatizations (for example, the railways) not included in the total here.

28. B. Hugill, 'A Civil Service on its Last Legs', *The Observer*, 29 May 1994, p. 22.

29. D. Sandberg, 'The Pirate Privateers', *New Internationalist*, September 1994; see also R. T. Naylor, *Hot Money and the Politics of Debt* (Toronto: McClelland & Stewart, 1989).

30. World Bank, *Global Development Finance, 1997* (Washington DC: World Bank, 1997), p. 121.

31. For examples of this, see A. Showstack-Sassoon (ed.), *Women and the State* (London: Hutchinson, 1987).

32. H. Shutt, *The Trouble with Capitalism. An Enquiry into the Causes of Global Economic Failure* (London: Zed Books, 1998), esp. ch. 8.

33. Pierre Bourdieu, 'L'Architecte de l'euro passe aux aveux', *Le Monde Diplomatique*, September 1997, p. 19, cited in Z. Bauman, *Globalization, The Human Consequences* (Cambridge: Polity Press 1998), p. 99.

34. M. Castells, *The Rise of the Network Society* (Cambridge, Mass.: and Oxford, UK: 1996), p. 469.
35. P. Gowan, *The Global Gamble: Washington's Faustian Bid for World Dominance* (London: Verso, 1999) p. 5.
36. Ibid., p. 23.
37. Ibid., p. 29.
38. Ibid., p. 104. This argument has also been made by others, see Ronald McKinnon and Kenichi Ohno, *Dollar and Yen: Resolving Economic Conflict Between the United States and Japan* (Cambridge, Mass.: MIT Press, 1997).
39. There is no doubt about the strong US backing for the IMF course. See the ringing endorsement of it in the *Economic Report of the President* (Washington DC: February 1999), pp. 245ff. See also Stephen Gill, 'The Geopolitics of the Asian Crisis', *Monthly Review*, 50(10), 1999.
40. For further discussion, see Chapter 10 of this book.
41. Cited in Gowan, *The Global Gamble*. (Note 35 above), p. 3.
42. UNCTAD, *Trade and Development Report, 1999*, p. 107.
43. See 'The Fortune 500', *Fortune Magazine*, May 1994 and May 1998.
44. W. K. Tabb, 'The East Asian Financial Crisis', *Monthly Review*, 50(2) 1998, p. 25.
45. UNCTAD, *Trade and Development Report, 1999*, p. 57.
46. D. Henwood, *WallSt* (London and New York: Verso, 1998), p. 125.
47. Gowan, *The Global Gamble*, (Note 35 above), pp. 35–6.
48. Antonio Negri, quoted in Henwood, (Note 46 above), p. 231.
49. Economic Report of the President, 1999, (Note 39 above), p. 302.
50. Ibid., p. 262.
51. See, for example, W. A. Sahlman, 'The New Economy is Stronger than You Think', *Harvard Business Review*, November–December 1999, p. 100.
52. See P. Baran, *The Political Economy of Growth*, (New York: Monthly Review Press, 1957), ch. 4.
53. G. Soros, *The Crisis of Global Capitalism* (London: Little, Brown, 1999).
54. S. Huntington, 'The Lonely Superpower', *Foreign Affairs*, March/April 1999, pp. 35–49.
55. WTO, *Annual Report 1999* (Geneva: WTO, 1999), ch. vii.
56. J. Davis and Ch. Bishop, 'The MAI', (Note 17 above), p. 164.
57. P. Patnaik, 'Whatever Happened to Imperialism', *Monthly Review*, November 1990, p. 1.
58. A. Gamble, 'Marxism after Communism: Beyond Realism and Historicism', *Review of International Studies*, 25, special issue, December 1999, pp. 127–44.
59. S. Crispin and S. Lawrence, 'In Self-Defence', *Far Eastern Economic Review*, 1 July 1999, pp. 22–6.
60. J. Wolf, 'Going Ballistic', *Far Eastern Economic Review*, 18 February 1999, p. 26–7; and 'The New Star Wars', *Newsweek*, 22 February 1999.
61. http://www.channel4.org.uk (December 1999).
62. D. Shirmer, 'Access: Post-Cold War Imperialist Expansion', *Monthly Review*, 45, 1993, pp. 38–51.

63. http://www.fco.gov.uk/news/speechtext.html
64. N. Chomsky, *The New Military Humanism: Lessons from Kosovo* (Common Courage Press, 1999); http://www.commoncouragepress.com.

Part III Introduction

1. For example, F. Jameson, 'Actually Existing Marxism', *Polygraph: an International Journal of Culture and Politics*, 6/7, 1993, pp. 171–95. In his earlier, best-known, work, Jameson focused on postmodern culture as the logic of late capitalism. Today, Jameson appears to equate a subsequent development in late capitalism, 'late, late' capitalism with postmodern capitalism. F. Jameson, *Postmodernism, or, the Cultural Logic of Late Capitalism* (Durham: Durham University Press, 1990).
2. 'Institutional endorsement' is particularly noticeable in the US where courses in 'postcolonial studies' and 'postcolonial' literature abound. See E. Shohat, 'Notes on the "Post-Colonial"', *Social Text*, 31/32, 1993, pp. 99–113, **99**. In the UK too the term 'postcolonial' is beginning to work its way onto curricula of university courses.
3. For an excellent argument, see N. Fraser, 'From Redistribution to Recognition? Dilemmas of Justice in a "Post-socialist Age"', *New Left Review*, 212, 1995, pp. 68–93.
4. A. Portes and D. Kincaid, 'Sociology and Development in the 1990s: Critical Challenges and Empirical Trends', *Sociological Forum*, 4 (1989) pp. 479–503; quoted in M. J. Watts, 'Development I: Power, Knowledge, Discursive Practice', *Progress in Human Geography*, 17 (2), 1993, pp. 257–72, **262**.
5. C. Wright Mills, *The Sociological Imagination* (Oxford & New York: Oxford University Press, 1959), pp. 165–7.
6. E. Meiksins Wood, 'What is the "Postmodern" Agenda? An Introduction', *Monthly Review,* July/August 1995, special issue 'In Defense of History', pp. 1–12.
7. A. Dirlik, 'The Postcolonial Aura: Third World Criticism in the Age of Global Capitalism', *Critical Inquiry*, 20 (2), 1994, pp. 328–56.
8. E. Shohat, (Note 2 above), p. 101.
9. Ibid., p. 103.
10. A. Dirlik, (Note 7 above), p. 329.
11. A. Dirlik, (Note 7 above), pp. 330–1. Dirlik notes, however, these exceptions: A. Appadurai, 'Global Ethnoscapes: Notes and Queries for a Transnational Anthropology', in R. G. Fox (ed.), *Recapturing Anthropology: Working in the Present* (Santa Fe, N. Mexico: 1991); and A. Ahmad who, like Dirlik himself, relates postcoloniality to contemporary capitalism, see A. Ahmad, *In Theory: Classes, Nations, Literatures* (London: Verso, 1992).
12. E. Shohat, (Note 2 above), p. 110. Also, A. McClintock, 'The Angel of Progress: Pitfalls of the Term "Post-Colonialism"', *Social Text*, 31/32, 1993, pp. 84–97.

13. B. Ashcroft, G. Griffiths and H. Tiffin, *The Empire Writes Back: Theory and Practice in Post-colonial Literatures* (London: Routledge, 1989).
14. P. Williams and L. Chrisman (eds), *Colonial Discourse and Postcolonial Theory* (New York: Harvester Wheatsheaf, 1993).
15. Thiongo'o Ngugi wa, *Decolonising the Mind: The Politics of Language in African Literature* (London: James Currey/Heinemann, 1986).
16. J. Nederveen Pieterse and Bhikhu Parekh, 'Shifting Imaginaries: Decolonization, Internal Decolonization, Postcoloniality', in J. Nederveen Pieterse and Bhikhu Parekh (eds), *Decolonization of Imagination, Culture, Knowledge and Power* (London: Zed Books, 1995).
17. Quoted in F. Mulhern, 'The Politics of Cultural Studies', *Monthly Review*, July/August 1995, pp. 31–40, **32**.
18. H. Bhabha has been especially important in the discussion of hybridity, see 'The Commitment to Theory', *New Formations*, 5, 1988, pp. 5–25.
19. G. Prakash, 'Postcolonial Criticism and Indian Historiography', *Social Text*, 31/32, 1992, p. 8.
20. H. Bhabha, *passim*, in R. J. C. Young, *Colonial Desire: Hybridity in Theory, Culture and Race* (London: Routledge, 1995), p. 175.
21. H. Bhabha, 'Commitment to Theory', (see Note 18 above), p. 21.
22. A. Escobar, *Encountering Development, the Making and Unmaking of the Third World* (Princeton, NJ: Princeton University Press, 1995), p. 219.

8   Africa: Exclusion and the Containment of Anarchy

1. M. Castells, *The Rise of the Network Society* (Cambridge, Mass. and Oxford, UK: Basil Blackwell, 1996), p. 106.
2. Centre d'Études Prospectives et d'Informations Internationales (CEPII), *L'economie mondiale 1990–2000: l'imperatif de la croissance* (Paris: Economica, 1992), cited in M. Castells, *The Rise of the Network Society* (Note 1 above), p. 134.
3. See UNCTAD, *Trade and Development Report, 1998* (New York and Geneva: UN; 1998) p. 127.
4. World Bank, *Global Development Finance, 1997* (Washington, DC: World Bank, 1997), p. 202.
5. Kofi Annan, 'The Causes of Conflict and the Promotion of Durable Peace and Sustainable Development in Africa' (www.un.org/ecosoc-dev/geninfo/afrec), cited in S. Lone, 'Confronting Conflict in Africa', *Africa Recovery*, August 1998, p. 20.
6. J. Ihonvbere, *Economic Crisis, Civil Society, and Democratization: The Case of Zambia*, (Trenton, NJ: African World Press, 1996), p. 25.
7. This calculation is based on the statistical tables in Annexes of the 1970 and 1982 issues of OECD, *Development Cooperation, Review of the OECD Development Assistance Committee* (Paris: OECD, 1970 and 1982).

8. R.T. Naylor, *Hot Money and the Politics of Debt* (Toronto: McClelland & Stewart, 1987).

9. Bank for International Settlements, *59th Annual Report 1989* (Basle: BIS, 1989), pp. 135–6.

10. M. Castells, *End of Millennium* (Cambridge, Mass. and Oxford, UK: Basil Blackwell, 1998), p. 135.

11. R. T. Naylor, *Hot Money* (Note 8 above), p. 59.

12. UNCTAD, *Trade and Development Report, 1989* (New York: United Nations, 1989), p. 38, table 19.

13. The *Guardian*, 9 January 1987.

14. For a thorough discussion on the process and effects of these IMF- and World Bank-imposed reforms, see M. Chossudovsky, *The Globalisation of Poverty, Impacts of IMF and World Bank Reforms* (London and New Jersey: Zed Books, 1998).

15. A. Leftwich, 'Governance, Democracy and Development in the Third World', *Third World Quarterly*, 14(3), 1993, p. 607.

16. Ibid., p. 608.

17. Besides a mountain of country case studies, critical 'generic' reviews of structural adjustment programmes have appeared in special issues of the *Journal Review of African Political Economy (ROAPE)*, 47, 1990 and 62, 1994. More recently, *ROAPE* has published good overviews by: P. Carmody; 'Constructing Alternatives to Structural Adjustment in Africa', *ROAPE*, 75, 1998, pp. 25–46; Stefano Ponte, 'The World Bank and "Adjustment in Africa" ', *ROAPE*, 66, 1995; and S. Bromley, 'Making Sense of Structural Adjustment', *ROAPE*, 65, 1995, pp. 339–48. For more general critiques that are not restricted to Africa, see E. Helleiner, *States and the Re-emergence of Global Finance: From Bretton Woods to the 1990s* (Ithaca, NY: Cornell University Press, 1994); S. George and F. Sabelli, *Faith & Credit, the World Bank's Secular Empire* (Boulder, Col.: Westview Press, 1994); D. Ghai (ed.), *The IMF and the South* (London: Zed Books, 1991).

18. African NGO Declaration to UNCTAD ix, prepared by the parallel NGO Conference to UNCTAD ix, held 24–28 April 1996, Midrand, South Africa; circulated by email – contact ifaa@wn.apc.org

19. D. Ghai and C. Hewitt de Alcantara, 'The Crisis of the 1980s in Africa, Latin America and the Caribbean: An Overview', in D. Ghai (ed.), *The IMF and the South* (London: Zed Books, on behalf of United Nations Research Institute for Social Development, 1991), pp. 14–17.

20. D. Ghai and C. Hewitt de Alcantara 'The Crisis of the 1980s' (Note 19 above), p. 16.

21. Reported in *The Economist*, 5 March 1994.

22. World Bank, *Adjustment in Africa: Reform, Results, and the Road Ahead, a World Bank Policy Research Report* (New York: Oxford University Press, 1994).

23. UNCTAD, *Trade and Development Report*, 1998, p. 125.

24. UNCTAD, ibid., p. 125.

25. International Monetary Fund, *World Economic Outlook* (Washington DC: IMF, October, 1999), statistical appendix.

26. UNCTAD, *Trade and Development Report*, (Note 23 above), p. 127.

27. K. Watkins, 'Debt Relief for Africa', *Review of African Political Economy*, 62, 1994, pp. 117–27, **126**. For further reading on the evolution of poverty, social conditions and income inequality under structural adjustment, see also G. Cornia, S. Jolly and F. Stewart (eds), *Adjustment with a Human Face: Protecting the Vulnerable and Promoting Growth* (Oxford: Clarendon Press, 1987); and P. Gibbon, 'The World Bank and African Poverty 1973–91', *Journal of Modern African Studies*, 30(2) 1992, pp. 193–220. See also M. Chossudovsky, *The Globalisation of Poverty, Impacts of IMF and World Bank Reforms*, (London and New Jersey: Zed Books, 1998).

28. D. Avramovic, 'Depression of Export Commodity Prices', *Third World Quarterly*, July 1986.

29. UNCTAD, *Trade and Development Report*, (Note 23 above), p. 119.

30. M. Castells, *End of Millennium*, (Note 10 above), p. 117.

31. B. Martin, 'Gains without Frontiers', *New Statesman and Society*, 9 December 1994, pp. 22–3. The senior manager whom Martin quotes is Davison Budhoo. See also B. Martin, *In the Public Interest? Privatisation and Public Sector Reform* (London: Zed Books, 1994).

32. B. Martin, 'Gain without Frontiers', (Note 31 above), p. 23.

33. See B. Riley, 'Funds Pour Into New Growth Regions', *The Economist*, 7 February 1994.

34. World Bank, *Global Development Finance* (Washington DC: World Bank, 1997), pp. 120–1.

35. See M. Mandani, 'Uganda: Contradictions in the IMF Programme and Perspective', in D. Ghai (ed.), *The IMF and the South: The Social Impact of Crisis and Adjustment* (London: Zed Books, 1996); P. Lewis and H. Stein, 'Shifting Fortunes: The Political Economy of Financial Liberalization in Nigeria', *World Development*, 25(1), 1997, pp. 5–22.

36. P. Carmody, 'Constructing Alternatives to Structural Adjustment in Africa', (Note 17 above), p. 29.

37. A. Leftwich, 'Governance, Democracy and Development in the Third World', *Third World Quarterly*, 14(3), 1993, pp. 605–24, **610**. For further reading on the pressures towards democratization in Africa, see other contributions to the same issue of *Third World Quarterly*, including the literature review by E. Reinierse, pp. 647–64.

38. C. L. Baylies, 'Political Conditionality and Democratisation', *Review of African Political Economy*, 65, 1995, pp. 321–37.

39. A. Leftwich, 'Governance, Democracy and Development', (Note 37 above), p. 606.

40. For an excellent review of the literature on the links between political and economic reform in Africa, see C.L. Baylies, 'Political Conditionality and Democratisation', (Note 38 above).

41. B. Gills, J. Rocamora and R. Wilson (eds), *Low Intensity Democracy, Political Power in the New World Order* (London: Pluto Press, 1993).

42. A. Sawyer, 'The Politics of Adjustment Policies', ECLA Document ECA/ICHD/88/29, quoted in Ghai and Hewitt de Alcantara, 'The Crisis of the 1980s' (Note 19 above), p. 27. See also J.-J. Barya, 'The

New Political Conditionalities of Aid: An Independent View from Africa', *IDS Bulletin*, 24(1), 1993, pp. 16–23.

43. For example, R. Sandbrook, *The Politics of Africa's Economic Recovery* (Cambridge University Press, 1993); C.L. Baylies, 'Political Conditionality and Democratisation' (Note 38 above), p. 333 *passim*.

44. J. Walton and D. Seddon, *Free Markets and Food Riots: The Politics of Global Adjustment* (Oxford: Basil Blackwell, 1994). See also M. Chossudovsky, who holds the World Bank team in Rwanda directly responsible for the political and social repercussions of shock therapy that brought the country to civil war, in 'IMF/World Bank Policies and the Rwandan Holocaust', *Third World Resurgence*, 52, 1994. He makes a similar argument in the case of Somalia.

45. W. Reno, 'Markets, War, and the Reconfiguration of Political Authority in Sierra Leone', *Canadian Journal of African Studies*, 29(2), 1995. See also W. Reno *Corruption and State Politics in Sierra Leone* (Cambridge University Press, 1995).

46. Ibid., p. 217.

47. S.P. Huntington, *Political Order in Changing Societies* (New Haven, Conn. and London: Yale University Press, 1968).

48. J.C. Scott, *Comparative Political Corruption* (Englewood Cliffs, NJ: Prentice-Hall, 1972) p. 35.

49. R. Kaplan, 'The Coming Anarchy: How Scarcity, Crime, Overpopulation and Disease are Rapidly Destroying the Social Fabric of Our Planet', *Atlantic Monthly*, February 1994, pp. 44–76, **46**.

50. Ibid., p. 72, Kaplan approvingly quotes Martin van Creveld, who suggests in the *Transformation of War* that by compelling the senses to focus on the here and now, people at the edge of existence can find liberation in violence.

51. Kaplan, 'The Coming Anarchy', (Note 49 above), p. 46.

52. W. Reno, 'Corruption and State Politics in Sierra Leone', (Note 45 above), describes the involvement of the Nimba Mining Company (NIMCO).

53. I. Smillie, L. Gberie and R. Hazelton, *The Heart of the Matter: Sierra Leone, Diamonds and Human Security* (Toronto: Partnership Africa Canada: 1999), available at www.web.net/pac

54. See C. Collins, 'Reconstructing the Congo', *Review of African Political Economy*, 74, 1997, p. 591–600; Quentin Outram, 'It's Terminal Either Way: An Analysis of Armed Conflict in Liberia, 1989–1996', *Review of African Political Economy*, 73, 1997; pp. 355–71. On Angola, see Ian Hunt, 'Rough Diamonds', *The Guardian*, 14 September 1999. Also, in *Africa Report 1998* (Note 5 above) Kofi Annan observed (while not naming names) that foreign interests continue to play a large role in sustaining some conflicts in the competition for oil and other African resources.

55. 'A Crude Awakening: The Role of the Oil and Banking Industries in Angola's Civil War and the Plunder of State Assets', *Global Witness*, December 1999.

56. See Notes 53 and 55 above.

57. E. Braathen, M. Boas and G. Saether, *Ethnicity Kills? The Politics of War, Peace and Ethnicity in Sub-Saharan Africa* (London: Macmillan; 2000).

58. M. Duffield, *The Symphony of the Damned: Racial Discourse, Complex Political Emergencies and Humanitarian Aid*, Occasional paper, School of Public Policy, University of Birmingham, 2 March 1996.

59. See M. Barrett, *The Politics of Truth* (Oxford: Polity Press, 1991), p. 130 *passim*.

60. Examples of this 'discourse analysis' approach to the new aid agenda are A. Leftwich, 'Governance, the State and the Politics of Development', *Development and Change*, 25, 1994, pp. 363–86; M. Robinson, 'Aid, Democracy and Political Conditionality in Sub-Saharan Africa', in G. Sorensen (ed.), *Political Conditionality* (London: Frank Cass, 1993), pp. 85–99; and 'Strengthening Civil Society in Africa: The Role of Foreign Political Aid', *IDS Bulletin*, 26(2), 1995, pp. 70–80.

61. ODI, *NGOs and Official Donors*, Briefing Paper 1–4, August 1995, (London: Overseas Development Institute), quoted in M. Duffield, (Note 58 above), p. 8. For a comprehensive review and detailed advocacy of the NGO approach to 'development' see M. Edwards and D. Hulme (eds), *Making a Difference, NGOs and Development in a Changing World* (London: Earthscan, 1992). See also J. Clark, *Democratizing Development: The Role of Voluntary Organisations* (London: Earthscan, 1991). Clark notes some 4000 development NGOs working in OECD member countries, dispersing almost US$3 billion-worth of assistance every year, and that they work with between 10 000 and 20 000 southern NGOs. For a critical assessment on the role of NGOs in development, see A. Fowler, 'Distant Obligations: Speculations on NGO Funding and the Global Market', *Review of African Political Economy*, 55, 1992, pp. 9–29.

62. M. Duffield, *The Symphony of the Damned* (Note 58 above). Much of this section of Chapter 8 is based on Duffield's thesis as developed in this work. Note, however, that Duffield has also elaborated his thesis in connection with other zones of insecurity on the edge of the global economy, notably the Balkans. In an outstanding report for UNICEF in 1994, Duffield first developed his theory of 'complex political emergencies', with reference to both Angola and Bosnia. See M. Duffield, 'Complex Political Emergencies', An Exploratory Report for UNICEF' (School of Public Policy, University of Birmingham, 1994).

63. R. Richards, *The New Racism* (London: Junction Books, 1992).

64. R. Kaplan, 'The Coming Anarchy: How Scarcity, Crime, Overpopulation and Disease are Rapidly Destroying the Social Fabric of Our Planet', *Atlantic Monthly*, February 1994, pp. 44–76. This article formed the basis of the BBC's dramatic documentary, *Pulp Futures*, in 1995.

65. M. Duffield, *The Symphony of the Damned*, (Note 58 above), p. 10. See P. Richards, 'Fighting for the Rain Forest: Youth, Insurgency and Environment in Sierra Leone', Mimeo (London: University College, Department of Anthropology, 1995); For a critique of Richard's thesis,

see Yusuf Bangura, 'Understanding the Political and Cultural Dynamics of the Sierra Leone War: A Critique of Paul Richard's "Fighting for the Rain Forest"', *Africa Development, Afrique & Développement*, XXII (3 & 4), 1997, pp. 117–47.

66. M. Duffield, *The Symphony of the Damned*, (Note 58 above). p. 12. For a discussion of 'complex emergency' theory, see J. Edkins, 'Legality with a Vengeance: Famines and Humanitarian Relief in "Complex Emergencies"', in S. Owen Vandersluis and P. Teros, *Poverty in World Politics* (London: Macmillan in association with *Millennium: Journal of International Studies*, 2000), pp. 59–90.
67. M. Duffield (Note 58 above), pp. 42–3.
68. Ed Vulliamy, 'How Drugs Giants Let Millions Die', *The Observer*, 19 December 1999.
69. *The Guardian*, 1 May, 2000.
70. Comment in an interview on the BBC TV documentary programme, '*Horizon*: The Battle for Aids', 4 December 1995.

9 Islamic Revolt

1. *The Economist*, Editorial, 'Living with Islam', 18 March 1995.
2. S. Huntington, 'The Clash of Civilizations?', *Foreign Affairs*, Summer 1993, pp. 22–49.
3. F. Fukuyama, *The End of History and the Last Man* (London: Hamish Hamilton, 1992).
4. S. Huntington, The Clash of Civilizations', (Note 2 above), p. 26.
5. See the discussion of this in Chapter 6 of this volume.
6. S. Huntington, 'The Clash of Civilizations', (Note 2 above), p. 24.
7. G. H. Jansen, *Militant Islam* (London: Penguin, 1978) p. 1, quoting K. Ahmad, 'Islam, Its Meaning and Message'.
8. See W. M. Patton, 'Shi'ahs', in J. Hastings (ed.), *Encyclopaedia of Religion and Ethics* (Edinburgh: T. & T. Clark, 1908), pp. 453–8.
9. E. Gellner, *Postmodernism, Reason and Religion* (London: Routledge, 1992).
10. E. Gellner, ibid., p. 7.
11. G. H. Jansen, *Militant Islam*, (Note 7 above), p. 29.
12. S. Bromley, 'The Prospects for Democracy in the Middle East', in D. Held (ed.), *Prospects for Democracy* (Oxford: Polity Press, 1993), pp. 380–412, **383**. See also S. Bromley, *Rethinking Middle East Politics, State Formation and Development* (Oxford: Polity Press, 1994).
13. E. Gellner, *Postmodernism, Reason and Religion*, (Note 9 above), p. 9.
14. E. Gellner, ibid., p. 10.
15. E. W. Said, *Orientalism* (London: Routledge & Kegan Paul, 1978).
16. M. Rodinson, 'The Western Image and Western Studies of Islam', in J. Schacht with C. E. Bosworth (eds), *The Legacy of Islam* (Oxford: Clarendon Press, 1974), pp. 9–62, **11**.
17. M. Rodinson, ibid., p. 37.
18. M. Rodinson, ibid., pp. 49–50.

19. E. Said, *Orientalism* (London: Penguin Books, 1985), p. 259.
20. M. Rodinson 'The Western Image', (Note 16 above), p. 48.
21. M. Rutven, *Islam in the World* (London: Penguin, 1991), p. 292.
22. E. Said, *Orientalism*, (Note 19 above), p. 240, quoting T. E. Lawrence.
23. See Chapter 2 of this book on the roots of neocolonialism.
24. G. H. Jansen, *Militant Islam*, (Note 7 above), p. 14.
25. G. H. Jansen, ibid., p. 62.
26. E. Said, *Culture and Imperialism* (New York: Vintage Press, 1994).
27. E. Said, *Orientalism*, (Note 19 above), p. 3.
28. G. H. Jansen, *Militant Islam*, (Note 7 above), p. 68.
29. G. H. Jansen, ibid., p. 75.
30. O. Roy, *The Failure of Political Islam* (London: I. B. Tauris, 1995), p. 3.
31. O. Roy, ibid., p. 83. For similar classifications, see also G. H. Jansen, *Militant Islam*, (Note 7 above), p. 134.
32. P. Aarts, quoting N. Chomsky, in 'Democracy, Oil and the Gulf War', *Third World Quarterly*, 13(3), 1992, p. 527.
33. S. Bromley, *American Hegemony and World Oil: The Industry, the State System and the World Economy* (Oxford: Polity Press, 1991), p. 250.
34. S. Bromley, 'The Prospects for Democracy in the Middle East', in D. Held (ed.), *Prospects for Democracy* (Oxford: Polity Press, 1993), pp. 380–406.
35. O. Roy, *The Failure of Political Islam*, (Note 30 above), p. 4.
36. Ibid., p. 93.
37. Ibid., pp. 98–9.
38. Ibid., p. 196.
39. Khosrokhavar, in M. Castells, *The Power of Identity* (Malden, Mass., USA and Oxford, UK: Basil Blackwell, 1997), p. 20 passim.
40. Castells, ibid., p. 20.

10   The Developmental States of East Asia

1. World Bank, *The East Asian Miracle* (New York: Oxford University Press, 1993), p. xv.
2. B. Balassa, 'Trade Policies in Developing Countries', *American Economic Review*, 61, May 1971; *Policy Reform in Developing Countries* (New York: Pergamon Press, 1977); and *The Newly Industrializing Countries in the World Economy* (New York: Pergamon Press, 1981).
3. C. Johnson, *MITI and the Japanese Miracle* (Stanford, Calif.: Stanford University Press, 1982). See also 'Political Institutions and Economic Performance: The Government–Business Relationship in Japan, South Korea and Taiwan', in F. C. Deyo (ed.), *The Political Economy of the New Asian Industrialism* (Ithaca, NY: Cornell University Press, 1987), pp. 136–64.
4. E. K. Y. Chen, *Hyper-growth in Asian Economies: A Comparative Study of Hong Kong, Japan, Korea, Singapore and Taiwan* (New York: Holmes & Meier, 1979).

5. A. Amsden, 'The State and Taiwan's Economic Development', in P. Evans, D. Rueschemeyer and T. Skocpol (eds), *Bringing the State Back In* (New York: Cambridge University Press, 1985), pp. 78–106. See also A. Amsden, *Asia's Next Giant: South Korea and Late Industrializiation* (New York: Oxford University Press, 1989).
6. F. Fröbel, J. Heinrichs and O. Kreye, *The New International Division of Labour: Structural Unemployment in Industrialized Countries and Industrialization in Developing Countries* (Cambridge University Press, 1980).
7. See M. Castells, 'Four Asian Tigers with a Dragon Head: A Comparative Analysis of the State, Economy, and Society in the Asian Pacific Rim', in R. P. Appelbaum and J. Henderson, *States and Development in the Asian Pacific Rim* (California: Sage, 1992), pp. 33–70.
8. One of the first such attempts was D. Senghaas, *The European Experience: A Historical Critique of Development Theory* (Leamington Spa: Berg, 1985). The neo-Listian position is fully developed by G. White and R. Wade in their introduction to G. White (ed.), *Developmental States in East Asia* (London: Macmillan, 1988).
9. See R. Wade, 'State Intervention in "Outward-looking" Development: Neoclassical Theory and Taiwanese Practice', in G. White (ed.), *Developmental States*, (Note 8 above), pp. 30–67.
10. P. L. Berger, *The Capitalist Revolution, Fifty Propositions about Prosperity, Equality and Liberty* (Aldershot: Wildwood House, 1987).
11. See for example, L. Pye, 'The New Asian Capitalism: A Political Portrait', in P. L. Berger and Hsin-Huang M. Hsiao (eds), *In Search of an East Asian Development Model* (New Brunswick: Transaction, 1988), pp. 86–7.
12. P. L. Berger, 'An East Asian Development Model?' ch. 1, in P. L. Berger and Hsin-Huang M. Hsiao (eds), *In Search of an East Asian Development Model* (New Brunswick: Transaction, 1988; second printing, 1990), p. 7.
13. See R. MacFarquhar, 'The Post-Confucian Challenge', *The Economist*, 8 February 1980; M. Morishima, *Why has Japan Succeeded? Western Technology and the Japanese Ethos* (Cambridge University Press, 1982); G. Rozman (ed.), *The East Asia Region: Confucian Heritage and its Modern Adaptation* (Princeton, NJ: Princeton University Press, 1991); Wong Siu-lun, 'Modernization and Chinese Culture in Hong Kong', *The China Quarterly*, 106, 1986, pp. 306–25; and J. P. L. Jiang (ed.), *Confucianism and Modernization: A Symposium* (Taipei: 1987).
14. See W. Bello and S. Rosenfeld, *Dragons in Distress: Asia's Miracle Economies in Crisis* (Harmondsworth: Penguin, 1990): in Taiwan, more than 2900 labour disputes were registered in 1987 and 1988 alone, and over 4540 disputes went into arbitration in the district courts (pp. 227, 223); emigration from Singapore, negligible in the 1960s, rose to 2000 families a year in the mid-1980s, and to 4700 by 1989 (p. 333); and in South Korea, between 1987 and 1989 more than 7100 labour disputes erupted, while the number of unions more than doubled, from 2725 to 7358 (p. 41).

15. See *New Internationalist*, January 1995; and W. Bello and S. Rosenfeld, *Dragons in Distress: Asia's Miracle Economies in Crisis* (Note 14 above).

16. This section on the geopolitical factors affecting East Asian development draws on an interesting essay by an MA student on the University of Sheffield's graduate programme in international studies, Anne Holgate Lowe, 'Geopolitical and Historical Factors in the East Asian Development Model', University of Sheffield, Department of Politics, 1995.

17. CIA figures cited by B. Cummings, 'The Origins and Development of the North East Asian Political Economy: Industrial Sectors, Product Cycles and Political Consequences', in F. Deyo (ed.), *The Political Economy of the New Asian Industrialism* (Ithaca, NY: Cornell University Press, 1987), pp. 44–83.

18. S. Haggard and Tun-jen Cheng, *Newly Industrializing Asia in Transition, Policy Reform and American Response* (Berkeley, Calif.: Institute of International Studies, University of California Press, 1987).

19. M. Castells, *'Four Asian Tigers with a Dragon Head'*, (Note 7 above), p. 53.

20. S. Krasner, 'Trade Conflicts and the Common Defense: The United States and Japan', in S. Haggard and Chung-in Moon (eds), *Pacific Dynamics: The International Politics of Industrial Change* (Boulder, Col.: Westview Press, 1989), pp. 251–74, **252**.

21. S. Haggard, 'Introduction', in S. Haggard and Chung-in Moon (eds), *Pacific Dynamics*, (Note 20 above), pp. 1–21, **8**.

22. S. Haggard, *Pathways from the Periphery* (Ithaca, NY: Cornell University Press, 1990).

23. P. Berger, *The Capitalist Revolution* (Aldershot: Wildwood House, 1987), p. 142.

24. W. Bello and S. Rosenfeld, *Dragons in Distress*, (Note 14 above), p. 337.

25. W. Bello and S. Rosenfeld, ibid.

26. *New Internationalist*, 'Unmasking the Miracle', January 1995, pp. 18–19.

27. See World Bank, *The East Asian Miracle*, (Note 1 above), figure 1.3, p. 31, and table 1.1, p. 33. For its data, the World Bank relies on submissions by governments. Authoritarian governments are hardly likely to admit to shortcomings in social distribution and equity. Meanwhile, local critics are often censured and cowed, making it difficult to achieve a correct assessment of the situation.

28. W. Bello and S. Rosenfeld, *Dragons in Distress*, (Note 14 above), pp. 37, 38. Here they cite Choi Jang-Jip, 'Interest Control and Political Control in South Korea: A Study of the Labor Unions in Manufacturing Industries, 1961–1980', PhD Dissertation, Department of Political Science, University of Chicago, August 1983, pp. 270–1; and Song Byung-Nak, 'The Korean Economy' (unpublished manuscript, Seoul, 1989), p. 27.

29. Kim Dae Jung, *Mass-participatory Economy* (Lanham, Md.: University Press of America, 1985), p. 37, quoted in M. Hart-Landsberg, 'South Korea, The Fraudulent Miracle', *Monthly Review*, December 1987.

30. E. Paul, 'Prospects for Liberalization in Singapore', *Journal of Contemporary Asia*, 23(3) 1993, pp. 291–305, **294**.
31. N. Harris, 'States, Economic Development, and the Asian Pacific Rim', in R. P. Appelbaum and J. Henderson (eds), *States and Development in the Asian Pacific Rim* (California and London: Sage, 1992), p. 78.
32. UNCTAD, *World Investment Report, 1994* (New York: United Nations, 1994), p. 76.
33. J. Yam, cited in P. Gowan, *The Global Gamble, Washington's Faustian Bid for World Dominance* (London: Verso, 1999), p. 52.
34. Ngai-Ling Sum, 'The NICs and Competing Strategies of East Asian Regionalism', in A. Gamble and A. Payne, *Regionalism and World Order* (London: Macmillan, 1996), pp. 207–46.
35. P. Bowles and B. MacLean, 'Understanding Trade Bloc Formation: The Case of the ASEAN Free Trade Area', *Review of International Political Economy*, 3 (2), pp. 319–48. See also R. Higgott and R. Stubbs, 'Competing Conceptions of Economic Regionalism: APEC versus EAEC in the Asia Pacific', *Review of International Political Economy*, 2 (3), 1995, pp. 516–35, **523**.
36. Bowles and MacLean, 'Understanding Trade Bloc Formation', (Note 35 above), p. 343.
37. Ibid., Note 35.
38. P. Bowles and B. MacLean, ibid. (Note 35 above), p. 333, quoting J. Reidel, 'Intra-Asian Trade and Foreign Direct Investment', *Asian Development Review*, 8 (1), 1991, pp. 111–46.
39. OECD, *Economic Survey, Japan*, (Paris: OECD, 1995), p. 154.
40. W. K. Tabb, 'Japanese Capitalism and the Asian Geese', *Monthly Review*, 45 (10), March 1994, pp. 29–40, **32**. See also M. Bernard and J. Ravenhill, 'Beyond Product Cycles and Flying Geese: Regionalisation, Hierarchy, and the Industrialisation of East Asia', *World Politics*, 47 (2), 1995; and W. Hatch and K. Yamamura, *Asia in Japan's Embrace: Building a Regional Production Alliance* (Cambridge University Press, 1996).
41. K. Fukasaku, *Economic Regionalization and Intra-industry Trade: Pacific Asian Perspectives*, OECD Technical Papers, No. 53 (Paris: OECD Development Centre, 1992); quoted in P. Bowles and B. MacLean, 'Understanding Trade Bloc Formation', (Note 35 above), p. 336.
42. P. Bowles and B. MacLean, 'Understanding Trade Bloc Formation' (Note 35 above), pp. 336–7, quoting L. Lim, 'ASEAN: A New Mode of Economic Cooperation', Paper presented to the conference 'The Political Economy of Foreign Policy in Southeast Asia in the New World Order', University of Windsor, Canada, September 1992.
43. P. Bowles and B. MacLean, 'Understanding Trade Bloc Formation' (Note 35 above), p. 341.
44. For authoritative papers on these two opposing camps, see the special issue of *Cambridge Journal of Economics*, 2, 1998.
45. For a blow-by-blow debunking of these various Western explanations of the 'Asian' crisis, see Ha-Joon Chang, 'The Hazard of Moral

Hazard, Untangling the Asian Crisis', *World Development*, 28(4), April 2000, pp. 775–88.

46. US Government, *Economic Report of the President*, transmitted to the Congress, February 1999, p. 279.
47. Cited by W. Bello, 'The Asian Economic Implosion: Causes, Dynamics, Prospects', in *Race & Class*, 40(2/3), March 1999, special issue on 'The Threat of Globalism', p. 138.
48. Between 1994 and 1996 net external financing into Asia-5 (Indonesia, Malaysia, the Philippines, the Republic of Korea and Thailand increased from US$47.5 billion to US$92.8 billion. See Institute of International Finance, *Capital flows to emerging market economies* (Washington, DC: 29 January 1998, p. 2) cited in UNCTAD, *Trade and Development Report*, (New York and Geneva: United Nations, 1998), p. 66.
49. For a discussion on how short-term flows and particular risk arbitrage dominated such flows, see J. Kregel, 'Derivatives and Global Capital Flows: Applications to Asia', *Cambridge Journal of Economics*, (22), 1998, pp. 677–92.
50. Within one year of the crisis, a net inflow of US$97.1 billion into Asia's emerging markets in 1996 had become a net outflow of almost US$12 billion. See UNCTAD, *Trade and Development Report,* (Note 48 above), p. 69.
51. Robert Wade, 'From Miracle to Cronyism: Explaining the Great Asian Slump', *Cambridge Journal of Economics* (22), 1998, pp. 693–706, **693**.
52. For an easy-to-read explanation about the role of hedge funds in the East Asia crisis, see Paul Krugman, *The Return of Depression Economics*, (Harmondsworth: Penguin 1999), pp. 133 ff.
53. On the implication of custom-based derivatives in the East Asia Crisis, see J. Kregel, 'Derivatives and Global Capital Flows', (Note 49 above).
54. UNCTAD, *Trade and Development Report*, (Note 48 above), p. 103.
55. P. Gowan, *The Global Gamble*, (Note 33 above), p. 104.
56. R. McKinnon and K. Ohno, *Dollar and Yen: Resolving the Economic Conflict between the United States and Japan* (Cambridge, Mass.: MIT Press, 1997), cited in R. McKinnon, 'Wading in the Yen Trap', *The Economist*, 24 July, 1999, pp. 83–6. See also R. Taggart Murphy, *The Weight of the Yen: How Denial Imperils America's Future and Ruins and Allliance* (New York: W.W. Norton, 1996).
57. There is no space in this chapter to discuss the decline and long recession of Japan in the 1990s. But for a quick resumé see Paul Krugman's chapter on Japan's crisis in *The Return of Depression Economics*, (Note 52 above). And Chalmers Johnson, 'Economic Crisis in East Asia: The Clash of Capitalisms', in *Cambridge Journal of Economics*, 22, 1998, p. 653–61.
58. P. Gowan, *The Global Gamble*, (Note 33 above), pp. 97–9.
59. W. Bello, 'The Asian Economic Implosion', (Note 47 above), p. 136.
60. IMF, *World Economic Outlook* (Washington DC: IMF, October 1999), p. 64, box 2.6. Note that the IMF has estimated these output losses on

the basis of a non-crisis output scenario of 4 per cent per year from 1997 onwards. This non-crisis scenario assumed a slowdown in the growth rate of about 4 per cent.

61. See World Bank, *World Bank Poverty Update: Trends in Poverty,* (Washington DC: World Bank, 1999), available on the internet at http://wb.forumone.com/poverty/data/trends See also T. Manuelyan Atine and M. Walton, *Social Consequences of the East Asian Financial Crisis,* (Washington DC: World Bank, 1998) available at http://www.worldbank.org/poverty

62. See W. Bello, 'The Asian Economic Implosion', (Note 47 above), p. 139.

63. P. Gowan, *The Global Gamble,* (Note 33 above), p. 128.

64. For discussions on the failed AMF initiatives, and the US role in this, see R. Higgott, The Asian Economic Crisis: A Study in the Politics of Resentment', *New Political Economy* 3(3), 1998, pp. 333–57; S. Gill, 'The Geo-politics of the Asian Crisis', *Monthly Review,* March 1999, pp. 1–9; and W. K. Tabb, 'The East Asian Financial Crisis', *Monthly Review,* June 1998, pp. 24–38.

65. J. Garten, 'Lessons for the Next Financial Crisis', *Foreign Affairs,* March/April 1999, pp. 76–92, **84**.

66. The distinguished neo-liberal economist, J. Baghwati, provides a compelling demonstration of how the actors, values and interests of the group he identifies as the 'Wall Street–Treasury' complex have been at the heart of the US and IMF policy response. J. Bhagwati, 'The Capital Myth: The Difference between Trade in Widgets and Trade in Dollars', *Foreign Affairs,* 77(3), 1998, cited in R. Higgott, 'The Asian Economic Crisis' (Note 64 above), p. 344; J. Garten too has argued that, when Asia blew up, it was the Treasury Department, and not the State Department which had 'the crucial relationships with finance ministers and central bank directors, and understood both the technical details and policy issues', 'Lessons for the Next Financial Crisis' (Note 65 above), pp. 84–5. See also Gowan, *The Global Gamble* (Note 33 above), pp. 107ff. In all this literature two names are regularly cited as key actors – Robert Rubin and Larry Summers of the US Treasury Department.

67. Cited in P. Gowan, *The Global Gamble,* (Note 33 above), p. 115. Korea in particular has been forced to grant foreign investors control over Korean companies and banks, something it steadfastly refused to do until forced by the crisis. For examples, see W. K. Tabb, 'The East Asian Crisis', *Monthly Review,* June 1998, pp. 24–38, **37**.

68. *The Economist,* 'Survey of South East Asia', 12 February 2000.

69. World Bank, *World Bank Poverty Update,* (Note 61 above).

70. IMF, *World Economic Outlook* (October 1999), p. 54, box 2.4.

71. This is the view of Alan Greenspan of the US Federal Reserve Bank, as expressed in *Far Eastern Economic Review,* 14 May 1998, p. 65. Cited in R. Higgott, 'The Asian Economic Crisis', (Note 64 above), p. 349.

72. For a balanced assesment of the 'regional' effects of the crisis, see R. Higgott, (Note 64 above).

11   Democracy, Civil Society and Post-development in Latin America

1. N. Lechner, 'De la Revolución a la Democracia', *La Ciudad Futura*, 2, 1986, p. 33, quoted by R. Munck, 'Political Programmes and Development: The Transformative Potential of Social Democracy', in F. J. Schuurman, *Beyond the Impasse: New Directions in Development Theory* (London: Zed Books, 1993), pp. 113–21, **115**.
2. J. G. Castañeda, *Utopia Unarmed* (New York: Vintage Books, 1994), p. 177.
3. Ibid., p. 177.
4. Ibid., p. 183.
5. Ibid., p. 183.
6. Ibid., p. 179.
7. Ibid., p. 196.
8. V. I. Lenin, *Imperialism, the Highest Stage of Capitalism* (New York and London: International Publishers, 1939; first published 1916), p. 85.
9. R. Prebisch, *The Economic Development of Latin America and Its Principal Problems* (New York: Economic Commission for Latin America, 1950). This paper was later reworked and served as the founding document for the United Nations Conference on Trade and Development (UNCTAD), of which Prebisch became the first Secretary General. See R. Prebisch, 'Towards a New Trade Policy for Development', vol. II of *Proceedings of the United Nations Conference on Trade and Development* (Geneva: UNCTAD, 1964).
10. A. M. M. Hoogvelt, *The Third World in Global Development* (London: Macmillan, 1982), pp. 167–8.
11. D. Green, *Silent Revolution, the Rise of Market Economics in Latin America* (London: Cassell and Latin America Bureau, 1995), p. 16.
12. Ibid., p. 17.
13. A. G. Frank, *Capitalism and Underdevelopment in Latin America* (New York: Monthly Review Press, 1967) (originally published in Spanish in 1957).
14. T. dos Santos, 'The Structure of Dependence', in C. K. Wilber (ed.), *The Political Economy of Development and Underdevelopment* (New York: Random House, 1970).
15. C. Furtado, *Diagnosis of the Brazilian Crisis* (Berkeley, Calif.: University of California Press, 1965).
16. N. Girvan, 'The Development of Dependency Economics in Latin America', *Social and Economic Studies*, 22 (1), 1973.
17. O. Sunkel, 'National Development Policy and External Dependency in Latin America', *Journal of Development Studies*, 6(1), 1969.
18. For a review of these arguments, see A. M. M. Hoogvelt, *The Third World in Global Development*, (Note 10 above), Ch. 5.
19. R. Gott, 'Introduction', *Rural Guerillas in Latin America* (Harmondsworth: Penguin, 1973), pp. 51–2.

20. K. Roberts, 'Democracy and the Dependent Capitalist State in Latin America', *Monthly Review* October 1985, pp. 12–26.
21. J. Schatan, *World Debt: Who Is to Pay?* (London: Zed Books, 1987), p. 74.
22. P. Calvert, 'Demilitarisation in Latin America', *Third World Quarterly*, 7(1), January 1985, pp. 31–43.
23. See E. Galeano, *Open Veins of Latin America*, especially his introduction to the new edition (New York: Monthly Review Press, 1978), reprinted in *Monthly Review*, 30(7), December 1978. On the American backing for the coup that toppled President Allende in Chile, see also A. Sampson, *Sovereign State, the Secret History of ITT* (London: Hodder & Stoughton, 1973).
24. N. Chomsky and E. S. Sherman, *The Washington Connection* (Nottingham: Spokesman, 1978). Note in particular the illuminating picture of 'the Sun and its Planets' on the inside cover of the book. This gives statistics on US financial backing and army training for countries using 'torture on an administrative basis in the 1970s'. In Chile, a group of economists who came to power with Pinochet were dubbed 'the Chicago Boys' because many of them had studied at Chicago University under Milton Friedman, guru of neo-liberal economics (see S. Branford and B. Kucinski, *The Debt Squads, the US, the Banks and Latin America* (London: Zed Books, 1988), p. 85.
25. E. Galeano, *Open Veins of Latin America*, (Note 23 above), p. 21.
26. Jackie Roddick presents figures for the respective shares of public and private net inflows into the region, 1961–78. In the period 1961–5, banks contributed only 2.1 per cent of a total of US$1.6 billion, while public flows (bilateral and multilateral lending) contributed 60.2 per cent. In 1978, of a total of US$21.8 billion, public flows contributed a mere 7.3 per cent, while banks contributed the lion's share of 56.6 per cent. See J. Roddick, *The Dance of the Millions, Latin America and the Debt Crisis* (London: Latin America Bureau, 1988), pp. 27–8.
27. Quoted in J. Roddick, ibid., p. 65.
28. See S. Branford and B. Kucinski, (Note 24 above), esp. ch. 9, 'Reaganomics against Latin America'.
29. J. Petras, 'Chile and Latin America', *Monthly Review*, 28(9), February 1977, pp. 13–24, **17**.
30. Ibid., p. 18.
31. A term originally coined by G. O'Donnell in *Modernization and Bureaucratic-Authoritarianism. Studies in South American Politics* (Berkeley, Calif.: University of California Press, 1973).
32. See, in particular, F. Cardoso and E. Faletto, *Dependency and Development in Latin America* (Berkeley, Calif.: University of California Press, 1979), esp. their introduction to the American edition.
33. D. Green, *Silent Revolution*, (Note 11 above), p. 164.
34. See in particular, N. Bobbio, *Democracy and Dictatorship* (Minneapolis, Minn.: University of Minnesota Press, 1989), and D. Held, 'Democracy, the Nation-state and the Global System', in D. Held (ed.), *Political Theory Today* (Oxford: Polity Press, 1991). Both are referred to in D.

Slater's excellent review of the region's new social movements: D. Slater, 'Power and Social Movements in the Other Occident', *Latin American Perspectives*, issue 81, 21(2), Spring 1994, pp. 11–37.

35. D. Held, ibid., p. 231.
36. R. T. Naylor, *Hot Money and the Politics of Debt* (Toronto: McClelland & Stewart, 1987), ch. 22.
37. J. Roddick, *The Dance of the Millions* (Note 26 above), p. 109.
38. In 1982, Ronald Reagan launched a new project 'exporting democracy world wide', setting up a special organization for the purpose. The function of the National Endowment for Democracy (NED) was to distribute government money to citizens, organizations and unions fighting for the 'restoration of democracy in totalitarian countries' or in countries where democracy is still precarious', see *International Labour Reports*, 13, January/February 1986, p. 7.
39. Eduardo Galeano gives a vivid description of this in the new edition of *Open Veins of Latin America* (Note 23 above):

> *To operate effectively, the repression must appear arbitrary.* Apart from breathing, any human activity can constitute a crime. In Uruguay torture is applied as a routine system of interrogation: anyone may be its victim, not only those suspected or guilty of acts of opposition. *In this way panic fear of torture is spread through the whole population, like a paralyzing gas that invades every home and implants itself in every citizen's soul...Each crime builds horrible uncertainty in persons close to the victim and is also a warning for everyone else.* State terrorism aims to paralyze the population with fear.
>
> (Galeano, p. 32, emphasis in original)

40. Cited in J. G. Castañeda, *Utopia Unarmed*, (Note 2 above), p. 202.
41. J. G. Castañeda, ibid., p. 197.
42. There is a plethora of statistics on the region's economic decline and increased poverty over the whole of the period 1970–95. Here I shall mention just a few salient facts of the critical period in the 1980s when structural adjustments were imposed:

- In the period 1980–8, the combined GDP for Latin America and the Caribbean declined by 6.6 per cent. Add to this the losses incurred as a result of a deterioration of the terms of trade (–3 per cent) and those caused by resource transfers out of the region (–6 per cent), and the fall in per capita income was 16 per cent over the period. Meanwhile, the rate of inflation rose from 46 per cent in 1978–9 to 336 per cent in 1987–8. Breaking down the decline in per capita income by two sectors, owners of capital and workers, their respective declines were 12 per cent and 26 per cent. See D. Ghai and C. Hewitt de Alcantara, *The IMF and the South, the Social Impact of Crisis and Adjustment* (London: Zed Books, 1991). The authors base their calculations on CEPAL, *Notas sobre la economía y el desarrollo*, December 1987 and 1988.

- Absolute poverty: During 1980–9 the estimated number of the absolute poor in Latin America increased from 136 million to 183 million. See C. Reilly, *New Paths to Democratic Development in Latin America* (Boulder, Col.: Lynne Rienner), p. 5. By 1993 the figure had risen to over 200 million, or 46 per cent of the total population (D. Green, *Silent Revolution*, (Note 11 above), p. 202).

43. S. Ellner, 'Introduction', in B. Carr and S. Ellner (eds), *The Latin American Left: From the Fall of Allende to Perestroika* (Boulder, Col.: Westview Press, 1993).
44. See D. Green, *Silent Revolution*, (Note 11 above), p. 188.
45. Ibid., p. 192.
46. R. Munck, *Politics and Dependency in Latin America* (London: Zed Books, 1985), p. 117.
47. Cited by C. Reilly (ed.) in 'Introduction' to *New Paths to Democratic Development in Latin America, the Rise of NGO–Municipal Collaboration* (Boulder, Col.: Lynne Rienner, 1995) p. 1.
48. J. G. Castañeda, *Utopia Unarmed*, (Note 2 above), ch. 7, 'The Grass Roots Explosion'.
49. J. Daudelin and W. E. Hewitt, 'Churches and Politics in Latin America: Catholicism at the Crossroads', *Third World Quarterly*, 16(2) 1995, pp. 221–36, **224**. Note the decline of these groups in recent years, which these authors blame in part on the Vatican's response (stimulated also by the contemporary Protestant Evangelical invasion), and partly by the general failure of the Catholic left to set the social agenda of the Church firmly. They argue that today there is developing something more akin to a throwback to traditional state–Church relations.
50. P. Berryman, 'Basic Christian Communities and the Future of Latin America', *Monthly Review*, 36(3) July/August 1984 pp. 27–40, **28**.
51. Ibid., pp. 29–30.
52. J. G. Castañeda, *Utopia Unarmed*, (Note 2 above), p. 223.
53. H. Oporto, *La Revolución democrática: una nueva manera de pensar Bolivia* (La Paz: Los Amigos del Libro, 1991), cited in D. Slater, 'Power and Social Movements', (Note 34 above), p. 23.
54. C. Reilly, *New Paths to Democratic Development*, (Note 42 above), p. 13.
55. Food rioting and the deterioration of the urban poor led the World Bank in 1990 to initiate a series of social emergency programmes in some Latin American countries to cushion the worst effects of the structural adjustment programmes. As Reilly observes, 'these emergency funds occasioned the Bank to begin dealing directly with subnational political actors and NGOs – perhaps initiating new patterns for a multilayered presence for the development bank in the region', (C. Reilly, ibid., p. 14).
56. A recently published *Guide to Directories of NGOs* by the Inter-American Foundation refers to over 11 000 Latin American NGOs. Various

contributors in C. Reilly's edited volume trace the interactions between NGOs and their financial backers with the municipal authorities.

57. See C. Reilly, *New Paths to Democratic Development*, (Note 42 above), p. 263.
58. J. S. Jacquette, 'Conclusion', in J. S. Jaquette (ed.), *The Women's Movement in Latin America* (Boston Mass.: Unwin Hyman, 1989).
59. The best-known example was the 'Madres de la Plaza de Mayo' in Argentina – the mothers of the disappeared who held rallies for years in Buenos Aires. They became a symbol not only of the 'need to know' but also of the necessity for Argentine society to come to terms with the dirty war. There were similar groups in other countries, for example the 'Confederation of Widows' of Guatemala; see J. G. Castañeda, *Utopia Unarmed*, (Note 2 above), p. 227.
60. The emancipatory story of Domitla Barrios de Chugara, leader of the Housewives Committee of the Siglo xx Mines in Bolivia, became world famous, partly also as an example of the power of the ethnographic methodology in which Latin American scholar intellectuals went out of their way to record the authentic voice of the people; see D. Barrios de Chungara (with M. Viezzier), 'Let Me Speak', *Monthly Review* (New York; 1979) (see also 'Excerpts', *Monthly Review*, 30(9), February 1979.
61. F. Calderon (ed.), *Los Movimientos Sociales ante la Crisis* (Buenos Aires: CLASCO, 1986). Cited in A. Escobar, 'Imagining a Post-Development Era? Critical Thought, Development and Social Movements', *Social Text*, 31/32, 1992, pp. 20–55, **32**.
62. A. Escobar, ibid., p. 33.
63. A. Peterson, 'Social Movement Theory', *Acta Sociologica*, 32(4), 1989, pp. 419–26, cited in D. Slater, 'Power and Social Movements' (Note 34 above), p. 29.
64. A. Escobar, *Encountering Development: The Making and Unmaking of the Third World* (Princeton, NJ: Princeton University Press, 1995), p. 221.
65. R. Mangabeira Unger, *False Necessity, Anti-necessitarian Social Theory in the Service of Radical Democracy* (Cambridge University Press, 1987), p. 362. See also his *Social Theory: Its Situation and its Task* (Cambridge University Press, 1987). Although Unger acknowledges no debt to Foucault, the message and the effort of his anti-enlightenment project is much the same as that of other postmodernists. Where he differs, however, is in the illusion of revolutionary reformism, in which the development of new participatory democracy can be a path of cumulative institutional innovation that can reconcile objectives of economic growth with the overcoming of the present brutal inequalities.
66. A. Escobar, 'Imagining a Post-Development Era', (Note 61 above), p. 27.
67. A. Escobar, *Encountering Development*, (Note 64 above), p. 219.
68. Ibid., p. 216.
69. A. Escobar, 'Imagining a Post-Development Era', (Note 61 above), p. 44.
70. D. Slater, 'Power and Social Movements', (Note 34 above), p. 29.

71. W.I. Robinson, 'Latin America and global capitalism', *Race & Class*, special issue, 'The threat of globalism', 40 (2/3), October1998–March 1999, pp. 133–144.
72. Economic Commission for Latin America and the Caribbean (ECLAC), 'Social Panorama of Latin America, 1999', http://www. eclac.cl/conference/g-2071
73. 'Great reforms, nice growth, but where are the jobs?', *The Economist*, 21 March 1998, cited in W. I. Robinson, 'Latin America and global capitalism' (Note 71 above).

Conclusion

1. These are, of necessity, very rough calculations. Will Hutton has argued, as others have done, that in the rich countries there is an emerging social structure of 40–30–30%, while the consensus among Third World observers is that the the proportions there are reversed. See W. Hutton, *The State We're In* (London: Jonathan Cape, 1995), pp. 105ff. The World-watch Institute, quoting the International Labor Organization, has estimated that over 1 billion people, or about a third of the global workforce, are unemployed or under-employed, working substantially less than full-time, or earning less than a living wage. The global work-force is set to swell by 1.5 billion new job seekers by 2050, almost all living in the developing world, where about half of the population is under the age of 25. See http://www.worldwatch.org/alerts/pop2.html
2. P. Kennedy, 'The Global Gales Ahead', *New Statesman/Society*, 3 May 1996, pp. 28–9.
3. For a balanced, sensitive and detailed account of the differences between the social policy discourses of various global agencies, see B. Deacon, with M. Hulse and P. Stubbs, *Global Social Policy, International Organizations and the Future of Welfare* (London: Sage, 1997). Also B. Deacon, *Globalization and Social Policy, The Threat to Equitable Welfare*, United Nations Research Institute for Social Development, Occasional Paper 5 (Geneva: UNRISD, 2000).
4. Positive grassroots strategies are documented in M. Barratt Brown, *Africa's Choices* (Harmondsworth: Penguin, 1995); in W. Rau, *From Feast to Famine, Official Cures and Grassroots Remedies to Africa's Food Crisis* (London: Zed Books, 1991); and in J. Gelinas, *Freedom from Debt, The Re-appropriation of Development through Financial Self-reliance* (London and New York: Zed Books; Ottawa: Inter Pares; and Dhaka: University Press; 1998).
5. *The Guardian*, 22 June 2000.
6. For a robust defence of this position, see A. Giddens, *The Third Way and its Critics* (London: Polity Press, 2000).
7. See Ch. Leadbeater, *Living on Thin Air, The New Economy* (London: Viking, 1999), p. 109.
8. D. Harvey, *Justice, Nature & the Geography of Difference* (Cambridge, Mass. and Oxford, UK: Basil Blackwell, 1996), p. 360.

9. A. Hoogvelt, 'Prospects in the Periphery for National Accumulation in the Wake of the Cold War and the Debt Crisis', in B. Gills and S. Qadir (eds), *Regimes in Crisis* (London: Zed Books, 1995), pp. 72–81. For a similar argument, see also C. Hines and T. Lang, *The New Protectionism* (London: Earthscan, 1993).

10. A. Quijano, *Estética de la Utopia, David y Goliath* (Lima: Sociedad y Politica Endiciones, 1990) p. 37; quoted *passim* in A. Escobar, *Encountering Development, The Making and Unmaking of the Third World* (Princeton, NJ: Princeton University Press, 1995), p. 221.

11. See D. Boyle, 'Time Is a Great Social Healer', *New Statesman*, (23 August 1999), p. 18. There is now a growing literature on such local exchange trading schemes. See, for example, P. Lang, *LETS Work: Rebuilding The Local Economy* (Bristol: Grover Books, 1994); J. Croall, *LETS Act Locally: The Growth of Local Exchange Trading Systems* (London: Calouste Gulbenkian Foundation, 1997); M. Pacione, 'Local Exchange Trading Systems as a Response to the Globalization of Capitalism', *Urban Studies*, 34(8), 1997, pp. 1179–99. And C. Williams, 'The New Barter Economy: An Appraisal of Local Exchange and Trading Systems (LETS)', *Journal of Public Policy*, 16(1), 1996, pp. 85–101.

12. Cited, *passim*, in G. Mulgan, 'Creating a Twin Economy', *Demos*, 2, 1994. See also D. Boyle, *Funny Money: In Search of Alternative Cash* (New York: HarperCollins, 1999).

13. P. Hawken, A. Lovins and L. Hunter Lovins, *Natural Capitalism: Creating the Next Industrial Revolution* (London: Little, Brown, 1999).

14. Cited, *passim*, in U. Beck, 'Beyond the Nation State', *New Statesman*, 6 December 1999, pp. 25–7, **26**. The *New Statesman's* article is an edited extract from Beck's book *What Is Globalization?* (London: Pluto Press, 1999). A senior staff member of the IMF, V. Tanzi, has warned that there are 'termites' working away at the foundations of the fiscal house of governments. He lists the growth of e-commerce, the use of transfer price mechanisms, the spread of tax havens and hedge funds, and the mobility of capital and labour. He concludes that the world must prepare itself for what could prove to be significant falls in tax levels. See V. Tanzi, *International Dimensions of National Tax Policy*, Paper presented at the Expert Meeting on International Economic and Social Justice, UN Division for Social Policy and Development, New York, 12–14 November, 1998; cited in B. Deacon, *Globalization and Social Policy*, (Note 3 above), p. 3.

15. Personal communication from Environmental Information Services, London, 1997.

16. *World Watch, 1999*, cited in *The Economist*, 11 December 1999, p. 24.

17. An NGO swarm has been defined by a recent RAND study as 'amorphous groups of NGO's, linked on line, descending on a target – it has no central leadership or command structure; it is multi-headed, impossible to decapitate'; cited in *The Economist*, (Note 16 above).

18. *Yearbook of International Organizations*, cited in *The Economist*, (Note 16 above).

Index